W9-BVP-022

BR
560
.L67
E54
1992

Engh, Michael E.,
  1949-

Frontier faiths.

930648

DATE			
MY 09 '14			

BAKER & TAYLOR BOOKS

Frontier Faiths

Michael E. Engh, S.J.

FRONTIER FAITHS

Church, Temple, and Synagogue

in Los Angeles

1846–1888

SMS UNIVERSITY
WEST PLAINS CAMPUS

University of New Mexico Press   *Albuquerque*

Library of Congress Cataloging-in-Publication Data

Engh, Michael E., 1949–
Frontier faiths : church, temple, and synagogue in Los Angeles,
1846–1888 / Michael E. Engh. — 1st ed.
p.   cm.
Includes bibliographical references and index.
ISBN 0-8263-1343-4
1. Los Angeles (Calif.)—Church history—19th century. 2. Los
Angeles (Calif.)—Religion—19th century. I. Title.
BR560.L67E54   1992
277.94'94081—dc20
91-39297
CIP

© 1992 by the University of New Mexico Press. All rights reserved.
First edition.

For my parents,
Donald Eric Engh and Marie Therese Airey,
who have been authors in their own way.

CONTENTS

Contents

Illustrations:
following pages 67 and 120

TABLES

MAPS

—◦•❈•◦—

PREFACE

—⸙⟶⟿⟿⟵⸙—

When residents of Los Angeles celebrated the centennial of the nation's independence, in 1876, they reveled in an outburst of homespun patriotic pageantry. Yards of red, white, and blue bunting hung from buildings, a "noble triple arch" spanned Main Street, and flags flew from scores of front porches and balconies throughout town. Escorting a series of richly festooned "triumphal cars," ethnic, fraternal, and business groups proudly marched through the streets in a lengthy morning parade. A young Jewish girl riding in the lead, Miss Carrie Cohn, had the honor of portraying the Goddess of Liberty. Other units, ranging from the Société Française de Bienfaisance Mutuelle to Fire Company #38, with their decorated hook-and-ladder truck, represented the diverse segments of the settlement's populace of six to eight thousand souls.[1] This "procession," which one observer boasted took thirty minutes to pass the reviewing stand, was only the beginning of the day's festivities.

The two chaplains for the subsequent "literary exercises" were Reverend David Temple Packard, who conducted an "impressive" opening prayer, and Rabbi Abraham Wolf Edelman, who offered the closing benediction. Packard had pastored the First Congregational Church for the past two years, while Edelman had presided at Congregation B'nai B'rith since its foundation, in 1862.[2] At first

[1] J. J. Warner, Benjamin Hayes, and J. P. Widney, *An Historical Sketch of Los Angeles County, California* (Los Angeles: Louis Lewin & Company, 1876; reprint ed., Los Angeles: O. W. Smith, 1936), pp. 141–47, 149, 159.
[2] These two congregations still serve the Los Angeles community, though both have relocated west of their old sites; Congregation B'nai B'rith is now known as the Wilshire Boulevard Temple.

glance these services may not appear to differ from the festivities of other small towns across the nation in 1876. However, the highly visible roles of Edelman and Miss Cohn reveal important aspects of community consciousness and composition. Organizers had selected both the Polish-born rabbi and the daughter of one of his immigrant congregants for prominent positions in their centennial ceremonies.[3]

These decisions manifest a religious tolerance and social acceptance with limits that did not extend to the members of all creeds. Planners evidently did not invite the local blacks or Chinese to contribute to the day, while ecclesiastics of Roman Catholicism, the town's largest and oldest denomination, absented themselves from sharing a platform with clergymen of other faiths. These intriguing details only hint at the sometimes sensitive dynamics of religious life in Los Angeles. The centennial celebrations were one episode in the interplay among residents of diverse ethnic backgrounds, with their plurality of faiths and strongly held opinions on race. The origins and consequences of such interaction among believers merit closer examination, offering us telling glimpses into the society and civic life in a frontier settlement then known as the "Queen of the Cow Counties."

In this volume, I study those persons and events who contributed to the creation of a distinctive urban culture in Los Angeles in the tumultuous mid-nineteenth century. Specifically, I am interested in the religious roots of Angelenos, whether they sprang from the soil of the Mexican *frontera* (frontier), Puritan New England, or Confucian and Taoist China. Tensions had arisen among members of diverse ethnic and racial groups in the *pueblo* who were caught up in the drastic political and economic transformations that followed American conquest. Beginning in 1848, settlers in Los Angeles haltingly fashioned patterns of tolerance and even cooperation in the midst of social upheaval and growing spiritual diversity. The settlers of this frontier town adapted their religious practices to suit the region's peculiar climate, terrain, sensibilities, and social conditions.

Distinct from earlier national frontiers such as western New York and the Old Northwest, Los Angeles counted a Roman Catholic majority in its population well into the 1870s. Vibrant Jewish and

---

[3] Miss Carrie Cohn was the daughter of an important wholesale grocer, Bernard Cohn, who had arrived in Los Angeles in 1855, from his native Poland. See Norton B. Stern, "The First Jew to Run for Mayor of Los Angeles," *Western States Jewish Historical Quarterly*, XII (April, 1980), p. 249.

Chinese communities thrived alongside Spanish-speaking Catholic congregations and brought an unusual plurality to the religious life of the settlement. The mixture of languages, races, and creeds more closely resembled the populace in communities such as Santa Fe and Tucson than in Des Moines, Indianapolis, or even San Francisco. This is evident in the laws, customs, and the very processes of the evolution of Los Angeles into an American town. The southern counties of California developed in ways distinct from those earlier frontiers east of the Sierra Nevadas, which have often been considered the religious paradigms of this nation. The religious distinctions persisted throughout the latter half of the nineteenth century and set this area apart even from the northern portion of the state.

The years 1846 to 1888 form an easily demarcated period of transition, during which Los Angeles changed from a Hispanic pueblo to an Anglo-American city. The war between the United States and Mexico concluded in 1848, and California passed to the conquering *norteamericanos*. Not only did the victors introduce a new flag, but religious pluralism as well. In subsequent years, the town of Los Angeles slowly expanded, and in the process absorbed denominations and nationalities new to southern California. The arrival of the Santa Fe railroad, in 1885, inaugurated a dramatic population influx that irrevocably changed the character of the community.

Few historians have focused their attention on the religious life of western pioneers, and fewer still have examined the spiritual aspect of the history of Los Angeles during this important era. The studies of William Warren Sweet were the earliest and most extensive works on frontier churches, though he made little mention of southern California.[4] Since the time of Sweet, church historians and others have integrated the frontier experience into treatments of American reli-

---

[4] *The Story of Religion in America*, New York: Harper and Row, 1930, revised, 1950; see also "The Churches as Moral Courts of the Frontier," *Church History*, II (June, 1933), pp. 3–21; and "The Frontier in American Christianity," in *Environmental Factors in Christian History*, edited by J. T. McNeill, et al., (Chicago: University of Chicago Press, 1939), pp. 380–98. Sweet outlined the work of four major denominations in his series of edited documents, entitled *Religion on the American Frontier*; the "religion" was Protestant Christianity; the "frontier" was the trans-Allegheny Midwest between 1783 and 1840. The volumes in the series were: *The Baptists*, New York: Henry Holt and Company, 1931; *The Presbyterians*, New York: Harper and Brothers, 1935; *The Congregationalists*, Chicago: University of Chicago Press, 1939; and *The Methodists*, Chicago: University of Chicago Press, 1946.

gious history. Sydney E. Ahlstrom, Robert T. Handy, Winthrop S. Hudson, Edwin Gaustad, and Martin E. Marty have all noted the importance of the West in the nation's spiritual growth.[5] Nonetheless, Ferenc Morton Szasz has noted that religious history in the trans-Mississippi West is "largely 'terra incognita.' "[6] And what of this unique corner of the continent, this "island on the land," as Helen Hunt Jackson and Carey McWilliams have called southern California?[7]

Los Angeles has not lacked its share of historians of local religion, and the earliest histories of the community all included at least a section on the town's religious life. A trio of pioneers, J. J. Warner, Benjamin P. Hayes, and Joseph Pomeroy Widney, boasted of church growth in their 1876 volume, *An Historical Sketch of Los Angeles County, California*, the first town history. Four years later appeared the *History of Los Angeles County, California*, which sandwiched the section on "Churches" between "City Water" and fraternal "Societies," all signs of local progress. Later publications, known as "mugbooks" for their collection of biographies and portraits, included requisite entries on the houses of worship. James M. Guinn, Henry D. Barrows, and Marco R. Newmark witnessed many of the changes in Los Angeles and extensively recorded these developments between 1880 and 1946. Sometimes colorful, but always valuable, information on religious life appears in their prolific publications on the city's history.[8]

Several scholars have turned their attention to the field of religious history in the City of the Angels and have produced valuable

[5] Sydney E. Ahlstrom, *A Religious History of the American People*, (New Haven: Yale University Press, 1972), pp. 385–510; Robert T. Handy, *A History of the Churches in the United States and Canada* (New York: Oxford University Press, 1977), pp. 153–59, 162–76; Winthrop S. Jordan, *Religion in America* (2nd ed., New York: Charles Scribner's Sons, 1973), pp. 131–57; Edwin S. Gaustad, *A Religious History of America* (New York: Harper and Row, 1966, 1974), pp. 112–254; and Martin E. Marty, *Righteous Empire: The Protestant Experience in America* (New York: Dial Press, 1970), pp. 53–54; and by the same author, *Pilgrims in Their Own Land: 500 Years of Religion in America* (Boston: Little, Brown, and Company, 1984), pp. 92–99.

[6] Szasz, *The Protestant Clergy in the Great Plains and Mountain West, 1865–1915* (Albuquerque: University of New Mexico Press, 1988), p. 6.

[7] Carey McWilliams, *Southern California: An Island on the Land* (revised ed., Santa Barbara: Peregrine Smith, Incorporated, 1973), p. 7.

[8] Warner, Hayes, and Widney, *An Historical Sketch of Los Angeles County, California* (Los Angeles: Louis Lewin, 1876; reprint ed., Los Angeles: O. W. Smith, 1936), pp. 89–93; John Albert Wilson, *History of Los Angeles County, California* (Oakland,

works. Harland E. Hogue authored one of the earliest works, "A History of Religion in Southern California, 1846–1880." Unfortunately, this 1948 dissertation included little on the Chinese religious experience. A slim, though thoughtful, volume appeared in 1976, edited by Francis J. Weber: *The Religious Heritage of Southern California: A Bicentennial Survey*. The six chapters each summarized the local growth of a particular religious tradition. In 1979, Gregory H. Singleton contributed *Religion in the City of the Angels: American Public Culture and Urbanization, Los Angeles, 1850–1930*. In this volume, he examined the significant Protestant experience in the city, with greatest emphasis on the period after 1885. Sandra Sizer Frankiel has included the City of the Angels in her recent study, *California's Spiritual Frontiers: Religious Alternatives in Anglo-Protestantism, 1850–1910*.[9] As her title states, Frankiel has limited her subject to one segment of the state's diverse religious populace.

In terms of strictly denominational studies, there is a constellation of writers who have chronicled the labors of their fellow believers. A mere sampling requires mention of works by Thomas A. Chinn, Clifford A. Cole, Charles C. Conroy, Clifford M. Drury, Ivan C. Ellis, Zephyrin Engelhardt, O.F.M., Leland D. Hine, Edward Drewry Jervey, Douglas O. Kelley, William M. Kramer, Leo J. Muir, Norton B. Stern, and Francis J. Weber.[10] Each church and temple has also

---

California: Thompson and West, 1880; reprint, ed., Berkeley: Howell-North, 1959), pp. 119–21; *An Illustrated History of Los Angeles County*, Chicago: Lewis Publishing Company, 1889), pp. 290–305; Guinn, *Historical and Biographical Record of Los Angeles and Vicinity* (Chicago: Chapman Publishing Company, 1901), pp. 147–55; Barrows, "Early Clericals in Los Angeles," Historical Society of Southern California *Annual Publications* (1902), pp. 127–33; and Newmark, "The Story of Religion in Los Angeles, 1781–1900," Historical Society of Southern California *Quarterly*, XXVIII (March, 1946), pp. 35–50.

[9] Hogue, Ph. D. dissertation, Columbia University, 1958; Weber, Los Angeles: Interreligious Council of Southern California, 1976; Singleton, Ann Arbor: UMI Research Press, 1979; and Frankiel, Berkeley: University of California Press, 1988.

[10] Chinn, Mark H. Lai, and Philip P. Choy, *A History of the Chinese in California: A Syllabus*, San Francisco: Chinese Historical Society of America; Cole, *The Christian Churches of Southern California*, St. Louis: Christian Board of Publications, 1959; Conroy, *The Centennial*, Los Angeles: Archdiocese of Los Angeles, 1940; Drury, *The Centennial of the Synod of California*, San Francisco, Office of the Stated Clerk, 1952; Ellis, "Baptist Churches in Southern California," Ph.D. dissertation, Northern Baptist Theological Seminary, Chicago, 1949; Engelhardt, *Missions and Missionaries of California*, 4 vol., San Francisco: James H. Barry and Company, 1908–15; Hine, *Baptists in Southern California*, Valley Forge, Pennsylvania: Judson Press, 1966; Jervey,

benefited from its cadre of biographers and memorialists. In addition, there are the dozens of congregational and institutional histories that have appeared over the years to record various anniversaries.

As valuable as these denominational works are, there is still a need to weave together the diverse threads of the religious history of Los Angeles. Scholars are increasingly turning their attention to comparative studies in history, and religious developments in the West warrant similar treatment. Hogue, Singleton, and Frankiel have compared certain aspects of religious experience in Los Angeles and have pointed the way for further studies. Broadening the scope further, in this study I examine the reasons why traditionally hearty pioneer denominations initially fared so poorly in the City of the Angels. Baptists and Methodists had successfully pioneered on other frontiers of the nation, yet in Los Angeles they were among the later arrivals. Women's contributions are another neglected topic, particularly in nineteenth-century Los Angeles. Here we find women of diverse religious, ethnic, and racial backgrounds actively involving themselves in a startling number of cross-denominational undertakings. The work of churchfolk in temperance and Sabbath law campaigns to "tame" and refine frontier society has also been overlooked. Finally, Los Angeles differed from other, more homogeneous, communities because of the challenges to evangelization posed by peoples of diverse ethnic and racial backgrounds. To limit this study to a manageable length, however, certain matters had to be left for future study, particularly the social mobility of congregation members. I believe that the topics addressed in this volume warrant examination from a perspective broad enough to survey the full range of religious experience in Los Angeles in the last century.

In considering these matters, I have identified five specific areas or

The History of Methodism in Southern California and Arizona, Nashville: Parthenon Press, 1960; Kelley, *History of the Diocese of California, from 1849 to 1914*, San Francisco: Bureau of Information and Supply, Diocese of California, 1915; Kramer and Stern have published extensively in the *Western States Jewish History*; Muir, *A Century of Mormon Activities in California*, 2 volumes, Salt Lake City: Deseret News Press [1952]; and Weber, *California's Reluctant Prelate*, Los Angeles: Dawson's Book Shop, 1964, which is only one of many publications by the dean of historians of the local Roman Catholic community. His latest publication, *Century of Fulfillment: The Roman Catholic Church in Southern California, 1840–1947*, Mission Hills, California: Archival Center, Archdiocese of Los Angeles, 1990, arrived too late to be fully included in this study.

characteristics which marked the frontier religious experience in Los Angeles. The first two chapters explain how the polyglot racial and ethnic diversity among residents influenced the order in which organized congregations appeared during the transitional era 1846 to 1888. Subsequent chapters examine the other singular features of religious development. These include the nature and extent of interreligious cooperation; the unique opportunities for evangelization; the diverse roles that Roman Catholic religious women played; and the displacement of Roman Catholicism from its traditional position of local influence at the time of the "Protestantization" of Los Angeles. These five attributes of religious life distinguish the spiritual development of citizens in southern California and set this community apart from other frontiers in other regions and even from the northern portion of the state.

In the course of writing this book I have repeatedly received cooperation and gracious assistance from numerous people. My primary indebtedness is to Allan G. Bogue, University of Wisconsin-Madison, whose careful reading of the text and cogent comments have immeasurably enhanced this manuscript. Mr. Thomas J. Archdeacon and Mr. Robert C. Ostergren, of the same institution, read this work in its dissertation form, offered thoughtful suggestions, and encouraged me to offer this study to a wider audience. Doctor Angelo Collins, O.P., of Florida State University, discussed many points of theory in this work and aided me in clarifying my thought over the several years in which the book developed.

A host of scholars, librarians, and archivists have proven extraordinarily helpful, but several stand in the forefront of this distinguished assembly. Professor Eldon G. Ernst first introduced me to the comparative method of history in interdenominational or "ecumenical" studies, in his seminars at the Graduate Theological Union, Berkeley, California. I owe him an immense intellectual debt. Ellen Burke, Inter-Library Loan Librarian of the State Historical Society of Wisconsin, located materials that I despaired of ever finding. Time and again she speedily came to my rescue with volumes I thought unobtainable. Monsignor Francis J. Weber graciously put the records of the Archives of the Archdiocese of Los Angeles at my disposal. Mrs. David S. Forsyth, of the Historical Society of the Centinela Valley, California, not only made me the beneficiary of her vast knowledge of Los Angeles history, but also critically reviewed an earlier draft of this manuscript.

The citations of primary documents in the bibliography provide a complete list of the centers where I met many other helpful and hospitable persons. Church and synagogue officials from pastors to clerks welcomed me and made available the documents in their care. The Santa Barbara Mission Archive-Library funded a portion of my research, through its Maynard Geiger Memorial Fellowship for 1988. Sister Mary William Vinet, D.C., guided me through the rich collections of the Archives of the Daughters of Charity in Los Altos Hills, California. In Berkeley, the librarians of the Graduate Theological Union Library went beyond the call of duty to answer my inquiries. Mrs. Florence E. Borders, Reference Librarian at the Amistad Research Center, Tulane University, New Orleans, furnished extensive correspondence from the archives of the American Missionary Association. At both the Henry E. Huntington Library, in San Marino, California, and the Presbyterian Church (U.S.A.) Department of History, in Philadelphia, staff members provided me with ready and expert assistance during the months of my research.

Special mention ought to be made of the members of the academic community at Loyola Marymount University, where I resided during the course of this project. Doctor Seth Thompson reviewed each chapter and made valuable suggestions for improving the text. Doctor Anthony F. Turhollow, former professor of History and Dean of the Graduate School, also read the manuscript and made valuable suggestions. Christina Anderson and Sylvia Kreng, of the Charles Von Der Ahe Library, graciously handled my many interlibrary loan requests. Sister Bridget McNamara, R.S.H.M., took time during her sabbatical to produce extensive translations from Latin and Italian manuscripts.

Finally, fellow members of the Society of Jesus merit particular mention for their sustained interest in my progress. Charles J. Kavanagh, S.J., Theodore Fisher, S.J., Thomas Deasy, S.J., Jeffrey S. Seeger, S.J., and Gerald J. Phelan, S.J., provided me with translations of Latin, Italian, German, and French materials. John R. Moniz, S.J., deciphered and transcribed a series of nineteenth-century holograph documents. Edward J. McFadden, S.J., read the entire manuscript in both its forms, made more corrections of syntax and grammar than I cared to count, and thereby saved me much embarrassment.

Other Jesuits offered me timely encouragement and manifested a genuine concern throughout the long months of research and writing. Two who stand out in this regard are John R. Bisenius, S.J., and Anthony B. Brzoska, S.J.

Even from this short list, it is obvious that my debts of gratitude from this project are immense. This manuscript is the best expression of appreciation I can offer to all the people who so graciously assisted me in this enterprise. They have enabled me to study the religious dimension of pioneer life during an era of momentous change in Los Angeles. From these women and men I have garnered a vast amount of historical information. Many people have assisted in my growth as a historian and have taught me that research, analysis, and writing are truly cooperative endeavors. Finally, I have also learned that I reserve to myself, alone, the responsibility for any shortcomings or omissions in this volume.

----•+❇+•----

"THE FIRST SHALL BE LAST"

The Foundation of Congregations in Los Angeles

William Money, a self-taught physician, theologian, astrolo-
ger, and historian, claimed to have been born with "the likeness of a
rainbow" in his right eye. As founder of the Reformed New Testament Church, he was the self-proclaimed "Bishop, Deacon and De-
fender" of what he considered to be "true" Christianity. He proudly
led twelve followers in disputing the religious practices in Roman
Catholic Los Angeles. In 1855, Money boasted that the Catholic
clergy had dubbed him as "the most obstinate heretic on the earth."
His pastoral and "encycle" [sic] letters in the town's leading paper, the
Star, reveal the thoughts of one of the first of a long line of prophets
and eccentrics attracted to southern California over the years.[1] As a
pioneer in local religious dissent, Bishop Money offers a strong contrast to the deeply rooted Hispanic piety prevalent in the pueblo in
the mid-1850s.[2]

Over the years, those dissatisfied with orthodox religion have often
found a safe and even friendly environment in the Los Angeles area.
Since the time of William Money, believers and those seeking spiri-

---

[1] The priests had apparently also threatened with excommunication any who read
Money's twenty-two-page book, *Reform of the Church of the New Testament of Our Lord
Jesus Christ*; Los Angeles *Star*, 5 January 1856. Other letters from Money appeared in
this newspaper on 17, 24, and 31 March, 11 August, 27 October, 3 and 17 November
1855; and in *El Clamor Publico* on 1 and 22 March 1856, 30 May 1857, 4 December 1858, and 12 March and 25 June 1859. Thereafter, he apparently pursued other
interests.

[2] The most complete treatment of Money is in William B. Rice's delightful *William
Money: A California Savant*, Los Angeles: Privately Printed, 1943.

tual enlightenment have transplanted themselves and found a welcome reception. Los Angeles has notably become home to the Church
of the Nazarene as well as to Aimee Semple McPherson's Four Square
Gospel. Growing alongside the more traditional, mainline denominations, these churches have contributed to the religious pluralism for
which Los Angeles is renowned. In this chapter we examine how this
began; in later chapters we will consider the impact of such growing
religious diversity upon the community.

It is important to bear in mind that southern California was a frontier that stood as an exception to the patterns of religious pioneering
in the United States. Members of the evangelical Protestant churches
(Baptist, Congregational, Disciples of Christ, Methodist, and Presbyterian) were the more common religious pathbreakers pressing
westward in the nineteenth century.[3] California and the Southwest
were different. In these two regions, Roman Catholicism was his-
torically strong. It is therefore important to note that evangelistic
church groups were not the first nor the most successful in organizing congregations in Los Angeles. Accustomed to pioneering in the
Old Northwest and other frontier regions, adherents of these creeds
faced new and unfamiliar challenges in this section of California. The
regional characteristics of the foundation and growth of creeds in
southern California therefore warrant serious consideration for what
they reveal of the settlement process in this region.

In the Spanish borderlands of the southwestern United States, the
religious frontier had been advancing and retreating since the *conquis-
tadores* first attempted settlement along the upper Rio Grande Valley,
in New Mexico, in the 1590s.[4] A three-fold system of religious, mili-

---

[3] It is interesting to note that historian William Warren Sweet considered Congregationalists, along with Episcopalians, as "apostles to the genteel" on the frontier.
Never numerous among pioneers in the far West, they exerted an influence beyond
what their numbers alone might suggest; *American Churches: An Interpretation* (New
York: Abingdon-Cokesbury Press, 1948), p. 39.

[4] D. W. Meinig's definition of the Southwest has proven to be most helpful, and I
have attempted to follow his concepts of historical geography in order to distinguish
California as a separate region. His comment on the vagueness of the boundaries
of the American Southwest is worth recalling at this point. "The Southwest is a
distinctive place to the American mind but a somewhat blurred place on American
maps . . . everyone knows that there is a Southwest but there is little agreement
as to just where it is." Meinig concluded that the Southwest is best limited to the
area of New Mexico and Arizona. See his valuable book, *Southwest: Three Peoples in
Geographical Change, 1600–1970* (New York: Oxford University Press, 1971), p. 3.

tary, and secular institutions secured the frontier regions by means of missions, forts, and settlements. Crown officials and churchmen had worked steadily to extend the protection of the laws of their monarch, "His Most Catholic Majesty," to the Floridas, Texas, New Mexico, and the Californias. The privileged position of the Roman Catholic church in the Spanish empire received careful treatment in the *Recopilación de leyes de los reynos de las Indias,* the "Laws of the Indies," published in 1681.[5]

Designating the Church of Rome as the official religion of the state, Spanish (and later Mexican) law permitted no other creeds within the realm. Statutes even mandated that the parish church in a new settlement must face the central *plaza,* a tangible expression of the importance of Roman Catholicism in communal life. In the subsequent century, civil and religious authorities extended these legal customs to Spain's final frontier. Friars and soldiers trekked into Alta California in 1769 and founded the first of four *presidios* (forts) and twenty-one missions intended to secure the northern flank of Spain's North American empire. In an effort to populate the province, families of colonists from other portions of New Spain later settled in three pueblos: San José (1777), Los Angeles (1781), and Branciforte (1797).

The first Spanish explorers to view southern California by land passed through the future site of Los Angeles in August of 1769. Franciscan diarist Fray Juan Crespi noted that the expedition reached "a very spacious valley" the day after the feast of Our Lady of the Angels of the Porciúncula. Seeing a "beautiful river," the visitors named it the Río Porciúncula.[6] Crespi recorded a series of earthquakes over two days and surmised that there must be volcanoes in the region to produce the repeated shocks. The priest also commented:

> This plain where the river runs is very extensive. It has good land for planting all kinds of grain and seeds, and this is the most suitable site of all that we have seen for a mission, for it has all the requisites for a large settlement.[7]

---

[5] Oakah L. Jones, Jr., *Los Paisanos: Spanish Settlers on the Northern Frontier of New Spain* (Norman, Oklahoma: University of Oklahoma Press, 1979), pp. 6–8.

[6] The Río Porciúncula is now known as the Los Angeles River.

[7] Herbert E. Bolton, *Fray Juan Crespi, Missionary Explorer* (Berkeley: University of California Press, 1927), quoted in John and LaRee Caughey, eds., *Los Angeles: Biography of a City* (Berkeley: University of California Press, 1977), p. 50.

Extending from modern Santa Monica, in the north, to San Juan Capistrano, in the south, the plains that Crespi described vary from thirty to one hundred miles in breadth. A series of mountain ranges, peaking at eleven thousand feet, rim the basin on the north, east, and southeast. To the west and south lies the Pacific Ocean. These mountains separate the region from the hot and dry Mohave Desert, to the east, and trap the moisture resulting from Pacific storms. Smaller, rugged ranges divide the plains of Los Angeles from the adjoining San Fernando, San Gabriel, and San Bernardino valleys.

Had Crespi remained longer, he would have discovered that the region enjoys a temperate, semiarid climate, wettest and coldest in February and driest and hottest in July. Both the climate and vegetation of southern California differ greatly from those of the northern two-thirds of the state, because local rainfall annually averages only twelve inches.[8] Alternating cycles of drought and flooding also characterize the southland. At the time of Spanish exploration, chaparral growth densely covered the hillsides, while California scrub and black oak dotted the grasslands of the Los Angeles basin.[9] Crespi and his companions also encountered an Indian population engaged in fishing, hunting deer and rabbit, and gathering acorns and roots.

Spanish soldiers and friars returned in September 1771 and founded the mission of "El Santo Arcángel San Gabriel de los Temblores," in the fertile valley of the same name.[10] The Franciscan *padres* selected a site in the midst of an estimated 4,000 Indian people, of the tribal group that came to be known as the Gabrielino. These Indians resided in some forty permanent village communities, located near the natural resources on which they subsisted. The Gabrielinos inhabited what is today Los Angeles County and half of Orange County, along with the islands of Santa Catalina and San Clemente. When the Mexican government secularized the missions, in 1833, the Indian converts

---

[8] In addition to the Porciúncula, or Los Angeles, River Crespi mentioned, three other watercourses cross the basin: the Rio Hondo, San Gabriel, and Santa Ana.

[9] For an extended and engaging discussion of the natural history of the Los Angeles basin, see Elna Bakker, *An Island Called California: An Ecological Introduction to Its Natural Communities* (second edition, Berkeley: University of California Press, 1984), pp. 344–69. See also Howard J. Nelson and William A.V. Clark, *Los Angeles: The Metropolitan Experience* (Cambridge, Massachusetts: Ballinger Publishing Company, 1976), pp. 7–20.

[10] The mission's title translates as "The Holy Archangel, Saint Gabriel of the Earthquakes."

drifted to neighboring pueblos and *ranchos* in search of employment. Contagious diseases and intra-Indian conflicts repeatedly ravaged the Gabrielinos, so that by 1870 there were only 219 Indians in all Los Angeles County.[11]

The first of two ethnographic accounts of the Gabrielino people was the work of the Franciscan missionary Gerónimo Boscana, who based his work, "Chinígchinich," on observations from 1812 to 1826. The second source is a series of letters penned by a Scottish immigrant turned *ranchero,* Hugo Reid, who was married to a Gabrielino woman, Victoria, of the Comacrabit *ranchería.* The Gabrielinos believed in a Giver of Life, who had created the world and all living things before ascending to heaven. Contact with the spirits resulted from use of the hallucinatory Jimson weed, which also gave strength, cured certain maladies, and provided hunters with good luck. Active practice of this religion declined rapidly during the mission era, with virtually all vestiges of its beliefs eradicated by 1870.[12]

The first *pobladores,* or settlers, arrived in 1781 from Sinaloa and Sonora, over one thousand miles to the southeast, to establish a new town under the impressive name of "El pueblo de Nuestra Señora de los Angeles del Río Porciúncula."[13] The new community, located west of the mission, initially comprised forty-four persons of mixed Spanish, black, and Indian ancestry who engaged in agriculture and stock raising. San Gabriel's Franciscan missionaries served the com-

---

[11] George Harwood Phillips carefully explained the factors involved in this dramatic Gabrielino decline in his article, "Indians in Los Angeles, 1781–1875: Economic Integration, Social Disintegration," *Pacific Historical Review,* XLIX (August, 1980), pp. 427–51.

[12] Boscana entrusted his manuscript, "Chinigchinich: An Historical Account of the Origins, Customs, and Traditions of the Indians of Alta-California," to Alfred Robinson, who first published it in 1846, appended to his own work, *Life in California During a Residence of Several Years in That Territory* (New York: Wiley and Putnam, 1846; reprint ed., Salt Lake City: Peregrine Publishers, 1970), pp. 1–74. Hugo Reid's letters were first published in the Los Angeles *Star,* in 1852. See Robert F. Heizer, ed., *The Indians of Los Angeles County: Hugo Reid's Letters of 1852,* Los Angeles: Southwest Museum, 1968. Two other valuable sources of information are Bernice Eastman Johnson, *California's Gabrielino Indians* (Los Angeles: Southwest Museum, 1962), pp. 37–74; and Lowell John Bean and Charles R. Smith, "Gabrielino," in William C. Sturtevant, gen. ed., *Handbook of North American Indians,* 20 vols. (Washington, D.C.: Smithsonian Institution, 1978), vol. 8: *California,* edited by Robert F. Heizer, p. 538.

[13] This translates as, "The town of Our Lady of the Angels on the Porciúncula River."

munity's spiritual needs, though various other priests ministered intermittently over the years.[14] Completed in 1822, a new church served a growing community and spared the people the weekly ten-mile journey to the mission for Sunday services.[15]

The early nineteenth-century *padrones* (censuses) for the Los Angeles area indicate the religious solidity of Roman Catholicism in the community. With independence, in 1821, Mexican officials first began to encourage the immigration of foreigners to Alta California and other northern provinces, in efforts to bolster population and trade. The Colonization Law of 1824 and subsequent acts stipulated where these new residents could locate and what property they might possess. There was no provision requiring that these settlers embrace Roman Catholicism, though many of them did so, in order to gain Mexican citizenship or to win the hand in marriage of the daughter of a prominent citizen.[16] The Los Angeles district, including the town and its surrounding ranchos, numbered some 2,228 souls in 1836, of which 533 were Indian and 50 non-Hispanic. Of this latter group, 29 were from the United States, and all were men.[17]

Eight years later, a second census for the same district showed only a limited increase in population. The figures for 1844 reveal that the 2,250 inhabitants included 650 Indians and 53 foreigners. Of the latter, 31 reported the United States as their place of birth, an increase of only 2 since the previous census.[18] The immediate potential for a religious congregation other than Roman Catholic was practically nil.

[14] Zephyrin Engelhardt, O.F.M., *San Gabriel Mission and the Beginnings of Los Angeles* (San Gabriel, California: Mission San Gabriel, 1927), pp. 47–53, 95, 123–36. See also Thomas Workman Temple, "Se Fundaron Un Pueblo de Espanoles," Historical Society of Southern California *Annual Publications*, XV (1931), pp. 69–98; and Harry Kelsey, "A New Look at the Founding of Old Los Angeles," *California Historical Quarterly*, LV (Winter, 1976), pp. 326–39.

[15] Construction of the chapel entailed the services of Joseph Chapman, a captured pirate, and financing through the sale of donated livestock and barrels of brandy. This led historian J. Thomas Owen to remark that it was a church "conceived in brandy, roofed by a pirate, and dedicated to the Holy Mother." See his valuable article, "The Church by the Plaza: A History of the Pueblo Church of Los Angeles," Historical Society of Southern California *Quarterly*, XLII (March, 1960), pp. 15–16.

[16] David J. Weber, *The Mexican Frontier, 1821–1846: The American Southwest under Mexico* (Albuquerque: University of New Mexico Press, 1982), p. 162.

[17] J. Gregg Layne, ed., "The First Census of the Los Angeles District," Historical Society of Southern California *Quarterly*, XVIII (September–December, 1936), p. 83.

[18] Marie E. Northrop, ed., "The Los Angeles Padron of 1844," Historical Society of Southern California *Quarterly*, XLII (December, 1960), pp. 360–62.

Every one of the norteamericano settlers was male, and most were married to Hispanic women. Not a single couple or family from the United States was then resident in Los Angeles.

Los Angeles and all California initially were the juridical responsibility of the bishop of Sonora, resident in the city of Alamos, Sonora, and later in Culiacán, Sinaloa. No hierarch of that diocese ever undertook the difficult journey to such a remote province. Furthermore, the bishopric was unoccupied from the death of its incumbent in 1825 until 1838, due to papal opposition to Mexican independence.[19] Consequently, the Hispanic population developed rich, family-centered devotional practices to maintain their faith life. If and when a clergyman was present in a settlement or rancho, he supplemented these familial devotions from old Mexico with the rituals of the sacraments and the blessings of fields and crops.[20]

In 1840, Pope Gregory XVI erected the Diocese of Both Californias and appointed a Mexican-born Franciscan as first bishop, Friar Francisco García Diego y Moreno. Only twenty-one priests, many aged or infirm, were available to staff the diocese: four Dominicans for all Baja California, and seventeen Franciscans for Alta California. Tithes proved so difficult to collect that the new diocesan seminary struggled to survive, and plans for constructing a cathedral in Santa Barbara were forgotten. To the day of his death, in 1846, the bishop saw his grandiose plans frustrated by a scarcity of funds and the indifference of the laity.[21] Not until 1850 did José Sadoc Alemany, a Spanish Dominican missionary then active in the Upper Midwest, succeed to García Diego's vacant post.

Until 1846, the community of Los Angeles enjoyed a cultural and religious hegemony, in which Roman Catholicism held sway by law and custom.[22] Immigrating settlers were so few that they could easily be assimilated into the existing society and church. This began to change when the United States fought Mexico (1846–1848), and the

[19] Weber, *The Mexican Frontier*, pp. 69–70.

[20] For the period 1822 to 1846, David Weber describes the state of religion on the frontera in his volume, *The Mexican Frontier*, chapter 4: "The Church in Jeopardy," pp. 69–84. I examine the family-centered folk piety of Angelenos at greater length, in chapter 6.

[21] Francis J. Weber, *A Biographical Sketch of Right Reverend Francisco García Diego y Moreno, O.F.M.* (Los Angeles: The Borromeo Guild, 1961), pp. 25–29.

[22] See chapter 7 for an extended discussion of the position of the Roman Catholic communion under Spanish and Mexican rule.

victorious norteamericanos introduced new forms of law and government in the conquered territories. Then, the discovery of gold
in 1848 sparked in the following year a rush of people from many
nations to mineral-rich northern California. While Los Angeles never
received the massive numbers of "forty-niners" who overwhelmed
the Hispanic population to the north in a mad dash for treasure and
territory, changes in the pueblo were significant. There was a pro-
portionally profound economic and demographic impact upon this
town nestled bucolically amidst the fields and vineyards on the banks
of the Río Porciúncula.

In the census of 1850, the first in California under United States
rule, enumerators unfamiliar with the Spanish language seriously
underrepresented Hispanics in their tallies throughout the state.[23] A
direct comparison with previous census returns is complicated by the
differing boundaries for the civic entity constituting Los Angeles. In
the new, American system, the county as an administrative territory
replaced the previous Los Angeles "district," with greatly expanded
boundaries, encompassing 34,500 square miles.[24] For the first time,
however, it was possible to get an exact count of the population of
the town alone: 1,610. The vast county contained only 3,530 people.

The division of the population by gender exhibits an imbalance
typical of frontier regions. Los Angeles was home to 895 males,
but only 715 females. The contrast in the surrounding county was
even more dramatic: 1,138 men appear on the rolls, but only 782
women. It is also possible to recognize significant shifts in population. Those born in the United States and its territories (excluding
California) numbered 512 in the county, with many of these residing in the pueblo. Foreigners in the county totaled 699, of whom
518 were recent arrivals from Mexico. These latter figures were enor-
mous increases over the 1844 tallies and indicate the demographic
consequences of both conquest and gold rush.[25]

[23] For a discussion of the problems census enumerators faced, see Richard Griswold del Castillo, *The Los Angeles Barrio, 1850–1890: A Social History* (Berkeley: University of California Press, 1979), pp. 34, 178–80.

[24] The creation of the counties of San Bernardino and Orange, in 1853 and 1889,
respectively, reduced Los Angeles to its present size of 4,083 square miles. Helen L.
Jones and Robert F. Wilcox, *Metropolitan Los Angeles: Its Governments* (Los Angeles:
The Haynes Foundation, 1949), pp. 12–13; and Robert Glass Cleland, *The Cattle on
A Thousand Hills* (San Marino, California: Huntington Library, 1951), p. 138.

[25] Maurice H. Newmark and Marco R. Newmark, eds., *Census of the City and*

The census figures also document the presence in Los Angeles of the first Anglo-American families, only eleven in number, yet important for the course of future events. Single adult males predominated in the non-Hispanic population, but a handful of Anglo-American women had already arrived and established residence. These newcomers found a society vastly different from their New England Sabbaths or log-cabin schoolhouses. The prevailing Hispanic religious customs of the time received repeated notice in the diaries, letters, and newspaper accounts of newcomers and visitors to the community. One of the earliest of such writers was a member of the Mormon Battalion stationed in Los Angeles between March and July of 1847, to augment the occupying forces of the United States Army during the war with Mexico.[26]

In his diary entry for 3 June 1847, this Latter-Day Saint gave an outsider's description of the annual Corpus Christi procession around the plaza.[27] Henry Standage noted that even one of the six companies of the New York Volunteers then engaged in the military occupation was pressed into service as an honor guard:

> The inhabitants of the Pueblo have been sweeping the public
> square for 2 days past, and this morning they erected 4 stages,
> one in each corner of the square, also erecting an altar at each
> place, making it of green bushes, and decorated with roses, strips
> of white cloth and very handsome [*serapes*] or a kind of out-
> side covering thrown around the man while on horseback, were
> thrown on the ground. . . . As soon as mass was performed in the

---

County of Los Angeles, California, for the Year 1850 (Los Angeles: Times-Mirror Press, 1929), pp. 115, 117.

[26] It is important to note that the Latter-Day Saints held religious services during their time in Los Angeles, one of the earliest denominations to do so. See Frank Alfred Golder, Thomas A. Bailey, and J. Lyman Smith, eds., *The March of the Mormon Battalion from Council Bluffs to California; Taken from the Journal of Henry Standage* (New York: The Century Company, 1928), pp. 223–24; Daniel Tyler, *A Concise History of the Mormon Battalion in the Mexican War* (Salt Lake City, n.p., 1881; reprint ed., Chicago: Rio Grande Press, 1964); and Hubert Howe Bancroft, *The Works of Hubert Howe Bancroft*, vol. XX, *History of California* (San Francisco: The History Company, 1886–90; reprint ed., Santa Barbara, California: Wallace Hebberd, 1970), pp. 396–98, 468–515.

[27] Bancroft, *Works*, vol. XXII, *History of California* p. 489; see also Harlan E. Hogue, "A History of Religion in Southern California, 1846–1880" (Ph.D. diss., Columbia University, 1958), pp. 31–34.

church the Priest with a long retinue came out into the Square, the Priest performing certain rites at each of the altars. The band belonging to the N. Y. Vols. playing while the procession was passing from corner to corner and the inhabitants showering roses all the time on the capital Priest's head and spreading costly garments on the ground for him to walk on. The cannon firing at intervals as the procession moved from place to place.[28]

Such processions were public demonstrations of the prevailing creed in the small community. With increasing prosperity in the following decade, these religious ceremonies grew larger and more elaborate. The editor of the Spanish-language paper, *El Clamor Público*, reported on each of these events, though with a differing perspective from that of his counterpart at the Los Angeles *Star*. In the 28 May 1853 edition of the *Star*, the editor commented on the Corpus Christi celebrations with less than pious sentiments:

The ceremonies were to us interesting—rather more interesting than intelligible—and the assemblage was greater than any we have heretofore seen on any like occasion. The bevy of Senoritas was unusually large, presenting as they wended their way along, their dark lustrous eyes peering from the rich rebosa which partially concealed the face, their graceful forms arrayed in costly and beautiful silks, and their dignified and elegant carriage, a most captivating sight.[29]

On the same issue's Spanish-language page, *La Estrella*, the editor's remarks were far more circumspect, possibly out of deference to the sensibilities of Hispanic readers. The differences between the report-

<hr>

[28] Golder, Bailey, and Smith, eds., *The March of the Mormon Battalion*, pp. 223–24. Other descriptions and comments upon Los Angeles religious customs are found in June Barrows, ed., "A Vermonter's Description of a Sunday in Los Angeles, California, in 1852," *Vermont History*, XXXVIII (Summer, 1970), pp. 192–94; and Marjorie Tisdale Wolcott, ed., *Pioneer Notes from the Diaries of Judge Benjamin Hayes, 1849–1875*, (Los Angeles: privately printed, 1929), pp. 71–73, 102, 107, 119, 123, 168–69, 199, 284. Francis D. Clark listed the members of the regimental band of the New York Volunteers in *The First Regiment of New York Volunteers Commanded by Colonel Jonathon D. Stevenson in the Mexican War* (New York: George S. Evans and Company, 1882), p. 23.
[29] "Corpus Christi," p. 2.

ing of the two publications, *El Clamor Publico* and the *Star*, offer some of the numerous examples of the growing bifurcation in Los Angeles society. Divisions were appearing in many areas besides religion, contrasts arising from the increased and diverse immigration swelling the local populace.[30]

Cattlemen throughout southern California took advantage of the lucrative market that hungry miners and prospectors provided in the northern end of the state. Herds driven from the Los Angeles area yielded immense profits throughout the 1850s for the rancheros in the "Queen of the Cow Counties." Like any prosperous cow town, however, the community also attracted its share of shiftless gamblers and unemployed cow hands. Saloons, gambling dens, and brothels opened along the Calle de los Negros, a narrow lane connecting the southwest corner of the plaza with Los Angeles Street. Gunshots frequently punctuated the night, when arguments led to boisterous brawls along "Nigger Alley," as this street came to be known. Violence was so common in the town that the *Southern Californian* of 16 November 1854 laconically reported on the mayhem:

> The week has been comparatively quiet; four persons have been killed, it is true, but it has been considered a poor week for killing; a head or two has been split open, and an occasional case of cutting has occurred, but these are minor matters, and create but little feeling.[31]

California's spectacular increase in population prompted Pope Pius IX, in 1853, again to split the immense diocese of California. The pontiff named Bishop Alemany to the newly created archbishopric of San Francisco and erected the diocese of Monterey for the sprawling southern counties of the state. For the bishop of this new see the pope selected Tadeo Amat, a Spanish theologian then serving as a Philadelphia seminary rector. Amat prepared to assume his missionary post

---

[30] Leonard Pitt studied the instances of conflict between Hispanics and people coming into the community in the 1850s. See *The Decline of the Californios: A Social History of the Spanish-Speaking Californians, 1846–1890* (Berkeley: University of California Press, 1966), pp. 148–66.

[31] Violence in the community prompted repeated vigilante action, as described in Pitt, *Decline of the Californios*, pp. 156–58, and Horace Bell, *Reminiscences of a Ranger* (Los Angeles: Yarnell, Caystile, and Mathes, 1881), pp. 79–82.

by making an extended tour of Europe to raise funds and to secure personnel for the institutions he envisioned founding. He did not reach California until late in 1855. In his company came Italian and Spanish priests and seminarians, as well as Spanish and American Sisters of Charity of St. Vincent de Paul. He had obtained some $14,000 in contributions, along with the promise of an annual donation from the French mission association, the Société de la Propagation de la Foi.[32] Amat's arrival and reception in Los Angeles was a public event heralded by pealing church bells, Indians dancing in costume, and throngs of the faithful and curious.[33]

Ministers of more traditional Protestant denominations preceded Amat's arrival. Leaders of Methodist, Baptist, and Presbyterian communions had each dispatched ministers to the pueblo so distant from "The City" of San Francisco. The growth in the Anglo-American populace in southern California prompted these assignments and promised fruitful results.[34] Local lawlessness, however, quickly dispelled any illusions of success held by even the most seasoned minister. The gun-toting individuals then attracted to Los Angeles rarely carried a Bible or frequented a camp meeting.

Typical of so many frontier-seasoned Methodist ministers, John W. Brier, with his wife and family, crossed the continent by covered wagon and reached Los Angeles in the spring of 1850. Reverend Brier, the first Protestant clergyman to preach in the pueblo, soon left this demanding field for more promising harvests in the northern mining regions. Brier's later clerical colleagues would encounter the same lack of success in gathering a lasting congregation. Reverend John W. Douglas, a New-School Presbyterian, arrived several months after Brier's departure and taught school in the home of William Wolfskill. However, the prospects of success in Los Angeles were far too

[32] "Cash Book," vol. I, entries for 1855, Archives of the Archdiocese of Los Angeles, Mission Hills, California, hereafter cited as AALA; see also Francis J. Weber, *California's Reluctant Prelate* (Los Angeles: Dawson's Book Shop, 1964), pp. 26–27.

[33] Weber, *California's Reluctant Prelate*, p. 42; *El Clamor Público*, 15 December 1855.

[34] A "Baptist" writing to the editor of the *Pacific*, in San Francisco, in the issue of 4 June 1852, lamented that "No place needs the Gospel more than Los Angeles." Here was a native population that was "ignorant and degraded," still attached to the "ridiculous observances of the Roman Church." A preacher from any denomination would suffice. Local needs for religion were pressing, and the prospective congregants would probably have "little regard as to the particular views of the minister."

poor, so by August of 1851, Douglas departed for more promising fields in San Francisco, where he edited the new religious journal, *The Pacific*.[35]

In February 1853, the Northern Methodists dispatched the Reverend Adam Bland to the newly created circuit of southern California, which included the rowdy pueblo. On 19 July 1853, Bland wrote to a fellow minister that local religious progress was slow in a society he rated as "the worst." In true Methodist tradition, Bland soon planned a series of camp meetings to kindle a greater fervor, while his wife conducted school in the newly whitewashed former barroom of the converted El Dorado saloon. The Virginia-born Bland withdrew, in 1854, in favor of Reverend J. McHenry Caldwell, a former sailor who had graduated from Dickinson College, in Carlisle, Pennsylvania.[36] Bland had made a definite impression upon residents, one of whom remembered the minister as a "smart preacher and a shrewd horse trader," in a field he regarded as "hopeless."[37]

The camp meeting became a recurrent religious exercise in Los Angeles county for the following three decades. The first gathering, the one mentioned by Bland, was held several miles east of Los Angeles, in the town of Lexington, during the week of 15 September 1854. According to one press account, several preachers joined Bland in the grove of "Mr. Sheldon's farm," and preached from an improvised pulpit to "anxious worshipers."[38] In a telling remark about the challenges of such labors, one minister noted at the following year's revival that there were "some hard nuts there yet."[39] Several aspects

[35] For John Brier, see J. M. Guinn, "Los Angeles in the Adobe Age," *Historical Society of Southern California Annual Publications*, IV, Part I (1897), pp. 49–55. Harland E. Hogue discussed Douglas's work in his "The History of Religion in Southern California," pp. 55–56; see also *The Pacific*, XLVIII (2 November 1899), p. 19.

[36] Charles V. Anthony, *Fifty Years of Methodism: A History of the Methodist Episcopal Church Within the Bounds of the California Annual Conference, from 1847 to 1897* (San Francisco: Methodist Book Concern, 1901), p. 99.

[37] Letter, Bland to Reverend Isaac Owen, 19 July 1853, Los Angeles, in typescript, "Correspondence of the Rev. Isaac Owen," Transcript C-B 337, pp. 233–34, Bancroft Library, Berkeley, California, hereafter cited as BL; *Los Angeles Star*, 26 February, 1853, p. 2, noted Bland's arrival in this "hard place," and the issue of 6 August 1853 reported the opening of a school, which his wife conducted; and H. D. Barrows, "Early Clericals of Los Angeles," *Historical Society of Southern California Annual Publications*, V (1902), p. 129.

[38] *Los Angeles Star*, 14 and 21 September 1854.

[39] *Los Angeles Star*, 13 October 1855.

of these events are significant for what they reveal about the initial Protestant approaches to ministries in Los Angeles.

The location chosen indicated that the clergymen anticipated a response from Anglo-American farmers and their families, living in and around Lexington. Later renamed El Monte, Lexington was a settlement of Texas Baptists, known for their antipathy toward the local Hispanic population. Los Angeles, by way of contrast, was thoroughly Roman Catholic. So few Anglo-American families resided in the pueblo that preachers could not find there a sufficient number of souls for the religious awakening they sought to arouse. At the 1854 camp meeting, Baptist and Methodist clergymen joined their efforts to reach these "hardened sinners," much as other clerics had done in earlier revivals, dating back to the Cane Ridge revival in Kentucky, at the turn of the nineteenth century.

Language proved a further important consideration. No Protestant minister could speak Spanish, until the arrival of Reverend William Mosher, in 1871, and even he did not engage in full-time Hispanic ministry until 1876.[40] Camp meetings were therefore Anglo-American religious gatherings, which remained incomprehensible to most Hispanics. In the ten years after 1854, Protestant ministers preached in surrounding towns, with only occasional visits to Los Angeles. Not until the end of that decade would the Anglo-American population sufficiently increase to support full-time pastorates.

For the fourteen years after Reverend Bland's departure, in 1854, the northern Methodist Episcopal Church's California Conference could only intermittently supply Los Angeles as part of its Southern California District, because of a lack of personnel and the poor prospects for success. Southern Methodists were not much more successful, despite Methodism's well-deserved reputation for attracting the heartiest of circuit riding ministers. The minutes of the Pacific Conference of the Methodist Episcopal Church, South, record annual clergy appointments to the Los Angeles District and even a membership of forty-two worshipers by 1856. Nonetheless, a permanent congregation of this denomination would not appear in the community until 1869. Too few Methodists of either branch of that church

---

[40] William C. Mosher "Scrapbook," (n.d.), p. 115; Henry E. Huntington Library, San Marino, California, hereafter cited as HL.

LOS ANGELES AREA, 1870

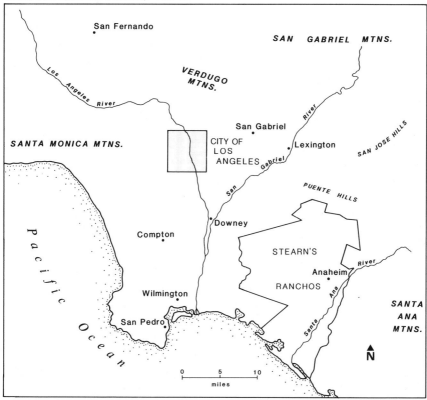

lived in Los Angeles in the 1850s and early 1860s to sustain organized denominational life.[41]

Baptist efforts in Los Angeles would not develop for several years. Lexington's Baptists, however, had organized a church in November of 1853, with four members drawn from a community of only thirty-

[41] George Foster Pierce, D.D., undertook an official visitation to California on behalf of the Methodist Episcopal Church, South, in 1859. The bishop kept a journal of his cross-country stage journey and recorded a visit to Los Angeles, though he made no reference to encountering any fellow Southern Methodist clergy or members. The journal was reprinted from George S. Smith, *The Life and Times of George Foster Pierce, D.D., L.L.D.* (Sparta, Georgia: Hancock Publishing Company, 1888), in "Parson's Progress to California," Historical Society of Southern California *Quarterly*, XXI (June-September, 1939), pp. 45–78. Other data from Anthony, *Fifty Years of Methodism*, p. 115, 124, 133, 294; "Minutes of the Pacific Annual Conference"

four families. Baptist evangelization in Los Angeles also originated in rustic Lexington, which had hosted the first camp meetings of the region. In 1859, Lexington's minister, Reverend John Freeman, initiated regular weekly preaching in the pueblo in Schoolhouse Number One. But Baptist progress was slow in the City of the Angels; usually in the forefront of pioneering Christianity in the United States, Baptists were among the last of the mainline Protestant denominations to establish themselves in Los Angeles.[42] Baptist strength lay in the surrounding farming areas, such as Lexington, which manifested the rural orientation, family population, and appeal of this faith found on other frontiers.

Presbyterian clergy suffered similar discouragements. Reverend James Woods arrived in Los Angeles in October of 1854, and commenced his ministry there on 12 November. The Massachusetts-born Woods had received his education at Wesleyan University, in Middleton, Connecticut, and the Theological Seminary of Charleston, South Carolina. His reactions to Hispanic customs and local conditions were repeatedly negative. Sunday bullfights, gambling, horse races, and cock fights appalled him as desecrations of the Sabbath. The general lawlessness of the community further repulsed him and inspired him to preach some of his strongest sermons. On 29 April 1855, Woods confided to his diary: "I preached this morning upon the destruction of Sodom and Gomorrah and had I wanted material for supposed scenes in those cities I could have found them in the very scenes now transpiring around me."[43]

This Old-School Presbyterian minister was thoroughly a product of his times, embodying the religious beliefs and cultural prejudices of the age. He earnestly sought to preach the Gospel message of a redeeming Savior, but he confined his efforts solely to Anglo-Americans. Jailed criminals and wealthy ranchers alike received his

---

[Methodist Episcopal Church, South], vol. I, passim, Archives of the Pacific and Southwest Annual Conference of the United Methodist Church, Claremont, California, hereafter cited as APSAC; and Leon L. Loofbourow, *In Search of God's Gold* (San Francisco: Historical Society of Northern California–Nevada Conference of the Methodist Church, 1950), vol. II, p. 164.

[42] Ivan C. Ellis, "Baptist Churches of Southern California" (Ph.D. dissertation, Northern Baptist Theological Seminary, Chicago, 1948), pp. 90–91, 105.

[43] Quoted in Lindley Bynum, ed., "Los Angeles in 1854–5: The Diary of Rev. James Woods," Historical Society of Southern California *Quarterly*, XXIII (June, 1941), pp. 83–84.

ministerial attention, though one of the former expressed the desire that he would rather see a wild bear in his cell. Local Roman Catholic religious practices led him to confide to his diary: "Called this afternoon into the Catholic church while passing. Idolatry, idolatry, idolatry." He further commented that the Hispanic men of the town's "aristocracy" were "a dark complexioned set with darker minds and morals."[44]

Despite many discouragements from low attendance at his Sunday services and recurring poor health, Reverend Woods organized a church, on 18 March 1855, with twelve members. This was the first Protestant religious body formally to constitute itself as a congregation in Los Angeles. Woods reflected often in his diary upon his sermons, the low attendance at services, female immodesty in dress, and the adverse effect of local society upon his children. When poor health forced Woods to depart, six months later, Reverend Thomas K. Davis replaced him and remained until mid-1856.[45] Three years then elapsed until a successor appeared. Reverend William E. Boardman and his wife arrived from Philadelphia early in 1859, only to find a dispersed and dispirited congregation. No Protestant denomination was meeting on a regular basis or conducting services in Los Angeles at that time.

Author of the popular volume *The Higher Christian Life*, Reverend Boardman proved an engaging preacher and practical organizer who quickly sized up the religious prospects of the community.[46] Soon after his arrival, he instituted the "First Protestant Society of the City of Los Angeles," in May 1859, to bring together the disparate adherents of Reformed religion. Ten men and five women inscribed their names to the preamble and constitution, adopted on the fourth day

[44] Bynum, ed., "Diary of Rev. Woods," entries for 24 December 1854, p. 78, and 25 April 1855, p. 83.

[45] Davis later wrote that he and his family departed Los Angeles due to an outbreak of violence that paralyzed the community and "broke up" the church and the schools. "Autobiographical Sketch" (January, 1867), p. [4], Manuscript D2971, Presbyterian Office of History, Philadelphia, hereafter cited as POHP; and *The Davis Family* (Norwood, Massachusetts: The Plimpton Press, 1912), p. 111.

[46] Bynum, ed., "Diary of Rev. Woods," p. 67; William S. Young, untitled manuscript, (11 April 1923), pp. 3–4, "First Presbyterian Church of Los Angeles" file, Archives, San Francisco Theological Seminary, San Anselmo, California, hereafter cited as ASFTS; *The Higher Christian Life* (Boston: Hoyt, 1858); and Mrs. [William E.] Boardman, *Life and Labours of the Reverend W. E. Boardman* (New York: D. Appleton and Company, 1887), p. 113.

of that month. The stated purpose was "the present maintenance, permanent establishment and successful progress of Protestant Worship in this city."[47] What individual denominations had attempted and failed to attain, this nonsectarian Protestant body now hoped to achieve. By August of that year, $315 was in the treasury in order to pay the first three-month installment of Boardman's salary. The women of the church formed a sewing society and industriously sought to raise the funds needed for the construction of a church structure.[48]

The minister was such a popular figure in Los Angeles society that he received an appointment to the superintendency of the town's public school system. In a locale where one-year terms were the normal tenure for this office, Boardman had the unusual distinction of recurrent reappointment to that post every year of his pastorate, 1859–62. Boardman also entered into the fraternal life of the community, affiliating, in January 1862, with the pioneer Masonic Lodge #42. His extensive contacts also led to a lifelong friendship with one of the wealthier men of the county, Benjamin Davis Wilson, a Tennessean then resident, east of the town, at his farm, Lake Vineyard. According to one account, it was through Wilson that Boardman received title to a lot in Los Angeles that enabled the minister to proceed with the realization of one of his dreams: the erection of a church building.[49]

On 2 November 1860, a meeting was held to organize "the first Presbyterian church 'Old-School,'" and to elect officers and trustees. By April of the following year, Boardman and his congregation laid the foundation stone for a church edifice on the northwest edge of town. The order of procession of the day is worth noting, for what it reveals of the broad support the sole Protestant body enjoyed in the community. Participants included a band; members of the German "Teutonia" society, Odd Fellows Lodge #35, and Masonic Lodge #42; Boardman and the trustees of the church; the mayor and Common Council of Los Angeles; and interested individuals from "the

[47] "Constitution and By-Laws of the First Protestant Society of Los Angeles," pp. 1–3, HL; hereafter cited as "Constitution."

[48] "Constitution," p. 8.

[49] "Records," vol. II, p. 6, Lodge 42, Free and Accepted Masons, Los Angeles, California; Barrows, "Early Clericals," p. 130; Boardman-Wilson correspondence, 1859–1868, Wilson Collection, HL; and Midge Sherwood, *Days of Vintage, Years of Vision* (San Marino, California: Orizaba Press, 1982), vol. I, p. 318.

general citizenry." The parade assembled at the Masonic Hall and marched first to the United States courthouse and then on to the building site. The Masonic order presided over the ceremonies, the Teutonians rendered an ode, and Boardman preached a discourse disavowing any spirit of religious prejudice in the project at hand.[50] To local Anglo-Americans, Protestant Christianity appeared to be on the rise in backward Los Angeles.

But progress was short-lived. The church building was roofed by the time Reverend Boardman and his wife left the community for Philadelphia, in February 1862. The advent of the Civil War had prompted the minister to return to the East and search for some means by which he might contribute to the Union cause.[51] The Los Angeles congregation then languished, and the church itself suffered the indignity of being sold at a sheriff's auction for nonpayment of taxes, in February 1863. The Los Angeles *Star* was quick to chide Angelenos for their poor religious spirit: "What heathens we must be, sure enough, when we find the church offered for sale by the Sheriff. . . ."[52] One anonymous soul redeemed the structure on behalf of the First Protestant Society, but Angelenos gathered there only sporadically for scheduled services over the next three years. Despite several unsuccessful attempts, a Presbyterian congregation could not be reestablished until 1874, by which time title to the church had passed to the Episcopalians.

Methodist, Baptist, and Presbyterian church leaders had dispatched dedicated clergymen to serve the spiritual needs in Los Angeles, only to see one divine after another give up the demoralizing field. Gamblers, prostitutes, and fugitives from the law far outnumbered local God-fearing folk. Too few Anglo-American women and families had settled to sustain a viable congregation. Evangelization of the local

[50] "Constitution," p. 9; Los Angeles *Star*, 29 April 1861; "Records," vol. I, p. 349, Lodge #42, Free and Accepted Masons, Los Angeles, California.

[51] Boardman served as secretary for the United States Christian Commission throughout the course of the Civil War. In its efforts to improve the lot of the men in the military, this group benefited greatly from Boardman's organizational skills. Regarding the work of the Commission, see Boardman's letters to Benjamin D. Wilson, 8 October 1862 and 4 February 1863, both from Philadelphia; Wilson Collection, HL. See also *Christ in the Army: A Selection of Sketches of the Work of the U. S. Christian Commission* (Philadelphia: Ladies' Christian Commission, 1865), pp. 1–16, 23–46.

[52] 31 January 1863.

Hispanic population was not a pressing concern of the early Protestant clerics, despite the acknowledged need to rescue them from the "idolatry" of Roman Catholicism. Regions other than Los Angeles appealed to the ministers because of opportunities for serving English-speaking settlers in the northern portion of California. Protestant church authorities concluded that increased settlement by the "right sort of people" in the town was the only solution to this religious dilemma.

Immigrants to Los Angeles by 1854 included not only members of the usual denominations found on the midwestern frontier, but other believers as well. The federal census completed in January of 1851 had listed eight men in Los Angeles who were working in adjoining shops in the business block known as Bell's Row. These seven merchants and one tailor were the first Jews in the community. The same six Germans and two Poles would gradually welcome additional relatives and friends, as well as other Jews from the United States, England, and France. The Los Angeles *Star* was able to report, on 8 July 1854, that the "Israelites of this city" had organized the Hebrew Benevolent Society and elected a slate of officers. The printed constitution and by-laws that appeared the following year listed thirty members, who committed themselves to securing a cemetery, following Jewish funeral customs, and providing benevolent aid to the needy.[53]

The officers of this society moved quickly to secure a proper burial site for the members of their faith. They incorporated their organization on 6 July 1854, and the very next day they petitioned the Los Angeles Common Council for a parcel of land. That civic body approved their request two months later, and conveyed title for three acres just northeast of town on 9 April 1855.[54] This group also gathered each year between 1854 and 1862 to observe Jewish religious holidays.[55] For the first six years, High Holy Days services were

[53] Norton B. Stern, "Location of Los Angeles Jewry at the Beginning of 1851," *Western States Jewish Historical Quarterly*, V (October, 1972), pp. 25–31; *Constitution and By-Laws of the Hebrew Benevolent Society of Los Angeles, California* (Los Angeles: Southern Californian Office, 1855), pp. 3, 12.

[54] Thomas Cohen, "First Jewish Community Site," in *Bicentennial Digest: A Perspective of Pioneer Los Angeles Jewry* (Los Angeles: Jewish Federation–Council of Greater Los Angeles, 1976), pp. 5–6.

[55] For example, see Los Angeles *Star*, 15 September 1855, for an account of the local observance of Passover that year. In the 11 October 1856 edition of the same newspaper appeared the article, "Hebrew Festivals," explaining the history and local ceremonies for Rosh Hashanah.

conducted by one of their own members, while in 1860 and 1861 they secured a visiting rabbi.[56] By 1862, the local Jewish population had grown to an estimated 200 souls, which prompted the society's members to seek a permanent rabbi.[57]

Among the men of the organization was a lay rabbi who had first inspired the formation of the benevolent society. Joseph Newmark, a native of Poland, had trained to preside at marriages and other religious ceremonies in the absence of an ordained rabbi. He also held a license as *schochet,* kosher ritual butcher. He had emigrated to the United States in 1824, assisted in the establishment of two synagogues in New York City, conducted business in the Midwest, and then established himself in San Francisco in 1852. With his wife and family, Newmark moved to Los Angeles, in September 1854, where they long remained in the forefront of Jewish community life. Newmark conducted worship for the High Holy Days sponsored by the Hebrew Benevolent Society, until a formal congregation was instituted, of which he was founding president.[58]

Newmark and Moritz Morris visited San Francisco and officially tendered the nascent Congregation B'nai B'rith's invitation to Abraham Wolf Edelman to serve as rabbi and teacher. Edelman's acceptance marked the beginning of twenty-three years of service to the pioneer Jewish religious body in Los Angeles. Like Newmark, the rabbi was of Polish birth and education. He and his wife had emigrated to the United States shortly after their marriage, in 1851, and had resided in several communities prior to their 1859 move to San Francisco. Edelman had further studied Hebrew language and law in that city under Rabbi Henry A. Henry, of Congregation Sherith Israel, as well as perfecting his English while working as a dry-goods salesman.[59]

---

[56] The Los Angeles *Star* of 7 September 1861 reported that M. Golland of San Francisco had led the services that year in the community.

[57] Norton B. Stern and William M. Kramer, "Jewish Padre to the Pueblo: Pioneer Los Angeles Rabbi Abraham Wolf Edelman," *Western States Jewish Historical Quarterly,* III (July, 1971), p. 193.

[58] Harris Newmark, *Sixty Years in Southern California, 1853–1913* (4th ed., revised by Maurice H. Newmark and Marco R. Newmark, Los Angeles: Zeitlin and Ver Brugge, 1970), pp. 121–22; and William Kramer and Norton B. Stern, "The Layman as Rabbinic Officiant in the Nineteenth Century," *Western States Jewish History,* XVI (October, 1983), pp. 49, 52. The original name for the 1862 organization was the Congregation B'nai Berith, later changed to B'nai B'rith.

[59] Stern and Kramer, "Jewish Padre to the Pueblo," pp. 194–95.

In Los Angeles, Edelman found thirty-two charter members of the religious community, who met for worship in a rented hall in the Arcadia Block. Like himself, the majority were European immigrants who had been attracted to the opportunities that gold-rush California offered. Many in the congregation had arrived in Los Angeles as the result of a chain migration of relatives and friends from overseas. Sixteen-year-old Isaias W. Hellman, for example, departed Reckendorf, Bavaria, in 1859, with his brother Herman, to join their merchant cousins Samuel and Isaias M. Hellman in Los Angeles. Relatives and friends of the Haas and Fleischman families also came from Reckendorf. From Loebau, Prussia, J.P. Newmark had arrived in the pueblo in 1851, and was later joined by his brother Harris, his uncle Joseph Newmark with a wife and six children, cousins Samuel and Kaspare Cohn, as well as members of the Jacoby and Lewin clans. Solomon Lazard and his cousin Maurice Kremer came from the same town, in the Alsace region of France. The three Elias brothers (Jacob, Raphael, and Israel) together established a partnership in Los Angeles, in 1853. Thus, the eight "Israelites" found in the *pueblo* in 1851 grew to approximately two hundred by 1860 and were closely interrelated by family ties and marriage.[60]

Local Judaism was also concerned and deeply involved in the formative stages of Los Angeles society in the initial decades of American rule. Members of the small Jewish community actively participated in a wide range of local affairs, including fraternal, political, economic, and charitable endeavors. Several examples illustrate their significant associations. Four of the sixteen founding members of the first Masonic lodge in 1853 were Jews, and by 1865, five Jews had already served on the town's Common Council. Edelman himself soon affiliated with Masonic Lodge #42, the Royal Arch Masons, the Odd Fellows, the Independent Order of Chosen Friends, and the

---

[60] Mitchell Gelfand, "Progress and Prosperity: Jewish Social Mobility in Los Angeles in the Booming Eighties," *American Jewish History*, LXVIII (June, 1979), p. 429. Of the twenty-four founders of Congregation B'nai Berith, the nationalities of twenty are known. Of these, seventeen were Polish or Polish-Prussian in origin. See William S. Kramer and Norton B. Stern, "The Major Role of Polish Jews in the Pioneer West," *Western States Jewish Historical Quarterly*, VIII (July, 1976), p. 342. Regarding the Hellman and Newmark families, see Newmark, *Sixty Years*, p. 13, 26, 122, 248. Solomon Lazard and the Elias brothers are treated in Max Vorspan and Lloyd P. Gartner, *History of the Jews in Los Angeles* (San Marino, California: Huntington Library, 1970), pp. 8–9.

Ancient Order of United Workmen. In each group, he found prominent coreligionists. The involvement of Jews in local mercantile pursuits was significant, due to their European training as well as their
commercial contacts through members of the Jewish community in
San Francisco. When the first of several smallpox epidemics plagued
Los Angeles in 1862, these "Hebrews" made important contributions
through their benevolent society, a gesture they repeated in each of
the later relief efforts.[61]

The interest of the growing Jewish populace in religious instruction of their young and the desire for formal worship services did not
differ significantly from the aspirations of frontier believers of other
faiths. The actions of local Jews paralleled the organizational attempts
other denominations made in Los Angeles. The Jewish experience
was different only in that it was more successful, at an earlier date,
than that of their Protestant brothers and sisters. This accomplish-
ment was in large part due to the role of the 1854 Hebrew Benevolent
Society. The all-male association set local Judaism on a firm institutional basis, provided leadership and training in organizational skills,
and supplied a locus for Los Angeles Jewry to meet. Society members contributed greatly to the successful establishment and survival
of Congregation B'nai B'rith. Edelman's flock achieved distinction
as the second oldest denomination among enduring religious bodies
in Los Angeles.

When the Joseph Newmark family sailed to Los Angeles, in 1854,
from San Francisco, they brought in their employ a Chinese servant.
This man followed two of his countrymen, Ah Luce and Ah Fou,
who had been listed in the 1850 federal census as house servants.[62]
These pioneers were typical of many Chinese who would settle in the
pueblo in the following years: they were single, young males seeking
employment in unskilled positions. By 1860, the Chinese population totaled 16: 14 men and 2 women.[63] The 1870 figures document

[61] "Records," vol. I, p. 7, Lodge #42, Free and Accepted Masons, Los Ange-
les; J. Albert Wilson, *History of Los Angeles County, California* (Oakland, California:
Thompson and West, 1880; reprint ed., Berkeley: Howell-North, 1959), pp. 114–15;
Stern and Kramer, "Jewish Padre to the Pueblo," pp. 196–99; Los Angeles *Tri-Weekly
News*, 13 February 1863.

[62] Newmark and Newmark, eds., *Census of the City and County of Los Angeles . . .
1850*, pp. 30–31. The Los Angeles *Star* of 24 January 1857 reported that the three Chinese working in the Los Angeles Laundry recently had celebrated the lunar new year.

[63] One year later, the Los Angeles *Star* of 27 April 1861 noted that twenty-one

SMS UNIVERSITY
WEST PLAINS CAMPUS

a dramatic increase to 170 Chinese people in the city, of whom half lived in one block south of the plaza.[64] The vast majority of these Chinese immigrants were men engaged in manual labor, who sought to save enough money from the "Golden Mountain" (California) to return enriched to their homeland. What the census figures do not indicate, however, is the structure of Chinese society, the nature of their religious customs, nor the early date at which such worship commenced.[65]

The historian Suchen Chan offers important insights into Chinese urban society in her valuable study of California agricultural workers from China.[66] In Chinatowns throughout the state, the entrepreneurial elite occupied the position of greatest status, followed by the independent professionals and artisans. Those who labored as cooks, servants, and laundry and construction workers comprised the lowest class. To maintain their leadership position, the elite controlled businesses and organizations with direct links to the homeland. They served as brokers of goods, foods, and information from China for those eagerly seeking contact with their native land. Chan also notes that the urban Chinese had far less contact with whites and less dependence upon whites for their employment than their rural counterparts. It is not difficult to understand why the Chinese quarter was considered a "foreign" district, in which the customs and social systems of China persisted among the residents.

The overwhelming majority of these Asian immigrants followed the traditional folk religion of China, which was deeply embedded in their culture. They did not conduct weekly formal worship services, held at regularly scheduled hours. Supplicants offered prayers when need arose, often lighting "joss" sticks or burning paper money to win the favor of a particular figure in the pantheon. As early as 1857,

---

Chinese men and eight women were working in Los Angeles and vicinity. Some labored as cooks, but most were employed in laundries.

[64] William Mason, "The Chinese in Los Angeles," *Museum Alliance Quarterly*, V (Fall, 1967), p. 16. In the county, census enumerators counted 234 Chinese: 196 men and 34 women. See Robert M. Fogelson, *The Fragmented Metropolis: Los Angeles, 1850–1930* (Cambridge: Harvard University Press, 1967), p. 56.

[65] Gunther Barth described the characteristics of Chinese immigration to the United States in *Bitter Strength: A History of the Chinese in the United States, 1850–1870* (Cambridge: Harvard University Press, 1964), p. 157.

[66] Suchen Chan, *This Bitter-Sweet Soil: The Chinese in California Agriculture, 1860–1910* (Berkeley: University of California Press, 1986), pp. 404–405.

newspaper accounts documented the observance of the lunar new year.[67] Religious sanctuaries stood in neighborhoods or in homes, to house figures of the deities and memorial tablets honoring ancestors. Because priests, as such, were not necessary except for the more sophisticated rituals, they could be invited for solemn occasions from San Francisco.[68]

Religious beliefs in China combined a polytheistic system of deities with philosophical insights garnered from Buddhism, Confucianism, and Taoism, known as the Three Teachings. The syncretic approach emphasized the search for harmony within oneself and with all creation. Creed was less important than tolerance, moral conduct, cooperation, simplicity, and tranquility. Pursuing these values, the observant Chinese "had a Confucian cap, wore a Taoist robe, and put on a Buddhist sandal."[69] The various gods and goddesses assisted humans in the search for harmony and peace. The more popular divinities reverenced in California included Kuan Kung (god of literature and valor, peace and war), Hsuan Ti'en Shang Ti ("True Lord of the Black Pavilion," conqueror of the demon king), Tou Mu (goddess of light, queen of heaven), and Kuan Yin ("One who hears prayers," goddess of mercy). Kung Fu-tse (Confucius) received veneration as a sage, not a god. Particular groups sought the divine aid of specific gods, such as Chih Nu ("Weaver Maid," whom women supplicated) and Lu Pan ("The Craftsman," whom carpenters worshiped). The cycle of the year's holy days included six festivals, two of which were most popular in Los Angeles. Newspaper accounts refer annually to the lunar new year celebrations, as well as to the commemoration of the dead during Ch'ing Ming ("Pure Brightness" festival).[70]

These rites, not to mention the beliefs and gods involved, appeared

[67] Los Angeles *Star*, 24 January 1857.

[68] An excellent description of Chinese religious life in Los Angeles is contained in Raymond Lou, "The Chinese American Community of Los Angeles, 1870–1900: A Case of Resistance, Organization, and Participation" (Ph.D. dissertation, University of California, Irvine, 1982), pp. 270–78.

[69] Shih-Shan Henry Tsai, *The Chinese Experience in America* (Bloomington: Indian University Press, 1986), p. 43.

[70] Thomas W. Chinn, H. Mark Lai, and Philip P. Choy, *A History of the Chinese in California* (San Francisco: Chinese Historical Society of America, 1969), pp. 74–77; "Celebration of Chinese New Year, January, 1876," reprinted from the Los Angeles *Daily Star*, January, 1876, in *Gum Saan Journal* of the Chinese Historical Society of Southern California, III (May, 1979), pp. 10–11; and Los Angeles *Herald*, 12 October and 24 November 1881.

so different to Anglo-American residents of Los Angeles that they received derision and even outright rejection. The earliest evidence of Chinese religion gaining a formal location in the community was the dedication of the first temple, in the winter of 1875. When worship commenced, so did local journalistic commentary: "In solemn conclave the other day the Chinamen formally decided on the jews-harp, bones and trombone, with a dash of piccolo and kettledrum, for their joss-house worship."[71] Such newspaper accounts of Chinese rituals emphasized the colorful or bizarre aspects of ceremonies, but provided little information to promote greater understanding of the beliefs involved. Three years after the temple opened, the funeral ceremonies for the local poet Lee Pai prompted a lengthy and biased journalistic description that included references to the Asian dirge as "a camp-meeting hymn run wild," while the cemetery rites were "heathenish ceremonies."[72]

One of the greatest difficulties between the races was the unfamiliarity of the Chinese priests with the English language. The philosophical underpinnings of Asian religious beliefs were fundamental matters that these holy men could not convey to their Occidental neighbors. Nor did many non-Chinese have any familiarity with the Chinese tongue. Dialogue was thus limited to descriptions of the deities revered and the rites performed. Chinese priests went so far as to invite the public to visit their temples, and many of those who toured the sanctuaries were Christian women intent upon learning more about religion in the Chinese quarter.[73] Beginning in the mid-1870s, two major Chinese festivities in particular attracted Anglo attention: the lunar new year celebrations, with their religious components; and the triennial fall ceremony, honoring the dead. Again, the local press fastened on the aspects that appeared unusual to Western eyes.

This unflattering and even hostile newspaper coverage had begun in the Los Angeles press in the early 1860s and had continued throughout the decade. The Los Angeles *Star* carried an article, in August

---

[71] Los Angeles *Express*, 20 October 1875.

[72] Los Angeles *Daily Evening Express*, 30 August 1878, as reprinted in the *Gum Saan Journal*, II (July, 1979), pp. 3–4.

[73] For one woman's description of such a temple visit, see Janette Lewis Young's diary entry for 25 October 1885, in *William Stewart Young*, by Nellie Mae Young (Glendale, California: Arthur H. Clark Company, 1967), p. 51.

1861, announcing the first local complaints against the Chinese. The writer noted that the community already had enough of the "substratum of the human family" without the addition of the "outcasts of the Flowery Kingdom." The *Southern News* that same year echoed similar sentiments and endorsed "anti-coolie" legislation. The arrival in 1869 of Chinese laborers attracted to road construction jobs provoked renewed newspaper vituperation.[74] The Los Angeles *Daily Star*, in particular, printed biased articles denigrating "pagans of the Chinese persuasion," "heathen Chinee," and other "Johns."[75]

One violent result of such ignorance, combined with local racial prejudice, was the so-called "Chinese Massacre," of 7 October 1871. Nineteen Chinese met their deaths at the hands of rampaging crowds of angry Angelenos in the area of Chinese habitation along "Nigger Alley," southwest of the plaza.[76] While relations between the races in subsequent years never again reached such fatal results, local residents only grudgingly permitted Asian worship a place within the religious pluralism emerging in Los Angeles. Protestant Christian denominations, in 1871, had begun a fervent campaign to evangelize the Chinese and thus Americanize them as well. Methodist, Presbyterian, Congregationalist, and Baptist clergy and laity returned repeatedly to "Chinatown" to attempt to arouse in the residents an interest in Jesus Christ, personal salvation, and the English language.[77]

Most Chinese, however, responded to the riot and racism in the 1870s by drawing upon the riches of their ancient religious traditions. Emphasizing the need for the restoration of harmony within the broader community, they began an annual celebration of the

---

[74] The Chinese arrived in May 1869 to construct a wagon road near Newhall, to the north of Los Angeles. By the following year, there were 172 Chinese living in the community. Mason, "The Chinese in Los Angeles," pp. 15–16.

[75] See instances of this prejudiced reporting in the issues of 5 February and 24 December 1870; and 31 January, 16, 18, and 25 February, 8 and 10 March, 15, 17, and 30 June 1871.

[76] Surprisingly little has been published regarding the Chinese Massacre, particularly about the religious overtones of this violence. Descriptions of varying worth are found in Wilson, *History of Los Angeles County*, pp. 84–85; C.P. Dorland, "The Chinese Massacre at Los Angeles in 1871," *Historical Society of Southern California Annual Publications*, III, Part II (1894), pp. 22–26; and Paul M. De Falla, "Lantern in the Western Sky," *Southern California Quarterly*, XLII (March, 1960), pp. 57–88, and (June, 1960), 161–85.

[77] These Protestant efforts at Chinese evangelization are discussed in chapter 6.

Chiao, or world renewal, ceremony.[78] Over four nights and three days, Taoist priests conducted liturgies within a specially constructed temple, to propitiate gods and appease evil ghosts. Chinese workers enjoyed a holiday from work, in order to participate in the rituals, settle debts and feuds, and partake in the procession to the river to launch paper "prayer boats." The festival was celebrated each year from 1875 to 1911, when rising republican nationalism disrupted the community.

With their ethnic identity strengthened by this celebration, the Chinese endured the hostile reception afforded them in Los Angeles in the late nineteenth century. Like the Jews, they also proceeded to affiliate themselves with organizations of their coreligionists in San Francisco. Such economic and social ties with their respective counterparts in the northern city enabled both Chinese and Jews to strengthen their religious endeavors in Los Angeles. These networks allowed the members of these two groups to organize their worship on a more permanent basis, at an earlier date, than their Protestant neighbors. They surmounted the obstacles facing all religious pioneers, but did so while laboring under the added burdens of local perceptions of them as foreigners and not "typically American." The respective foundations of these two faiths at such early dates manifest developments in the religious diversity that was beginning to characterize southern California's leading settlement.

In addition to these two groups, the historic presence of the Roman Catholic communion further accentuates the region's distinct spiritual heritage. Under the charge of a resident bishop, by 1859, this denomination benefited from the ministrations of clergy and nuns, outside funding, and capable administration. Roman Catholics also remained a numerical plurality in the pueblo through these early years, and their clergymen spoke the Spanish of the Californio residents. The institutions of local Catholicism therefore endured the tumultuous 1850s and 1860s with a stable church organization, staffed by clerics conversant in the language of the majority of the citizenry.

In the establishment of lasting congregations, Protestant settlers were initially far less fortunate than Roman Catholics, Jews, and Chi-

---

[78] For further information about this event, see Paul G. Chace, "The Turtledove Messenger, A Trait of the Early Los Angeles Chiao Ceremony," in *Gum Saan Journal* of the Chinese Historical Society of Southern California, XII (December 1989), pp. 1–9.

nese in Los Angeles. The greatest obstacle faced by pioneers of the Reform tradition was the division of a small number of people into separate denominations. These "godly folk" struggled with a scarcity of clergy, a paucity of funds, local violence, and the distance from fellow believers. Lack of familiarity with Spanish also precluded outreach to the broader local community. Increased Anglo-American immigration was necessary for the survival of the churches so long identified with westering Christianity. Neither the circuit-riding Methodist nor the Baptist farmer-preacher could succeed initially in this isolated pueblo on the banks of the Río Porciúncula.

Reverend William Boardman's effort was the most successful endeavor among Protestants in these early years, but also one of the more unusual ones. The First Protestant Society of Los Angeles depended not only upon the personality and organizational skills of Boardman, but also upon preaching that avoided the dogmatic rigidity of denominationalism. Boardman was perceptive enough to recognize that an insistence upon doctrinal purity would quickly divide the handful of evangelical Christians. Few clerics in later years proved to be as sensitive to such local religious conditions. Subsequent Protestant clergymen struggled to found traditional and specifically denominational congregations along the model that pioneers would have known in the Midwest. As we will explore in the following chapter, few of these preachers appreciated the adaptations geography and demographics required for a successful pastorate in Los Angeles.

STARTING CHURCHES AND "STARVING OUT PREACHERS"

Religious pluralism continued to grow in Los Angeles during the 1860s, but not in a manner contemporary Protestants would have expected. Denominational leaders, in particular, marveled at the churches that pioneered in this community. Certain denominations, which one historian dubbed "apostles to the genteel," proved more successful at founding permanent establishments in the pueblo at an earlier date than communions traditionally associated with the frontier. Once again, geography, demographics, and ministerial methods exerted important influences upon faith life in southern California. Focusing on the era between 1865 and 1885, this chapter continues the examination of congregational expansion begun in the previous chapter.

The Episcopalians, not typical denominational pioneers on other frontiers, made an early appearance in Los Angeles and secured a precarious, though lasting, foothold. The scholarly bishop of the Episcopal Diocese of California, the Right Reverend William Ingraham Kip, ventured south from San Francisco to visit the pueblo as early as October of 1855. Holding services in the small Methodist saloon-turned-chapel, Kip attracted approximately eighty people to his liturgy during the day and an even larger crowd in the evening. Various residents informed the prelate of their interest in a church that did not preach "Nebraska or Kansas, slavery or antislavery," and matters that were "not identified with any of the isms of the day."[1] In his later report, Kip informed the Third Triennial Convention of the diocese that he believed Los Angeles the "only place we can at present profitably occupy in southern California."[2] A serious shortage of clergy frustrated the prelate in his desire to establish a mission station in this portion of his far-flung see.

On his return to San Francisco, Kip proceeded by way of Fort Tejon, where men from the First Regiment of United States Dragoons were stationed. Located a two-day journey north of Los Angeles, the Army outpost served to pacify nearby reservation Indians and to command Tejon Pass. The bishop learned that all six officers were members of his flock, one of whom was even a licensed lay reader.[3] In other military stations Kip had made similar discoveries of church members. The presence of Episcopalians in the officer corps would prove to be important in later years for the growth of this denomination in Los Angeles.

Two years after his visit, Los Angeles had no Protestant minister, so in May of 1857, Bishop Kip authorized Doctor Mathew Carter, a local physician, to serve as a lay reader for a mission congregation.[4] The English immigrant read from the Book of Common Prayer and from published collections of popular sermons. In August 1857, the worshipers organized as St. Luke's parish and elected three trustees. Despite what the locals considered an "excellent" choir, enthusiasm slackened by December of that year, and the church disbanded.[5] The Presbyterian divine, William Boardman, arrived early in 1859 and departed in 1862. No Protestant clergyman returned to a pastorate in Los Angeles until late 1864, and this clerical pioneer was Episcopalian.[6]

Reverend Elias Birdsall had left an Indiana "missionary" charge in response to one of Bishop Kip's repeated appeals for assistance in

[1] William Ingraham Kip, *The Early Days of My Episcopate* (New York: T. Whittacker, 1892), p. 211.

[2] *Journal of the Proceedings of the Third Triennial Convention of the Protestant Episcopal Church in California* (San Francisco, May 1856), p. 13.

[3] Kip, *The Early Days of My Episcopate*, pp. 212–13.

[4] Los Angeles *Star*, 6 May 1857; and Diocese of California, *Journal of Proceedings*, Eighth Convention (May 1858), p. 13.

[5] Los Angeles *Star*, 6 May, 18 and 25 July, 29 August, 3 October, 21 November, and 12 December 1857.

[6] Frederick G. Bohme, "Episcopal Beginnings in Southern California: The Centennial of Los Angeles' First Parish," *Southern California Quarterly*, XLVII (June, 1965), p. 171; J. Albert Wilson, *History of Los Angeles County, California* (Oakland,

his vast California diocese. Arriving with his family in December of 1864, Birdsall commenced weekly services in the Odd Fellows' Hall at eleven o'clock on Sunday mornings. The following March, he supervised the election of a vestry as part of the formal organization of a parish known as St. Athanasius Protestant Episcopal Church.[7] One month later, the growing congregation obtained the use of the Presbyterian chapel, vacated by Reverend Boardman. In May and June of that year, Birdsall and several of his parishioners delivered a series of high-toned lectures in the *adobe* city hall, though one press account noted that the room could have held more listeners.[8] The energetic pastor was able to report to the annual convention of the diocese that the initial results of less than one year's labor included ten communicants, six Sunday school teachers instructing fifty-five students, Communion Alms totaling $28.00, and current expenses of $167.00.[9]

The surviving roster of communicants for 1865 lists only nine names: one vestryman and eight women.[10] The most prominent individual recorded was Ada Hancock, the wife of General Winfield Scott Hancock. She had served as organist at Boardman's congregation and sang "with as much zeal and interest as though she were a member of all the churches represented."[11] The Hancocks had located in Los Angeles in May of 1859, when the general arrived as the army quartermaster charged with the establishment of a military supply base for southern California, Arizona, and New Mexico. Camp Drum, or

---

California: Thompson and West, 1880; reprint ed., Berkeley: Howell-North, 1959), p. 121; *El Clamor Público*, 12 December 1857; and Roy F. Schippling, "A History of the Diocese of Los Angeles" (unpublished S.T.M. thesis, Nashotah House, Wisconsin, 1972), pp. 39–40.

[7] The name of the parish was changed, in 1883, to St. Paul's.

[8] Los Angeles *Tri-Weekly News*, 4 April, 16 and 20 May 1865; and undated newspaper clipping, "Lectures at City Hall in Aid of St. Athanasius Protestant Episcopal Church," found in the scrapbooks of Judge Benjamin I. Hayes, vol. 50, part 2, #477; Hayes Scrapbook collection, Bancroft Library, Berkeley, California, hereafter cited as "Hayes."

[9] Birdsall's report is found in the *Journal of Proceedings* of the 1865 diocesan convention, p. 23, as quoted from Stephen C. Clark, *The Diocese of Los Angeles: A Brief History* (Los Angeles: Diocese of Los Angeles Committee on Diocesan Anniversaries, 1945), p. 16.

[10] "Register A," p. 86, St. Athanasius–St. Paul's Church, Los Angeles, California.

[11] Emma H. Adams, *To and Fro in Southern California* (Cincinnati: W.M.B.C. Press, 1887; reprint ed., New York: Arno Press, 1976), p. 89.

Drum Barracks, as the depot came to be known, later served as an important garrison for Union troops to dampen the ardent secessionist spirit among many Angelenos. The officers and their wives first augmented the ranks of Reverend Boardman's church and later bolstered Reverend Birdsall's congregation.[12] Many were Episcopalians, whose presence enhanced the prestige of the parish and attracted the members of prominent local families.[13]

Given the social standing of the worshipers at St. Athanasius and the scarcity of other ministers, the Episcopal priest was the natural selection to deliver the principal oration marking the death of Abraham Lincoln, in the Los Angeles city hall, on 19 April 1865. Birdsall was also appointed that year to the post of superintendent of the town's public schools, the second time a Protestant cleric had held that position. Such prominence in the community greatly assisted Birdsall in his next project, securing Episcopal title to the Presbyterian church building in which he held services. Begun as a nondenominational undertaking of Boardman's First Protestant Society, the structure eventually became the home of the first permanent Protestant congregation in the community.[14]

The remaining trustees of the defunct First Presbyterian Church, "Old-School," stipulated two conditions by which the property might be transferred. The first was that the Episcopalians repay the $500 construction loan originally extended by the Presbyterian Board of Domestic Missions. The second requirement was the regular scheduling of Protestant services in the structure; the absence of any minister for more than three months would cause title to revert to the trustees. Bishop Kip was ready to agree to these requirements,

---

[12] J.J. Warner, Benjamin Hayes, and J.P. Widney, *An Historical Sketch of Los Angeles County, California* (Los Angeles: Louis Lewin, 1876; reprint ed., Los Angeles: O.W. Smith, Publisher, 1936), p. 91; and Harris Newmark, *Sixty Years in Southern California, 1853–1913* (4th ed., revised by Maurice H. Newmark and Marco R. Newmark, Los Angeles: Zeitlin and Ver Brugge, 1970), p. 301.

[13] Birdsall's first vestrymen included, among others, the town's postmaster (George C. Clarke), the local Wells, Fargo agent (Samuel E. Briggs), a leading freight and lumber operator (John M. Griffith), one of the town's more prosperous druggists (Theodore Wollweber), an established physician (Doctor T.R. Hayes), and the editor of the Los Angeles *News* (C.R. Conway). See Bohme, "Episcopal Beginnings in Southern California," p. 179.

[14] Los Angeles *Tri-Weekly News*, 22 April 1865; J.M. Guinn, "Pioneer School Superintendents of Los Angeles," Historical Society of Southern California *Annual Publications*, IV, Part I (1897), p. 78.

and so the trustees conveyed title to him by February 1866. However, the problem faced earlier by the Presbyterians, i.e., the lack of a cleric, soon confronted the bishop and threatened his possession of the property.

Birdsall evidently was not universally popular with his congregation, nor was he thoroughly enamored with Los Angeles, as the California agent of the American Home Missionary Society learned, in a visit to the community in the early spring of 1866. James H. Warren wrote his Congregationalist superiors that the bishop was pressing Birdsall to remain. Kip was unsuccessful in his appeal, and Reverend Birdsall departed for a Stockton rectorship, in late spring 1866, leaving an organized parish, an elected vestry, and the recorded title to a brick church edifice. His successor, Reverend H.H. Messenger, assumed charge and continued services for approximately one year, thus relieving the bishop of any immediate worry of losing ground in southern California.[15]

The clerical observer who had recorded these Episcopal difficulties also sought to gain a foothold for his creed in Los Angeles. James H. Warren, like Birdsall, was not from one of the more successful denominations among traditional pioneering churches. Writing to his superiors in the American Home Missionary Society, Warren reported his impressions from a visit to southern California. The energetic and dynamic minister noted that, "It would take Mr. Birdsall a hundred years to plough up, sow down and harvest in good heavy crops." He went on to acknowledge the tremendous difficulties any missionary would face in an area which was the "Egypt of California . . . religiously and politically," a region given up to "darkness, popery, and Mormonism. . . ."[16]

Reverend Warren was enthusiastic as well as realistic about the prospects of Congregational preaching in Los Angeles. His balanced assessment received consideration at the mission society headquarters and by the Permanent Committee on Home Missions, in San Francisco. The committee met on 2 July 1866 and approved the dispatch of

[15] Letter, James H. Warren to M[ilton] Badger, 27 April 1866, San Francisco, American Home Mission Society records, file: "California 1866, S–Z, sec. 2," found on Microfilm #C-B 393, reel 4, BL, hereafter cited as AHMS; Parish Register "A," p. 6, St. Athanasius–St. Paul's Episcopal Church, Los Angeles, California.

[16] Letter, James H. Warren to Rev. M[ilton] Badger, 10 February 1865, San Francisco, Microfilm C-B 393, reel 3, of AHMS file, "California 1865, W–Z, sec. 2," BL.

two missionaries to southern California: the Reverends J.A. Johnson, for San Bernardino, and Alexander Parker, for Los Angeles. Three days later, the two clergymen and their families sailed through the Golden Gate, with Warren's abundant advice fresh in their minds. The agent prepared Scottish-born Parker, in particular, for a "long siege" of slow work "laying the foundations" for the Pilgrim church in Los Angeles.[17]

Alexander Parker was a curious choice to lead this church, in a community where Southern sentiment had been strong during the Civil War. Parker was an alumnus of Ohio's hotbed of reform, Oberlin College, and a Union Army veteran whose highly opinionated letters to superiors reveal a critical attitude toward the populace of Los Angeles. He estimated that there were five thousand people in town and noted that, "In politics they are rebels and in religion Catholic." The Roman Catholic priests and nuns he found "getting to be enormously wealthy." Worse yet, all of this was accomplished in part through the support of Protestants, who seem "to have left their religion at the river and their principles somewhere on the plains. They are emphatically without God." Furthermore, they have "starved out" every preacher so far sent to them.[18] Parker sought to remedy these problems through careful preaching, thorough planning, and an ever-vigilant eye on the progress of other creeds.

The numerous letters Parker penned to New York church authorities reveal as much about the activities of other denominations as about the progress of Congregationalism in Los Angeles. Parker and his traveling companion Johnson began by preaching morning and evening upon their arrival in July 1866. He eventually began holding services in the courthouse when he could get the key from the judge. Parker suspected the judge of being a member of "the Episcopal party," intent on ridding the town of this noisome Union man. It was Parker's Sunday school, of all things, that brought the harshest reactions upon the clergyman, after less than six months in the

---

[17] James H. Warren to M[ilton] Badger, 9 July 1866, San Francisco, and 18 July 1866, San Francisco, Microfilm C-B 393, reel 4, AHMS file, "California 1866, S-Z, sec. 2," BL.

[18] Letter, Alexander Parker to "Bro." [A. Huntington] Clapp, 18 December 1866, Los Angeles, Microfilm C-B 393, reel 3, AHMS file, "California 1866, A-P, sec. 1," BL.

community. His principles of racial equality led him to organize an integrated Sabbath school for both black and white children.

Many churchgoing Angelenos were shocked. While Parker noted that the Episcopal Sunday school was educating the children of the two races separately, he was not afraid to stand "alone in this city" and integrate his own Sabbath school. To gain a congregation by proceeding otherwise would not "answer my purpose nor satisfy my conscience." He became known locally as a "radical" on this account and smugly enjoyed the notoriety.[19] Parker concluded that the Episcopal minister, Reverend Messenger, made religion too easy for the people. Yet Parker's hard-line approach did not retard his progress entirely, because three months later, agent Warren reported that Parker had bought a home, initiated the purchase of a lot for a church, and begun work to found a congregation. All this he achieved in a community inhabited with certain "Philistines, i.e., Catholics, Copperheads, Secessionists . . . and some Episcopalians."[20]

On 21 July 1867, Parker organized the First Congregational Church of Los Angeles, in the parlor of Amanda Wallace Scott, on South San Pedro Street. One other man and three women joined Parker and his wife in this religious undertaking, which would require their sustained efforts to insure even minimal success. Many local people believed that Los Angeles could not then support more than one Protestant clergyman. The infant congregation relied for several years upon the financial aid of the American Home Mission Society for the minister's support. Parker set sail that autumn for San Francisco, to solicit donations from prominent coreligionists for the planned church building. A series of concerts in the winter of 1868 produced further funds to purchase seats for the structure. Parker's determination to remain debt-free provoked a row between the pastor and the deacon, which eventually led to the former's resignation.

Dedication day for the small frame meetinghouse was 28 June 1868, and one pioneer recorded the recollections of an eye witness.

[19] Letter, Parker to Clapp, 18 December 1866; and J. T. Ford, "Early Days of Congregationalism in Southern California," published in the *Pacific*, XLIX (2 November 1899), p. 19.

[20] Letter, James H. Warren to M[ilton] Badger, 18 March 1867, San Francisco, Microfilm C-B 393, reel 4, AHMS file, "California 1867, O-Z, sec. 2," BL.

Aunt Margaret [Mrs. Jotham Bixby] noticed a certain constraint in the air and a black eye on the minister. After service she discovered that the afternoon before the minister and the deacon had gotten into a fist-fight in the furniture store over a red carpet for the church that the deacon had purchased without authority. Poor minister, he was red headed. He was so mortified that he resigned . . .[21]

A thoroughly discouraged man, Parker withdrew from Los Angeles in the first week of July 1868, in favor of a northern California pastorate, in Nevada City. In a letter of 16 July 1868, he revealed some of the difficulties pioneer clergymen such as himself had to face in frontier communities where organized religion exercised such slight influence in local society.

Parker informed Congregationalist authorities that for his livelihood he had relied entirely upon receipt of his monthly one-hundred-dollar salary from the American Home Mission Society. He also had anticipated that pew rentals in the completed church would generate sufficient income to satisfy pressing construction debts. Rain damage and other difficulties, however, had unexpectedly increased expenses. He was forced to sell off his own property in order to keep the congregation solvent. With this information, Parker's altercation with his deacon is far more understandable: the church debt stood at $500; he had not been paid his salary in three months; and continued local opposition toward his racial ideals had worn him down. He was far too discouraged to continue in the "Egypt" of Los Angeles.[22]

James Warren, the missionary society's California agent, gamely rose to the occasion and sought both to bolster Parker and to rally the sharply divided Los Angeles congregation. Warren visited Parker in Nevada City that summer, did all he could to lift his spirits, and then headed to Los Angeles in the fall to introduce the clergyman replacing Parker.[23] Reverend Isaac W. Atherton arrived with his wife, Adelia, in October 1868. Encountering similar financial difficulties

[21] Sarah Bixby Smith, *Adobe Days* (fourth edition, Fresno, California: Valley Publishers, 1974), p. 117.

[22] Letter, Alexander Parker to Dr. [Milton] Badger, 16 July 1868, San Francisco, Microfilm C-B 393, reel 4, AHMS file "California 1868, M-Z, sec. 2," BL.

[23] Parker remained in Nevada City two years and then accepted the first of several pastoral calls in Iowa, where he died, in 1885. *Congregational Year-Book* (1887), p. 31,

to those faced by Parker, Atherton's milder disposition fostered the church's gradual growth in a town he considered as "the *worst place in all this godless* country."[24] Warren returned, in November, to assist in the reorganization of the church into a society, which included the selection and ordination of a new deacon, the election of a board of five trustees in accord with state law, and a subscription drive that yielded pledges totaling one thousand dollars.[25]

Warren's vision of a great future for the Los Angeles church under Atherton's pastorate was borne out by the subsequent, though gradual, growth in membership and finances. The 1870 report to the General Session of California showed an increase of thirty members over the six in 1868, and eighty children in the Sabbath school, twice as many as the 1868 total. The congregation had also raised $900 toward annual expenses, while only $30 had been reported for the same purpose in 1868.[26] Much of the credit for this successful establishment of Congregationalism must be given to the state agent of the mission society, James Warren. Warren wrote, in obvious amazement, "It seems almost odd that Congregationalists should be acting as Pioneers instead of the Methodists."[27]

Northern Methodist activity had begun midway through Parker's tenure with the Congregationalists, and the local press had noted the town's religious progress, with three ministers resident in the community. Rev. Asbury P. Hendon had revived Methodism's active proselytism in Los Angeles in the fall of 1867, and still could submit an annual report listing forty members for his initial term on this circuit.[28] Progress was so rapid that a new church was under construc-

---

quoted in Royal G. Davis, *Light on a Gothic Tower*, (Los Angeles: First Congregational Church, 1967), p. 10.

[24] Letter, Atherton to David B. Coe, 1 November 1870, Los Angeles, Microfilm C-B 393, reel 5, AHMS file, "California 1870, A-H, sec. 1," BL.

[25] Letters, James H. Warren to Milton Badger, 4 November 1868 and 16 December 1868, both on Microfilm C-B 393, reel 4, AHMS file, "California 1868, M-Z, sec. 2," BL.

[26] *Minutes*, Annual Meeting of the General Session (San Francisco: General Session, 1868), pp. 3, 22; (1870), pp. 5, 26.

[27] Letter, Warren to M[ilton] Badger, 18 March 1867, San Francisco, on Microfilm C-B 393, reel 4, AHMS file "California 1867, O-Z, sec. 2," BL.

[28] Hendon apparently succeeded a Reverend Columbus Gillet at some point in 1867, though the extent of Gillet's ministry is unclear. According to Edward Drewry Jervey, "the Conference apppointments for 1866–1867 list Los Angeles 'to be sup-

tion by November 1867, on Fort Street. In the meantime, Hendon held church services in a room of the county courthouse. Membership rose to fifty-four by September of that year, while the new Sunday school enrolled eighty students, all in a circuit assignment encompassing "a region of uncertain dimensions."[29]

The minister's prolonged bout with typhoid left the congregation temporarily leaderless, so that attendance at church meetings fell off dramatically. Reverend Alanson Coplin, also of frail health, succeeded Hendon in 1868, but remained only eight months. At this point, growing discouragement with ministerial leadership seriously threatened Methodist prospects for the immediate future. Then, as if an answer to prayers, there appeared a seasoned cleric with a devoted spouse, a couple able to rally the local church. Driving a buckboard to Los Angeles, Reverend A.M. Hough came from Salt Lake City, with his wife at his side and "a heavy Army revolver buckled round him." He had been a missionary in Montana for four years and was also a seasoned veteran of the Indian wars. One church member who welcomed the Houghs later wrote of them, "He belonged to the Church Militant and was a muscular Christian. . . . Mrs. Hough, his lifelong companion, was one of God's saints upon earth."[30]

Another Angeleno offers an unusual perspective on just how "muscular" the new pastor's faith actually was. Horace Bell penned two volumes of colorful reminiscences, in which he displayed an occasional propensity to stretch the truth, and his recollections must be used with that caution in mind. However, Bell does offer memories of events that certain prominent people wished would remain forgotten, such as the execution of jailed murder suspect Michel Lache-

---

plied.' However . . . *An Historical Sketch of Los Angeles County*, 89–90, lists 'Rev. C. Gillett' as pastor 1866–1867. This source claims to be indebted to the Methodist Church Record in the city. This record was subsequently either lost or destroyed. At least the fall of 1867 can be definitely established since the Conference appointment lists A. P. Hendon." See *The History of Methodism in Southern California and Arizona* (Nashville: Historical Society of the Southern California–Arizona Conference, 1960), p. 231, n. 3.

[29] Anthony, *Fifty Years of Methodism*, pp. 145, 264–65, 294; Los Angeles *Republican*, 2 and 9 November 1867; and Joseph Pomeroy Widney, "History of the Early Methodist Church in Los Angeles," (Typescript, 1938), p. 1, HL.

[30] A. M. Hough, "Dictation of A Life's Story," (Typescript, n.d.), Dictation C-D 810, pp. 1–2, BL; Anthony, *Fifty Years of Methodism*, pp. 145, 276, 304; Widney, "Methodist Church," pp. 3–4.

nais, in December of 1870. Rushing the town jail after a secret organizational meeting, a "Methodist mob" seized the yet-untried culprit and lynched him in a corral at the corner of Temple and New High streets. Bell concludes,

"The pastor of what is now called the First Methodist Church marched at the head [of the mob] with a double-barreled shotgun resting in the hollow of his left arm. . . . I knew that Methodist pastor and always thought him a pretty good fellow. . . . But what a state of affairs, when a minister of the Gospel descends from his pulpit to become himself a law-breaker and murderer in an alleged vindication of decency." [31]

The ensuing developments show that, in 1869, the local community was finally ready for Methodism's message and manners. Church women formed a Ladies' Social circle, the same year that parishioners completed their house of worship and Hough himself commenced building a parsonage, on an adjoining lot. Taking its name from its location, Hough's congregation organized as the Fort Street Methodist Episcopal Church. The pastor expanded his activities to include cooperation with Congregationalist minister Atherton in joint prayer meetings. That year the two denominations also held Thanksgiving services together, with Hough preaching. The pastor then revived the Sunday school, recruited six of the female members of the congregation to teach, and soon counted over ninety students in weekly attendance. In 1870, Hough joined with three other clergymen to initiate Sunday-afternoon street preaching, in front of the courthouse, along with Monday-morning "preachers' meetings." [32]

Because statistics record only bare facts, the ordinary daily life of the denomination does not emerge clearly. The disappearance of the church's registers also exacerbates the sketchiness of this evidence.

[31] Bell, *On the Old West Coast, Being Further Reminiscences of a Ranger* (New York: William Morrow and Company, 1930), pp. 179–80; for another version of what was reputedly the last lynching in the city, see also Newmark, *Sixty Years in Southern California*, pp. 419–20.

[32] Los Angeles *Republican*, 13 May 1869, 25 November 1869. See unidentified newspaper clippings in "Hayes:" "Prayer Meetings," 23 October 1869, vol. 54, p. 2; "M.E. Church and Sunday School," [March, 1870], vol. 54, p. 62; "Street Preaching" and "Preachers' Meeting," 20 January 1870, vol. 54, p. 47; BL.

One member of the Fort Street congregation, however, recorded in her diary her family's close involvement in their parish. Sarah Johnston Barnes lived with her son-in-law and daughter, Robert and Mary Barnes Widney, and noted their daily family routine in 1871 and 1872. Weather and household matters were of far greater interest to Sarah Barnes than local events that rocked the community. She fails to mention either the Chinese Massacre, in 1871, or Judge Widney's subsequent trial of the instigators of that riot, matters we will examine in chapter 5.

Mrs. Barnes viewed her world from a domestic perspective. It was more important to her that Reverend Hough had assumed the position of Presiding Elder of the Los Angeles District, and Reverend P. Y. Cool and his wife had moved into the church parsonage. The diarist's daughter organized children's concerts for Sunday evenings, held noisy rehearsals at home and in the church, spearheaded fundraising for the Sabbath school, and served in the church ladies' Fourth of July dinner. Sarah Barnes noted many other events over the months, such as the church collection taken up for the widow and children of a parishioner killed in an accident (February 17), her participation in a church Quarterly Meeting and Love Feast (April 28), her grandchild's baptism at home (June 2), and her attendance with her daughter at Episcopal services (June 9).[33]

The Barnes daily journal permits a glimpse of the significant role religion played in the life of a family deeply involved in the development of their community. This domestic record affords glimpses of the familial activities of a man who had immersed himself in the development of Los Angeles. Arriving in 1868, Robert Widney opened a law and real-estate office and commenced publishing the *Los Angeles Real Estate Advertizer*, the first newspaper of its type in the community. Widney was capitalizing upon the opportunities afforded by the projected breakup of the vast Stearns ranch empire. The Robinson Trust, of San Francisco, had gained control of 177,000 acres in Los Angeles and San Bernardino counties amassed by Abel Stearns over the preceding two decades. Through its subsidiary land company, Trust officials planned to subdivide the Stearns empire into farms ranging from 20 to 160 acres.[34]

---

[33] Diary of Sarah Johnston Barnes, passim; HL.

[34] Robert Glass Cleland, *The Cattle on a Thousand Hills: Southern California, 1850–1880* (2nd edition, San Marino, California: Huntington Library, 1951), pp. 198, 203–205.

Widney saw the population of the town of Los Angeles reach a total of 5,728 people in 1870, a substantial increase from 4,385 residents in the previous decennial census. Named a state judge in 1871, Widney also worked that year to obtain federal financing of San Pedro harbor improvements. The following year he spearheaded the lengthy and acrimonious campaign to gain voter approval of a county bond issue designed to induce officials of the Southern Pacific Railroad to include Los Angeles on their main line. In 1873, he joined other promoters to form the Los Angeles Board of Trade, while at the same time he supervised the first street railway in the community. When it came to the development of Los Angeles, Robert Widney was one of the town's most active promoters, a true "booster." Moving in other circles, Mrs. Widney long provided leadership both for the church and for wider civic affairs, such as the first kindergarten in Los Angeles, in 1876.[35] Working with other members of their congregation, the Widneys were central characters in the efforts to transform Los Angeles ever more completely into a thoroughly Anglo-American community.

Unmentioned in the Barnes diary or the J.P. Widney memoirs was the presence of one Georgia-born charter member of the 1868 Northern Methodist congregation. This was Biddy Mason, an enterprising black woman first brought to California as a slave by emigrants, in 1851. She won freedom for herself and her three daughters in a Los Angeles courtroom on 19 January 1856.[36] Robert Owens and his wife, Minnie, welcomed the Masons into their home. Owens had earned his own release from slavery; he also had purchased his wife and daughter from bondage and settled in Los Angeles, in 1853. It is said that the first group of blacks assembled for prayer in the Owens home in 1854, and evidence suggests that worshipers continued to meet there in subsequent years.[37]

---

[35] Census statistics quoted from U.S. Census Office, *Report on the Social Statistics of Cities*, Part II: *The Southern and Western States*, (Washington, D.C.: Government Printing Office, 1887), p. 779. Information about the Widneys is found in Newmark, *Sixty Years in Southern California*, pp. 370, 426, 442, 449, 460, 503, 515–16, and 521; Boyle Workman, *The City That Grew* (Los Angeles: Southland Publishing Company, 1935), pp. 188–89; and Ella Giles Ruddy, ed. *The Mother of Clubs: Caroline M. Seymour Severance* (Los Angeles: Baumgardt Publishing Company, 1906), p. 87.

[36] Los Angeles *Star*, 2 February 1856. For an excellent overview of Biddy Mason's accomplishments, see Dolores Hayden, "Biddy Mason's Los Angeles, 1856–1891," *California History*, LXVIII (Fall, 1989), pp. 86–99, 147–49.

[37] Rudolph M. Lapp, *Blacks in Gold Rush California* (New Haven: Yale University

Chapter 2

Working as a nurse and midwife, Biddy Mason slowly accumulated property and established the financial stability of her family. She later opened her South Spring Street residence to local blacks, who gathered for prayer and worship.[38] Her name appears along with those of thirteen other "ladies of the A[frican] M[ethodist] E[piscopal] Church" in an 1869 newspaper notice of a "Grand Festival" to benefit their church construction fund.[39] Later fundraising events included lectures and an annual "Ratification Ball," to celebrate the anniversary of the Fifteenth Amendment.[40] By April 1871, the Los Angeles *Star* could report that the black congregation had "recently completed" construction of their "Little Church on the Hill" at Fourth and Charity (now Grand) streets.[41]

According to one account, the Right Reverend T.M.D. Ward, presiding bishop of the A. M. E. Conference of California, assigned a pastor to this congregation. This minister and his clerical successors encountered serious difficulties in sustaining their flock.[42] Only ninety-three blacks made their homes in Los Angeles in 1870, and even ten years later the census listed an increase of only nine persons.[43] Preachers also discovered that certain blacks preferred to worship in the predominantly white churches of the town. The church struggled

Press, 1977), p. 118; Wilson, *History of Los Angeles County*, p. 120; Ellis, "Baptist Churches in Southern California," p. 96, quoted an undated issue of the Los Angeles *Star* of 1854 regarding the visit to the community of Reverend John Williams, "a Methodist brother of the colored persuasion."

[38] Delilah L. Beasley, *The Negro Trail Blazers of California* (Los Angeles: Privately Printed, 1909), pp. 109–10; Lawrence B. de Graaf, "Race Sex, and Region: Black Women and the American West, 1850–1920," *Pacific Historical Review*, XLIX (May, 1980), p. 301; and "History of First African Methodist Episcopal Church of Los Angeles," (n.p., n.d.), p. 13, in copies of historical materials supplied to the author by the First African Methodist Episcopal Church, Los Angeles, California, hereafter cited as FAME.

[39] The names of six men also appear on the announcement for the dinner and dance, to be held at Stearn's Hall. The event proved quite successful, and those in attendance had "very good time generally." Los Angeles *Star*, 25 September and 2 October 1869.

[40] Los Angeles *Star*, 9 and 16 April, 19 October 1870; 18 December 1871.

[41] 11 April 1871.

[42] Fred M. Baker and Jesse H. Sterling, "History," n.p. (n.p., n.d.), historical materials supplied to author by FAME, Los Angeles. See also, *A Treasury of Tradition, Innovation and Hope: History of Second Baptist Church, Los Angeles* (Los Angeles: Second Baptist Church, 1975), p. 7.

[43] *Compendium of the Ninth Census*, p. 126; and J. Max Bond, *The Negro in Los Angeles* (San Francisco: S and E Research Associates, 1972), p. 20. This work is a photo-

for several years, but in 1877 the chapel was listed on the delinquent tax roster and was later sold.[44]

Judge Anson Brunson purchased the A.M.E. church for its unpaid taxes, and one source explains that he did this because he did not want a black church near his Grand Avenue estate. The congregation continued undaunted by such prejudice and resumed meeting in the homes of members, at least until 1885.[45] In that year, the expanding black population warranted the reestablishment of this denomination. The challenges faced by early black believers paralleled the problems which white Protestants confronted in frontier Los Angeles. However, in addition to a pioneer congregation's usual limited numbers and scarce funds, members of the African Methodist Episcopal Church carried the further burden of local racial discrimination.[46]

While the Widneys and Biddy Mason were engaged in the affairs of their respective congregations, members of the Methodist Episcopal Church, South, were also establishing a permanent presence in Los Angeles. Unionist activities during the Civil War had seriously disrupted the operation of this denomination throughout the state, and not until 1867 did a minister return to the community. While Reverend J.C. Miller held the assignment for the Los Angeles circuit, real progress did not commence until Reverend Abram Adams succeeded him, in 1869. Membership in the circuit totaled some 228 that year, though only 11 resided in the pueblo. Southern Methodists, like their Baptist neighbors, were still a rural denomination in Los Angeles county at that time, with their greatest concentration in the area of Los Nietos. There they conducted for many years their annual camp meetings.[47]

---

static reproduction of a previously unpublished 1936 Ph.D. dissertation, written at the University of Southern California, Los Angeles.

[44] The town's city directory, in 1875, noted the "Colored Church" held only "occasional services" that year. *Directory of Los Angeles for 1875* (Los Angeles: Mirror Book and Job Printing, 1875), p. 78. The tax assessor valued the church lot at $350 and its improvement at $150; taxes for the year amounted to $11.31. Los Angeles *Daily Star*, 7 January 1877.

[45] Baker and Sterling, "History," n.p., FAME.

[46] It is important to remember that Angelenos had strongly supported the Confederacy during the Civil War, established segregated Sunday schools, and kept the children of the races in separate public schools after the war between the states. For notice of the "Colored" school, see the Los Angeles *Star*, 23 May 1868, 9 January and 3 July 1868, 12 February 1870, and 24 June 1871.

[47] "Minutes of the Pacific Conference," [Methodist Episcopal Church, South], vol. I, pp. 347, 356, 376, 386, 403, APSAC; J.C. Simmons, *The History of Southern*

Reverend Adams, then 38, persisted with his small congregation in the town, organized Trinity Church in 1869, and registered an increase of three members by the next year. Undaunted, Adams embarked on new projects and joined with other Protestant clergymen in the "union street preaching" of January 1870. When Bishop William M. Wight organized the Los Angeles Conference, later that year, Adams was one of only ten Southern Methodist clergymen in all of southern California. Like members of their denomination on other frontiers, the leaders of this new conference were soon promoting higher education. Local Southern Methodists assumed responsibility for Los Nietos College, which, in March 1869, had opened its doors south of Los Angeles, in the thriving agricultural community of Los Nietos, near present Downey. With enrollment never exceeding ninety students, the school struggled for ten years and finally closed in 1879.[48]

In August 1873, Southern Methodists began a second educational "institute," after they received a pledge of a $5,000 cash endowment fund from local rancher and developer Benjamin D. Wilson. The former state senator also donated ten acres of land and two buildings at the army's vacated Drum Barracks, in Wilmington. The following March, Wilson conveyed title for the property, as he had for the first Protestant church building, during Reverend Boardman's day. Wilson College, as it was known, opened within sight of the harbor for Los Angeles. The initial enrollment of twenty-two students increased over time, but gradually the school declined and closed after fifteen years. The Northern Methodists opened their own school, in 1880, and this grandly named "University of Southern Califor-

---

Methodism on the Pacific Coast (Nashville: Southern Methodist Printing House, 1886), pp. 377–79; Los Angeles *Star*, 29 August, 5 and 12 September 1868, 28 August 1869, and 7 October 1871; and Los Angeles *Evening Express*, 4, 12, and 14 September 1874.

[48] "Minutes of the Pacific Conference," vol. I, p. 403, APSAC; Simmons, *History of Southern Methodism*, p. 378; *Centennial Anniversary* (Los Angeles: Trinity United Methodist Church, 1969), n.p.; Harlan E. Hogue, "A History of Religion in Southern California, 1846–1880" (Ph.D. dissertation, Columbia University, 1958), pp. 233–34; Los Angeles *Semi-Weekly News*, 15, 18 March 1869, quoted in Cleland, *Cattle on a Thousand Hills*, p. 329, n. 32; Wilson, *History of Los Angeles County*, pp. 145, 149–50; Los Angeles *Star*, 25 March 1874, quoted in Midge Sherwood, *Days of Vintage, Years of Vision*, (San Marino, California: Orizaba Press, 1982), vol. I, p. 330; and Deed, Benjamin D. Wilson to W. A. Spurlock, 29 August 1873, Los Angeles, Wilson Collection, HL.

nia" eclipsed both Los Nietos College and Wilson College of their southern brethren.

The arrival of a Presbyterian missionary organizer initiated the re-establishment of that faith in a process that matched the slow growth of Southern Methodism in Los Angeles. Members of the Synod of the Pacific designated Reverend Thomas Fraser as "synodal mission-ary," in 1869, for the region stretching from Mexico to the "aurora borealis." That spring, Fraser endured two months of travel by stage-coach over rough roads to assess Presbyterian prospects in southern California. In Los Angeles, he conducted a disheartening two-week search for any evidence of the congregation left by Reverend Board-man in 1862. All he could locate was the county recorder's record of the 1866 deed, by which the former trustees conveyed title to the church property to Bishop Kip.[49] Preaching in the Methodist and Congregational churches, Fraser decided that Los Angeles was ready for a Presbyterian church and should be held "regardless of expense, as England holds Gibraltar . . ."[50]

Reverend William C. Harding came to Los Angeles from the East, in 1870, and organized a church of eight members by that October. Harding, unsuited to local conditions, "failed totally" and withdrew to the adjacent community of Wilmington, where he was more suc-cessful. But three other Presbyterian divines came in as many years and could do no better. Officials of the Presbyterian Home Missions Office in New York City could not understand Fraser's insistence on maintaining a presence in Los Angeles, after these repeated fail-ures. The synodal missionary laid the groundwork for yet another attempt, when in 1872 he organized the six Presbyterian congrega-tions in southern California into the Presbytery of Los Angeles. Still finding no clergyman equal to the challenges that Los Angeles pre-sented, Fraser returned two years later, surveyed the situation yet again, and founded the church himself.[51]

[49] Fraser recognized that the trustees had acted without proper authorization in the transfer of the property, leaving Bishop Kip with an imperfect title. Local Pres-byterians later undertook a series of legal actions against the Episcopal authorities, until the courts settled the matter. See *Manual of First Presbyterian Church, Los Angeles, California* (Los Angeles: First Presbyterian Church, 1884), pp. 3–4.

[50] Letter, Thomas Fraser to "Brother Hill," 21 January 1902, Oakland, California, in the Fraser Collection, ASFTS.

[51] Records, 1873–1887, vol. 1, pp. 3–5, Los Angeles Presbytery (Presbyterian

To Fraser's way of thinking, the two major drawbacks in those years had been the personalities of the four previous clergymen and, as was the case with other Protestant denominations, the absence of a sufficient number of families to sustain a congregation. Gradual migration had changed the latter situation, so that on 11 January 1874, there were enough "substantial" members to pledge themselves to form the First Presbyterian Church of Los Angeles. The congregation ordained two men and installed them as elders one month later, and thereby completed the church's organization.[52] By August, a Sunday school was functioning. An intense search was also underway to locate a suitable minister, with Fraser maintaining close contact with local leaders. Jonathon Sayer Slauson, later an elder and trustee, corresponded at length with the missionary about these church matters. Fraser repeatedly advised church officers through Slauson on the selection of a minister appropriate to Los Angeles.[53]

Jonathon S. Slauson was the type of church member whom Fraser appreciated as "substantial." President of the Los Angeles County Bank, backer of the Los Angeles and Independence Railroad, and ardent real-estate developer, Slauson earnestly sought the advancement of Presbyterianism in the local community.[54] His correspondence is the rare instance of surviving evidence that reveals the thinking of a prominent and forthright layman of the time. Slauson desired a pastor who would seek out people who were religiously "indifferent" and "those of no religious conviction." The town evidently had many more such persons than those who attended church out of "conscientious conviction." The pastor should also be young and healthy enough to sustain the demands of such evangelization, and be a man "whose wife can enter socially upon the work." The small church needed the right man to start this ministry, because it would

---

Church in the U.S.A.), POHP; and Edward A. Wicher, *The Presbyterian Church in California, 1849–1927* (New York: Frederick H. Hitchcock, 1927), p. 148.

[52] Session Minutes and Records, 1874–1879, vol. I, pp. 3–4, First Presbyterian Church of Los Angeles, POHP; Letters, Fraser to Hill, 21 January 1902, Oakland, California, and W. C. Harding to Thomas Fraser, 23 May 1871, Wilmington, [California], both in the Fraser Collection, ASFTS; *Pacific*, XIX (17 May 1870), p. 4, and (27 October 1870), p. 5; *Occident*, V (11 February 1874), p. 48.

[53] Letter, Fraser to Hill, 21 June 1902, ASFTS; E. F. Field, "Historical Address," (Los Angeles: typescript, 4 February 1894), pp. 4–5, HL.

[54] Glenn S. Dumke, *The Boom of the Eighties in Southern California* (San Marino, California: Huntington Library, 1944), pp. 209–10.

be difficult "at the best." Slauson considered Los Angeles Presbyterians as a "missionary congregation who have emigrated from very near a community of Feet washing Baptists in Tennessee or a real Camp meeting Western Methodist community of the west."[55]

The first minister the local church called was Reverend A.F. White, whom Slauson considered too elderly, and who had an "unsuitable" wife. Known as a pioneer clergyman, White had served as pastor in Carson City, Nevada, as well as Nevada state geologist. The presbytery installed White on 29 August 1875, and in the two years of his service, he added 135 new members to the congregation. Halfway through his tenure, Los Angeles ceased to be missionary territory, as far as Presbyterian officials were concerned. It was through the influx of new residents into the community that the First Presbyterian Church obtained sufficient worshipers to become self-sustaining. In 1875 and 1876, this communion received 118 new members, 96 of whom had transferred from other Presbyterian bodies. Reverend White was not engaged in the type of pastoral outreach that Slauson desired, yet the denomination was slowly progressing because of immigration.[56]

New arrivals speaking another tongue also found their ways to Los Angeles early in that decade. In 1872, Carl Zahn, a German dentist recently relocated from Australia, gathered several local residents to found an independent "*deutsch-evangelisch*" church. Zahn shepherded this small group, for whom he purchased a lot on Spring Street between Fourth and Fifth streets and erected a small sanctuary. In 1876, Reverend Gottlieb H. Bollinger of the Northern Methodists' California Annual Conference met with Zahn and arranged the transfer of the congregation to a newly founded German Mission of the Los Angeles Circuit. Membership increased slowly, with only thirty-eight on the rolls and fifty children in the Sabbath school by 1879.[57]

---

[55] Letters, J.S. Slauson to Thomas Fraser, 18 July 1874, Los Angeles, and 14 December 1877, n.p., Fraser Collection, ASFTS.

[56] Interestingly, at the time of White's resignation, in 1879, the congregation declared a three-month "vacation" because of its inability to raise funds for a replacement pastor's salary. See Session Minutes and Records, 1874–1879, vol. 1, p. 74, First Presbyterian Church of Los Angeles, POHP; *Occident*, V (3 September 1874), p. 276, and VI (16 September 1875), p. 292; Field, "Historical Address," pp. 4–5; Presbyterian Board of Home Missions *Annual Reports* (New York: Presbyterian Board of Home Missions, 1875–1877), 1875: p. 90, 1876: p. 206.

[57] *Minutes* of the Twenty-seventh Annual Session of the California Annual Confer-

Nonetheless, in that year the members built and paid for a new church on Fourth Street, legally incorporated the parish, and elected five trustees, including Zahn, who was also licensed as a lay preacher.[58]

In the early years of this congregation, Doctor Zahn and the members had extended their hospitality to the final major Protestant denomination to establish a foothold in Los Angeles. Baptist activity in the county had been increasing, though regular preaching had ceased in Los Angeles in 1863. Twenty-three delegates from five churches met in rural El Monte in August, 1869, to draw up the constitution and articles of faith of the Los Angeles Baptist Association. The first session of the new association met the following month, in Los Nietos, and elected officers, solicited funds, and selected a missionary for the area. Membership that year in the association totaled five congregations with 118 people, residing in two counties; by 1876, there were sixteen assemblies with 633 people affiliated, in five counties.[59]

As with the Presbyterians, the Baptist denomination profited from the steady immigration of new residents into the town of Los Angeles. Reverend William Hobbs and his wife were two such settlers, arriving from Sydney, New South Wales, Australia. Through their efforts, some twenty people met on 6 September 1874 to form the First Baptist Church of Los Angeles. Eight people (four men and four women) officially constituted this body. This small congregation then proceeded to call Hobbs as pastor, elect a clerk, adopt a church covenant and articles of faith, hear a sermon, and conclude with services in Chinese by "Brother" Lee Key. Significantly, four of the eight founders were from the southern states, while the other four were from the Los Nietos church, which itself was predominantly comprised of Southerners.[60] Nineteen others joined in the following year, all but

---

ence (1879), pp. 42–43; *75-Jährige Jubiläums-Feier der Ersten Deutschen Methodisten-Kirche* (Los Angeles: German Methodist Church, 1951), [p. 1]; Wilson, *History of Los Angeles County*, p. 121; and William A. Spalding, *History and Reminiscences of Los Angeles City and County, California* (Los Angeles: J.R. Finnell and Sons, 1931), vol. 3, pp. 555–56.

[58] The other four trustees were Herman Newman, Daniel Schieck, Conrad Hafen, and F. Galways; *75-Jährige Jubiläum*, [p. 2]. Bollinger continued as pastor until 1883, when William Schudt assumed the pulpit; *Historical Journal of the Pacific and Southwest Annual Conference* (Pasadena: United Methodist Center, 1981), p. 45. This congregation is currently known as the First German United Methodist Church in downtown Los Angeles.

[59] Ellis, "Baptist Churches in Southern California," pp. 131–32, 150.

[60] "Official Records," ledger vol. I, pp. 1–11, First Baptist Church, Los Angeles, California, hereafter cited as FBC.

one by presenting a "letter of dismission" from another congregation. This pattern of affiliation mirrored that of the First Presbyterian Church and continued for the first years of the congregation. The local community, however, soon was embroiled in a bitter dispute that split the small group. When Reverend Hobbs resigned as pastor, in June 1875, certain individuals were displeased with the manner in which the church clerk acted in the search for a replacement. Heated discussions throughout the summer of 1876 regarding the clerk's correspondence with prospective pastors led to an "insolent letter," in August, in which nine departing members charged the "so-called" church with "abominations and gross immorality."[61]

Eventually, the reduced denomination secured the services of Reverend Winfield Scott, in September 1876, though there was soon disagreement over the length of his term and the renewal of his call. Lack of funds precluded further discussion and forced the termination of his ministry by January 1878. Such financial difficulties permitted only short-term pastorates until 1881.[62] It is significant to note the intensity with which these communicants took the governance of their church. The clerk's records are replete with notations on extended discussions, lists of names of those who spoke to various issues, and the tabulations of voting to resolve matters. Local Baptists vigorously exercised a democratic church polity, which finally manifested in Los Angeles the spirit considered so typically "American" among pathbreakers and pioneers.[63]

Two final groups formally organized in the mid-1870s, though only one was able to survive the vicissitudes so often plaguing small frontier congregations. Two men led an effort, in the summer of 1874, to survey Los Angeles in search of fellow believers in the Christian Church, otherwise known as the Disciples of Christ. Together with their wives, W.J.A. Smith, a preaching elder, and G.W. Linton, a fellow layman, ascertained that approximately twenty-five people in town were interested in gathering as a church. Until that time, "Disciples" were forced to travel to San Bernardino, Los Nietos, and El

---

[61] "Official Records," vol. I, pp. 36, 39–45, 50, FBC.

[62] "Official Records," vol. I, pp. 63–68, 71, 73, FBC.

[63] "Constitution and By-Laws, Articles of Faith, Church Covenant and Roll of Members of the First Baptist Church of Los Angeles" (ledger volume, 1876–1891), n.p., FBC.

Monte in order to worship together.[64] Regular services commenced in Los Angeles in October 1874, in conjunction with a Sunday School for approximately thirty students.[65]

Twenty-six people formally "covenanted together," on 28 February 1875, at a meeting in the county courthouse, where they also pledged to accept the Bible as their "only rule of faith and practice." They elected four elders, including the prosperous dry-goods merchant, Benjamin F. Coulter, who began his long and generous association with this local church. The presiding minister that day was G.R. Hand, from the neighboring town of Downey, where the Disciples were firmly established. Like the Baptists and Presbyterians, the Disciples derived support and leadership for their Los Angeles efforts from the brothers and sisters of their denomination in surrounding farming communities.[66] In later years, local Disciples of Christ invited "all the friends of our Lord Jesus Christ who earnestly desire to worship as the early Christians worshiped" to gather annually at Downey for summer camp meetings. There they sought to improve cooperation among Disciples in the area, as well as to "proclaim the 'good news' to the world."[67]

The work of women in the foundation of the Church of Unity in Los Angeles is far easier to document than for the Disciples or most any other denomination. It is safe to say that without the leadership of Caroline M. Seymour Severance, the local Unitarians most probably would not have organized as early as they did. Severance and her husband, the retired banker T.E. Severance, were Bostonians recently settled in Los Angeles. Early in March of 1877, another newcomer, Reverend John D. Wells, called at the Severance home in search of fellow Harvard graduates. The resulting conversations revealed that Wells was the former pastor of the First Unitarian Church of Quincy, Massachusetts, and had relocated in the West for the sake of his health.

These transplanted seekers sought out fellow Unitarians and other friends and held services in the Severance home, in March 1877.

---

[64] See the Los Angeles *Star*, 25 September 1869, for one notice of a "Christian Meeting" in San Bernardino, some sixty miles east of Los Angeles.

[65] Clifford A. Cole, *The Christian Churches of Southern California* (St. Louis: Christian Board of Publication, 1959), p. 40.

[66] Wilson, *History of Los Angeles County*, p. 121.

[67] E. B. Ware, *History of the Disciples of Christ in California* (Healdsburg, California: F. W. Cooke, 1916), pp. 189–90.

William A. Spalding was present for that first gathering and later recalled the key role that Caroline Severance exercised in subsequent meetings, when Reverend Wells was absent. She involved herself by

> generally suggesting the topic, leading off with a brief statement stimulative of thought, and then calling on various members of the group to express themselves. And before the session was concluded, everybody who had any ideas to express was given an opportunity to express them—and believe me, he gave the best that was in him. Madame Severance was a great programmer.[68]

Severance's energetic spirit attracted such notice that the small group soon had to seek larger quarters in a rented hall.

"Madame Severance" actively sought out other religious enquirers like herself and also engaged in a variety of reform activities over the next three decades. She led the formal organization of a Unitarian society in Los Angeles, in May 1877, with twenty-seven charter members, and then started the Sunday school. The initial signatories undertook a series of entertainments to raise funds for the denomination. Soon known as "Unitarian Thursdays," these popular weekly readings, recitations, plays, and instrumental recitals were held in conjunction with a dinner and a dance. The minister's wife, Mrs. Wells, added further cultural luster to these gatherings, inasmuch as she let it be known that she was a cousin of the poet Henry Wadsworth Longfellow.[69]

When Reverend Wells suffered deteriorating health, Mrs. Severance managed to maintain the religious meetings until early 1880. But services ceased when the Severances returned to Boston for several years. Back in Los Angeles by 1884, Mrs. Severance reassumed her position of leadership in the women's rights movement and the free kindergarten association.[70] In the fall of that year, the increase in local population enabled Madame Severance and others to reestablish

---

[68] Spalding quoted in John D.K. Perry, *A History of the First Unitarian Church of Los Angeles, California, 1877–1937* (Los Angeles: First Unitarian Church, 1937), p. 7.

[69] Perry, *First Unitarian Church*, pp. 8–10; and Kate Douglas Wiggin, *My Garden of Memory: An Autobiography* (Boston: Houghton Mifflin Company, 1923), pp. 100–103. Severance had recruited Kate Douglas Wiggin to train in the first experimental kindergarten in Los Angeles, in 1876, which initiated Wiggin's lifelong work with children. Wiggin is best remembered as the author of *Rebecca of Sunnybrook Farm* and other children's literature.

[70] Ruddy, ed., *Mother of Clubs*, p. 87.

regular worship. Once more a Harvard man stood in a Unitarian pulpit in Los Angeles; Reverend J.H. Allen presided at the first gathering
of the revived Church of Unity. The new members of this assembly
included many women prominent in community affairs, but none
gained the fame and respect accorded to Caroline Seymour Severance.[71]

The influx of the first Unitarians and non-Hispanic settlers into Los
Angeles, in the 1870s, permitted the foundation of a host of additional
religious groups. It is clear that Los Angeles was the scene of unusually diverse religious growth as early as the mid-nineteenth century.
"Bishop" Money's New Testament Church challenged local Catholic hegemony. Within a matter of only a few years, Rabbi Edelman's
synagogue, Biddy Mason's African Methodist Episcopal congregation, and the Chinese were all contemporary worshipers alongside
Congregationalists and Methodists. The factors leading to these developments warrant our investigation in the following section. Such
attention will help us understand who these believers were and why
they were able to establish themselves so early. Then it will be possible to understand more clearly the significance of their presence in
the pueblo, as well as their many contributions to the growth of Los
Angeles.

[71] Allen was a member of the faculty of Harvard University. See the "History, Preamble, and Constitution of the Church of Unity, Los Angeles, Cal.," pp. 1–3, (ledger
volume, 1886–1892), First Unitarian Church, Los Angeles; Perry, *First Unitarian
Church*, pp. 11–12.

"PEOPLE OF THE RIGHT SORT"

Few American cities have experienced the explosive growth that plays such a central role in the history of Los Angeles. Historian Robert M. Fogelson examined the increase in population and measured the staggering rate of expansion shown in the table below. The boosters of Los Angeles gloried in this growth. To modern readers, unchecked expansion connotes traffic congestion, housing shortages, and pollution of the environment; to proponents of "progress" in the last century, more residents meant more businesses, schools, churches, and a quicker end to frontier conditions.

The population increase in the decade of the 1870s brought the type of immigrants that Protestant clergymen had so long desired:

Table 1: Population Growth in Los Angeles, 1850–1910[1]

Year	Total Population	Rate of Growth
1850	1,610	——
1860	4,385	172%
1870	5,728	27%
1880	11,183	95%
1890	50,395	351%
1900	102,489	103%
1910	319,198	212%

[1] Fogelson, *Fragmented Metropolis: Los Angeles, 1850–1930* (Cambridge: Harvard University Press, 1967), pp. 21, 78, 79.

Anglo-American Protestants, with their families.[2] The ministers had the Southern Pacific Railroad to thank for many of their newfound parishioners. The tracks finally connected Los Angeles with San Francisco in September of 1876. Real-estate developers, such as the Methodist Robert Widney, were quick to herald the glories of "semi-tropical California" to prospective buyers arriving at the Arcade depot at Main and Alameda streets. Buffeted between ballyhoo and barbeques, newcomers settled in Los Angeles at a pace reminiscent of the rowdy and raucous years of the 1850s.

The county population also grew dramatically in the decade of the 1870s, doubling from a total of 15,309, in 1870, to 33,381, ten years later. Initiating a trend that persisted to the turn of the century, American-born settlers arrived in increasing numbers from New York, Missouri, Illinois, Ohio, Indiana, and Pennsylvania.[3] These newcomers traveled west by train and spurred the subdivision of the vast Spanish and Mexican ranchos into smaller landholdings and town sites. Several colonies of like-minded religious settlers appeared in the county, such as the Presbyterians, of Westminster, and the Disciples of Christ, in Downey. The churches of these rural communities were initially stronger than their Los Angeles counterparts. As church-endorsed settlements, these towns were able to organize strong and lasting religious organizations. In the ensuing years, the outlying colonies provided the bases from which these denominations formed their first permanent Los Angeles congregations.[4]

Religious growth in Los Angeles appeared most clearly in four specific ways: increased membership, the construction of new religious edifices, the formation of new ecclesiastical jurisdictions, and the appearance of further new denominations. Membership records

[2] The birthrate among Hispanic Roman Catholics in Los Angeles had also been declining, as noted in the studies by Richard Griswold del Castillo. The birthrate per 1,000 childbearing women in 1850 he estimated at 341, while the figure for 1870 was down to 150. This decline coincided with the economic collapse of the Hispanic pastoral economy in the 1860s in southern California, brought on by extended drought, taxation, and legal difficulties over ownership of land. See *The Los Angeles Barrio, 1850–1890: A Social History*, (Berkeley: University of California Press, 1979), p. 80.

[3] U.S. Census Office, *Compendium of the Ninth Census* (Washington, D.C.: Government Printing Office, 1872), p. 400; and *Statistics of the Population of the United States* (Washington, D.C.: Government Printing Office, 1883), p. 498.

[4] The histories of these respective denominational colonies are discussed in Harland E. Hogue, "A History of Religion in Southern California, 1846–1880" (Ph.D. dissertation, Columbia University, 1958), pp. 256–57, 261–73, 335–36.

do not exist for the Roman Catholic and Jewish bodies, though the Los Angeles *Times*, in 1886, carried an article estimating that 5,000 people were affiliated with the former communion and 50 persons with the latter.[5] Protestant growth is evident from annual reports for the three oldest parishes.[6] Episcopalians totaled 40 in 1870, but grew to 200 in 1885, while Congregationalists expanded from 37 to 301 during those same years. The most dramatic growth in that period occurred in the Northern Methodist fold, with an increase from approximately 60 to 999 registered members.[7] Denominations established after 1870, such as the Baptists and Presbyterians, counted hundreds of additional worshipers at their respective services.

Only four religious structures stood in the community prior to 1869. In that year, the Roman Catholics extensively remodeled their 1822 adobe church, to alleviate crowded conditions on Sundays. The Episcopalians continued to met in the brick chapel that the defunct First Protestant Society had erected in 1862. The Congregationalists and Northern Methodists completed their respective meetinghouses in 1868. During the 1870s, seven new houses of worship appeared. Between 1880 and 1889, the city's population increase led three established congregations to construct larger facilities, while members of nine new parishes erected their first houses of prayer.[8]

The denominations that chose to erect larger churches on new sites were the Episcopalians, in 1883, and the Congregationalists and Southern Methodists, in 1885. The Northern Methodists opted to split their congregations and to erect small churches in the growing neighborhoods of the city. Four such new chapels appeared between 1880 and 1885. Other groups, such as the Baptists, Presbyterians, and

[5] Los Angeles *Times*, 7 March 1886.

[6] It is difficult to ascertain the actual growth in the membership of each denomination, because of incomplete congregational records. See table 3, in chapter 7, for the most complete listing of communicants that could be found for the period from 1870 to 1890.

[7] *Journal*, Annual Convention of the Protestant Episcopal Church of the Diocese of California, (1871), p. 67, and (1886), statistical table, n.p.; *Minutes*, Annual Meeting of the General Session of California (1870, 1885), statistical tables, n.p.; Los Angeles *Star*, 26 March 1870; and *Minutes*, Southern California Methodist Episcopal Church, North, Annual Conference (1885), statistical table, n.p.

[8] *An Illustrated History of Los Angeles County, California* (Chicago: Lewis Publishing Company, 1889), pp. 290–305; and Marco R. Newmark, "The Story of Religion in Los Angeles, 1781–1900," Historical Society of Southern California *Quarterly*, XXVIII (March, 1946), pp. 35–50.

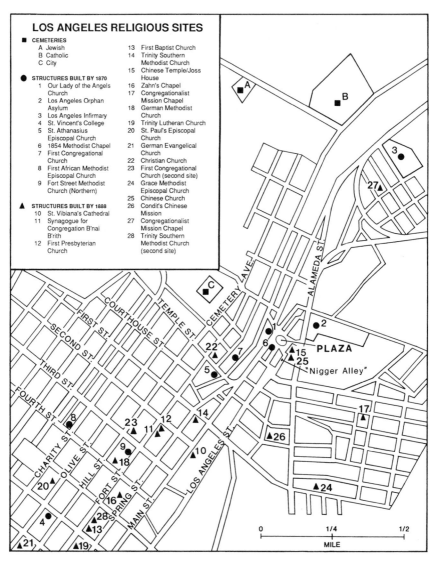

LOS ANGELES RELIGIOUS SITES

■ CEMETERIES
- A Jewish
- B Catholic
- C City

● STRUCTURES BUILT BY 1870
1. Our Lady of the Angels Church
2. Los Angeles Orphan Asylum
3. Los Angeles Infirmary
4. St. Vincent's College
5. St. Athanasius Episcopal Church
6. 1854 Methodist Chapel
7. First Congregational Church
8. First African Methodist Episcopal Church
9. Fort Street Methodist Church (Northern)

▲ STRUCTURES BUILT BY 1888
10. St. Vibiana's Cathedral
11. Synagogue for Congregation B'nai B'rith
12. First Presbyterian Church

13. First Baptist Church
14. Trinity Southern Methodist Church
15. Chinese Temple/Joss House
16. Zahn's Chapel
17. Congregationalist Mission Chapel
18. German Methodist Church
19. Trinity Lutheran Church
20. St. Paul's Episcopal Church
21. German Evangelical Church
22. Christian Church
23. First Congregational Church (second site)
24. Grace Methodist Episcopal Church
25. Chinese Church
26. Condit's Chinese Mission
27. Congregationalist Mission Chapel
28. Trinity Southern Methodist Church (second site)

Unitarians, moved for the first time in the 1880s from rented quarters into newly completed edifices. Three parishes also instituted mission chapels for Chinese, Hispanic, and German evangelization. By 1889, Los Angeles boasted seventeen houses of prayer, as compared to the four structures existent a scant two decades previously. The addition of so many spires to the skyline enabled civic boosters to promote the community as a thoroughly modern city, where residents assembled in "elegant and commodious places of worship."[9]

The leaders of the churches were also busily engaged in establishing new ecclesiastical jurisdictions. The Baptists led the movement, with the formation of the Los Angeles Baptist Association, in 1869, while the Southern Methodists followed, one year later, with the Los Angeles Conference. The Presbytery of Los Angeles appeared in 1872.[10] The Southern California Annual Conference of the Northern Methodists first met in 1876. Among the Episcopalians, St. Athanasius church passed from "mission church" to formal parochial status, when it legally incorporated, in 1874. In 1877, diocesan authorities based in San Francisco then proposed a set of districts, to be known as "convocations." The clergy of the vast Convocation of Southern California, however, did not gather until 1883 to discuss affairs for their churches in the southern half of the state. National leaders established the Diocese of Los Angeles, in 1895, and Joseph Horsfall Johnson assumed office as first bishop the following year.[11]

Other religious denominations began appearing in Los Angeles with every passing year. Between 1880 and 1885, Seventh-Day Adventists, United Presbyterians, "German" [Missouri Synod] Luther-

---

[9] *Los Angeles City and County Directory, 1884–1885* (Los Angeles: Atwood and Ernst, 1885), pp. 11–12; J. Albert Wilson, *History of Los Angeles County, California,* (Oakland, California: Thompson and West, 1880; reprint ed., Berkeley: Howell-North, 1959), pp. 119–21; and Los Angeles *Times,* 7 March 1886.

[10] On the national level, the Presbyterian denomination had divided into "new-school" and "old-school" factions, in 1837. Both sects further split into northern and southern branches over the issue of slavery; the New School in 1857 and the Old School in 1861. Subsequent to the Civil War, the two southern branches united as the Presbyterian Church in the United States. The northern branches combined, in 1870, as the Presbyterian Church in the United States of America, more commonly known as the Presbyterian Church, U.S.A (or "Northern Presbyterians"). In California, the northern church's synod after 1870 was titled the Synod of the Pacific. The Presbytery of Los Angeles formed in 1872 was the local division of this body. See Sydney E. Ahlstrom, *A Religious History of the American People* (New Haven: Yale University Press, 1972), p. 660.

[11] Ivan C. Ellis, "Baptist Churches in Southern California" (Ph.D. dissertation, Northern Baptist Theological Seminary, Chicago, 1948), p. 124, and Leland D. Hine, *Baptists in Southern California,* (Valley Forge, Pennsylvania: Judson Press, 1966), pp. 31–43; Leon L. Loofbourow, *In Search of God's Gold* (San Francisco: Historical Society of the Northern California–Nevada Conference, Methodist Church, 1950), p. 164; William Stewart Young, "Address on the Fiftieth Anniversary of the Founding of First Presbyterian Church, Los Angeles" (Typescript, 1923), p. 5, "First

ans, Holiness Bands, Reorganized Latter Day Saints, Spiritualists, and "a society of American Buddhists" held their first services, while the Unitarians reappeared as a formal body.[12] In the same period, local blacks withdrew from the Fort Street Methodists, in order to form the Second Baptist Church.[13] In surrounding towns, other denominations established themselves, such as the Society of Friends, in Whittier, and the German Brethren ("Dunkards"), in Lordsburg (present-day LaVerne).[14] People of other diverse creeds, such as the Latter-day Saints, were also settling in Los Angeles, hosting missionary clergy, and working toward the eventual formation of their own congregations, later in the decade.[15] This proliferation of religious bodies provided one further indication that Los Angeles had passed its frontier period.

Such a plethora of faiths could only appear and establish themselves in a community with the population and prosperity of rapidly urbanizing Los Angeles. The members of the growing and diverse congregations shared enough values and attitudes to provide the basis for a new civic ethos that replaced the Hispanic and cosmopolitan characteristics of an earlier age. The westering churches of earlier frontiers finally established themselves in this corner of southern California. By 1885, the long-desired Protestant families arrived in numbers great enough to erase most vestiges of the city's Hispanic and frontier heritage. Members of this increasing new majority of residents ever more resolutely promoted nationally prevalent concepts of society, government, and religion.[16]

In the decade of the 1870s, members of the traditional pioneer-

Presbyterian Church, Los Angeles" file, Archives, San Francisco Theological Seminary, San Anselmo, California; Charles V. Anthony, *Fifty Years of Methodism*, (San Francisco: Methodist Book Concern, 1901), p. 351; Frederick G. Bohme, "Episcopal Beginnings in Southern California," *Southern California Quarterly*, XLVII (June, 1965), p. 185; and Stephen C. Clark, *The Diocese of Los Angeles: A Brief History*, (Los Angeles: Committee on Diocesan Anniversaries, 1945), pp. 22, 34–37.

[12] Los Angeles *Times*, 7 March 1886.

[13] For a listing of the churches in 1885, see the Los Angeles *City Directory* (1885), pp. 11–12.

[14] Glenn S. Dumke, *The Boom of the Eighties in Southern California* (San Marino, California: Huntington Library, 1944), pp. 6, 246–57, discusses these later religious groups and their educational endeavors.

[15] Leo J. Muir, *A Century of Mormon Activities in California* (Salt Lake City: Deseret News Press [1952]), vol. I, pp. 109–10.

[16] Gregory H. Singleton presents an interesting discussion of the nature of the

LOS ANGELES AREA, 1888

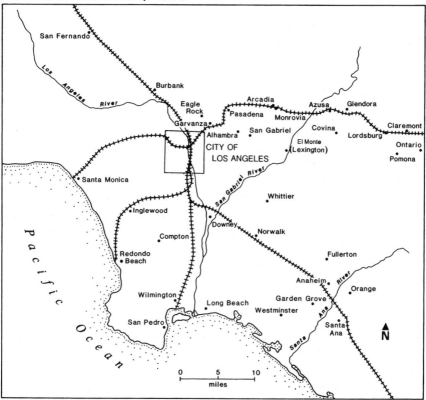

ing Christian denominations established themselves in Los Angeles with the strength they had known in earlier frontiers in the trans-Appalachian regions. American Protestants finally began to exercise an influence in this community similar to what they had known in settlements extending from the Old Northwest to the Midwest. Anglo-American residents of Los Angeles easily recognized the goals of these late-arriving church folk. As historian William Warren Sweet first noted, such believers had long been the bearers of a distinctive national culture, who worked to defend democratic institutions, pro-

"voluntaristic" denominations that came to dominate the religious scene in Los Angeles at the turn of the century. See his *Religion in the City of the Angels: American Public Culture and Urbanization, Los Angeles, 1850–1930* (Ann Arbor, Michigan: UMI Research Press, 1979), pp. 49–96.

vide the foundations for morality, and foster education and civility.[17] For example, church members had helped tame these frontiers and exerted godly influence on local society by publically opposing violence and card playing, while advocating temperance, family life, and higher levels of decorum in personal behavior. Three principal factors explain the delay in the establishment of more traditional pioneers of American religious expansion in Los Angeles: geographic isolation, ministerial methods, and frontier demographics in the southern counties of California.[18]

Early settlers, traveling by wagon, struggled through the vast deserts and over the ring of rugged mountains surrounding the Los Angeles basin. Reverend James Brier and his family barely survived one such crossing, in 1849, through the wasteland they named "Death Valley." Prevailing northwesterly winds also impeded immigrants in vessels attempting to sail northward along the coast. These topographical and climatic conditions long curtailed communications with the pueblo. The advent of steam-driven ships and trains, the overland stage, telegraph lines, and new wagon roads enabled the regular movement of passengers and freight in and out of the community.[19]

The gradual improvement in transportation services enabled increasing numbers of people to reach Los Angeles more easily. Military personnel traveled on government assignment to posts in this remote corner of California. Immigrants convinced of the commercial opportunities of the southern portion of the state left friends and relatives in gold-rush San Francisco for cow town Los Angeles. Businessmen engaged in railroad construction imported the inexpensive labor force they needed from China. Other immigrants made their way to Los Angeles, particularly from the southern states, but the difficult conditions of overland and coastal travel limited their numbers. Once the railroad tracks were laid, immigration changed appreciably. The Southern Pacific connection, in 1876, linked Los Angeles for the

[17] For a brief explanation of Sweet's ideas, see "The Churches as Moral Courts of the Frontier," *Church History*, II (June, 1933), pp. 8–10, 21.

[18] Historian Sandra Sizer Frankiel adds a fourth characteristic for Los Angeles believers: the type of settler that California attracted. For her discussion of this fascinating point, see *California's Spiritual Frontier: Religious Alternatives in Anglo-Protestantism, 1850–1910* (Berkeley: University of California Press, 1988), pp. 1–18.

[19] Harris Newmark discussed these improvements in communications and transport in his *Sixty Years in Southern California, 1853–1913* (4th ed., revised by Maurice H.

first time with transcontinental rail service. The Santa Fe Railroad augmented this link in 1885, and the ensuing competition for patronage enticed hordes of midwestern passengers to book passage, when fares dropped as low as one dollar for transport from Kansas City to Los Angeles.[20]

The second factor contributing to the unique order of frontier churches in Los Angeles arose from the demographics of the local population. Immigrants arriving in the two decades after 1848 discovered a Hispanic community that was predominantly Roman Catholic, both in its religious affiliation and in its vibrant cultural heritage. Only certain denominations could take hold because of the varied origins of these pioneers, but every improvement in transportation enabled additional settlers to reach the pueblo. These newcomers, in turn, further altered the local religious composition, until it was as multihued as a Mexican serape. Dramatically affecting the composition and character of the community, immigration into Los Angeles after the completion of the transcontinental railroad, in 1869, proceeded at an ever accelerating pace.

No group felt the impact of this influx of new residents more than the descendants of the founders of Los Angeles. Spanish-speaking Roman Catholics comprised the earliest of the community's pioneers, and their communion constituted the oldest of the creeds, not only in this settlement, but throughout California and the Southwest. The presence of long-settled Hispanics distinguished the demographics of both the community and the region. Because of numbers and influence, this denomination remained the most important of the town's institutional religions until well into the 1880s. The Hispanic ethos of communal life changed noticeably between 1848 and 1870, with the economic and political reversals of the Californios. A further factor contributing to this change in cultural ethos was the difference in religious sensibilities among arriving newcomers.

During the earliest years of population change, 1850 to 1870, immigrants to Los Angeles showed a preference for Jewish, Episcopal, Congregational, Chinese, and African Methodist Episcopal wor-

---

Newmark and Marco R. Newmark, Los Angeles: Zeitlin and Ver Brugge, 1970), pp. 152–53, 187, 229, 234, 242, 290, 385–88.

[20] Boyle Workman, *The City That Grew, 1840–1936* (Los Angeles: Southland Publishing Company, 1936), p. 230.

ship. Not one of these creeds was a notable pioneer denomination east of the Mississippi River. The local religious institutions of these newcomers persisted in large measure because these settlers shared a common background of class, ethnicity, or race. Locally stationed army officers, like their comrades across the nation, favored the Episcopalian church. Providing an element of social respectability, the presence of the military elite in the local parish attracted other believers whose background or professional standing afforded them some claim (or dream) of greater local status.

The Jews and, to a lesser extent in later years, the Congregationalists engaged in early chain migrations of coreligionists from their respective homelands in the German states and New England. These familial and ethnic ties permitted strong business and social connections to develop both within and beyond the local community. Many Los Angeles Jews, for example, had relatives in San Francisco. Organized religion benefited from these connections, because such bonds provided a coherence among congregants beyond the denominational realm. Kinship, along with national origins, reinforced the sense of group association and identity necessary for these nontraditional groups to survive as spiritual pioneers in Spanish-speaking Los Angeles.

The federal census for 1870 reported that Los Angeles County included 162 residents born in Massachusetts and 141 who gave Maine as their place of birth. Congregationalism was traditionally strong in both states, and many relocated New Englanders could be expected to support the church of their ancestors. Members of the Llewellyn and Jotham Bixby families were representative of southern California settlers who had relocated from Maine. Arriving in 1866, the two brothers operated extensive ranches, twenty miles south of Los Angeles, and supported the town's Congregational church devotedly and generously, from the time of its foundation. Additional members of the extended family later joined the Bixby brothers in their farming enterprise, while other residents of their native county followed them out from Maine.[21] Martha Hathaway Bixby was one member of this clan whom we will encounter in a later chapter.

---

[21] Llewellyn Bixby's daughter later wrote her memoirs, in which she described the chain migration of her father's seven siblings and numerous cousins from Maine to California. See Sarah Bixby Smith, *Adobe Days* (4th ed., revised, Fresno, California: Valley Publishers, 1974), pp. 2–6.

In 1869, three men from Somerset County, Maine, purchased a tract of two hundred acres, almost midway between the town of Los Angeles and the Bixby ranches. Within five years, some sixteen families, half of them related to one another by marriage, had relocated in what came to be known as the "State of Maine" colony.[22] Missionary agent James Warren doggedly sought out such New Englanders and successfully recruited their support on behalf of the local church of the Pilgrim faith.[23] The presence of such an organizer from the American Home Missionary Society was a significant factor in the early establishment of Congregationalism, as compared to other religious pioneers. They amazed themselves with their success, particularly when they stole a march on the Methodists in Los Angeles and founded their church first.

A sense of community also developed among two other groups, but more directly in response to persecution and discrimination. In the face of continued antipathy and occasional violence, Chinese and black worshipers gathered for prayer, struggled to accumulate funds, and erected their own sanctuaries. Members of both groups found few job opportunities open to them, beyond laundries and small stores, or truck gardens and construction gangs. But such occupations were lucrative, in comparison with wages paid respectively in either China or the American South. Those who gathered to celebrate the lunar new year or sing Gospel hymns at the African Methodist Episcopal church were contemporaries of the earliest religious groups in Los Angeles. For the Chinese and the blacks, both their racial heritage and the experience of local prejudice reinforced the bonds that enabled their respective religious associations to endure, when other denominations faltered.

Railroad connections after 1870 were only one factor explaining the eventual arrival in Los Angeles of such traditional pioneering groups as the Northern and Southern Methodists, the Baptists, and the Presbyterians. A further inducement attracting many farmers was the breakup of the vast Mexican ranchos in southern California. One important example of such subdivision was that of the Abel Stearns ranch empire, described in the last chapter. Beginning in 1868, two

[22] Wilson, *History of Los Angeles County*, pp. 138, 189.
[23] U.S. Census Office, *Compendium of the Ninth Census* (Washington, D.C.: Government Printing Office, 1872), p. 400; and Royal G. Davis, *Light on a Gothic Tower* (Los Angeles: First Congregational Church, 1967), p. 22.

decades of rapid agricultural development ensued in the southern portion of Los Angeles county on these landholdings alone. The establishment of church-sponsored colonies there and elsewhere further strengthened Protestant denominations, with the arrival of additional believers who came to work the soil.[24] This scenario was repeated throughout the Los Angeles basin and adjacent valleys.

A third, and final, factor contributed to the unusually slow progress of the traditional American pioneer churches in Los Angeles. The hearty frontier ministers who first reached the pueblo were unprepared in language and religious attitudes to deal successfully with the cow town's polyglot society. They preached a conservative and orthodox Christianity, which emphasized dogmas of sin and personal repentance.[25] Finding few Protestant American families, clergymen repeatedly grew frustrated with local conditions. In the period between 1848 and 1870, these preachers showed slight interest in approaching either the town's Hispanic majority or the smaller Chinese population. Only a very few ever learned the Spanish language or attempted to master Cantonese; those who did so appeared after 1876. Roman Catholic Hispanics, foreign-born Jews, and Chinese were unlikely subjects for camp meeting conversions, when the hymns and sermons were delivered entirely in the English language.[26] Such reluctance to alter methods left the ministers with little choice but to hope and pray for a "new class" of people to inhabit the settlement. When these Anglo-American congregations finally began, the clergy could then turn their attention to the local "foreigners."

Only one minister offered an exception to this unwillingness to adapt to the demographic conditions peculiar to southern California.

[24] Other church-related settlements included the "Indiana Colony" of Presbyterians from Indiana, who founded Pasadena, in 1874; and the Northern Methodists, who settled, in 1885, at Willmore City, now known as Long Beach. See Dumke, *Boom of the Eighties*, pp. 70–72, 85–90.

[25] The most complete information on sermons preached concerns the Presbyterian James Woods, who strongly emphasized an orthodox and conservative Christianity. The Huntington Library preserves his diary, which contains references to topics he treated in his sermons. See Lindley Bynum, ed., "Los Angeles, 1854–1855: The Diary of Reverend James Woods," Historical Society of Southern California *Quarterly*, XXIII (June, 1941), pp. 65–86. Some 183 of Woods's sermons survive, including the texts for at least 12 preached in Los Angeles between November 1854 and September 1855. See the James Woods Collection, Box 1, ASFTS.

[26] Later Protestant evangelization would in fact adopt the language of the Chinese and Hispanics. This gradual change is discussed in chapter 5.

Recognizing that too few Presbyterians resided locally to support a congregation, Reverend William Boardman proposed a nondenominational Protestant church. The resultant First Protestant Society of Los Angeles proved a notable success, for two principal reasons. The preacher first discovered that the small number of English-speaking people felt so isolated that they designated themselves as the local "Americans." So great was their desire to band together in the pueblo that they were willing to compromise on their respective creeds in order to construct a common house of worship.

Boardman also recognized that such a joint effort required that the pastor and members of this association minimize doctrinal or denominational differences. Inclined toward the "higher life," or holiness, movement, the Presbyterian cleric emphasized a less dogmatic form of faith for the town's Protestants. This approach to orthodox belief was the first instance of a phenomenon that would reappear in later years.[27] Such unique clerical insight into local conditions further highlights the shortcomings of the traditional methods by which other ministers evangelized, down through the 1870s.

Religious life in Los Angeles differed significantly from that in other frontier regions of the nation because of these influences of geographic isolation, local demographics, and ministerial methods. The settlement's religious endeavors were important manifestations of a broader and distinctively regional phenomenon. Southern California's cultural heritage and range of immigrating populations differed dramatically from other portions of the country. The most outstanding pioneer churches from other frontiers in the United States were unprepared to adapt their message or lifestyle to fit this unusual society. The clergymen of these faiths opted to await the day when emigration from other regions of the nation would sufficiently change the complexion and creeds of Angelenos. Their decisions suggest that these clerics accepted the prevailing cultural presuppositions of the inherent superiority of American Protestant Christianity over any other faith. Given such limiting attitudes and choices, the traditional religious pioneers who considered themselves to be the "true" Americans only established themselves in Los Angeles after members of a diverse array of more flexible creeds managed to do so.

---

[27] For a discussion of the holiness movement in southern California, see Frankiel, *California's Spiritual Frontiers*, pp. 103–108.

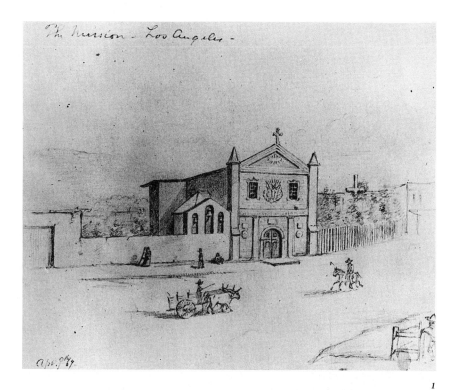

The mission - Loos Angeles -

Apr.9th.

1

1. Sketch of Our Lady of the Angels
Church by William Henry Jackson in 1867.
The building shows the 1856 alterations by
Father Blas Raho, C.M., such as the remodeled facade, the ornamental pillasters
(or "Cleopatra's needles"), and the fresco
over the door by Henri Penelon. Compare
this sketch with the 1857 painting. (Courtesy National Park Service, Scott's Bluff
National Monument.)

2

3

2. A common sight at Los Angeles parades and processions after 1856 were the blue-clad Sisters of Charity and their charges in white dresses and veils. In this 1857 painting, the Sisters lead the children from the Our Lady of the Angels church on the *plaza* back to the Orphan Asylum on Alameda Street at Macy.

This view of the church depicts the structure with a flat roof, probably covered

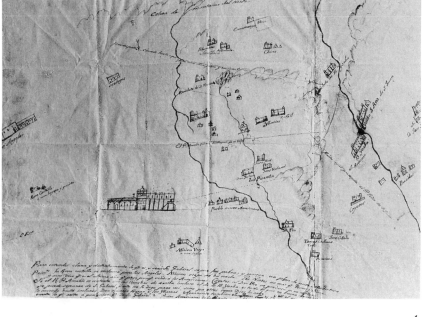

in *brea* (tar), and its unremodeled facade. (California Historical Society/Ticor Title Insurance, Los Angeles, Department of Special Collections, University of Southern California Library.)

3. This is one of the earliest known photographs of the *plaza* of Los Angeles, circa 1865. The church of Our Lady of the Angels is in the left foreground facing eastward toward fields along the Los Angeles river in the distance. The homes of the *rico* families face the town's square, such as the red-tiled *adobe* of José Antonio Carrillo on the far right. In the center of the *plaza* is the water reservoir, and above that is the two-story Vicente Lugo home which in subsequent years successively housed St. Vincent's College, a Roman Catholic parochial school, and Chinese shops and apartments until it was razed in 1951. Ygnacio del Valle's one-story adobe is to the right of the Lugo home. The alley to the

right of del Valle's adobe is the Calle de Los Negros, site of the "Chinese massacre" of 1871. (Seaver Center for Western History Research, Los Angeles County Museum of Natural History.)

4. Map showing the divisions of territory served by the priests from Los Angeles, San Gabriel, and San Juan Capistrano. Traveling much like Methodist circuit riders, Roman Catholic clergy traversed the countryside to hold services on the *ranchos* of their far-flung congregations. The references to the *pueblo nuevo Americano*, the "new American town" later known as El Monte, "Padre Amable" [Petithomme, SS.CC.], and "Padre Pedro" [Bagaria] of San Juan Capistrano suggest that this map dates from 1854. (California Historical Society/Ticor Title Insurance, Los Angeles, Department of Special Collections, University of Southern California Library.)

5. The Cathedral of St. Vibiana, Second and Main Streets in 1887. Designed by Los Angeles architect Ezra F. Kysor, it is based on the church of Puerto de San Miguel in Barcelona. Construction and furnishing of this $75,000 structure severely taxed the resources of the Roman Catholic diocese in the early 1870s when the population of Los Angeles was less than 5,000. To the left is the bishop's residence, erected in 1877–78. (Seaver Center for Western History Research, Los Angeles County Museum of Natural History.)

6. Bishop Thaddeus Amat, C.M., (1810–1878). A member of the Vincentian order, Amat served in Missouri and Pennsylvania before being named the first Bishop of the Roman Catholic diocese of Monterey-Los Angeles in 1853. Amat established his residence in Los Angeles in 1859 and lived here until his death in 1878. (Reproduced by permission of the Huntington Library, San Marino, California.)

7. Reverend Blas Raho, C.M., (1806–1862). A Neapolitan by birth, this Vincentian priest served in the American South prior to volunteering for the diocese of Monterey-Los Angeles. As pastor of Our Lady of the Angels church, Los Angeles, Raho won wide respect for his openness and liberality. (Archival Center, Archdiocese of Los Angeles.)

8. Reverend Joaquin Bot (1836–1903), pastor of San Gabriel, at entrance of the mission church, with acolytes, Raymundo Balderama and Antonio Ruiz, 1865. One of Amat's Catalonian clerical recruits, Bot was ordained in 1862 in Los Angeles and served in various parishes throughout the diocese of Monterey-Los Angeles until his death. He also imported religious art from Spain, which he retailed to parishioners. (California Historical Society/Ticor Title Insurance, Los Angeles, Department of Special Collections, University of Southern California Library.)

6

7

8

9

10

9. Sister Celeste Duffel, of the Daughters of Charity, with children of the Los Angeles Orphan Asylum on Alameda Street, circa 1885. (Courtesy of Maryvale, (Los Angeles Orphan Asylum), Rosemead, California.)

10. The Los Angeles Infirmary of the Sisters of Charity, erected in 1870 at Ann and Naud Streets. Beginning with the first hospital in Los Angeles in 1858, the Sisters offered public health care services under contract with the county Board of Supervisors until 1879. The Infirmary relocated from this site in 1884 and is now known as St. Vincent's Medical Center.

Note the presence of two of the Sisters on the balcony. (California Historical Society/Ticor Title Insurance, Los Angeles, Department of Special Collections, University of Southern California Library.)

11. St. Vincent's College, founded in 1865, at its second site at Sixth and Broadway, circa 1868. Mr. Ozro W. Childs (Episcopalian) donated the land; Rosa (Levy) Newmark (Jewish) organized the first fund raising efforts; and Reverend Miguel Rubio, C.M., (one of the Roman Catholic founders) designed the building. (Courtesy of the Archives of Loyola Marymount University, Los Angeles.)

12. Members of the congregation and their pastor, Reverend H. H. Messenger at the entrance of St. Athanasius Episcopal church, circa 1867. Built by the First Protestant Society of Los Angeles under Reverend William E. Boardman in 1862, the structure passed to the Episcopalians in 1866, who later sold it to the county of Los Angeles in 1883. (Seaver Center for Western History Research, Los Angeles County Museum of Natural History.)

13. Reverend Elias Birdsall, (1831–1890), pastor of St. Athanasius Episcopal church, 1864–1866, and 1880 to 1890. Born in Hammondsport, New York, and educated at Nashotah House, Wisconsin, Birdsall left a rectorship in Evansville, Illinois, in response to Bishop William Ingraham Kip's call for volunteers to the Diocese of California. (Seaver Center for Western History Research, Los Angeles County Museum of Natural History.)

13

4

THE RISE AND FALL OF "SYMPATHY, TOLERANCE, AND GOOD FEELING"

When Angelenos celebrated the nation's centennial, in 1876, they commissioned three men to record their community's history. J.J. Warner, Benjamin I. Hayes, and Joseph Pomeroy Widney collaborated in the first book-length history of Los Angeles. Like so many writers of the nineteenth century, they emphasized progress and growth. They avoided distasteful topics, which would reflect poorly on their town and its hardy pioneers and boosters. They neglected to mention instances of unchecked violence, such as the riot only five years previous, in which a mob stabbed, shot, and lynched nineteen Chinese residents in the center of the town.[1]

The historian Robert R. Dykstra has documented this "taboo on social conflict," which he discovered in the accounts written about five Kansas communities involved in the cattle trade. Glowing descriptions of a community's humble origins and prospects of future greatness were far more popular than dreary notices of hangings or bitter contention among pioneers.[2] True to this pattern, Warner, Hayes, and Widney concluded their volume: "It is meet and proper . . . that old hatreds, old enmities, should be buried with the dead century, to be remembered no more. . . ."[3] However, it is important

---

[1] The entry for 1871 describes harbor and irrigation improvements, along with the appearance of the first edition of the Los Angeles *Daily Evening Express*. See *An Historical Sketch of Los Angeles County, California* (Los Angeles: Louis Lewin and Company, 1876; reprint ed., Los Angeles: O.W. Smith, Publisher, 1936), pp. 127–28.

[2] See *The Cattle Towns* (New York: Alfred A. Knopf, Inc., 1968; reprint ed., New York: Athaneum, 1974), pp. 361–64.

[3] *Historical Sketch*, p. 132.

to resurrect what our Victorian predecessors considered unseemly, in order to gain a more accurate sense of how Angelenos dealt with differences in their pluralistic and polyglot frontier society.

In this chapter we focus on the nature and extent of the inter-religious contacts among residents during the years when violence so frequently plagued the pueblo. Certain scholars, such as Leonard Pitt, Albert Camarillo, Richard Griswold del Castillo, Antonio Ríos-Bustamente, and Pedro Castillo, have examined this era from several perspectives. However, there is need for additional study, to reveal the further dimensions of interreligious contacts in this rustic settlement.[4] We know that ethnic and racial hatreds erupted and deepened the fissures in local society. What we also need to consider are the ways in which residents in the City of the Angels came to develop respect for one another and toleration for each other's creeds.

Early Angelenos "pulled together," as pioneers were fond of recalling, but what specifically was it that brought immigrant Jews, newly freed blacks, and native-born Californios to work together? How well did the members of diverse communions cooperate in common causes? In this chapter we analyze the specific challenges they faced and the varied responses they developed. The chapter begins with a discussion of lawlessness and ethnic strife, and then considers how religious believers struggled to found and maintain educational, health, and social services.

Common threats to the health and well-being of Los Angeles resi-

---

[4] Leonard Pitt has devoted the most attention to the religious ramifications of the clash of Hispanic and Anglo-American cultures in California. He limited himself, however, to a discussion of the role of Roman Catholicism, the communion of the majority of Hispanics. Later historians have contributed little, beyond Pitt's investigation, to the study of religion in the clash of cultures. See Leonard Pitt, *The Decline of the Californios: A Social History of the Spanish-Speaking Californians, 1846–1890* (Berkeley: University of California Press, 1966), chapter XIII, pp. 214–28; Richard Griswold del Castillo, *The Los Angeles Barrio, 1850–1890: A Social History* (Berkeley: University of California Press, 1979), pp. 161–70; Antonio Ríos-Bustamente and Pedro Castillo, *An Illustrated History of Mexican Los Angeles, 1781–1985* (Los Angeles: Chicano Studies Research Center, University of California, 1986), pp. 72–73; and Rudolfo Acuña, *Occupied America: A History of Chicanos* (New York: Harper and Row, Publishers, 1981), pp. 114–15. The broader perspective of religious involvement among Christians of various communions, Jews, Chinese, and Latter-Day Saints does not appear in any of these works. The closest study is a slim monograph, edited by Francis J. Weber, *The Religious Heritage of Southern California* (Los Angeles: The Inter-Religious Council of Southern California, 1976).

dents first stirred people to action in joint remedial efforts, in the two decades after 1848. Most immediate and pressing was the extent of murder and other crimes in the pueblo. One source recorded that, from August 1850 to October 1851, not one conviction resulted from the forty-four homicides committed in the county of less than 2,300 souls for those fifteen months. The mayor and Common Council took recourse to what became a common remedy for such lawlessness, by formally calling into being a "vigilance committee," on 13 July 1851, to establish order in a settlement swarming with cowboys, card dealers, drifters, and other gun-packing characters of questionable repute.[5]

The first of a twenty-year series of committees of public safety convened twelve months later and hanged two Mexicans for the murder of two Yankees. Local tempers again were excited in November, when the popular Indian fighter, Major-General Joshua Bean, was murdered in nearby San Gabriel. An angry public meeting at the Los Angeles courthouse led to immediate action. A self-constituted court tried six suspects and condemned two, Cipriano Sandoval and Reyes Feliz, to the hangman's noose. The evidence of racial bias in these incidents greatly agitated the Hispanic community, particularly because of Sandoval's reputation as a devoted family man and peaceful citizen.

The Los Angeles Rangers were organized, in the summer months of 1853, because of the continued concern for the safety of the community.[6] Approximately forty riders constituted the initial corps of the Rangers, many of them Texans, from the neighboring settlement of Lexington (also known as El Monte). Anglo-Americans predominated at first, though prominent Hispanics later joined, including Agustín Olvera, Juan Sepúlveda, and Rafael Guirado, who as *ricos*, or "rich ones," were members of the pueblo's traditional elite class.[7] Anglo-American men of means also pledged their support, well-known figures such as Stephen C. Foster, state senator; John G. Downey, druggist; I.S.K. Ogier, lawyer; Phineas Banning, operator

[5] Los Angeles *Star*, 11 October 1851, cited in Pitt, *Decline of the Californios*, p. 149.

[6] Los Angeles *Star*, 24 July, 31 July, 27 November 1852; Pitt, *Decline of the Californios*, pp. 156–58; and William B. Rice, *The Los Angeles Star, 1851–1864* (Berkeley: University of California Press, 1947), p. 45.

[7] The *ricos* commanded a deferential respect from Hispanic residents of lower standing in the pueblo.

of a transportation line, and his partner, David Alexander, a member of the Common Council and a dry-goods merchant; and Benjamin Hayes, federal district judge.[8]

One of the principal consequences of this collaboration in the Rangers between prominent Anglo-Americans and Hispanics was the precedent which emerged for continued cooperation. Necessity demanded such interethnic mutual assistance, to avert an explosion of violence between these two segments of society. Tensions ran particularly high after grisly murders in January 1855, July 1856, January-February 1857, November 1858, October 1861, and December 1863. Different approaches to law and justice added to the tensions. The intricacies of the United States judicial system baffled many Hispanics, and it appeared to them that Anglo-Americans more often went free, while prisoners with Spanish names were executed. Citizens meted out vigilante justice, however, to members of both races. Only the repeated presence of the ricos prevented further bloodshed in retaliation for the real and supposed injustices that Hispanics endured.

Hangings, whether by mobs or vigilance committees, occurred with bloodcurdling frequency in Los Angeles in the 1850s. Men of property and influence participated in both sorts of activities. Mayor Stephen C. Foster led one such mob, on 12 January 1855. Foster had promised to resign his office and lead a lynch party, if the courts interfered with the execution of David Brown, a convicted murderer. When news of a court-ordered stay of execution reached town, Foster fulfilled his promise and was then reelected to office. Phineas Banning, well-known forwarding agent and stage-company operator, led another vigilance committee in an episode that illustrates the violence of the times.

Banning had more than usual motivation for his actions, because Charles Wilkins had earlier killed Banning's brother-in-law, the rancher John T. Sanford. Known locally as a "veritable scoundrel," Wilkins had shot his employer, Sanford, for his money, while traveling on an isolated road near Fort Tejon. Tempers in Los Angeles flared when the murderer confessed that he felt no remorse for his

---

[8] Newmark, *Sixty Years*, p. 35; Rice, *Los Angeles Star*, pp. 88–89; Pitt, *Decline of the Californios*, pp. 158–59; and the colorful Horace Bell, who was often inclined to stretch the truth, in his *Reminiscences of a Ranger* (Los Angeles: Yarnell, Caystile and Mathes, Printers, 1881), pp. 108–17.

actions. While Wilkins was being held in the town jail, Banning had stormed in and attempted to shoot the culprit in his cell. Friends first restrained Banning, but, on 17 December 1863, they aided him in seizing Wilkins from the sheriff. These vigilantes dragged their victim to Tomlinson and Griffith's corral, where they hung him from the sturdy crossbeam spanning the gate.[9]

There is no complete and reliable account that tallies the exact number of vigilance committee meetings and executions, though it appears that the last was in December of 1870.[10] The distinctions were hazy between impromptu mobs and more deliberative vigilante actions. What stands out, however, is the cooperation of leading figures from across ethnic boundaries to confront lawlessness. Many of the leaders promoting law and order were also prominently involved in efforts to establish local schools on a firm basis.

The war between Mexico and the United States had brought all schooling to a halt in 1846. The 1849 state constitution mandated a free public-school system, although Angelenos manifested slight interest for several years. Legislative action in 1851 permitted the local division of monies received from the State School Fund between private and public instruction. Scanty tax receipts in Los Angeles permitted neither system to develop to any significant extent. Not until 1853 would the Common Council finally pass an ordinance creating a "City Board of Education" to supervise public instruction.[11] Prior to that, the council engaged various individuals, such as the parish priest, to teach what children could be assembled in the homes of the teachers.

Not surprisingly, education languished. In 1852, the council's school visitation committee consisted of John G. Downey and

[9] Newmark, *Sixty Years*, pp. 139–40, 327; Pitt, *Decline of the Californios*, pp. 160–62; J. Albert Wilson, *History of Los Angeles County, California* (Oakland, California: Thompson and West, 1880; reprint ed., Berkeley: Howell-North, 1959), pp. 81, 83–84.

[10] Robert M. Widney, the prominent Methodist layman, local developer, and member of the bench, led a "Law and Order" party, circa 1870–71. The exact nature and extent of the activities of this group is unclear, other than its instigation by "substantial citizens . . . to suppress crime." This is according to Widney's son-in-law, Boyle Workman, in his *The City That Grew, 1840–1936* (Los Angeles: Southland Publishing Company, 1935), p. 145.

[11] John Swett, *History of the Public School System in California* (San Francisco: A. L. Bancroft and Company, 1876), p. 15; and Wilson, *History of Los Angeles County*, p. 71.

Ygnacio del Valle. These gentlemen reported that the total number of children under instruction were twenty pupils, with Reverend Anacletus Lestrade, SS.CC., the French parish priest, and fifteen, in the care of a parishioner, Ygnacio Coronel. Some progress was made in the following year. With the arrival of the first resident Methodist minister came his wife, Ellen (Kimberlin) Bland, who opened a private school in her husband's saloon-turned-chapel. When the Blands departed, early in 1854, Reverend and Mrs. J. McHenry Caldwell replaced them and continued the "academy" for several months.[12]

Growing dissatisfaction with these arrangements eventually prompted action by the town council. The Los Angeles *Star*, in its Spanish-language section, criticized the efforts of the local curate on 15 January 1853:

> The school of Father Anacletus was not adequate to satisfy the needs of this community, and in spite of a great reduction [of students], one priest who has to fulfill the holy duties of his ministry is not able to devote himself with the dedication required for the education of youth . . .[13]

The newspaper editor went on to welcome the additional teacher whom Reverend Lestrade had engaged to assist him. Nonetheless, lawyer Benjamin I. Hayes wrote to a friend, that same month, that the "four little schools" in the community were "not of a high order." The solution, to his way of thinking, would be "two or three Sisters of Charity who understand English and Spanish" and would operate a school.[14]

In May of the following year, Mayor Stephen C. Foster took matters in his own hand, and persuaded the Common Council to con-

---

[12] William E. North, *Catholic Education in Southern California* (Washington, D.C.: The Catholic University of America, 1936), p. 113; Los Angeles *Star*, 26 February, 6 August, 22 October 1853 and 22 April 1854.

[13] The Spanish original text: "La escuela de R.F. Anacleto no era suficiente para satisfacer las necesidas de esto pueblo; pues apesar de su mucha contracción, un sacerdote que tiene que desempenar las sagradas ocupaciones de su ministerio, no puede consagrarse con la asiduidad que requiere la enseñanza de la juventud . . ."

[14] Letter, Hayes to B.M. Hughes, 24 January 1853, Los Angeles, quoted in Marjorie Tisdale Wolcott, *Pioneer Notes from the Diaries of Judge Benjamin Hayes, 1849–1875* (Los Angeles: Privately Printed, 1929), p. 91.

struct two schoolhouses and to appoint school officials.[15] That body named three of its own members as the initial Board of Education: Manuel Requena, Francis Mellus, and W.T.B. Sanford. Foster, a Yale graduate (class of 1840), was the logical choice to be the first school superintendent. Workmen were soon laying the bricks for Schoolhouse Number One, on the northwest corner of Spring and Second streets, while a second structure went up on Bath Street. The board engaged William McKee and Miss Louisa Hayes as teachers, and progress was in the air.[16] Controversy about the schools, however, soon arose and quickly engulfed the community.

Antipathy toward foreigners and Roman Catholics in the state emerged in the Know-Nothing movement and crystallized in two actions, in 1855, affecting public education. That May, the California legislature prohibited further public financing of sectarian education, and the state Bureau of Public Instruction curtailed the practice of public instruction in the Spanish language.[17] In cooperation with Roman Catholic clergy and others, Hispanics in Los Angeles responded with several attempts to institute private schools that would preserve their native tongue. The first of their endeavors commenced that December. Bishop Thaddeus Amat, newly arrived in California, visited Los Angeles for the first time and called a meeting of prominent residents of various faiths, to discuss plans to establish a girls' school in the community.

The bishop proposed to open an institution staffed by the Daughters of Charity of St. Vincent de Paul, commonly known as the Sisters of Charity. The assembled gentlemen, including at least one prominent Mason, heartily endorsed this project and appointed a committee to direct a public "subscription" to establish the Sisters in Los Angeles as soon as possible.[18] Many of those present were either Hispanic or

[15] J.M. Guinn, "Pioneer School Superintendents of Los Angeles," Historical Society of Southern California *Annual Publication*, IV, Part I (1897), p. 76.

[16] Wilson, *History of Los Angeles County*, p. 71.

[17] The mood of the times can be better understood when it is recalled that the Know-Nothing Party swept the 1855 state elections from the governorship on down. Hubert Howe Bancroft, *The Works of Hubert Howe Bancroft*, vol. XXIII *History of California* (San Francisco: The History Company, 1886–1890; reprint ed., Santa Barbara, California: Wallace Hebberd, 1970), pp. 692, 694–701. Regarding the schools, see Swett, *History of the Public School System*, pp. 23–24.

[18] *El Clamor Público*, 15 December 1855, reported that a committee of nine men had explored Bishop Amat's proposal and made their recommendations for its imple-

claimed a Hispanic spouse. Both the elected chairman and secretary of that meeting, Massachusetts-born Abel Stearns and John G. Downey, from Ireland, were married to women from prominent Californio families. The bishop's plan united the citizens' desires for improved educational opportunities with the preference for Spanish-language instruction they shared with friends and relatives.

The committeemen needed to act quickly, because six Sisters arrived by steamer three weeks later, on 6 January 1856, at the end of a two-month journey from Emmitsburg, Maryland. Sister Mary Scholastica Logsdon led the band of three American and three Spanish women, who were soon established in the former home of Benjamin D. Wilson, southeast of the plaza. The newspapers endorsed the project and urged support of female education. Contributions totaled some six thousand dollars, to fund the "Institución Caritativa," a combined school and orphanage. Within the month, Logsdon could report to her superiors in the East that the Sisters had enrolled sixty-eight "day scholars" and had received a number of orphan girls as well.[19]

Not every Angeleno was pleased with the presence of the Sisters, nor impressed with their work with the young. In a letter to her former neighbor, Anna Ogier complained about the new residents to whom Margaret (Hereford) Wilson's husband had sold their home.

> I am mad everytime I see one of the Sisters in the yard with their kites flying around, I mean their bonnets. I think Mr. Wilson sold his property very well, but I am sorry it did not fall into the hands of some nice American or Spanish family who would have been good neighbors for those Sisters are too ugly to tolerate. . . . I hope they won't be able to raise the money to pay for it. . . .[20]

---

mentation. These gentlemen included Benjamin Hayes, Abel Stearns, Thomas Foster (charter member of Masonic Lodge #42), Louis Vignes, Ezra Drown, Antonio F. Coronel, Manuel Requena, Ygnacio del Valle, and John Downey (another Mason). A committee of five solicited funds throughout the community: Hayes, del Valle, Coronel, Agustín Olvera, and David W. Alexander, with Requena serving as treasurer.

[19] Letter, Sister Scholastica Logsdon to Reverend Francis M. Burlando, 29 February 1856, Institución Caritativa de Los Angeles, "Correspondence of the Director," vol. II, Archives of the Western Province of the Daughters of Charity, Los Altos Hills, California, hereafter cited as AWPDC; *El Clamor Público*, 12 January 1856.

[20] Letter, Anna Ogier to Mrs. B. D. Wilson, 4 February 1856, Los Angeles, Wil-

The extent of such sentiments in the community are impossible to gauge, particularly when the nativism of the Know Nothings was so strong elsewhere in the nation. What is actually more remarkable for Los Angeles is the degree to which local residents disregarded the sectarian biases of their day and age.

Local Hispanic parents were uneasy, and they also sent students to an "Escuela católica," in the home of Louis Vignes. Published notices stated that classes would be conducted in Spanish, though students could also anticipate the "perfection" of their English conversation. This school relocated twice, to other homes, before ceasing operation, in September 1856. Hispanic parents were disappointed and took another course of action. In January 1857, "many prominent citizens" petitioned the Common Council for an equal division of the education funds to finance a school taught in the Spanish language. When the council did not respond, the new pastor of the Catholic parish, Reverend Blas Raho, C.M., proposed, in February 1857, to reopen the bilingual school. Instruction would commence once he located 100 people willing to pay fifty cents weekly tuition, a goal not achieved until January of 1859, when he engaged Pioquinto Dávila to conduct a school for boys.[21]

Sectarian strife over the curriculum of public schools had sundered many a city and town, including San Francisco to the north. That community's unique constellation of Know Nothings and vigilantes clashed with self-assured, Irish-born Roman Catholics, unwilling to compromise on public educational policy. As one recent historian has noted about events in the City by the Bay, "In the 1850's neither

---

son Papers, HL. The flying "kites" mentioned in the letter refer to the headgear of the Daughters of Charity, which then consisted of starched and pressed white linen, rather resembling wings. (Hence the sobriquet for the Sisters, "God's Geese").

[21] *El Clamor Publico*, 8, 15 March, 5, 12, 19 April, 28 June, 30 August, 13 September 1856; 24 January and 7 February 1857; 15 January, 30 April, 2 July 1859. Several other private schools also opened. A Mrs. Hartman operated a school in the first half of 1854; see the Los Angeles *Star*, 14 January and 6 May 1854. Mrs. Mary Hoyt instructed Hispanic and Anglo-American children in a "select school," 1857–59, according to *El Clamor Público*, 28 February 1857 and 24 December 1859. Santiago López attracted editorial notice when he proposed to open a school for Hispanics; see *El Clamor Público*, 26 September 1857. R. Mulot and H. DeLangre also taught children in several languages, advertising proficiency in English, Spanish, French, and the classical languages; see *El Clamor Público*, 29 October 1859.

the American Adam nor the bark of Peter really wanted to accom-
modate the other." [22] These opposing groups of San Franciscans had
already dispossessed the Spanish-speaking from their lands and status
in that community by 1855. The volume and type of immigration
had blunted the Anglo-Hispanic dimension of antagonisms in their
school controversies and highlighted instead ethnic and sectarian factors within the Anglo community.

In Los Angeles, however, demography and economics still favored
the Hispanic populace through the 1850s. Anglo-Americans proceeded cautiously in their criticisms of the Church of Rome and
persuaded themselves to enlist the aid of their Hispanic neighbors
in school promotion. The absence of overt denominational strife in
this era distinguished the City of the Angels. True, these religious
groups counted few local members and were still too weak to sustain
a clergyman. The "school issue" was, nonetheless, a volatile matter,
and given the town's underlying racial situation, education was a matter that aroused passionate emotions. Despite the potential conflicts,
amazing progress was made throughout the 1850s.

Bishop Thaddeus Amat and his clergy opposed Roman Catholic
patronage of the free schools, as did their clerical confreres nationwide, in the nineteenth century.[23] Amat's local communicants clearly
did not entirely concur with the bishop's sentiments; many Roman
Catholics held positions within the public educational system. For
example, the Roman Catholic Louisa Hayes conducted the girls' division in 1855, and was the first woman to teach in the public schools.
Within the year, she married the newly elected Superintendent of
Public Instruction, Dr. John S. Griffin. Despite this and other in-

[22] Robert M. Senkewicz, S.J., *Vigilantes in Gold Rush San Francisco* (Stanford, California: Stanford University Press, 1985), p. 143.

[23] For a discussion of the bitter sectarian disputes over public education in the eastern United States, see James Hennesey, S.J., *American Catholics: A History of the Roman
Catholic Community in the United States* (New York: Oxford University Press, 1981),
pp. 107–10. As for Amat's position, speaking privately to a nun, he confided his
fear that Roman Catholic children would lose their faith if they attended the town's
public schools. Letter, Sister Scholastica Logsdon to Francis Burlando, 28 December
1861, Los Angeles, "Correspondence of the Director," vol. II, AWPDC. In a public lecture before the Mechanic's Institute of Los Angeles, in 1857, he argued that
parents were obliged to support parochial schools because "Christian education is
far superior to any other." The full text of Amat's lecture, "Christian Education,"
appeared in the Los Angeles *Star*, 2 May 1857.

volvement in the free-school system by members of his flock, Amat remained opposed to public instruction.[24]

The experiences of collaboration in the promotion of both education and the end of violence prepared settlers to meet further crises in other mutually helpful ways. The improvement of local health care provided another instance of pioneer need overcoming ingrained sectarian bias and suspicion. As early as July 1855, Doctors John S. Griffin and Thomas Foster petitioned the county's Board of Supervisors to establish a county hospital. But the supervisers only voted to form a "Committee of Health" to oversee the care of the indigent sick.[25] In the absence of any further action, the Sisters of Charity petitioned the town's Common Council for two lots for a health care site, early in 1857.[26] Making an alternative proposal, the Board of Supervisors requested that the Sisters staff such a facility "North of the church," in a rented, four-room adobe residence. In June 1858, the Board of Health advertised in the town's newspapers that the "County Hospital" was receiving patients, to be tended by "the Sisters of Charity under the best doctors of the City."[27]

Sister Scholastica Logsdon named Sister Ann Gillen to superintend the work, alongside the designated county physician. Conditions were primitive in the hospital. Furnishings were sparse, and there was no well or source of water on the site.[28] Within four months, the Sisters moved from the rented adobe into a residence they purchased on a lot adjoining their orphanage. After visiting the new institution, the editor of the Los Angeles *Star* outdid himself with superlatives in describing the work of the Sisters. These "ministering angels" deserved the financial support of all citizens for "the many benefits conferred on our community" since the Sisters established this hospital.[29]

[24] Newmark, *Sixty Years*, p. 47; and Guinn, "Pioneer School Superintendents," p. 78.

[25] "Minutes" of the Board of Supervisors, vol. I, pp. 217, 225–26, Executive Office, Board of Supervisors, Los Angeles, California.

[26] "Minutes" of the Common Council, vol. VII, pp. 464–65, Archives of the City of Los Angeles, Piper Technical Center, Los Angeles, California; hereafter cited as ACLA; and Bishop Thaddeus Amat to Reverend Francis Burlando, C.M., 4 May 1857, Los Angeles, in "Correspondence of the Director," vol. 1, AWPDC.

[27] *Southern Vineyard*, 5 June 1858; and *El Clamor Público*, 5 June 1858.

[28] Quoted in "Remarks on Sister Mary Scholastica Logsdon," in *Lives of Our Deceased Sisters, 1903* (Emmitsburg, Maryland: St. Joseph's Central House, 1903), p. 113.

[29] Los Angeles *Star*, 18 December 1858, as quoted in Helen Eastman Martin,

Chapter 4

The contractual arrangement between the Sisters and the county endured until local expectations of medical services changed, in the late 1870s. Between 1858 and 1878, the Sisters provided public health care for both the daily needs of the community and during its periods of epidemic illness.[30] In those years, the spectre of smallpox repeatedly haunted the settlement and challenged the citizens to find adequate means of coping with repeated outbreaks. Contagion struck Los Angeles in 1862–63, 1869, and 1876–77. Each attack of the disease prompted a rush for vaccinations, quarantines of the victims, either at home or in an isolated "pest house," the closure of schools, relief efforts on behalf of patients and surviving relatives of the deceased, and demands for more effective government action. Private individuals and organizations volunteered their services, with church members frequently in the forefront of endeavors to care for the distressed and to protect the healthy.

Between November 1862 and March 1863, smallpox struck the community with particularly devastating force among the Indian and Hispanic segments of the population. Afflicted Indians, following the traditional medicinal practices of their culture, bathed to rid themselves of the malady. Many chose to wash in the town's open water ditches, the *zanjas,* which supplied water for domestic use. The County Board of Supervisors appointed the town's mayor, Damien Marchessault, and Cristóbal Aguilar to investigate and to take necessary measures to halt the spread of the disease. The board also appointed Dr. James C. Welch to render medical attention. Marchessault and Aguilar divided the town into five districts, and health officials inspected every house in each district. In February 1863, for example, 6 cases were reported in the second district and 150 in the fourth district, which was probably the area of greater Indian and Hispanic residence.[31]

The History of the Los Angeles County Hospital (1878–1968) and the Los Angeles County–University of Southern California Medical Center (1968–1978) (Los Angeles: University of Southern California Press, 1978), p. 8. Doctor John S. Griffin concurred with Hamilton's assessment in his annual report, which the county physician filed with the supervisors on the following 6 February 1859. See *El Clamor Público*, 12 February 1859.

[30] In October 1878, the county government opened its own hospital, a development treated at greater length in chapter 6 of this study. The Sisters continued to operate their facility. It is today known as St. Vincent's Medical Center, one of the major health-care facilities in Los Angeles.

[31] Newmark, *Sixty Years*, p. 322; Los Angeles *Star*, 31 January and 21 February

The mayor turned to the Sisters of Charity to nurse the sick, in a house he procured, four miles outside of town. Sisters Scholastica Logsdon and Anne Gillen initially found the conditions in this facility deplorable, yet Gillen and other Sisters set to work to remedy the situation. Accurate statistics do not exist, though on 31 January 1863, the Los Angeles *Star* reported that 200 people were afflicted and 200 others had already died. One later account reported, "Nearly every house in Sonora town had out a yellow flag, and as many as fourteen were known to die in one day."[32] The members of the Hebrew Benevolent Society provided $150 to feed the sick and established a committee to solicit further funds on behalf of the afflicted.[33]

This alliance of governmental and religious institutions set a precedent for the following two outbreaks of the disease. The authorities evidently had learned how to cope better with such epidemics, when smallpox hit the community again, in May of 1869. "Health Regulations" from the County Board of Health appeared in the town's newspapers, and county officials again approached the Sisters of Charity to nurse the stricken. Sister Scholastica Logsdon once more dispatched two members of her staff, Sisters Phileta McCarthy and Margaret Weber, to "take charge" of the pest house. Doctor H.S. Orme, designated as the attendant physician, reported on the progress of the disease to the weekly press.[34]

The dreaded scourge once more spread through Los Angeles, from November 1876 through April 1877. In February of 1877, a citizen's meeting convened, under the gavel of Myer J. Newmark, a prominent Jewish businessman. Assembled residents drafted a set of resolutions, petitioning the community authorities to combat the disease more forcefully. The Common Council responded immediately, with a series of ordinances establishing a "Pest House Fund" and regulating

---

1863, cited in George Harwood Phillips, "Indians in Los Angeles, 1781–1875: Economic Integration, Social Disintegration," *Pacific Historical Review*, XLIX (August 1980), p. 449, n. 94.

[32] "Sonoratown" was the section of the community east of the plaza, where large numbers of Hispanics resided. The yellow flags designated the residences of the smallpox victims. Wilson, *History of Los Angeles County*, p. 97.

[33] Los Angeles *Tri-Weekly News*, 21 November, 19 December 1862, 13 February 1863; Los Angeles *Star*, 22 November 1862; unidentified clipping, 7 March 1863, "Board of Health," in the Benjamin Hayes Scrapbooks, vol. 50, part 2, #396, BL; and "Remarks on Sister Mary Scholastica Logsdon," p. 113.

[34] Los Angeles *Star*, 22 May 1869. See also Letter, Logsdon to Burlando, 21 May 1869, Los Angeles, in "Correspondence of the Director," vol. II; and Letters, Rev-

sanitary conditions and the quality of drinking water. Town officials also engaged the Sisters of Charity once again, to serve as pest-house nurses. Members of the fledgling Los Angeles County Medical Association also discussed the disease at two meetings and submitted to the press and local authorities their recommendations for action in future appearances of the pestilence.[35]

The collaboration among members of the town's ethnically mixed citizenry indicates the nature of the local response to these epidemics. The virulent disease threatened the entire community, cutting across ethnic and religious boundaries. The responses of government, religious, and private individuals suggest how seriously these residents considered the need for joint efforts. This was particularly the case in the initial epidemic, of 1862–63. Because of the rapid spread of disease and the high death rate, Angelenos were forced to act cooperatively and quickly to prevent the spread of the contagion.[36] The Hebrew Benevolent Society and the Sisters of Charity tendered important aid that both set a precedent for later relief efforts and garnered the respect of their fellow citizens.

Community leaders began to expand their horizons in the course of the later 1850s to address concerns beyond their immediate needs. In working to insure the rule of law, residents developed patterns of cooperation that benefited later projects to provide health care and educational facilities. Dreams of continued town growth and improvement inspired greater collaboration. Two other projects brought Angelenos together, in the interests of "progress" in the community. Though denominational differences also began to emerge, religious biases were hardly pronounced or strident.

---

erend James McGill, C.M., to Burlando, 16 May, 15 and 18 June 1869, Los Angeles, "Correspondence of the Director, vol. I; AWPDC.

[35] Los Angeles *Daily Star*, 8 February 1877, cited in Norton B. Stern, "Myer J. Newmark," *Western States Jewish Historical Quarterly*, II (April 1970), pp. 160–61; Minutes of the Common Council, vol. XII, pp. 613, 615, 627–32, ACLA; Weekly reports concerning Pest House patients, in the file, "City Treasurer, Bills to the City, February, 1877," ACLA; Minutes, vol. I, pp. 28, 37–38, Los Angeles County Medical Association, found on Microfilm Cal. 4-A L89, reel two, in the Library of the Los Angeles County Medical Association, Los Angeles, California.

[36] George Harwood Phillips stated that immunization was not compulsory, and Indians initially resisted this medical treatment. Authorities did not maintain accurate mortality statistics, but the toll among the Indians was particularly high. See Phillips, "Indians in Los Angeles, 1781–1875," pp. 448–49.

The 1856 Institución Caritativa, of the Sisters of Charity, housed a school and an orphanage, both for girls. The care of the orphans was a matter of strong and lasting community interest. As early as November 1857, the superior wrote of plans for a fair to raise funds, "something new here."[37] The highly successful "ladies' tea," as Sister Scholastica termed the fall affair, developed into an annual event, involving community-wide support. These "Orphans' Fairs" provided an opportunity for local residents, particularly the non-Hispanic populace, to gather and socialize. Aside from the *bailes* and *fandangos* favored by the Californios, few other opportunities for organized entertainment existed in the town. The yearly fair satisfied both the philanthropic and social needs of the people. The advance notice and subsequent reports in the town's newspapers repeatedly reveal the decidedly nonsectarian nature of the preparation and patronage of these galas. The women solicited donations throughout the community, shopkeepers sold tickets in their stores, attendance was invariably large, and dancing was known to proceed "to an advanced hour."[38]

The plight of the orphaned children, and the desire to socialize, were strong enough factors to motivate people to disregard denominational and ethnic distinctions. These fairs set a precedent for later fundraising endeavors, staged on behalf of diverse projects for improving the community. This was particularly the case with denominational expansion. Every congregation in the town was too small and too financially weak to exist without aid from both citizens of other creeds and from outside sources, until the mid-1870s. Newspaper notices of events such as suppers and "balls" began to appear in the early 1860s for a variety of religious concerns.

The most immediate revenue needs were for construction and operating expenses of the pioneer denominations. Reverend William E. Boardman departed Los Angeles in February 1862, but the Ladies' Sewing Society of his congregation continued to meet and

---

[37] Letters, Sister Scholastica Logsdon to Reverend Francis Burlando, 23 November 1857 and 8 October 1858, Institución Caratativa [Los Angeles], "Correspondence of the Director," vol. II, AWPDC; and *El Clamor Público*, 18 September 1858.

[38] Newspaper accounts include the Los Angeles *Star*, 22 and 29 November and 6 December 1862, 18 July 1868, 28 October 1871; the Los Angeles *News*, 9 November 1863; and unidentified clippings, dated 8 December 1865 and 25 July 1868, Hayes Scrapbooks, vol. 51, #53 and 475, BL.

raise funds, even without a pastor. They announced a "Calico Party," in the 11 April 1863 Los Angeles *Star*. The women of Congregation B'nai B'rith repeatedly organized dances, dinners, and concerts. Local editors encouraged Angelenos on more than one occasion to patronize in particular the events of the local "Hebrews." The writer for the *News* remarked, in 1864:

> This association of our citizens have ever lent a helping hand on all occasions when aid was most needed, and it is to be hoped that no one will withhold aid and encouragement on the approaching occasion . . .

Five years later, another editorialist praised the "well-known liberality" of the Jews toward diverse worthy causes in town and urged "a handsome reciprocity," in return.[39]

Bishop Thaddeus Amat could easily have testified to the broad-minded assistance of the Jews of the town. The regard for education that had first bridged sectarian lines, in the 1850s, found new expression in May 1865. Bishop Amat once more summoned prominent citizens to meetings at his residence, on the plaza. Not satisfied with the local educational opportunities for boys, the Spanish cleric proposed the foundation of a private, postelementary institution. Amat had secured the services of three priests from his own Congregation of the Mission, commonly known as Vincentians. He suggested that the boarding school be named in honor of the founder of that religious community: St. Vincent's College.[40] Citizen response was immediate, with the formation of a three-man "ways and means committee," and planning for a women's benefit fair, to be held within the month.

These initial efforts to raise funds for the school were notable on several counts. Both women and men of differing faiths were immediately involved in the endeavors to secure adequate contributions, manifesting a concern for local higher education that crossed sexual

---

[39] Los Angeles *News*, 15 December 1864; and Los Angeles *Star*, 22 May 1869.

[40] Los Angeles *News*, 16 May 1865; North, *Catholic Education*, pp. 115–16. The designation "college" was used in the nineteenth-century sense of the term: an institution that offered secondary and collegiate levels of instruction. St. Vincent's would not award its first Bachelor of Arts degree until 1885. No graduating class, down to the school's closure, in 1911, would number more than twelve students.

and denominational lines. District Attorney Volney E. Howard, a member of the ways and means committee, was a prominent Episcopalian.[41] The first "fair" also owed its inspiration to Rosa (Levy) Newmark, an English Jew. She had arrived in the settlement, with her family, in 1855, and her husband, Joseph, served as a lay rabbi in Los Angeles and also initiated the formation of Congregation B'nai B'rith, in 1862.[42] The support of Mrs. Newmark and other Jews not only helped launch this Roman Catholic educational institution, but continued the following year in a seemingly unusual manner.

When the Protestant Ozro W. Childs donated nine acres of land at Sixth and Broadway streets for a permanent college site, in 1866, Antonio F. Coronel and his sister Soledad staged a theater benefit to aid the construction fund. They directed, rehearsed, and produced a Hispanic Christmas play, the *Pastorela*, dramatizing a tale of the shepherds on the first Christmas night. Additional performances proved necessary, as one of the principal actors later recalled. "Strange as it may seem, the most liberal patrons and frequenters of this nativity drama were the Jewish people; so much so that the play was given an extra night at their earnest solicitation."[43] Once again, philanthropical and social inclinations combined to lead people to cross sectarian lines.

The appeal of educational development extended, as well, to local government authorities, who voted public funds, in 1866, to assist the erection of the first college building. The County Board of Supervisors appropriated $1,000 in October of that year, in response to a request from the school's president, Reverend James McGill, C.M. The clergyman encountered unexpected legal difficulties, however, when he approached the town's Common Council for a grant of

---

[41] While Howard's name does not appear among the list of communicants of St. Athanasius Protestant Episcopal Church in Los Angeles, there is an entry for his wife, in 1865. See Parish Register "A," p. 86, St. Athanasius–St. Paul Church, Los Angeles, California. Howard received election in 1872 as a vestryman for Our Savior Episcopal Church, in nearby San Gabriel. See Midge Sherwood, *Days of Vintage, Years of Vision* (San Marino, California: Orizaba Press, 1982), vol. I, p. 390. He later received appointment to the Superior Court and also sat in the California state constitutional convention, in 1878–79. See Newmark, *Sixty Years in Southern California*, pp. 356, 384, 529.

[42] Newmark, *Sixty Years*, pp. 120–21, 341, n. 1.

[43] Arturo Bandini, in *Navidad, A Christmas Day with the Early Californians*, edited by Susanna Bryant Dakin (San Francisco: California Historical Society, 1958), p. 20.

$500. W.B. Osburn, a local merchant of long standing, filed suit and obtained an injunction to prevent this expenditure of public monies from a depleted town treasury.[44] Upon the eventual dismissal of the injunction, the six council members proceeded, in January of 1867, to vote the appropriation. In what was clearly a pioneering case of conflict of interest, the mayor and one councilman voting the appropriation were members of the college's three-member ways and means committee![45]

The building was sufficiently completed by March of that year to permit the priests and students to leave their rented quarters on the plaza, in the Vicente Lugo adobe. Reverend Miguel Rubi, C.M., who had designed the building, conducted the dedicatory ceremonies, in the presence of many citizens, including the Sisters of Charity and their orphan wards. The first public "examination" followed in July 1867. Not only did the performance of the students justify the high hopes of those attending, but Los Angeles also could be proud of the college. Such were the florid sentiments expressed in the Los Angeles *News*, in a report marked by a surfeit of civic gloating.[46]

Such promotional reporting indicated a more magnanimous spirit toward the college than that expressed in the Osburn lawsuit, over expending public monies for the school. The editor of the *News* emphasized the benefits the institution provided for the cause of education, as well as for the improvement of the wider community. Such editors and local developers in the late 1860s repeatedly eschewed sectarian bickering. This forbearance would become progressively a more common practice in following years, when the pace of subdivision

[44] Osburn had at one time been prominent in the small band of local "Know Nothings," members of the short-lived American Party; see Los Angeles *Star*, 15 September 1855.

[45] The three members present at the meeting of the County Board of Supervisors, John G. Downey, E. H. Boyd, and Francisco Signoret, unanimously voted the appropriation requested by "James McGill, Esquire, chief magistrate of the Catholic College." Minutes of the County Board of Supervisors, vol. III, pp. 362–63, Executive Office, County Board of Supervisors, Los Angeles, California; [James McGill, C.M.], "Annals of St. Vincent College, Los Angeles, California," p. 186, in the Archives of the Province of the West of the Congregation of the Mission, Montebello, California, hereafter cited as APWCM; and unidentified newspaper clippings, Hayes Scrapbooks, vol. 51, #122, #141, BL. The town's mayor, Murray Morrison, and council member Antonio F. Coronel served alongside attorney Volney E. Howard on the college ways and means committee. See Newmark, *Sixty Years*, p. 341, n. 1.

[46] Los Angeles *News*, 2 July 1867.

and growth accelerated. Vestiges of denominationalism, however, surfaced within twelve months of the college exhibition.

When Reverend Elias Birdsall, the pioneer Episcopalian priest, left Los Angeles, in the spring of 1866, a series of short-term pastorates ensued. Reverend J.J. Talbott served from late 1867 to May of 1868, a brilliant orator "much admired, especially by the ladies."[47] Prior to departing, he submitted, in the press, a proposal for a private school that offended numerous local sensibilities. Talbott envisioned a "young ladies' seminary" for one hundred students, but under Protestant auspices. He noted that the Roman Catholics in town had provided well for their daughters, with a school that was "a credit to the city besides."[48]

The reverend gentleman reflected that similar institutions were necessary for Protestants of all denominations, but for a reason that was rather baldly stated in his article. "For our immediate city and county, we need institutions to which Jew or Gentile can send his daughter and son, assured that no sectarian influence will be brought to bear upon them . . ." Talbott further elaborated that the educational "wants of the Israelite and the Protestant are not supplied." His concluding argument was equally pointed. Roman Catholics do not send their children to Protestant schools; so too, Protestants and Jews do not want to send their children to Roman Catholic institutions.

These remarks were out of character for a community with close to two decades of religious cooperation in a variety of undertakings. Such ideas, though undoubtedly shared by others in the town, clashed with the practice of muting sectarian differences over educational policy. Talbott had resigned his clerical charge on 2 May 1868, and then submitted his article on 18 May.[49] Talbott may have suspected that his opinions were would be unpopular in the community, and thus chose to submit his idea after he resigned. A pointed reply was not long in appearing. On 6 June 1868, the Los Angeles *Star* carried a letter strongly rebutting Talbott's seminary proposal. Some estimate of the respondent's attitude can be deduced from the signatory sobriquet: "A Friend of Schools, but an Enemy to Humbug."

---

[47] H. D. Barrows, "Early Clericals of Los Angeles," Historical Society of Southern California *Annual Publications*, V, Part II (1900–1902), p. 131.

[48] Los Angeles *Star*, 30 May 1868.

[49] Los Angeles *Republican*, 2 May 1868 and Los Angeles *Star*, 23 May 1868.

The anonymous writer disputed at length the clergyman's estimation of the profitability of such a school to local merchants. The idea of businessmen realizing $50,000 in trade from this seminary was ridiculous. Far more troubling, however, was Talbott's attitudes toward local Jews, with the

> very patronizing manner in which he enlisted them [the children of Zion] in his crusade against the Church of Rome—nor in my judgment will they feel much flattered by being placed under the banner of Protestantism. They may, however, come to the conclusion that the Reverend Gentleman is a rather lymphatic fragment of the famous Blarney Stone.

This exchange of letters in the press strongly suggested that Reverend Talbott had not comprehended the extent or depth of tolerant accommodation developed among a significant segment of Los Angeles believers by the late 1860s.

An anonymous chronicler penned, in the parish register at St. Athanasius Church, that the pastor had been forced to resign because the "congregation was discouraged." One parishioner was more direct, when she wrote to her family: "Dr. Talbot turned out [to be] a regular scamp, a wolf in sheep's clothing and left here about three months ago with no enviable name. Among other sins drunkenness was by no means the worst. The church has suffered a severe blow."[50] Spirits revived with the advent of the next permanent pastor, who actually achieved quite peacefully what his predecessor had proposed. Reverend George Burton arrived in Los Angeles in June of 1869. Burton, his wife, and two assistants immediately opened a select school, later known as the College of Los Angeles. Harris Newmark recalled that Burton was a scholarly man, and his wife, who had been trained in France and Italy, was an accomplished linguist, vocalist, and instrumental musician. Enrollment the first year approached fifty students, male and female, with classes initially conducted in the vestry room of the church building.[51]

[50] Letter, Susan Glassell Patton to Sally Glassell, 7 December 1868, quoted in Midge Sherwood, *Days of Vintage, Years of Vision* (San Marino, California: Orizaba Press, 1987), vol. II, p. 165.

[51] "Parish Register A," p. 8, St. Athanasius–St. Paul's Church, Los Angeles, California; and Newmark, *Sixty Years*, pp. 356, n. 1, 373.

The Burtons later relocated their school to Fifth and Spring Streets and engaged a third assistant. The Newmarks and other leading families patronized the institution, which was noted for the competence of its teachers in literature and languages. Newmark listed several Jewish families whose children attended the college.[52] The nature and success of the school lead to the conclusion that Talbott's estimation of the need for such a "seminary" was actually quite accurate. Los Angeles was indeed ready for further diversification of educational offerings, but residents were not willing to pursue such development in a manner so obviously insensitive to the religious harmony they had gradually achieved over the years.

The year the Burtons opened their school coincided with the legal incorporation of St. Vincent's College. Nine residents of the town affixed their signatures to the formal petition, addressed to the state Board of Education.[53] Two, Reverends James McGill and Timothy O'Leary, were members of the faculty. The remaining seven were a more diverse array of prominent Los Angeles citizens, including at least four lawyers. Interesting to note, these men were not all Roman Catholics: two were active Episcopalians, one of whom was a local Masonic official.

Leading the list of laymen was an eminent Roman Catholic member of the bar, James G. Howard, who long provided legal counsel for the Vincentian Fathers. William McPherson was then serving as city attorney. Salisbury Haley, a retired sea captain, was married into one of the land-rich Californio families and claimed the county clerk and county judge as his brothers-in-law. Lawyer Aurelius W. Hutton later successfully sought election as city attorney (1873–76). The two parishioners of St. Athanasius Episcopal Church were attorney George H. Smith and Stephen H. Mott, deputy county clerk and junior warden of Masonic Lodge #42. William A. Mix completed the list of signatories attesting to the suitability of the college for state recognition.[54]

---

[52] The first exhibition of the Female Department of the College, held 23 December 1869, listed the names of nine students, including that of Harris Newmark's daughter, Emily; Los Angeles *Star*, 25 December 1869.

[53] "Petition of Incorporation," included in the Minute Book of St. Vincent's College, p. 5, St. Vincent's College Collection, APWCM.

[54] Newmark, *Sixty Years*, pp. 22, 82, 181, 350, 351, 363, 366, 405, 443, 597; *Saddleback Ancestors: Rancho Families of Orange County, California* (Santa Ana, California:

Chapter 4

The composition of this list suggests that the college administration desired a substantial representation from both the legal profession and local government. The Vincentian priests may have included the two Episcopalians because of friendship, or because of acquaintances these two gentlemen had with state officials. Whatever the reason may have been, their presence among the "Founders and Contributors" merits more than passing notice. This representation beyond the Roman Catholic communion underscored the more particularly civic aspect of the position of St. Vincent's College in the community. The school served the people of multiple denominations, a role that these gentlemen symbolized when they ascribed their names to the legal documents on 15 July 1869.

Another institution endorsed by members of differing denominations was the fraternal society, with its local lodge.[55] Both clergy and communicants were prominent in a wide range of these ostensibly nonsectarian societies. The pioneer Presbyterian divine, James Woods, affiliated with the Sons of Temperance, in 1855, and his successor, William E. Boardman, joined the Masonic lodge, with which Rabbi Abraham Edelman would later associate. Father Blas Raho, the Neapolitan pastor of Our Lady of the Angels church, enrolled in the French Benevolent Society, in 1862.[56] The Odd Fellows twice held their anniversary celebrations in St. Athanasius Episcopalian Church, and the pastor, Reverend J.J. Talbott, delivered remarks at the 1868 festivities. In 1870, the sociable Rabbi Edelman ventured into that Christian house of worship to perform the honors.[57] Not every man of the cloth looked favorably upon these fraternal societies, however; the Roman Catholic bishop actually denounced such organizations, repeatedly and by name.

Orange County Genealogical Society, 1969), p. 104; Wilson, *History of Los Angeles County*, pp. 50–51, 114; Parish Register A, p. 11, 22, St. Athanasius Church, Los Angeles, California; Record Book, vol. III, n.p., Lodge #42, Free and Accepted Masons, Los Angeles, California.

[55] For an interesting discussion of the role of the fraternal society in frontier society, see Don Harrison Doyle, *The Social Order of a Frontier Community: Jacksonville, Illinois, 1825–1870* (Urbana, Illinois: University of Illinois Press, 1983), pp. 178–90.

[56] Unidentified clipping, 16 January 1855, Hayes Scrapbooks, vol. 47. #270, BL; and Entry #69, "R.P. Raho," in the "Registre des Membres," Société Française de Bienfaisance Mutuelle, the French Benevolent Society office, Los Angeles, California.

[57] Los Angeles *News*, 8 May 1868; and Los Angeles *Star*, 30 April 1870.

Bishop Thaddeus Amat first prohibited Roman Catholics from joining Masonry in an 1862 decree of the first meeting in synod of the clergy of his diocese. The assembled clerics wrote that, as early as 1810, the bishops of the United States had warned their congregations of the dangers of membership in such "secret societies."[58] Amat vigorously pursued this restriction and threatened his flock with excommunication from the Church. The second diocesan synod, held in 1869, extended the ban. Roman Catholics no longer could affiliate with the Odd Fellows and Sons of Temperance, because the clergy believed that these, too, were secret societies, "against the good of the Church and of civil society."[59]

The records of Masonic Lodge #42 reveal that, with very few exceptions, local Roman Catholics heeded the bishop in this matter. Not a single Hispanic name appears on the rolls, even though representatives of other ethnic groups were affiliated. The Roman Catholic whose name stood out, however, was John Gately Downey. This Irish-born druggist-turned-financier had settled in the community in 1850, joined the lodge in 1854, and served as governor of California from 1860 to 1862. Downey long continued active in Masonic and civic affairs, yet was one of the most generous donors to the construction of Amat's cherished project, the Cathedral of St. Vibiana.[60] Perhaps because of Downey's influence and status, the bishop faced such an awkward situation that he decided to overlook this lodge affiliation.

Whatever the bishop's accommodation with Downey, Amat did not modify his longtime opposition to the mingling of Roman Catho-

---

[58] Decree 26, *Constitutiones Latae et Promulgatae ab Illmo. ac Revmo. D. Thaddaeo Amat, Congregationis Missionis, Episcopo Montereyensi et Angelorum, in Synodo Dioecesana Prima* (San Francisco: Vicente Torras, 1862), pp. 23–24. It should also be noted that several popes had forbidden Roman Catholics in Europe to join Masonic lodges, as early as 1723. See Lynn Dumenil, *Freemasonry and American Culture* (Princeton: Princeton University Press, 1984), pp. 11–12; and W. J. Whalen, *Christianity and Freemasonry* (Milwaukee: Bruce Publishing Company, 1958), pp. 100–109.

[59] Decree 16, and Appendix A, *Constitutiones Latae et Promulgatae . . . In Synodis Dioecesanis Prima et Segunda* (San Francisco: Mullin, Mahon and Company, 1869), pp. 91, 113–18.

[60] Wilson, *History of Los Angeles County*, pp. 176–77; and financial ledger, entitled, "Cuentas de la Catedral de Sta. Vibiana V[irgen] y M[ártir]," p. 8, Archives of the Archdiocese of Los Angeles, Mission Hills, California, hereafter cited as AALA. Downey donated $1,000 to the construction fund, one of the largest contributions recorded.

lics with members of other faiths. As early as 1856, he had established in the diocese an "Association for the Conversion of Heretics."[61] The society's members were committed to praying for fellow citizens "who walk in the chains of error and infidelity." The prelate also published a slim, though forceful, volume outlining at length his church's opposition to "mixed marriages." His *Treatise on Matrimony According to the Doctrine and Discipline of the Catholic Church* appeared in English in 1864, and in Spanish in 1867.[62] Roman Catholic officials had always forbidden marriage to "non-Catholics." Furthermore, "the Catholic Church has always abhorred and detested" these marital unions so "prejudicial to Christianity." Only because of the mixed sectarian population in the United States were religious authorities reluctantly tolerating such marriages and permitting them by dispensations from church law.[63]

In fairness to Amat, it is important to note a certain sensitivity toward one of the new religious bodies formed in the town where the bishop resided. The 1862 synod, held in May in Los Angeles, predated the foundation of the first Jewish congregation by two months. News of the impending arrival of a permanent rabbi may well have been widespread in such a small community. Decree Thirty "strictly" mandated the elimination of the Hispanic practice of hanging and "executing" an effigy of Judas Iscariot during Holy Week. The synod clergy sought to avoid the anti-Semitic "scandals that often result" when local Christians boisterously berated the betrayer of Jesus Christ in the plaza.[64]

Nonetheless, Amat was highly suspicious of the mixed religious population in Los Angeles and sought to erect stronger barriers of church precepts to protect members of his flock. Two men stand

[61] *Instrucción y Breve Compendio de Oraciones para Uso de los Miembros de la Obra de la Propagación de la Fé, de la Archicofradía del Santísima e Inmaculado Corazón de Maria, y de la Asociación para la Conversión de los Hereges* (San Francisco: Vicente Torras, 1856), p. 9. The bishops, meeting for their first national council, in Baltimore in 1852, had recommended the establishment of this society in every diocese of the nation.

[62] English edition, San Francisco: Michael Flood, 1864; Spanish edition, Barcelona: Pablo Riera, 1867.

[63] Amat, *Treatise on Matrimony*, p. 40, 45.

[64] *Constitutiones . . . Synodo Dioesesana Prima*, p. 26. Horace Bell offered a colorful description of this annual Holy Week spectacle of the "trial" and "execution" of Judas in effigy. See *Reminiscences of a Ranger* (Los Angeles: Yarnell, Caystile and Mathes, 1881), pp. 286–87.

in contrast to the portly bishop: his vicar general (and later successor), Francisco Mora, and the Jewish rabbi, Abraham Wolf Edelman. Like Amat, both men were European-born immigrants; the first arrived in Los Angeles in 1855, and the latter in 1862. Both enjoyed a circle of friends broader than their respective denominations. Edelman took advantage of the openness of Los Angeles lodges and was long active in fraternal circles.[65] Mora, while pastor of Our Lady of Angels Church, on the plaza, developed friendships with Edelman and other members of Congregation B'nai B'rith. These contacts benefited Mora and his communion in an unusual manner.[66]

Between 1865 and 1876, Mora handled the finances for three major Roman Catholic projects in Los Angeles. The detailed records he maintained for these endeavors offer a rare glimpse into the interdenominational support such church work enjoyed in a frontier community. The contributions came in varying amounts, from all segments of local society. These funds went to the improvement of the parish cemetery in 1865, the renovation of the parish church and schoolhouse in 1869, and the construction of the Cathedral of St. Vibiana, 1871–76. These specifically sectarian facilities nonetheless attracted the assistance of Jews and Protestants, in addition to Roman Catholics.

The 1865 contributions totaled $599.50 from 66 donors, of whom 2 were Jews and 1 was a Protestant. A further $250 came from the county government. Four years later, Mora counted $1,212.80 in funds, from 130 donors, including 8 Jews and 10 Protestants. Financing the erection of a cathedral was a long-term project of the entire diocese, from Monterey to San Diego. Construction between 1871 and 1876 provided the occasion for extensive fundraising, to meet costs of nearly $75,000. There were 505 individual contribu-

[65] Rabbi Edelman served as Worshipful Master of Los Angeles Masonic Lodge #42 in 1868, 1881, 1883, and 1884, as well as officiating as the founding Master of Wilmington Lodge #198, in 1869. In the Royal Arch Masons, Chapter 33, the rabbi was Captain of the Host, in 1867 and 1868. At the dedication of the Spring Street Masonic Temple, in 1869, Edelman delivered one of the orations of the day. He also associated with local chapters of the Ancient Jewish Order Kesher Shel Barzel and the Independent Order of B'nai B'rith. Stern and Kramer, "Jewish Padre to the Pueblo," pp. 197, 199, 200.

[66] For a further discussion of these interreligious friendships, see Francis J. Weber, "Precedent for Ecumenism," *Western States Jewish History*, XIX (January, 1987), pp. 158–60.

tors; 21 were local members of other faiths, whose donations totaled $1,199.65.[67]

The total amounts raised in each of these "subscriptions" also included the profits from the fairs and benefits, for which the ledgers do not list the names of those attending. Undoubtedly, many Angelenos of various faiths patronized these events as well, despite bishop Amat's skeptical attitude toward "non-Catholics." The records clearly reveal the noteworthy interest and support such specifically denominational projects could attract in the community. The collected funds manifested the generosity of Jews and Protestants, as well as their concern for the progress of religion in Los Angeles. The willingness of Mora to solicit donations from members of other local congregations merits comment as well.

Francisco Mora had arrived from Spain, in 1855, as a twenty-eight-year-old seminarian, who had volunteered for Amat's diocese. He served several pastorates, including Los Angeles, where he became acquainted with the exigencies of frontier settlements. After 1865, Mora acted in place of the bishop during Amat's extensive travels. Mora understood the evident interest of Angelenos in civic improvements, as well as their willingness to set aside sectarian differences while working in common cause. At the time of his retirement, in 1896, he urged his flock never to disparage Protestants and to treat them as "separated brethren."[68] While always a Spanish cleric at heart, Mora nonetheless adapted more readily to the evolving American urban situation than did Amat.

The only other denomination for which similar financial records survive also received significant contributions from members of other faiths. The 1883 building campaign of the First Congregational Church realized a total of nearly $11,000 in "subscriptions" from 140 donors.[69] At least 18, whose gifts totaled $640, were not parishioners. These included the Northern Methodists Robert Widney and

---

[67] Ledger volumes entitled "Book of Buildings," pp. 14–15, 19–23; and "Cuentas de la Catedral de Sta. Vibiana, V. y M.," pp. 7–23. The expense in erecting the cathedral, exclusive of furnishings, totaled $74,940.04. See "Cuentas," p. 4, AALA.

[68] Quoted in the [Los Angeles] *Tidings*, 24 October 1896. Mora's remarks are all the more important when placed in the context of the anti-Catholic feeling then being engendered locally by the American Protective Association.

[69] "Clerk's Records," vol. II (1883–1898), pp. 20–21, First Congregational Church, Los Angeles, California.

his brother Joseph Pomeroy Widney; the Episcopalians William H. Workman, Stephen Mott, and Ozro W. Childs; the Roman Catholics Joseph Mesmer and Victor Ponet; and the Jews Isaias W. Hellman and the firm of the Jacoby Brothers. All were business and professional men, a fact which suggests that business associations and friendships transcended narrow sectarianism.

It is unfortunate that financial records no longer exist from other congregations, to permit a broader comparative study among Los Angeles denominations in this early period. Such evidence would be particularly helpful for the era during which Bishop Amat increasingly restricted Roman Catholic association with other believers. Scattered materials do survive that reveal a vibrant intrachurch cooperation among Protestant bodies. The earliest efforts had proven short-lived, such as Reverend Adam Bland's first camp meetings, in 1854 and 1855, and Reverend William Boardman's First Protestant Society of Los Angeles, of 1859.[70] When a new clergyman visited Los Angeles, Angelenos invariably invited him to conduct services for all local Protestants. Two examples over the years include the appearance, in October 1852, of Reverend James G. Johnson, a "Cumberland Presbyterian," who preached in the county courthouse, and the traveling Southern Methodist circuit rider, C.M. Hogue, who ascended the pulpit in St. Athanasius Episcopal church, during one such visit in 1867.[71] Not until the Northern Methodists and Congregationalists established themselves, in the late 1860s could such cooperative efforts revive and flourish.

In chapter 9, we will examine more closely the expanding Protestant culture in Los Angeles, but it is important at this point to note how efforts at mutual assistance changed over time. The year 1869 stands as a watershed for the growth of specifically intra-Protestant cooperation. Arriving settlers commenced a variety of evangelizing projects designed to advance the cause of Reform religion in Los Angeles. Reverends A.M. Hough and Isaac W. Atherton were pastors of the Northern Methodist and Congregationalist churches, respectively. They initiated regular "Union" prayer and temperance meetings, which met alternately in their two meetinghouses. Parishioners

[70] *Star*, 14 September 1854, 21 July and 13 October 1855.
[71] Warner, Hayes, and Widney, *Historical Sketch of Los Angeles County*, p. 81; and Los Angeles *News*, 4 January 1867.

joined together that year for Thanksgiving Day services as well, with Hough preaching. The two ministers also opened their pulpits to one another, and to the traveling Presbyterian synodal missionary, Thomas Fraser.[72]

These activities continued in the following year, with additional projects that the clergymen extended to the two newest denominations in Los Angeles. When Hough and Atherton commenced Sunday afternoon preaching on the sidewalk in front of the courthouse, the pastors of the new Southern Methodist and Presbyterian congregations joined them. Reverends Abram Adams and William C. Harding took their turns in the weekly rotation of exhortation duties. The four men also gathered each Monday morning, and they also welcomed visiting preachers to join them. Setting an important precedent, this simple assembly antedated the more formal Ministerial Association, which existed in Los Angeles by 1881.[73]

In the decade that followed, the leaders of these and additional Protestant congregations continued the activities of 1869 and 1870. Union prayer and temperance meetings remained popular, as did the common Thanksgiving service, with the combined choirs drawn from several of the churches. The installation of new pastors frequently involved the presence of invited clergy of other denominations, and "pulpit exchanges" between local ministers became increasing frequent after 1880.[74] During their respective regional meetings, delegates welcomed observers and official visitors from other denominations, as a further expression of Protestant hospitality and mutual respect.[75] Beginning in 1871, further collaboration developed, when Congregationalists, Presbyterians, Baptists, and United Presbyteri-

[72] Los Angeles *Star*, 17 April 1869; unidentified newspaper clipping, 23 October 1869, Hayes Scrapbooks, vol. 54, part 2, #22, BL; and Los Angeles *Republican*, 25 November 1869; E.J. Harkness, "History of the Presbytery of Los Angeles, 1850–1928" (Ph.D. dissertation, University of Southern California, 1929), p. 22.

[73] Los Angeles *Star*, 8 and 22 January, 20 November 1870; "Letter from Los Angeles," the *Pacific*, XIX (3 February 1870), p. 1; and an unidentified newspaper clipping dated 20 January 1870, in the Hayes Scrapbooks, vol. 54, #47, BL.

[74] Los Angeles *Evening Express*, 10 and 12 September 1874, 7 December 1878; and "Official Records," vol. I, p. 83, entry for 9 January 1879, First Baptist Church, Los Angeles, California. Another aspect of this interdenominational contact involved the installation ceremonies of new pastors. For example, Congregational minister David T. Packard read a hymn at A.F. White's installation as pastor of First Presbyterian Church, in 1875; *Occident*, XIV (16 September 1875), p. 292.

[75] "Minutes," Presbytery of Los Angeles, vol. 1, p. 141 (27 September 1882), in

ans turned their attention toward evangelizing the local Chinese, endeavors that we will examine at length, in the following chapter. Culminating this decade of cooperative labor, the establishment of the University of Southern California, in 1880, ushered in a new era in the religious history of Los Angeles.

The Northern Methodist layman Robert M. Widney had secured, in 1879, the commitment of his church and the donation of the site for a college he had long envisioned. The Methodist school soon came to embody the twin dreams of many Angelenos for a Protestant community and a more developed city. Increasing numbers of arriving settlers judged St. Vincent's College as an unacceptable institution of higher learning. Not only were its facilities and course offerings too limited, but new residents desired a more specifically Protestant school. At the time of the laying of the cornerstone, in September of 1880, fulsome endorsements issued from the press and from the pulpits of the Presbyterian and other denominations. Local church members looked toward the day when temperance, tract, and benevolence workers would march from this school, intent on the moral uplift of the community.[76]

The donors of the land shared more fully in the second of the dreams, the town's continued expansion. Ozro W. Childs, Vermont native and Episcopalian, the Irish-born Roman Catholic John G. Downey, and the Bavarian Jew Isaias W. Hellman, had long collaborated in projects aimed at civic improvement. They had repeatedly worked together with people of all religions, to secure by all manner of means the growth of their community.

One surprising result of this long-sought local economic development and increase in population was the demise of the religious toleration with which these Angelenos were so familiar. Los Angeles came of age, in the 1880s, as an Anglo-American urban center, in

---

Records of the Presbytery of Los Angeles, 1873–1887, Presbyterian Office of History, Philadelphia; *Minutes*, Annual Meeting of the General Session of California, (1881), pp. 6, 12; and *Minutes*, Southern California Annual Conference of the Methodist Episcopal Church, North, (1877): p. 3, (1879): p. 14, and (1880): p. 7. Both branches of the Methodist Church exchanged delegates to their respective annual conferences.

[76] Leslie F. Gay, Jr., "The Founding of the University of Southern California," Historical Society of Southern California *Annual Publications*, VIII, Part I (1909–1911), pp. 45–46.

which Protestantism was on the ascendency. Thriving congregations rapidly developed and vigorously promoted an ethos and culture of voluntaristic Christianity. These believers turned to organized groups such as the Young Men's Christian Association and the Women's Christian Temperance Union to reform the social mores of their city of adoption. Later writers would conclude that Los Angeles was a thoroughly Protestant community in its laws, politics, and economic establishment, by the turn of the century.[77]

The increased prosperity of the churches in the 1880s, which resulted from the dramatic increase of population, also lessened the need for comprehensive mutual assistance among Jews, Catholics, and Protestants. The passing of the frontier brought changes in local conditions that actually diminished the need for broad religious cooperation. Population growth strengthened the sense of denominational identity and purpose. Members of the pioneer Jewish and Roman Catholic communions found themselves increasingly outnumbered and exercising ever-diminishing roles in local society. The elder generation of Childs, Downey, and Hellman continued to associate together, but their numbers were thinning and their status was waning. The people who arrived in increasing numbers in the 1880s brought with them the racial and religious biases that had largely been muted for so long in the pioneer community.

Harris Newmark later voiced the appropriate lament for the passing of "sympathy, tolerance, and good feeling," when Los Angeles achieved its long-sought urban status.[78] Small wonder that Newmark and members of the "Pioneers of Los Angeles County" fondly recalled a simpler, less contentious era, "when Jew and Catholic and Protestant all labored together and when there were no pronounced church or social coteries . . ."[79] Like most reminiscences, however, the tendency was toward the roseate. The religious cooperation which

[77] See Carey McWilliams, *Southern California: An Island On the Land* (2nd ed., Santa Barbara: Peregrine Smith, Incorporated, 1973), pp. 157–58; Gregory H. Singleton, *Religion in the City of the Angels: Protestant Culture and Urbanization, Los Angeles, 1850–1930* (Ann Arbor, Michigan: UMI Research Press, 1979), pp. 49–69; and Sandra Sizer Frankiel, *California's Spiritual Frontiers: Religious Alternatives in Anglo-American Protestantism, 1850–1910* (Berkeley: University of California Press, 1988), pp. 60–62.

[78] Newmark, *Sixty Years*, p. 383.

[79] Obituary, "Mrs. Cordelia Mallard," reprinted from the *Western Graphic*, in the Historical Society of Southern California *Annual Publication*, IV, Part III (1899), p. 281.

the community had enjoyed between 1848 and 1880, while real and striking, had actually been limited in extent, temporary in nature, and selective in its manifestations.

The rapid Hispanic decline in status and influence during this period had rendered their church amenable to the assistance of others in its projects for schools, health and child care, and cathedral construction. Originally the major religious communion in the pueblo, Roman Catholicism suffered declining fortunes after 1860. Migrating members of this church did not arrive in sufficient numbers to offset the effects of downward Hispanic mobility. Roman Catholic need coincided with the development of a small but vibrant Jewish community, led by successful businessmen. Their dearth in numbers and their immigrant backgrounds inclined these local Jews to seek out those societies and projects in which they might demonstrate their commitment to the larger community and its growth. Their generous benevolence won local Jews the acceptance of many Angelenos, while their rabbi proved to be a highly effective "ambassador to the Gentiles," through his friendship with leading Christians.[80]

Protestants had joined with members of the other two major faiths in Los Angeles to combat lawlessness and the other threats to civilized society. Though drawn from differing denominations and initially few in number, these believers enjoyed the significant advantage of greater familiarity with the legal and governmental systems of the United States. They nonetheless needed the active cooperation of their Jewish and Roman Catholic neighbors, to attain an orderly society. By the late 1860s, local Protestants were increasingly able to sustain, by themselves, both a well-regulated society and their respective denominations. Growing numbers enhanced congregational stability and permitted these Christians the means to transform the city along ever more Protestant lines.

More adequate law enforcement, economic development, new and growing institutions for health and child care, and permanent religious congregations all lessened the need for collaboration across denominational lines. Better provisions for the most unfortunate members of local society, such as orphans and the indigent sick, no longer required the concerted efforts of Angelenos of all backgrounds. Early efforts to enhance both public and private education had also helped

---

[80] Stern and Kramer, "Jewish Padre," p. 213.

to unite residents in common cause. Religious cooperation among pioneer settlers developed out of necessity and retained its vigor as long as primitive conditions prevailed. The waning of the need for this tolerant cooperation permitted the reemergence of contemporary cultural biases.

Newer generations of emigrants experienced little of the broadscale collaboration that an earlier era of residents had known in the former pueblo. By 1890, Los Angeles so resembled communities in the Midwest that many citizens would forget its formerly distinctive religious heritage. Such ignorance bred a bigotry that reflected no credit on its proponents. The vanished heritage, one of cooperation and respect, had first arisen in an earlier cultural isolation that permitted a unique society to form and flourish for a brief time, between 1848 and 1870. Older Angelenos discovered, in time, that religious toleration was a fragile commodity, susceptible to both shifting demographics and economic prosperity.

NEW OPPORTUNITIES FOR
EVANGELIZATION

An unusual array of religious pioneers made their homes in the City of the Angels. Hispanic Roman Catholics, Jews, Latter-day Saints, and Chinese worshipers were all local pioneers in advance of the members of more "typically American" communions.[1] As a result, religious life in frontier Los Angeles was amazingly diverse, for such a small and isolated settlement. This pluralistic community in Los Angeles was also distinctive because of the people who evangelized there, the challenges these missionaries faced, and the settlers they sought to evangelize. These three aspects of the planting of denominations form the subject matter for this chapter. Tried and true methods and ministers had to give way to novel techniques and teachers in southern California.[2]

[1] The Saints established an agricultural colony at San Bernardino, east of Los Angeles, which thrived until the 1,200 residents returned to Salt Lake, at the time of the Mountain Meadows massacre, in 1857. This settlement is the subject of Edward Leo Lyman's "The Demise of the San Bernardino Mormon Community, 1851–1857," *Southern California Quarterly*, LXV (Winter 1982), pp. 321–40.

[2] William Warren Sweet and subsequent historians have documented at length how parsons reached less-than-pious pioneers in earlier trans-Appalachian settlements. See Sweet, *The Story of Religion in America* (revised ed., New York: Harper and Brothers, 1950), pp. 244, 250–55. See also the standard study on the subject, Colin B. Goodykuntz, *Home Missions on the American Frontier, with Particular Reference to the American Home Missionary Society* (Caldwell, Idaho: Caxton Press, 1939); Ray Allen Billington, *The Protestant Crusade, 1800–1860* (New York: MacMillan Company, 1938; reprint ed., Chicago: Quadrangle Books, 1964), pp. 278–79; and for one denomination's history of foreign and home missions, see Clifford M. Drury, *Presbyterian Panorama: One Hundred and Fifty Years of National Missions History* (Philadelphia: Board of Christian Education, Presbyterian Church of the U.S.A., 1952).

Chapter 5

The experience of local Jews was sufficiently distinct from that of their Christian neighbors as to merit comment prior to consideration of the work of the churches. As members of a nonproselytizing creed, Jews were not engaged in seeking converts. The rabbi, according to European custom and tradition, did not legislate, but only interpreted and applied Talmudic law in the local community. He did not have the pastoral role of ministers in the Christian faiths. Only with the rise of the Reform movement among German, and later, American Jews did the rabbi assume a greater clerical role in the congregation. Proponents of this change sought to harmonize the customs and traditions surrounding their ancient faith with the discoveries and principles of the Enlightenment and the age of industrialization.[3] Unique challenges therefore faced the rabbi and members of the "cow-town congregation" in the far western frontier of Los Angeles.[4]

Rabbi Abraham Wolf Edelman, Polish-born and educated, shepherded his pioneer and immigrant flock during a period in which they confronted great change. While their recorded numbers increased from 161, in 1860, to 486, in 1880, the wealth and position of Jews in the community rose dramatically.[5] Edelman found his congregants undergoing profound socioeconomic change during his tenure. One study of local Jewish occupational, residential, and property patterns concluded that "the large majority of Jews, who remained in Los Angeles achieved a greater measure of social mobility than did non-Jews."[6] Such impressive achievements involved in particular the status-conscious Polish-Prussian Jews who sought recognition from

[3] Nathan Glazier, *American Judaism* (2nd ed., revised, Chicago: University of Chicago Press, 1972), pp. 25–28, 31–36.

[4] Valuable information on Rabbi Edelman and his flock is found in a paper by Stephen E. Breuer, "Cowtown Congregation: The Early Jewish Settlement of Los Angeles, from 1850 through 1885" (typescript, 1958), Office of the Executive Director, Wilshire Boulevard Temple, Los Angeles, California.

[5] Census statistics are from Norton B. Stern and William M. Kramer, "Jewish Padre to the Pueblo: Pioneer Los Angeles Rabbi Abraham Wolf Edelman," *Western States Jewish Historical Quarterly*, III (July 1971), p. 193, n. 2; and Mitchell Gelfand, "Progress and Prosperity: Jewish Social Mobility in Los Angeles in the Booming Eighties," in Moses Rischin, ed., *The Jews in the West: The Metropolitan Years* (Waltham, Massachusetts: American Jewish Historical Society, 1979), p. 27.

[6] Gelfand, "Progress and Prosperity," p. 44. For a comparison with the progress of Jews in another Western community, see William Toll, *The Making of an Ethnic Middle Class: Portland Jews over Four Generations* (Albany, New York: State University of New York Press, 1982), pp. 8–41.

their Gentile neighbors as members of a high-status group, the German immigrants.[7]

The quest for economic security and social standing profoundly affected the organized religious life entrusted to Rabbi Edelman. The time-honored strictures of Eastern European Judaism that the majority of Los Angeles Jews had known appeared increasingly anomalous on the southern California frontier. The rabbi quietly but steadily shed Orthodox rituals and inhibitions. His biographers record that, over the years, Edelman:

> conducted a congregation with a Sunday school, confirmation, a mixed choir [both male and female, Jewish and Gentile], an organ, mixed seating, English language sermons, some use of German, the addition of English prayers. . . . During some portion of the service male heads could be uncovered. . . . His wife cooked on the Sabbath![8]

The desire to keep pace with his ever more Americanized congregation led Edelman to move increasingly closer to Reform Judaism without, however, explicitly renouncing Orthodoxy.[9]

Like rabbis across the nation, Edelman made these religious adaptions to retain the local affiliation of young and ambitious Jews in the community. The rabbi also endorsed the Hebrew Benevolent Society and promoted the formation of two other Jewish fraternal organizations, the Ancient Jewish Order Kesher Shel Barzel, in 1870, and the Independent Order B'nai B'rith, in 1874.[10] His endeavors met with only limited success; evidence shows that, by an early date, significant numbers of Jews in Los Angeles were lapsing from religious observance.[11] In 1876, one observer noted that Congregation B'nai B'rith

---

[7] Regarding the rise of Jews in other communities in the West, see William Toll, *The Making of an Ethnic Middle Class*; and William M. Kramer and Norton B. Stern, "The Major Role of Polish Jews in the Pioneer West," *Western States Jewish Historical Quarterly*, VIII (July 1976), p. 331.

[8] Stern and Kremer, "Jewish Padre to the Pueblo," p. 210.

[9] For a discussion of the rise of Reform Judaism in the United States, see Nathan Glazer, *American Judaism*, pp. 31–42.

[10] J. Albert Wilson, *The History of Los Angeles County, California* (Oakland, California: Thompson and West, 1880; reprint ed., Berkeley: Howell-North, 1959), p. 123; and Stern and Kramer, "Jewish Padre to the Pueblo," p. 200.

[11] For example, see the comments of the president of Congregation B'nai B'rith,

counted only 60 members, while the 1870 census listed some 330 Jews in town.[12] When single young adults did not join these synagogue and fraternal institutions, there developed what a later scholar described as "a separation from organized Jewish life that was a harbinger of later and more massive non-affiliation."[13]

The quest for status and recognition finally led leaders of the congregation, in 1885, to select a "reverend doctor" to replace the less-polished Edelman.[14] Their choice fell upon the Berlin-trained Emanuel Schreiber. This selection manifested the desire for an enhanced denominational image and proved to be the greatest obstacle the venerable rabbi had faced since 1862. He had modified ritual, altered customs, confirmed the young, and befriended Gentiles. These highly significant accommodations were all elements of the rabbi's strenuous attempts to retain impetuous immigrants and their aspiring offspring in the ancient faith of Israel. Such willingness to undertake these alterations placed Edelman alongside Christian churchmen, who also struggled to reach their own congregants amidst the problems in a frontier community.

The economic and social transformation of the settlement was well underway by the first years of the 1850s, and no people were more profoundly affected than the Indian populace. The rapidly dwindling numbers of Indians in Los Angeles claimed the attention of Roman Catholic clergy and nuns. Spanish and Mexican Franciscans commenced evangelization of the indigenous tribes as early as 1771, at San Gabriel, and 1797, at San Fernando. The secularization acts of the Mexican government, between 1833 and 1836, dislodged the native people from mission lands and forced many Indians to turn to the ranchos and pueblos for employment. Gradually diminishing in number, prior to 1848, the Gabrielinos and Fernandinos rapidly

---

Isaias W. Hellman, in the Los Angeles *Star*, 19 August 1872. On the occasion of laying the cornerstone of the synagogue, Hellman lamented, "I am sorry to see that the Jewish young men, who certainly should be the first ones to join kindred institutions [to the Congregation], have so far not done it."

[12] Salvator Ludwig, Archduke of Austria, *Los Angeles in the Sunny Seventies*, translated by Marguerite Eyer Wilbur (Los Angeles: Bruce McAllister and Jake Zeitlin, 1929), p. 131; and Norton Stern, "Jews in the 1870 Census of Los Angeles," *Western States Jewish Historical Quarterly*, IX (October 1976), p. 71.

[13] Neil C. Sandberg, *Jewish Life in Los Angeles: A Window to Tomorrow* (Lanham, Maryland: University Press of America, 1986), p. 28.

[14] William M. Kramer and Reva Clar, "Emanuel Schreiber," *Western States Jewish Historical Quarterly*, IX (July 1977), pp. 354–55.

disappeared as distinct culture groups, in the following two decades.[15]

Reliable statistics for the Indian population are not available, though some idea of the relative decline in numbers can be discerned. The 1852 state census enumerated 3,693 Indians for Los Angeles County. Subsequent decennial counts show a decline to 2,014, in 1860, and to 219, in 1870. There was a modest gain by 1880, when the Indian population rose to 316. However, economic disruption, diseases such as smallpox, and migration out of the Los Angeles area had wrought havoc among this segment of the town's populace.[16]

No one religious communion, even the largest, was sufficiently well established to sustain effective ministry to these people. The pastor at San Gabriel and the priest from Los Angeles, who visited San Fernando, each spent what time he could spare with the Indian residents remaining in those areas. One of these hard-riding clerics, the Frenchman Edmond Venisse, SS.CC., described his labors in a letter of 1856. He visited the "Indiens" at San Fernando monthly to offer mass, teach catechism, hear confessions, baptize children, and visit the sick. In the pueblo, he also conducted mission-trained musicians, who accompanied his church choir with "the joyful violin, the melancholic flute, the metallic triangle, and the gay tambourine."[17]

Venisse observed firsthand the horrific destruction of the Indian populace through violence and disease. The priest tended the injured and dying after Saturday-night brawls, frequently hearing the confessions of the mortally wounded. The consumption of alcohol, which the *curé* sardonically termed "l'eau-de-vie," was the root cause of many Indian deaths.[18] Starting in 1856, the Daughters of Charity assisted the clergy and provided local Indians with service in time of need. From their Institución Caritativa, the Sisters provided shelter for orphaned children, instruction for students, nursing for small-

[15] William Mason, "Indian-Mexican Cultural Exchange in the Los Angeles Area, 1781–1834," *Aztlán*, XV (Spring 1984), pp. 140–41.

[16] *Statistical View of the United States* (Washington, D.C.: Government Printing Office, 1854; reprint ed., New York: Gordon and Breach Science Publishers, 1970), p. 394; Maurice H. Newmark and Marco R. Newmark, eds., *Census of the City and County of Los Angeles, California, for the Year 1850* (Los Angeles: Times-Mirror Press, 1929), p. 117, n. 4; George Harwood Phillips, "Indians in Los Angeles, 1781–1875: Economic Integration, Social Disintegration," *Pacific Historical Review*, XLIX (August 1980), p. 442, n. 67; and Sherburne F. Cook, *The Population of the California Indians* (Berkeley: University of California Press, 1976), pp. 55, 57–58.

[17] "Extrait d'une lettre de M. Venisse," *Annales de la Propagation de la Foi* (Lyon, France), XXX (1858), pp. 59, 61.

[18] Venisse, "Extrait d'une lettre," p. 59.

pox victims, placement service for domestics, and even attendance at burials.[19]

The Sisters also considered a request, in 1856, from Bishop Thaddeus Amat, to staff an Indian school in the southern portion of his diocese. Maryland superiors of the Sisters prevented a commitment to that endeavor, which forced the prelate temporarily to abandon his plans.[20] The few priests in Amat's 80,000 square-mile diocese could provide no more than occasional spiritual attention for the numerous Indian settlements. Seeing the desperate plight Indians faced in towns like Los Angeles, Amat provided them with dispensation from certain diocesan requirements. Marriage and burial regulations in 1862 mandated special consideration for Indians, recognizing the poverty and dislocated family situations which many suffered.[21]

Beset by a shortage of religious personnel, Bishop Amat concentrated his attention on Hispanics and on Roman Catholics arriving from the United States and Europe. He initiated no specific ministry on behalf of immigrants of two racial groups arriving in slowly increasing numbers: black and Chinese pioneers. Roman Catholic blacks worshipped at Our Lady of the Angels Church, on the plaza. In other communions, blacks attended worship services alongside whites, but received no special outreach or consideration. Their relative scarcity accounted for much of this neglect; blacks numbered 12 souls in 1850 and only 102 in 1880.[22]

---

[19] "San Francisco" ledger, pp. 97–99, AWPDC; Wallace E. Smith, *This Land Was Ours: The Del Valles and Rancho Camulos* (Ventura, California: Ventura County Historical Society, 1977), p. 116; and Sister Angelita Mumbrado, D.C., "Remembrance of My Youth," (typescript, [1917]), p. 12, Archives of the Central Province of the Daughters of Charity, Marillac Provincial House, St. Louis, Missouri.

[20] Letter, Sister Scholastica Logsdon to Reverend Francis Burlando, 21 November 1856, "Institución Caritativa," Los Angeles, in "Correspondence of the Director," vol. II. Bishop Amat tried again to secure Sisters to teach in the southern portion of his diocese in later years. See letter, Bishop Thaddeus Amat to Reverend Francis Burlando, 10 May 1867, St. Peter's Church, New York City, "Correspondence of the Director," vol. I; AWPDC.

[21] See decrees #31, #69, and #75, in *Constitutiones Latae et Promulgatae ab Illmo. ac Revmo. D. Thaddaeo Amat, Congregationis Missionis, Episcopo Montereyensi et Angelorum, in Synodo Dioecesana Prima* (San Francisco: Vincent Torras, 1862), pp. 44, 46–47, 26–27.

[22] Black population growth between 1850 and 1880 meant an increase in the percentage of blacks in the town population from .07 to .90. See J. Max Bond, *The Negro in Los Angeles* (San Francisco: R and E Research Associates, 1972), p. 20. This work is reprint of a previously unpublished 1936 Ph.D. dissertation in sociology, from

Another reason for ignoring the special spiritual needs of blacks derived from the Southern origins of many Los Angeles Christians. While black children were permitted to attend the Episcopalians' Sunday School, in 1866, they did so only in separate classes. This practice appalled the first Congregationalist pastor, Reverend Alexander Parker, a Union veteran and Oberlin graduate. Parker instituted integrated Sabbath instruction for the young at his chapel, provoking a controversy that kept Angelenos buzzing with indignation.[23] Blacks formed their own congregations once they amassed sufficient resources to do so, as in 1869 and 1885.

While local blacks struggled to support a minister through the 1870s, they received little outside evangelization from any denomination. In a similar, though gradually changing, situation was the Protestant outreach to local Hispanics. Traditionally affiliated with Roman Catholicism, Southwestern Hispanics posed an important challenge to Protestant evangelizers. The emigrant Christian communions rejected a language of worship and a plethora of customs they found novel and bewildering. Hispanics, for their part, were amazed to discover that the religious aspect of their culture was under assault not only from Protestants, but from their own denomination, as well.

The pioneer bishops of California and the Southwest, Jean Baptiste Lamy, of Santa Fe, Joseph Sadoc Alemany, O.P., of San Francisco, and Thaddeus Amat, C.M., of Los Angeles, faced similar challenges in their frontier dioceses. Problems ranged from personnel to policy and from poverty to piety. The bishops sought to maintain the allegiance of Hispanic Roman Catholics, while simultaneously attempting to alter cherished religious customs. The prelates also struggled to expand their ministry to the migrating Anglo-American, black, and European-born Roman Catholics. The arrival of non–Roman Catholics also bestirred the hierarchy and clergy to seek out converts, while at the same time fending off Protestant proselytization.[24]

---

the University of Southern California, Los Angeles. Bond also cited an interview with William Ballard, a Roman Catholic black born in Los Angeles, who attended services at Our Lady of Angels church; see p. 12, n. 44.

[23] See the letter of Alexander Parker to "Bro. [A. Huntington] Clapp," 18 December 1866, Los Angeles, Microfilm #C-B 393, reel 3, of American Home Missionary Society file, "California, 1866, A-P, sec. 1," AHMS, BL.

[24] Various aspects of these episcopal endeavors are discussed in Paul Horgan, *Lamy*

Chapter 5

The Roman Catholic bishop and padres in Los Angeles also participated actively in their denomination's evolving program of institutional growth. The clergy implemented a series of reforms over three decades to bring southwestern devotional practices into conformity with increasingly standardized "American" observances. The frontier-bred religious customs of Hispanics fell from official favor. The hierarchy of the United States met in successive conclaves, throughout the nineteenth century, to spell out increasingly more detailed regulations covering all facets of Roman Catholic life. The bishops sought to bring local practices into harmony with an "American," or national, church, which in turn was closely linked with the international institution based in Rome.

Starting in 1854, Bishop Amat repeatedly recruited priests, seminarians, and religious women in his native Catalonian region of Spain, to serve in his distant California see.[25] When he began his labors, in 1855, he found sixteen clergymen at work in his 80,000 square-mile diocese. Seven were Mexican clerics (mostly Franciscans), three were French members of the Congregation of the Sacred Hearts, and the remainder hailed from unknown other nations. The changes he introduced were clear by the time of his death, in 1878. In that year, the clergy totaled forty-one men: seventeen Spaniards, nine Irishmen, four Mexican Franciscans, two apiece from Italy and France, one American, and a scattering of other nationalities.

While successful in recruiting foreign priests, Amat was far less fortunate in attracting religious women from Spain and the rest of Europe. The fact that three of the first six Sisters of Charity to arrive in Los Angeles in 1856 were from Catalonia, in Spain, fueled his optimism, but when Spanish superiors refused to augment these

---

of Santa Fe (New York: Farrar, Straus, and Giroux, 1975), pp. 150–51, 176–84, 242–45; John B. McGloin, S.J., *California's First Archbishop: The Life of Jose Sadoc Alemany, O.P., 1814–1888* (New York: Herder and Herder, 1966), pp. 156, 162; and Francis J. Weber, *California's Reluctant Prelate* (Los Angeles: Dawson's Book Shop, 1964), pp. 51–71.

[25] The significance of the Catalonian origins of Amat and his clergy derives in part from the fact that the inhabitants of this region of Spain spoke a language distinct from the common tongue of the rest of that nation. When these clerics arrived in California, they considered their language more refined than that of their Californio and Mexican congregations. See Weber, *Reluctant Prelate*, pp. 24–25, 197; and letter of Amat to "V. Rev. Dowley," 23 June 1860, Marseilles; AALA. The same

numbers, Amat relied increasingly upon the American province of this religious order.[26] Twenty-three Sisters of Charity were at work in the city of Los Angeles by the time of the bishop's death, in 1878, with nineteen others laboring elsewhere in the far-flung diocese. By far the largest number of nuns were of Irish birth or descent, though at least four California Hispanic women are known to have entered this sisterhood.[27] The recruitment of men and women from Europe and the United States enabled Amat to alter the religious life of his flock.[28] Three times he convened his clergy in synods (meetings), in order to enact diocesan regulations that he favored or that the national hierarchy required. The first assembly, in 1862, mandated an end to a variety of Hispanic frontier observances. The clergy disapproved of the Christmas-season play of *Los Pastores*, peppered as it was with irreverent comments and asides, as well as the boisterous mock execution of Judas Iscariot, during Holy Week.[29] A host of common funeral customs also fell under clerical censure and gradually faded from parochial life.[30]

---

repository also retains the diocesan "Cash Book," listing expenses for educating and transporting foreign seminarians to California, 1856–76.

[26] The six pioneer Sisters of Charity in Los Angeles were Sisters Mary Scholastica Logsdon, Anne Gillen, and Corsina McKay, from the United States; and Francesca Fernandez, Angelita Mumbrado, and Clara Cisneros, from Spain. Mumbrado, "Remembrance of My Youth," p. 3, ACPDC; and *El Clamor Público*, 12 January 1856. Amat expressed his desire for additional Spanish religious women in letters to the American director of the Sisters of Charity, Reverend Francis Burlando, C.M., of 4 May 1857, from Los Angeles, and 7 September 1857, from Santa Barbara, California; see "Correspondence of the Director," vol. I, AWPDC.

[27] Charles I. White, *Life of Mrs. Eliza A. Seton* (tenth edition, New York: P.J. Kenedy and Sons, [1879]), pp. 503, 504. Scant material exists to document the ethnic and racial backgrounds of the Sisters of Charity in Los Angeles, as discussed at length in chapter 6.

[28] Amat finally secured the services of Spanish religious women in 1870, when a band of Sisters of the Immaculate Heart of Mary settled in the northern part of the diocese. However, they did not begin work in Los Angeles until 1886. Charles C. Conroy, ed., *The Centennial, 1840–1940* (Los Angeles: Archdiocese of Los Angeles, 1940), p. 143.

[29] Descriptions of these seasonal customs are found in Ana Begue de Packman, *Early California Hospitality* (Glendale, California: Arthur H. Clark Company, 1938), pp. 157–58; by the same author, *Leather Dollar Days* (Los Angeles: Times-Mirror Press, 1932), pp. 39–43; and Horace Bell, *Reminiscences of a Ranger* (Los Angeles: Yarnell, Caystile and Mathes, 1881), pp. 286–87.

[30] Arturo Bandini explained the demise of the Yuletide miracle play of *Los Pastores*

No longer were wakes to include drinking and dancing in the home where the body of the deceased was laid out, because such festivity "offends against gentility."[31] The processions to the church and cemetery with the corpse were to be more dignified, which meant a prohibition against the usual firing of guns and the lighting of firecrackers. Henceforth all coffins were to be closed, during both the procession and the funeral mass. The clergy were to refrain from permitting burials within the church building itself, despite the long tradition that had accorded this honor to deceased infants and prominent citizens. The synod mandated that all liturgical ceremonies conform to the rubrics of the Roman Ritual.[32]

Further instructions followed, in subsequent synods. The 1869 meeting made even clearer the prohibitions against intermarriage with Protestant Christians. By way of contrast, the pastor of Our Lady of the Angels Church, Reverend Blas Raho, C.M., had gladly blessed such unions on numerous occasions, until his death, in 1862.[33] Raho recognized that the scarcity of marriageable women was leading many Anglo-American Protestant men to seek out the daughters of Hispanic Catholic families. Such priestly tolerance diminished with each passing year throughout the 1860s, both in Los Angeles and across the nation. This is most evident in the final synod during Amat's bishopric.

---

as a local casualty of the Civil War. In actuality, the 1862 synod precluded further productions of this event. See his account, in *Navidad: A Christmas Day with the Early Californians*, ed. by Susanna Bryant Dakin (San Francisco: California Historical Society, 1958). The order for the termination of these traditional events is found in Decree #30, *Constitutiones . . . in Synodo Dioecesana Prima*, (San Francisco: Vicente Torras, 1862), p. 26.

[31] Anglo-Americans were, in fact, astonished when they observed Californios dancing in a home at the time of a wake. Reverend James Woods described such an event, of 24 January 1855, commenting in his diary, "Surely this is but a grade above paganism." Quoted from Lindley Bynum, ed., "Los Angeles in 1854–5: The Diary of Rev. James Woods," Historical Society of Southern California *Quarterly*, XXIII (June 1941), pp. 82–83.

[32] Decree 31, *Constitutiones . . . in Synodo Dioecesana Prima*, pp. 26–27. Arnoldo De Leon provides evidence for the regional character of these funeral customs, in his study of religious practices among Hispanics in Texas. See *The Tejano Community, 1836–1900* (Albuquerque, New Mexico: University of New Mexico Press, 1982), pp. 146–48.

[33] Decree 27, *Constitutiones . . . Synodis Dioecesanis Prima et Segunda* (San Francisco: Mullin, Mahon and Company, 1869), p. 95. For an example of Raho's openness

The 1876 synodal convocation issued fewer decrees than the preceding two gatherings, but it included one that pertained directly to yet another common *Californio* practice. The clerics again cited the Roman Ritual and ordered an end to the custom of baptizing children with "the Name of Jesus, the Divine Persons or mysteries." Hispanics had commonly christened their offspring with a litany of the newly prohibited names. Those now under the ban included Jesús, Trinidad, Espíritu, Salvador, Encarnación, Concepción, Ascención, Asunción, Presentación, Engracia, Altagracia, Cruz, Libramiento, and Resurrección. The baptismal registers of the town's church were replete with entries of infants so named by their parents.[34]

Bishop Amat had also attempted to alter the local religious life of Hispanics through his establishment of Roman Catholic schools for the young. Pupils (and instructors) were racially and ethnically mixed, from the first day that French clergy of the Congregation of the Sacred Hearts initiated parochial education in the pueblo, in June 1851. The female academy of the Sisters of Charity opened in February 1856, under the charge of Sister Corsina McKay, from New York City. A decade later, three Irishmen, of the Brothers of the Third Order of St. Francis, commenced schooling boys in the building on the plaza vacated by St. Vincent's College. The year-old college, begun by one Spaniard and two Americans, relocated and prospered under the care of additional Vincentian priests of Irish-American descent.[35]

Thaddeus Amat faced staggering challenges from the moment he stepped upon California soil. The churches lay in ruins, the clergy were few and aged, legal title to religious property was clouded, and

---

towards such intermarriage, see Sister Mary Ste. Therese Wittenburg, "A California Girlhood: Reminiscences of Ascención Sepúlveda y Avila," *Southern California Quarterly*, LXIV, (Summer 1982), pp. 137, 139.

[34] Decree 10, *Constitutiones . . . Synodo Dioecesana Tertia* (San Francisco: P.J. Thomas, 1876), p. 14; and Marie E. Northrop, *Spanish-Mexican Families of Early California: 1769–1850*, (Burbank, California: Southern California Genealogical Society, 1984), vol. II, passim.

[35] Harold A. Whelan, SS.CC., *The Picpus Story* (Pomona, California: Apostolate of Christian Renewal, 1980), pp. 175–79, 187; Venisse, "Extrait d'une Lettre," p. 57; *Los Angeles Star*, 30 July 1870; William E. North, *Catholic Education in Southern California* (Washington, D.C.: The Catholic University of America Press, 1936), pp. 120, 115–16; *Los Angeles Star*, 19 March 1870.

his financial resources were negligible. Amat mustered the assistance of other religious workers in his efforts to rebuild Roman Catholicism in southern California. The emphasis, however, was upon the "Roman" characteristics of this church, and not its more universal and "catholic" dimensions.

The matters that engaged bishop and clergy were those typically important to the representatives of institutional religion. Uniformity of belief, proper ritual, and conformity to outside norms were significant concerns to these European guardians of the faith, particularly the Catalonian clerics. Folk, or popular, practices among the Californios and Mexicans appeared crude to them. In this and other dioceses in which European clerics later came to dominate, there emerged a deep division between formal parish worship and the more personalized religious practices centered in Hispanic families.[36]

The divergence in religious practice affected Roman Catholic Hispanics far more deeply than their Anglo-American and European fellow congregants in Los Angeles. The restrictions enacted in church regulations and decrees were similar to those found elsewhere in the United States. Only in the Southwest had a religious expression developed that was so thoroughly indigenous to the region. Vestiges of this enforced separation between precepts and piety have continued to the present, a legacy that descends from the strict conformity demanded by a Catalonian bishop and his clerics.[37]

One form of devotion Amat introduced was the parish mission, an exercise resembling Protestant revival meetings in intent and in the numbers in attendance.[38] Visiting priests preached and conducted

[36] Other examples exist to document the frequency of division in the nineteenth century between non-Hispanic priests and the Spanish-speaking people of the Southwest. See De Leon, *Tejano Community*, pp. 139–40, 154; Horgan, *Lamy of Santa Fe*, pp. 148–52, 175–81; and Frances M. Campbell, "American Regional Catholicism: Dichotomous Developments in Anglo and Hispano Traditions, 1776–1885," paper delivered at the American Catholic Historical Association, 28 December 1983.

[37] For a discussion of the contemporary religious practices of Hispanics and their divergence from institutional Roman Catholicism, see the report produced by the Workshops on Hispanic Liturgy and Popular Piety, entitled "Faith Expression of Hispanics in the Southwest" (San Antonio, Texas: Mexican American Cultural Center, 1977); and Roberto O. Gonzalez, O.F.M., and Michael La Velle, *The Hispanic Catholic in the United States: A Socio-Cultural and Religious Profile* (New York: Northeast Catholic Pastoral Center for Hispanics, 1985).

[38] For an extended discussion of the parish mission in the nineteenth-century United States, see Jay P. Dolan, *Catholic Revivalism: The American Experience, 1830–1900* (Notre Dame: University of Notre Dame Press, 1978).

worship over a period of several days, seeking to inspire the laity and to win converts. The clerics heard confessions, dispensed Holy Communion, and prepared adults for Confirmation. While less emotional than outdoor camp meetings, these missions were the occasions for impassioned sermons, describing the pains of hell and the glories of heaven. Traveling preachers, such as the Jesuits Franz Xavier Weninger and James Bouchard, conducted these services locally, between 1870 and 1885, and prompted renewals of religious fervor in forms which the bishop and his clergy approved and guided.[39]

Arriving pioneer Protestants had quickly discovered many of the same difficulties that Bishop Amat faced in Los Angeles. Their financial resources were limited, their personnel were few in number, and the local population practiced a form of Christianity that appalled them. Lack of facility in the Spanish language was a further challenge they had to surmount. Not until the arrival of the Presbyterian parson William C. Mosher, in 1871, did there appear a Protestant minister able to converse with the Californios and Mexicans in their own tongue. Mosher, however, did not commence his ministry among these peoples until his "retirement," in 1877, from his last pastorate, that of the "Indiana Colony," in nearby Pasadena.[40]

Mosher had known service in difficult ministries before, having taught four years in Freedmen's schools in Georgia, after the Civil War. He pursued a course of preparatory work among Hispanics, readying them for later missionaries who would found formal congregations. As a licensed "colporteur," he traveled extensively to distribute tracts and Bibles. He devoted "much attention to the Spanish speaking people" and spoke their language "tolerably well."[41]

---

[39] The transcript of diary entries of Reverend Louis Cook, C.Ss.R., record Redemptorist efforts in Los Angeles, 4–18 January 1885. See Louis Cook, "Parish Missions in 1885," *Academy Scrapbook*, I (July, 1950), pp. 19–26. Weninger traveled on a circuit beginning in St. Louis and conducted separate missions to German- and English-speaking Roman Catholics between 20 February and 6 March 1870, according to an unidentified newspaper clipping in the Benjamin Hayes Scrapbooks, vol. 54, #52, BL; and the Los Angeles *Star*, 5 March 1870. Bouchard, based in San Francisco, traversed the far-western states and territories. See John B. McGloin, S.J., *Eloquent Indian: The Life of James Bouchard, California Jesuit* (Stanford, California: Stanford University Press, 1949), p. 201.

[40] Clifford L. Holland, *The Religious Dimension in Hispanic Los Angeles: A Protestant Case Study* (South Pasadena: William Carey Library, 1974), p. 226.

[41] William C. Mosher, "Scrapbook," pp. 73, 114–15; and clipping in same volume, p. 4, from *Annual Report*, Presbyterian Board of Publication (September 1878), HL.

Mosher's greatest satisfaction came from provoking religious questions in the minds of those who heard him.

In ten years of reports to his superiors, Mosher noted his travels across six southern California counties distributing Spanish-language publications. The scores of tracts he passed out included such anti-Catholic works as *Almost a Nun*, *Tracts on Popery*, and *History of the Inquisition*, as well as the *Shorter Catechism* and the *Little Brown Bible*. His buckboard also hauled a bundle of pamphlets entitled *Universalism Exposed*. The peripatetic parson seemingly thrived on religious combat, which set his approach apart from the more tolerant and cooperative stance of most clerics in Los Angeles during this period. His outright attacks on other faiths signaled the dawning of an era of diminished religious cooperation in a rapidly expanding community.

This bilingual combatant, however, was a man of his age, even if not fully acculturated to a more tolerant Los Angeles. Elsewhere in the nation, anti-Catholicism was on the rise, with the increasing numbers of immigrants arriving in the Atlantic-seaboard states. Mosher quarreled on more than one occasion with Roman Catholic clergy over the copies of the scriptures he provided. Mosher recounted, with some relish, episodes of Hispanic resistance to the priests' attempts to discourage use of the King James version of the Bible. He concluded a February 1879 report with the biting comment, "Thus we see the waning influence of the priests over a people whom they have so long enslaved, and whose religious education they have so long neglected."[42]

The former pastor's first convert was Antonio Diaz, an immigrant from Mexico who had briefly assisted Northern Methodists in their outreach to Los Angeles Hispanics. After meeting Mosher, Diaz quickly progressed along Presbyterian paths and received his license to preach in 1883. Ordained a minister, in April of 1884, Diaz was the first local Hispanic consecrated for ministry in any denomination between 1850 and 1885.[43] The presence of Diaz and additional Presbyterian workers led to the establishment of three small Hispanic

[42] "List of works remaining in the hands of W.C. Mosher, Dec. 31, 1884," Report to Presbyterian Board of Publication, in Mosher, "Scrapbook," pp. 296–99; and clipping dated February 1879, in Mosher, "Scrapbook," p. 5; HL.

[43] Minutes, vol. I, pp. 155–56, 190, Records of the Presbytery of Los Angeles (P.C.U.S.A.), 1873–1887, POHP; R. Douglas Brackenridge and Francisco García-

congregations in and around Los Angeles, by the end of 1883. The success of these enterprises owed much to Mosher and Diaz, as well as to a relative newcomer to this field.

Reverend Carlos Bransby, a former missionary in Bogotá, Columbia, assumed the superintendency of Spanish work in the Los Angeles Presbytery in April of 1882. Skilled as an organizer, Bransby was responsible for the formal institution of the three Presbyterian churches in the county for Hispanics. Despite the assistance of two additional clerics, he grew discouraged and withdrew. Bransby accepted a position at the University of California at Berkeley, to teach Spanish, in 1885. Evangelization languished for several years, until the appointment, in 1888, of Reverend Alexander Moss Merwin, another missionary returned from Latin America.[44]

Among those greeting Merwin upon his arrival was a woman who had been at work among Los Angeles Hispanics since 1883. Miss Ida L. Boone had opened a small school with the aid of her mother and the town's First Presbyterian Church. In 1884, she gained the support of the local branch of the Women's Presbyterial Home and Foreign Mission Society, as well as the New York–based Women's Executive Committee of Home Missions of the Presbyterian Church.[45] Certain of her projects resembled those of William C. Mosher. She visited the homes of the Spanish-speaking in her neighborhood and handed out tracts and Bibles as she went along. Like Mosher, she encountered a variety of obstacles to her labors.

The parents are all Catholics, and when they think that the children are learning too much about the Bible, they are withdrawn. . . . It is a hard place in which to work, because the priests have such complete control of the Spanish people. . . .[46]

Treto, *Iglesia Presbiteriana: A History of Presbyterians and Mexican Americans in the Southwest* (San Antonio, Texas: Trinity University Press, 1974), pp. 81–82; Mosher, Scrapbook," pp. 8, 9, HL; *Minutes*, Synod of the Pacific (1883), p. 41; and F.H. Robinson, "The Presbytery of Los Angeles," *The Occident*, XXV (23 April 1884), p. 1.

[44] Brackenridge and García-Treto, *Iglesia Presbiteriana*, pp. 80–81; *Minutes*, Synod of the Pacific (1883), p. 41; and Holland, *Religious Dimension in Hispanic Los Angeles*, p. 227.

[45] Minutes, vol. I, p. 203, Records of the Presbytery of Los Angeles (P.C.U.S.A.), 1873–1889, POHP.

[46] Quoted from Ida L. Boone's entry, in the "Words from Workers" section of the *Home Mission Monthly*, I (April 1887), p. 133.

Boone also served as a mission school teacher, and she continued in that vocation until 1907.[47]

Ida L. Boone engaged in an educational ministry that other Presbyterian women had commenced elsewhere in the Southwest as early as 1867. She represented locally what her denominational sisters had developed earlier in New Mexico and southern Colorado.[48] Boone, however, joined a distinctive local company when she commenced her labors in Los Angeles. A notable group of the town's women had dedicated themselves to religious outreach, in their service of racial minorities. Miss Boone and her mother stood alongside the Sisters of Charity, who nursed and taught local Indians, and those women of the American Missionary Association, who crossed the continent to instruct the Chinese.

Evangelization among Hispanics involved two other churches in limited ministry to the Spanish-speaking in Los Angeles. The Southern California Annual Conference of the Northern Methodists appointed a committee, in 1879, to investigate the feasibility of such outreach. The report the following year noted that Mr. and Mrs. Antonio Diaz were already at work. They spearheaded the mission of the Fort Street Church, which claimed some eighty new members. In 1881, the congregation underwrote the rent and part of the missioner's stipend for a chapel and Sunday school, on Rose Street. The district's presiding elder announced that this proselytization "continues efficient and a blessing. Many have renounced Roman Catholicism under the labors of the missionary."[49]

[47] Ida L. Boone entry, in "Who's Who in Presbyterian Missions" file, POHP; and Brackenridge and García-Treto, *Iglesia Presbiteriana*, pp. 85–86. The work of Presbyterian women in the home missions began in 1867, in New Mexico. That group and the 1878 Women's Executive Committee of Home Missions of the Presbyterian Church are described in Florence Hayes, *Daughters of Dorcas: The Story of the Work of Women for Home Missions Since 1802* (New York: Board of National Missions, Presbyterian Church of the U. S. A., 1952), pp. 54, 76; and Drury, *Presbyterian Panorama*, p. 200.

[48] Randi Jones Walker provides an excellent description of the Presbyterian and other Protestant schools in her study, "Religion in the Sangre de Cristos: Factors in the Growth and Decline of the Hispanic Protestant Churches in New Mexico and Southern Colorado" (Ph.D. dissertation, School of Religion, Claremont, 1983). See also Ruth Barber and Edith Agnew's specifically denominational study, *Sowers Went Forth: The Story of Presbyterian Missions in New Mexico and Southern Colorado* (Albuquerque, New Mexico: Menaul Historical Library of the Southwest, 1981).

[49] *Minutes*, Southern California Annual Conference (1881), p. 33; and Edward Drewry Jervey, *History of Methodism in Southern California and Arizona*, (Nashville, Ten-

Methodist prospects dimmed considerably in 1882, when Mr. and Mrs. Diaz abandoned the church of Wesley for that of Knox. The annual report noted that the incumbent at the Rose Street chapel was "only a layman, without ministerial training or standing." The district leader went on to issue two urgent appeals. From the bishop, he sought a cleric conversant in Spanish, and from the Board of Missions, he requested the funds to pay that recruit a salary of three thousand dollars. A new church building, he concluded, was available on Rose at First Street; all that was lacking was the person to staff the position.[50]

When a suitable person could not be found to undertake this work, the mission to Hispanics languished. Not until 1898 would this evangelical outreach resume, and then under the auspices of a different Northern Methodist congregation. By way of comparison, this denomination proved highly successful in its efforts among German immigrants in Los Angeles. By 1885, the German mission was the spiritual home to some eighty-four adults, while nearly an equal number of children attended the Sabbath school. A full-time pastor, resident in the parsonage attached to the church, reported to a presiding elder of the designated "German District" of the annual conference.[51]

The contrast in Methodist Episcopal results among Hispanics and Germans derived largely from dissimilar traditions of church affiliation. Hispanics were long attached to Roman Catholicism and had to be won away from an ancient allegiance to that faith. Migrating Germans brought their Methodist membership with them, or at least a Reformation heritage. In Los Angeles, they also were relatively prosperous and retained ministers without dependence upon other agencies of the denomination. Evangelization of the Spanish-speaking populace, however, was a more truly missionary endeavor, for which Methodism was not yet adequately prepared.

Limited evidence suggests the outlines of the Congregationalists' outreach to their Hispanic neighbors in Los Angeles. Sometime in 1883, this denomination established two missions, one on Chavez

---

nessee: Historical Society of the Southern California–Arizona Conference, 1960), p. 91.

[50] *Minutes*, Southern California Annual Conference, (1882), pp. 22, 33.

[51] Wilson, *History of Los Angeles County*, p. 120; and *Minutes*, Southern California Annual Conference (1885), pp. 53, 64.

Street at Railroad Street, southeast of the plaza, and another station on Sainsevain Street. Both structures were the sites of Congregationalist Sunday schools.[52] During the week, these facilities also housed the city's pioneer kindergartens, which Caroline Seymour Severance and other women initiated, in 1884.[53] In that same year, the Railroad Street Mission expanded operations as the Third Congregational Church of Los Angeles, with seventeen charter members.

Aside from the foundation of these missions, scant information survives regarding the Congregationalist proselytization among Hispanics prior to 1897. In that year, Reverend Alden Case returned from overseas missionary duties and established an interdenominational Protestant society for evangelization of the Spanish-speaking. No other church, however, developed an effective ministry to this people prior to 1900. As with the missions to the Chinese, treated in the following chapter, local communions only gradually obtained qualified personnel and the financial wherewithal to sustain such demanding work. Frequently lacking interest in such mission work, many pioneer clerics pinned their hopes for the growth of Protestantism on the arrival of "a new class of people settling here," godly Americans whom the ministers considered "the better class."[54]

Demographic factors long constituted the crucial ministerial challenge confronting pioneer pastors and congregants in Los Angeles. Their respective responses initiated the evolution of regionally distinct church practices and policy. Observant preachers quickly recognized that southern California was like no other territory they had known. No communion could escape the difficulties that effective ministry entailed among such polyglot parishioners.

Roman Catholics and Protestants alike turned their attention in varying degrees to the needs of the Hispanic population. Californios and Mexican immigrants discovered, however, that European-born

[52] *Manual of the First Congregational Church of Los Angeles, Cal.* (Los Angeles: First Congregational Church, 1886), pp. 10–11.

[53] Severance, a Unitarian, led these women in forming the Los Angeles Free Kindergarten Association. This organization eventually persuaded the city school officials to adopt this level of juvenile education throughout their system. Los Angeles *Times*, 9 September and 8 October 1884.

[54] Letter, Reverend Alexander Parker to "Bro. [A. Huntington] Clapp," 18 December 1866, Los Angeles, Microfilm #C-B 393, reel 3, of American Home Mission Society file, "California, 1866, A-P, sec. 1"; BL.

clerics evinced scant regard for local religious customs. Synodal decrees explicitly attacked certain traditional practices. Much of the religiosity of Hispanics became an increasingly familial and devotional matter, distinct from the formal dictates of institutional Roman Catholicism. The significant distance between Hispanics and the formal structures of the church of their birth is obvious in the inability of the clergy to attract even one Los Angeles male Hispanic to seek priestly ordination between 1850 and 1885.

While many of the Spanish-speaking remained culturally committed to the Roman faith, others were receptive to the message of Reformed Christianity. Protestant evangelization among Hispanics in this era was the beginning of what has proven to be a continuing pattern. Language and finance were crucial considerations. Racial prejudice was a further factor, given the tradition of Anglo-American bias directed against "people of color," as well as against the Church of Rome. During the period under study, Protestant missionizing among Hispanics lagged behind work with the Chinese, but this situation later reversed itself in the twentieth century, with the influx of population from Mexico.[55]

The demands of ministry to the Hispanics surpassed the clerical personnel available and prompted recourse to less conventional approaches. Roman Catholic women began service to Indians and Hispanics, with the Sisters of Charity performing a variety of services ranging from nursing to education. Protestant women assumed such roles at a much later date. Ida L. Boone's Hispanic mission school was among the early efforts of direct outreach by women of the Reformation churches. Such organized activity extended the role of women in religious institutions, in an era when increasing numbers of their sisters were demanding fuller equality and legal rights.

Women became increasingly engaged in both direct and indirect evangelization, works that could also be termed "formal" and "informal" ministries. As in so many settlements elsewhere, women taught in both private and Sabbath schools, imparting doctrine to the young.

---

[55] Clifford L. Holland investigated this growth in Protestant ministry to the Spanish speaking in his study previously cited, *The Religious Dimension in Hispanic Los Angeles*, pp. 71–80, 199–209. See also Felix Liu, "A Comparative Study of Selected Chinese Churches in Los Angeles County" (Ph.D. dissertation, Fuller Theological Seminary, Pasadena, 1981).

Characteristic of the Southwest, however, were the women's mission schools for Hispanics and Indian children, such as the 1883 Presbyterian endeavor in Los Angeles. More indirect evangelization occurred in settings where goals other than conversion were primary. The following chapter describes how Congregationalist women engaged in English-language instruction. These women's projects provided their churches with both versatility and flexibility in ministerial outreach, in times and places where clergy were in short supply.

The cultures and peoples served, the means of evangelization, and the particular groups engaged in ministerial outreach combine to set Los Angeles apart as a unique religious frontier. The Hispanic heritage provided the religious background for this aspect of the community's distinctively Southwestern character. Language initially offered a major challenge, but even with Spanish-speaking clergy, cultural differences were not easily or readily bridged in the churches and synagogues. The Catalonian clergy were uninterested in Mexican-derived Roman Catholicism, while American Protestants exhibited slight interest in learning the Spanish language. The accommodations of prospering pioneer Jews led some to new forms of worship and others away from their faith.

The recourse to women in ministry came early and broadened steadily over the period under study. They provided the denominations with the flexibility to meet diverse needs and to respond to regionally specific problems. Given the settlement's racial and ethnic pluralism, the requisite breadth of ministry and array of missionaries distinguished this community from any frontier outside the Southwest. This can be seen in the most extensive Protestant proselytism undertaken in the period. Not only was the mission to the Chinese in Los Angeles religiously daunting, but it was commenced in 1871, in a period of violent anti-Asian racism. Success in preaching the Gospel required not only trained personnel and innovative techniques, but the evangelizers needed the further quality of raw courage.

14

14. Joseph Newmark, with great-grand-daughter Rose Loeb, granddaughter Estelle Newmark Loeb, and daughter Sarah New-mark Newmark. Joseph Newmark (1799–1881) served as a lay rabbi in Los Angeles and then as the founding president of Congregation B'nai B'rith, now known as Wilshire Boulevard Temple. (Seaver Center for Western History Research, Los Angeles County Museum of Natural History.)

15. Rabbi Abraham Wolf Edelman (1832–1907), first rabbi of Congregation B'nai B'rith, now known as the Wilshire Boulevard Temple. Emigrating from his native Poland, Edelman worked in San Francisco before accepting the invitation from the Los Angeles congregation in 1862. He served until 1885, working to build bridges of understanding between his congregation and the Christian communions in Los Angeles. (Seaver Center for Western History Research, Los Angeles County Museum of Natural History.)

15

16

17

16. Synagogue of Congregation B'nai B'rith, on the east side of Fort (Broadway) Street between Second and Third Streets. Completed in 1873, Angelenos of all faiths participated in the fund raising activities to finance this structure designed by pioneer Los Angeles architect Ezra F. Kysor. The building was razed in 1896, though pieces of its ornamental stonework are preserved by the congregation, now known as Wilshire Boulevard Temple.

Note the unusual five-pointed star on the pinnacle of the facade. (Security Pacific Collection/Los Angeles Public Library.)

17. Interior of Congregation B'nai B'rith's synagogue, decorated with a floral canopy for the double-wedding ceremony of Jennette Lazard and Lewis Lewen, and Ella Newmark and Emil Seligman in 1885. Note the floral ship in the foreground, as well as the carpenter-gothic ark for the scrolls of the Torah in the background.

(Seaver Center for Western History Research, Los Angeles County Museum of Natural History.)

18. Entrance to a "Joss House" in the Chinese quarter of Los Angeles, possibly on Apablasa Street, circa 1895. The ornamentation suggests that this is a permanent temple structure. The panel to the right of the doorway carries a date of 1889, suggesting that the building was erected in that year. To the left is a tablet wishing the blessings of the gods on all visitors. Note the electric light bulbs over the doorway.

The large figures on either side of the temple represent the guardian deities of the temple. The paper inscriptions on the front posts announce that the door of good fortune is always open (left), and visitors ought to show proper respect when entering (right). (Courtesy of the Southwest Museum, Los Angeles. Photo #15740)

19

20

19. A shrine honoring the Legendary Heroes from the era of Chinese history known as the Three Kingdoms. From the left, the four lower figures represent ancient heroes who vowed loyalty to one another as virtual brothers. Second from the left is the image of the black-faced Chung Fei, a hot tempered fighter; and next to him is the red-faced, warm-hearted Kuan Kong, a highly popular deity. These figures were particularly important to Chinese from the Quandong region of China. Seated above is Lao Pei, while below him are two very small figures of ancient sages.

In the foreground are four large bowls for burning sticks of incense (joss). The vase on the far left holds *ch'ien* sticks with which supplicants consulted the gods for advice about decisions in their lives. (California Historical Society/Ticor Title Insurance, Los Angeles, Department of Special Collections, University of Southern California Library.)

20. A simple outdoor shrine in the Chinese quarter, decorated possibly for the lunar new year. Those who prayed here performed the *kow tow,* presented food for gods, and used the brick oven on the right to burn paper money for the benefit of deceased relatives. However, it is interesting that the traditional table for the offerings of food is not present.

The top-most banner proclaims a common greeting in Mandarin: "Prosperous age and a year of plenty." The lower scrolls read: "Wish you a thousand years" and carved in wood, "Blessing me with peace and health" and "Blessing my fellow members" [of my district association]. Similar tablets can still be found in the 1891 Kong Chow Temple now relocated on North Broadway in Los Angeles.

The side tablets proclaim belief in the power of the gods to bless people with prosperity even from afar. (California Historical Society/Ticor Title Insurance, Los Angeles, Department of Special Collections, University of Southern California Library.)

21. Congregationalist Mission to the Chinese, circa 1895. The man dressed in western clothing is probably Reverend Ng Poon Chew, who ministered to fellow Chinese in Los Angeles from 1894 to 1898, before relocating to San Francisco where he published a daily newspaper, the *Shung Sai Yat Po.*

The banner to the left of the men has the text for the Lord's Prayer, while the banner immediately behind the group is a poem, "Christianity is the light in the morning, and all people on earth come to worship." On the table are hymnals and Chinese language texts of the Bible. (California Historical Society/Ticor Title Insurance, Los Angeles, Department of Special Collections, University of Southern California Library.)

22

23

22. Caroline Maria Seymour Severance,
(1820–1914), reformer and pioneer of the
woman's club movement, and friend of
Lucy Stone, Julia Ward Howe, Ralph
Waldo Emerson, and William Lloyd Garrison. Severance championed women's rights
and organized the First Unitarian Church,
the Women's Club of Los Angeles, the Los
Angeles Free Kindergarten Society, the Los
Angeles Woman's Club and its successor,
the Friday Morning Club. (Security Pacific
Collection/Los Angeles Public Library.)

23. Biddy Mason, (1818–1891), one of the
principal founders of the First African
Methodist Episcopal Church in 1869. Born
in the South (probably in Georgia) and
brought to California by her owners in
1851, Mason successfully sued for the freedom of herself and thirteen others in 1856.
She supported herself as a nurse and midwife, and her philanthropy gained for her a
lasting reputation. (Seaver Center for Western History Research, Los Angeles County
Museum of Natural History.)

24

25

24. Mary Barnes Widney (1844–1924) was long active in the Fort Street Methodist Episcopal Church and a variety of community projects, including the Flower Festival Society, the Woman's Exchange, and the Los Angeles Free Kindergarten Society. Her mother, Sarah Johnston Barnes, chronicled life in the household of Mary and her husband, Robert M. Widney, prominent as a jurist, real estate developer, and one of the founders of the University of Southern California. (Reproduced by permission of the Huntington Library, San Marino, California.)

25. Fort Street Methodist Episcopal Church in the 1880s, located on the west side of Fort Street (now Broadway), between Third and Fourth Streets. The Northern Methodists had erected the brick building to the right of the church for their meeting place in 1867–1869. (Security Pacific Collection/Los Angeles Public Library.)

26

26. A view looking east on Second Street
from Hill Street in 1880. From left to right,
the religious structures include Trinity
Southern Methodist church; the baroque-
style cathedral of St. Vibiana at Second and
Main Streets; the First Presbyterian church
at Second and Fort (now Broadway); and
the 1873 brick synagogue of Congregation
B'nai B'rith. In the distance are the twin
towers of the depot of the Los Angeles
and Independence railroad. (Seaver Center
for Western History Research, Los Angeles
County Museum of Natural History.)

6

EVANGELIZATION OF THE CHINESE

From the debarkation of the first Chinese in San Francisco, in the early 1850s, various Christian communions sought them out as converts. The Presbyterians took a commanding lead in this ministry and gradually followed the Chinese to other communities throughout the state. Initiating this ministry in San Francisco, in November of 1852, Reverend William Speer was the first of three Presbyterian divines to return from China to work among the Chinese in the United States. Speer's successor, in 1857, was Reverend August Ward Loomis, with his wife. Loomis gained an assistant in 1870, Reverend Ira Condit, who had served a missionary tour in Guangzhou (Canton) and had learned to speak fluent Cantonese. Because so many of the Chinese in California hailed from Guangzhou, Condit was soon traversing the state to preach the Gospel message to them.[1]

Few clerics in the mid-nineteenth century exceeded these Presbyterian clergymen in their preparation for this difficult ministry and in the opposition they faced. Other clerics, for example, initially had to resort to the use of interpreters to express their message. Limited finances repeatedly plagued clergy of all denominations who served in California; ministry to the Chinese involved two further difficulties. The prejudice of their fellow Americans toward the Chinese

---

[1] Gunther Barth, *Bitter Strength: A History of the Chinese in the United States, 1850–1870* (Cambridge: Harvard University Press, 1964), pp. 159, 167; Ira M. Condit, *The Chinaman as We See Him and Fifty Years of Work for Him* (Chicago: Fleming H. Revell, 1900), pp. 90, 116; and Wesley S. Woo, "Protestant Work Among the Chinese in the San Francisco Bay Area, 1850–1920" (Ph.D. dissertation, Graduate Theological Union, Berkeley, 1983), pp. 33–45.

bedeviled the ministers in every community where they labored. The ministers also pursued a set of ethnocentrically biased goals, which further handicapped their efforts. Convinced of the superiority of United States culture and Protestant Christianity, the missionaries were determined both to acculturate and to convert their Asian audiences.

Even the sympathetic Condit described Chinese religious practices with such pejorative terms as "idolatry," "heathen worship," and "debasing superstitions."[2] American evangelists, evincing scant regard for ancient Chinese customs, did not consider adapting or modifying their religious message out of respect for Chinese sensibilities. For their part, many of the intended converts considered themselves only temporary residents of Gum San, the "Golden Mountain," as they termed California. Chinese sojourners sought to earn and save money, pay their debts, and then return as rapidly as possible to their native land. This outlook, along with the violence they suffered in a professedly Christian nation, led most Chinese to reject the culture and values they encountered in their strange host country, including its religion.[3]

Throughout the state, many in the Chinese communities went so far as to reject those of their countrymen who embraced Christianity and Western ways. Most offensive were those converts who cut their queues, adopted Western hair styles, wore Western clothes, and began to speak English. Reverend Condit documented the harassment that members of his flocks endured for their newfound faith in American trappings.[4] Despite the Chinese resistance to Christianity and what it represented culturally, Presbyterian and other Protestant Christians persisted in efforts to win new adherents. The growing Chinese population in Los Angeles attracted Condit and other missionaries to journey southward.

The 1860 federal census reported only eleven Chinese in the entire

---

[2] Condit, *The Chinaman as We See Him*, pp. 49, 50, 53.

[3] Shin-Shan Henry Tsai, *The Chinese Experience in America* (Bloomington: Indiana University Press, 1986), pp. 33–35; Barth, *Bitter Strength*, pp. 167–68; Raymond Lou, "The Chinese American Community of Los Angeles, 1870–1900: A Case of Resistance, Organization, and Participation" (Ph.D. dissertation, University of California, Irvine, 1982), p. 264.

[4] Condit, *The Chinaman*, pp. 157–61; and Lou, "Chinese American Community," p. 267.

county, though the editor of the Los Angeles *Star* closely watched any increase in those numbers.[5] In April 1861, the newspaper reported that twenty-one men and eight women worked in numerous kitchens or in some five wash houses in town. Another group, with seven or eight women included, arrived two months later and attracted notice as a new "invoice of Celestials." A Chinese merchant opened a store in mid-June, and the first manifestations of anti-Asian prejudice appeared soon after.[6] The editor grumbled, in the 17 August 1861 issue, about the "degraded of the almond eyed family." The community already had more than enough of the "sub-stratum of the human family" without swelling these ranks with the "outcasts of the Flowery Kingdom."

According to federal census enumerators, in 1870 there were 234 Chinese in the local area.[7] This growth had attracted the attention of members of the First Congregational Church, then under the pastorate of Reverend Isaac W. Atherton. No religious society had yet sought to minister to the local Chinese. In February of 1871, members of the parish initiated a Sunday-evening language school, in the white clapboard meetinghouse on New High Street.[8] Regardless of its ethnocentric motivations, this project's basic humanitarian character stood in stark contrast to the gross prejudice that the Chinese long endured in the community.

The Los Angeles *Star* had printed a steady stream of biased, anti-Asian information, which dwelled upon crime and violence involving the Chinese. For example, such reports appeared in this journal on 31 January, 16 and 25 February, and 8 and 10 March 1871. The editor voiced the approving though racist and condescending sentiments of many Angelenos, when he described the first month's progress of the Congregationalist class. "The Heathen Chinee [*sic*] Sunday school suits John Celestial to a dot; he eats of the tree of knowledge without money and without price, and swears it is cheaper than rice, if not

---

[5] Thomas W. Chinn, Mark Lai, and Philip P. Choy, *A History of the Chinese in California: A Syllabus* (San Francisco: Chinese Historical Society of America, 1969), p. 21. The Los Angeles *Star*, under the date of 24 January 1857, had noted the occurrence of the Chinese New Year, commenting that the three Chinese in town had celebrated in an appropriate manner.

[6] Los Angeles *Star*, 27 April, 8 June, 15 June 1861.

[7] Chinn et al., *Chinese in California*, p. 21.

[8] Los Angeles *Star*, 1 February 1871.

so fattening."[9] The strength of such feelings found full expression in an eruption of violence, later that same year. Misinformation fueled the flames of local bigotry, and a firestorm of hatred engulfed the unfortunate Chinese.

Early in October 1871, two rival societies, the Nin Yung and the Hong Chow associations, were locked in a dispute over the possession of a woman named Ya Hit.[10] The Nin Yung members had held her in bondage as a prostitute, until their rivals abducted her and forced Ya Hit to marry one of the Hong Chow group. On 23 and 24 October, hostilities commenced, with bullets flying in their quarter of town. This was in the infamous, block-long "Nigger Alley," the Calle de los Negros, where the Chinese inhabited aging adobe buildings, south of the plaza. One death resulted, which prompted the late-afternoon intervention of local law-enforcement authorities. Apparently confusing the members of the opposing factions, the first officers on the scene neglected the cries for help from the leader of the Nin Yung association.

The initial ineptitude of the deputies provoked renewed gunfire from the Chinese and resulted in the death of an assisting citizen, Robert Thompson, and the wounding of one of the police, Jesús Bilderrain. The crowd attracted by the gunfire soon turned into a mob of several hundred men, who returned the fire of the barricaded Chinese. At this point the mayor and the local police vanished. In time, the members of the mob rushed the buildings, dragged out and shot the inhabitants, and then seized any Chinese in the area and hung them from verandas and a nearby corral gate. Various citizens attempted to halt the slaughter, but the orgy of killing continued into the night, unabated by local officials.[11]

[9] Los Angeles *Star*, 28 March 1871.

[10] The associations were the Los Angeles branches of San Francisco–based Chinese social institutions. These organizations functioned as mutual aid societies and exercised great influence within local Asian communities. They also served to mediate Chinese interaction with the Anglo-American populace, who frequently confused these associations with more criminally oriented groups involved in gambling, prostitution, opium dens, and labor racketeering. See Lou, "Chinese American Community," pp. 25–26; Tsai, *Chinese Experience in America*, pp. 41–42; and Chinn, et al., *History of the Chinese in California*, pp. 66–67.

[11] This summation is drawn from Paul M. De Falla, "Lantern in the Western Sky," Historical Society of Southern California *Quarterly*, XLII (March and June 1960), pp. 67–86, 161–185. Other sources include Wilson, *History of Los Angeles County*, pp. 84–85; the account of a participant, C.P. Dorland, "Chinese Massacre at Los Angeles,"

The coroner convened a jury two days later, which viewed the bodies, heard the testimony of witnesses, and charged eight men with participation in the riot and subsequent looting. The inquest members also urged the county grand jury to indict those responsible for the murder of eighteen Chinese, including a fourteen-year old boy. The authorities charged between 100 and 150 alleged rioters. The grand jury then indicted an unspecified number of individuals from this roster, supplied by the coroner's jury. The mysterious destruction of these records in later years complicates a more complete examination of the proceedings. It is known that, of the eleven men who eventually stood trial, nine were convicted and served short prison terms, before the State Supreme Court released them on a procedural technicality.[12]

The press had listed only eleven men known to have been "instrumental in restoring order" on that riotous autumn evening. Several were prominent members of the laity in the community's handful of churches. Colonel George H. Smith, Cameron E. Thom, S.B. Caswell, and H.C. Austin were all affiliated with St. Athanasius Episcopal parish. Judge Robert M. Widney, of the Fort Street Northern Methodist Church, also presided at the trial of the accused murderers.[13] Each man had risked life and limb endeavoring to restore order or to rescue the victims from the hands of the mob.

The nature and extent of this violence offers a valuable insight into the anti-Asian prejudice long prevalent in wide segments of the Los Angeles population. During the riot, certain residents had hidden Chinese cooks and domestics in their homes, at considerable risk to themselves, and the attempt, two years later, to form an anti-Coolie club received a cool local response. Nonetheless, the prejudice that smoldered in town in 1873 soon flamed anew. Upwards of three

---

Historical Society at Southern California *Annual Publication*, III, Part II (1894), pp. 22–26; and Lou, "Chinese American Community," pp. 24–25.

[12] The district attorney, Cameron E. Thom, had prosecuted the eleven men for one specific murder, that of Doctor Chien Lee Tong, who had been shot through the mouth and then hanged. Upon appeal of conviction, the State Supreme Court ruled, on 21 May 1873, that the grand jury indictment had failed to allege that Chien had actually been murdered. The men in the state prison were therefore ordered released. De Falla, "Lantern in the Western Sky," part two, pp. 173–175, 178, 184; and Los Angeles *Star*, 28 October 1871.

[13] Los Angeles *Star*, 28 October 1871.

hundred Angelenos formed an "Anti-Coolie" Club in May of 1876 and circulated petitions seeking Congressional restriction of Chinese immigration to the United States. This society was professedly non-violent, but its general purpose manifested the same spirit of racial antagonism that had disgraced the community in 1871.[14]

Church leaders appear to have been cautiously silent through these years, at least as far as can be seen in their surviving public statements. Denunciations of violence had appeared, but few preachers advocated toleration or respect for the Asians in their midst. The problem, evidently, was Chinese in origin, not Christian. The "Methodist Conference" of the state responded to the 1871 riot by establishing a fund for "mission work" in Los Angeles.[15] Three other Protestant churches initiated endeavors on behalf of the Chinese, by 1876. Similar to other evangelical efforts throughout the state, Christians in these operations attempted to win the Chinese to the culture and religion of their sometimes bloody host country.

The Congregationalists, relying largely upon female parishioners to staff their program, had pioneered language instruction, six months prior to the riot. In February of 1871, these teachers offered instruction in English grammar and conversation; religion was not a formal part of the curriculum. Evincing his usual invective, the editor of the Los Angeles *Star* reported this effort to improve "the Heathens in our midst." In the following year, the church obtained the services of a volunteer teacher, who dedicated herself to this mission of education. Miss Agnes McCormick commenced her lessons at the meetinghouse in August 1872 and remained at this post for approximately nine months.[16]

McCormick arrived in Los Angeles in response to an appeal from the American Missionary Association for teachers desirous of working amongst the Chinese. Famed for their Freedman's Schools in the post-bellum South, members of the Association had voted to undertake evangelization of the Chinese in the United States, at their annual meeting in 1869.[17] Reverend John Kimball, and later Rev-

---

[14] William R. Lockyear, "The Celestials and the Angels: A Study of the Anti-Chinese Movement in Los Angeles to 1882," Historical Society of Southern California *Quarterly*, XLII (September 1960), p. 245.

[15] Wilson, *History of Los Angeles County*, p. 85.

[16] Los Angeles *Express*, 26 June 1873.

[17] *Annual Report*, American Missionary Association (1872), pp. 74–75. Regarding

erend William C. Pond, placed and supervised the volunteer teachers in California. Work commenced in Los Angeles in the summer of 1872 and continued until the society transferred sponsorship of the school to the Presbyterians, around 1875. The association engaged three women, who successively experienced discouraging church assistance, limited attendance, and deep-seated prejudice toward the Chinese.

The pioneer teacher, Agnes McCormick, hailed from Winona, Minnesota, and apparently arrived with no previous experience among the Chinese. She described her first month's arduous work as follows:

> I go to their [the Chinese] shops and beg them to go with me; sometimes [I] meet them on the street and insist upon their coming in to see the school, if they can not stay. They promise to come when they have time. They are *very* industrious, and their ruling motive is love of money. I have found it utterly impossible to establish a day-school. I can not get one to come.[18]

Her comments proved to be very accurate predictions of the approach that both of her successors would follow, in later years. In July of 1873, McCormick withdrew and Miss M.M. Woodbridge arrived to continue classes. The third teacher was Miss Mary P. Stewart, who taught in the school from the fall of 1873 until sometime in 1876.[19]

All three of these instructors were single Christian women, who relocated from elsewhere in the nation. Little is known about any of them prior to their arrivals in the Southwest or subsequent to their departures. The Minnesotan, McCormick, affiliated with the First Congregational Church in town, in November 1872. Miss Wood-

---

the history of this society, see "History of the American Missionary Association, with Facts and Anecdotes Illustrating Its Work in the South" (rev. ed., New York: American Missionary Association, 1874). This pamphlet reported that in 1867 the organization had 528 teachers and missionaries in diverse fields; see pp. 50–51.

[18] *Annual Report*, American Missionary Association (1872), p. 74.

[19] Letter, Mary P. Stewart to Reverend E.M. Cravath [Executive Secretary of the American Missionary Association], 22 October 1873, Los Angeles, found on Roll 1, microfilm of the "California-Colorado" correspondence files, American Missionary Association Manuscripts, Amistad Research Center, Tulane University, New Orleans, Louisiana; hereafter cited as CA-CO, AMA.

bridge hailed from Marietta, Ohio, and worshipped while in Los Angeles with the Episcopalians. Mary P. Stewart is the only one of the three who had any previous experience with the Chinese. She had left Vermont for a similar mission school in Portland, Oregon, one year before her arrival in southern California. Stewart later remained at her Los Angeles post when the American Missionary Association retired from the field, in favor of the Presbyterians.[20]

Each of the three women taught the weekly evening school for Chinese men, which initially met at the First Congregational Church, on New High street. Attendance at these classes never surpassed twenty-six, and sank as low as six students. McCormick and Stewart both extended their efforts to language instruction of Chinese women. Initial reactions to McCormick's invitation provoked a storm among Chinese men, who believed it unseemly for respectable women to appear in public. This unexpected controversy evidently greatly dispirited Miss McCormick and led to her resignation from the school, in June of 1873. Learning from this episode, Stewart resumed female education, but met with the twelve women in their homes, in the Chinese quarter of town, southeast of the plaza.[21]

Approximately two years later, Miss Stewart began both to evangelize in earnest and to instruct the growing numbers of Chinese children. With other volunteers, she further initiated referrals for employment through a placement service for domestics.[22] This agency assisted Chinese workers who could find only menial labor, arranged through individuals in their own associations. A church-sponsored office enabled a Chinese worker to move outside of the highly regulated society transplanted from China, which allowed for little upward economic mobility. New opportunities were available to individuals otherwise restricted to contracted manual labor.

Language classes had first met in the Congregationalist church, but

[20] *American Missionary*, XVI (June 1872), p. 247; XVII (September 1873), p. 201; XVIII (April 1874), p. 83; XIX (February 1875), p. 32; and XX (February 1876), p. 31, and (November 1876), p. 249. See also *Manual* (Los Angeles: First Congregational Church, June, 1886), p. 27; and *Annual Report*, American Missionary Association (1872), p. 74.

[21] Letters, Mary P. Stewart to Reverend E.M. Cravath, 22 October 1873, Los Angeles, and 6 November 1873, Los Angeles; and Stewart to Gen[eral] C.H. Howard, 19 November 1873, Los Angeles; CA-CO, AMA.

[22] Los Angeles *Express*, 26 June 1873; and Lou, "Chinese American Community," pp. 255–56.

later moved to the schoolhouse that during the week served as the public school for black children.[23] The conditions under which the women operated are quite evident in their letters to the superiors of the mission society. Woodbridge described the plain, whitewashed room, with its borrowed furniture:

> The walls are literally covered with printed cards of Scripture texts and hymns, and a large map of the United States, and ornamented with evergreens, sea mosses, flowers, flags, etc. A little clock ticks on a shelf near the organ, and everything I can contrive has been done to make the room respectably clean and attractive.[24]

She also explained that a policeman stood at her door during each class session, because "*some* Irishmen (haters of the Chinese) and the Hoodlums" threatened to repeat an attack made on the students and herself in July 1873.

None of the three women received much help from residents in town, even from members of the churches. Woodbridge had to hire three women assistants and pay from her own pocket whatever part of their salaries the missionary association could not afford.[25] Stewart approached both the Northern Methodists and Congregationalists, but discovered that "people manifest little interest in the Chinese."[26] When her supervisor, Reverend William Pond, queried the Congregationalist pastor about the school, he also received a startlingly candid response. This divine wrote that his denomination was "utterly unable to help," because "we are lean and poor & starved for means" to maintain their own parish. He went so far as to comment, "It seems a great mistake that she [Miss Stewart] ever came here, but it is useless to speak of that now."[27]

Supervisor Pond soon faced difficult decisions, when the finances of the American Missionary Association dwindled sharply in the

[23] Letter, Stewart to Cravath, 6 November 1873, Los Angeles; CA-CO, AMA.
[24] Letter of 4 August 1873, reprinted in *American Missionary*, XVII (October 1873), p. 225.
[25] Letters, M.M. Woodbridge to Gen[eral Charles] Howard, 10 September 1873, San Francisco, and 20 September, 1873, San Francisco; CA-CO AMA.
[26] Letter, Stewart to Cravath, 9 February 1874, Los Angeles; CA-CO, AMA.
[27] Letter, D.T. Packard to "Bro. [William C.] Pond," 17 April [1874], Los Angeles; CA-CO, AMA.

course of an economic depression gripping the nation. He initially forestalled the suspension of operations in Los Angeles, out of a sense of obligation to Stewart, who had crossed the continent at the association's invitation.[28] Pond closed the Los Angeles school for several "vacations," in 1874. Despite this and other attempts at retrenchment, Pond regretfully terminated instruction in December 1874.[29] Stewart apparently continued in Los Angeles and resumed her work at some time in 1875, though records are incomplete. Some type of education continued under her care, which the American Missionary Association transferred to Presbyterian colleagues, in mid-1876.[30]

Baptist street preaching offered a stark contrast to the broader approach the Congregationalists had given to their missionary work. Reverend John Francis and a Chinese assistant had began working in San Francisco, in 1870. Because the minister spoke no dialect of Chinese, he relied upon his companion for running translations as he spoke. Not until 1874 did Francis turn his eyes toward Los Angeles. In September of that year, the preacher and his assistant, Lee Kee, held forth from the sidewalk in front of the Temple Block in Los Angeles and attracted the notice of passersby and the local press.[31]

Several factors contributed to the disappointing results of these evangelical exhortations of Reverend Francis and his assistant. Local Baptists were only that month organizing their first congregation in Los Angeles. They invited "Brother Lee Kee" to address their initial meeting, on the sixth of September, and then wished him well.[32] Two weeks later, "See Key" [sic] preached alone, in the Chinese section of town, in a final appeal to his countrymen.[33] Evangelization of the Chinese, however, was known to be a lengthy and frustrating ministry. Seldom were there more than a few converts gained, and these came slowly and with much labor. The limited number of

[28] Letter, Pond to Cravath, 30 April 1874, San Francisco; CA-CO, AMA.

[29] Letters, Pond to "Ex[ecutive] Com[mittee], A[merican] M[issionary] A[ssociation], 11 June 1874, San Francisco, and to Cravath, 16 December 1874, San Francisco; CA-CO, AMA.

[30] The *Directory for Los Angeles* for 1875 lists Stewart's Chinese school, but with the annotation "Attendance irregular" (Los Angeles: Mirror Book and Job Printing, 1875), p. 82; see also letter, William C. Pond to Reverend E.M. Strieby, D.D., 24 August 1882, San Francisco; CA-CO, AMA.

[31] Los Angeles *Express*, 1, 5, 7 September 1874.

[32] "Official Records," vol. I, p. 1, First Baptist Church, Los Angeles, California.

[33] Los Angeles *Evening Express*, 19 September 1874.

saved souls did not inspire hard-strapped denominations, such as the Baptists, to allocate scarce resources of personnel or finances for such a missionary program.

Reverend Francis also limited his message to explicitly spiritual and Gospel-oriented matters and neglected the living and working conditions of the local Chinese. The Congregationalists, on the other hand, had recognized the importance of the more mundane, yet immediate, temporal concerns of their followers. The inability of Francis to converse directly with his audience in their native tongue further emphasized the distance between the Christian missionary and his Chinese listeners. Willingly or not, the Baptist preacher clearly communicated the cultural isolation of his faith from the workaday realities of Asian life.[34]

Reverend Ira M. Condit, the Presbyterian, came preaching a more socially informed message, in January 1876, during a brief visit among the seaside Chinese, at San Pedro. He returned with his wife and children in April of that year, at the request of various Angelenos and commenced a more permanent "South Coast Chinese Mission."[35] This endeavor combined existing local work with an expanded model of evangelization, as in San Francisco. The resultant Presbyterian Mission in Los Angeles capitalized upon the five years' work of the teachers of the American Missionary Association. In the meantime, sixty-four English-language students continued under the charge of the veteran Miss Mary P. Stewart, who remained at her teaching post for approximately one year.[36]

The following months were a busy time for the energetic Condit. He immediately utilized $1,500 of his own funds to purchase a lot on Wilmington Street, near First, and erect a five-room "Branch Mission Church," for worship and instruction. Over one hundred Chinese crowded the chapel, the doorways and windows for the dedication, on 21 May 1876. For the ceremonies that evening, Condit hosted the three local Congregational and Presbyterian ministers, as well as the

---

[34] Local Baptists did not again turn their attention to evangelization of the Chinese until 1896. This outreach resulted in the formation of the First Chinese Baptist Church, in 1903. Ivan C. Ellis, "Baptist Churches of Southern California" (Ph.D. dissertation, Northern Baptist Theological Seminary, Chicago, 1948), p. 219.

[35] Condit, *The Chinaman as We See Him*, p. 156; Lou, "The Chinese American Community," p. 259; *The Pacific*, XXV (21 September 1876), p. 4, and (2 November 1876), p. 4.

[36] *American Missionary*, XX (November, 1876), p. 249; Lou, "Chinese American

choir and members of the First Presbyterian Church.[37] Condit and his wife commenced a night school the next day. These efforts soon bore fruit, when eight Chinese presented themselves for baptism at First Presbyterian Church. At a special meeting, on 30 September 1876, members of the Session of the First Presbyerian Church placed the station "under the care" of their congregation. Three days later, the Session examined the eight candidates for admission and found their principles of faith and doctrine correct. Condit then administered the ordinance of baptism "in their native tongue."[38]

By the following January, Condit reported that he was assisted by his wife, "a native helper" (Shing Chack), and volunteers from "our Christian people" to conduct every week an evening class, three Chinese services, and a Sabbath school.[39] By April 1877, forty-six Chinese were in regular attendance at the mission and had raised sixty dollars toward its operation. The Sunday evening Sabbath school, staffed by First Presbyerian parishioners, counted forty students. Much of this progress can be ascribed to Condit's familiarity with Cantonese, as well as to the involvement of the missionary and his wife in Chinese community affairs. Anglo prejudice and vestiges of Chinese suspicion of Americans regularly challenged the couple in their work, but the cause of their rather abrupt withdrawal from Los Angeles came from another quarter.[40]

Community," p. 259; and Letter, Stewart to Reverend E.M. Cravath, 12 December 1877, Cincinnati, Ohio; CA-CO, AMA. Condit described Stewart's class as a "small dying" school, in a letter to John C. Lowrie [Executive Secretary, Presbyterian Board of Foreign Missions], 1 May 1876, Los Angeles, found in Presbyterian Board of Foreign Mission, Correspondence, 1829–1895, Record Group 31, Box 45, Folder 4, hereafter cited as PBFM; POHP.

[37] Letter, Condit to Lowrie, 22 May 1876, Los Angeles, with an unidentified newspaper clipping of 22 May 1876 describing the chapel dedication, in PBFM, Correspondence, 1829–1895, RG 31, Box 45, folder 4, POHP; Condit, *The Chinaman as We See Him*, p. 156; E.S. Field, "Historical Address," (typescript, 4 February 1894), p. 6, HL.

[38] The eight Chinese were Wong Kwong, Lem Loon, Mo Hing, Lim Shan, Ham Chin, Leung Hong Chung, Lee Foon Shing, and Wong Ark. Minutes, vol. I, p. 37, Session, Minutes and Records, 1874–1879, First Presbyterian Church, Los Angeles, POHP. This church is presently known as the True Light Presbyterian Church.

[39] Letter, Condit to Lowrie, 12 January 1877, Los Angeles, PBFM, Correspondence, 1829–1895, RG 31, Box 45, folder 4, POHP.

[40] *Occident*, XVII (6 September 1876), p. 285; and Lou, "Chinese American Community," p. 259.

A severe economic depression gripped the nation in 1877 and forced officials of the Synod of the Pacific to retrench and consolidate ministries. These budgetary problems coincided with the recommendation of Condit's doctor that he relocate to northern California for his health. Condit transferred to Oakland during the summer of 1877, and the Presbyterian Board of Foreign Missions surrendered the growing mission to the care of the United Presbyterian Church.[41] Disappointed with losing their former missionary, the Chinese converts were soon displeased with the new administration. Both the clergymen this latter denomination assigned to the Los Angeles station were former missionaries in China: H. V. Hoyes and J. C. Nevin. Unspecified yet mounting dissatisfaction over several years led this small band of Chinese Christians to rent rooms elsewhere for their worship and to seek assistance from the First Presbyterian Church, with which they had first associated.[42]

Both the minister of First Church and the officials of the Presbytery of Los Angeles responded to this appeal and negotiated with the denomination's foreign mission board. Officials were evidently impressed that thirty-nine Chinese had affiliated with First Presbyterian Church, Los Angeles, from the time of Condit's initial ministry in 1876 until 1884. The result was permission to form an independent First Chinese Presbyterian Church, in 1884. With renewed determination, this congregation proceeded to raise $1,450 to purchase a lot and to petition the Presbyterian Board for Church Erection for assistance in the construction of a chapel.[43] Presbyterian leaders assured the

[41] Condit was a member of the Presbyterian Church in the United States of America, commonly known as the Presbyterian Church, U.S.A. The United Presbyterian Church organized in 1865, in Iowa, and established a congregation in San Francisco the following year. Growth on the West Coast warranted the foundation of two presbyteries, in 1877. See *The Occident*, XVII (6 September 1876), p. 281. The mission for the Los Angeles Chinese long antedated the denomination's formation of a congregation among Anglo-Americans; that body did not come into existence until 1883. "Minutes" ledger, pp. 1–2, First United Presbyterian Church, Los Angeles, California.

[42] *Minutes*, Synod of the Pacific (1878), p. 30; Condit, *The Chinaman as We See Him*, pp. 156, 162; Wesley S. Woo, "Protestant Work Among the Chinese in the San Francisco Bay Area, 1850–1920" (Ph.D. dissertation, Graduate Theological Union, Berkeley, 1983), p. 48; *The Pacific*, XXVI (2 May 1877), p. 4, and (23 August 1877), p. 4.

[43] Minutes, vols. I and II, passim, Session, Minutes and Records, 1874–1892, First Presbyterian Church, Los Angeles, POHP; Minutes, vol. I, p. 214, Records of the

permanence of this mission, when they reassigned Condit as its director, in 1885. At least forty-one members comprised the parish when the minister assumed responsibility. He remained for five years, while also continuing to supervise his denomination's Chinese outreach.[44]

In his memoirs, published in 1900, Condit described at length the social and religious customs of the Chinese, their virtues and vices, and his assessment of their progress as a people. Condit believed that every Chinese desired to return to China one day, so the missionary sought to send the Gospel back with them. How he did this can be seen in sketches he penned about three members from his flock and their later careers. Two of the three assumed much of Western appearance and culture, Ham Chui as a physician and Kim Yow as a businessman and elder of the local congregation. The third, Mo Heng, returned to China as a missionary's assistant, where he endured the scorn of many for his rejection of key aspects of traditional Chinese culture.[45] In each of these stories, Condit displays the pride of a successful teacher and missionary who loved his converts, even if he did not fully understand the nuances of their sophisticated culture.

Other denominations eventually initiated missionary work among the Chinese, such as the Sunday school and congregation the Northern Methodists initiated in 1888. Within one year at least nine Chinese had accepted baptism in the Northern Methodist Church, on Fort Street. Their names, addresses, and occupations appeared among those of other parishioners listed in the congregation's *Annual Register* for 1889. One of these members, Chan Kiu Sang, later received his license to preach, the first Chinese in the United States that this denomination recognized. He then went on to serve as the pastor of the Los Angeles Methodist Chinese Church.[46]

Presbytery of Los Angeles (P.C.U.S.A.), 1873–1887, POHP; Woo, "Protestant Work Among the Chinese," p. 48; the *Occident*, XXV (23 April 1884), p. 1; *Minutes*, Synod of the Pacific (1884), p. 4, 50; "History of the Chinese First Presbyterian Church," (typescript, 1946), pp. 1–2, Chinese First Presbyterian Church file, "Presbytery of Los Angeles" box, ASFTS; and Pat Hoffman, *History of the First Presbyterian Church of Los Angeles* (Los Angeles: United University Church, 1977), pp. 3–4.

[44] Condit remained in charge of Presbyterian missions to the Chinese, and later the Japanese, from 1870 to 1903. Clifford M. Drury, *Presbyterian Panorama: One Hundred and Fifty Years of National Missions History* (Philadelphia: Board of Christian Education, Presbyterian Church of the U.S.A., 1952), p. 195.

[45] Condit, *The Chinaman as We See Him*, pp. 157–61.

[46] *Annual Register* (Los Angeles: Fort Street Methodist Episcopal Church, 1889), passim; *The Horizon* (Los Angeles: First Methodist Church, June 1938), pp. 18–19; and

The Congregationalists renewed their pioneer outreach in 1890, though immediate results were discouraging.[47] No other communion commenced evangelization until after 1900. Local churches confined themselves to more immediate concerns and contented themselves with assistance to missioners in other locales. Roman Catholic efforts, for example, were long restricted to San Francisco, where Bishop Francisco Mora contributed funds toward a priest and chapel, in 1882–84.[48] The common approach in Protestant circles was the establishment of a foreign mission society chapter to raise funds for Chinese and overseas missions.

The most significant missionary efforts among the Chinese were those the Presbyterians and Congregationalists founded and maintained. This evangelization exemplified the outreach that denominational leaders initiated in San Francisco, and then spread nationwide, particularly through the American Missionary Association. Mission workers helped acculturate the Chinese to American society, as well as to sensitize the two peoples to one another. These religious workers provided material and spiritual comfort to many of the Asian immigrants in times of need. The historian Gunther Barth noted that the Christian centers and chapels also offered some Chinese a measure of freedom from their highly regularized and tradition-bound way of life.[49]

Barth further maintained that missionaries experienced their greatest success when the services of the proselytizers coincided with particular needs of the Chinese.[50] The Congregationalist-Presbyterian undertaking provides a ready example of such achievement. A number of Chinese were quite anxious to master the English language, primarily for business purposes. Members of these two local churches were willing to undertake instruction in this subject, as one means to gain access to the inhabitants of the Los Angeles "Chinatown." This educational interaction between the two groups did, in fact, eventually gain converts to Christianity.

Marco R. Newmark, "The Story of Religion in Los Angeles, 1781–1900," *Historical Society of Southern California Quarterly*, XXVIII (March 1946), pp. 38, 41.

[47] Royal G. Davis, *Light on a Gothic Tower* (Los Angeles: First Congregational Church, 1967), pp. 58–59.

[48] Letters, Joseph S. Alemany to Francisco Mora, 18 June 1882, 13 November 1882, 30 March 1883, 1 August 1883, San Francisco; and copy of letter, Mora to Alemany, 9 October 1884, Los Angeles; AALA.

[49] Barth, *Bitter Strength*, p. 169; Lou, "Chinese American Community," p. 254.

[50] *Bitter Strength*, p. 167.

In a more recent study, the historian Shih-Shan Henry Tsai cautions that many of the Chinese converts to Christianity long maintained syncretic religious beliefs. Numerous Christians continued ancestor worship, wedding and funeral rite customs, and even visits to Taoist gods in Chinese temples. It is presently impossible to know the extent of such syncretism in late nineteenth-century Los Angeles. Whatever the extent of the mixture of spiritual and cultural traditions, local Chinese were sufficiently dedicated to their new faith to promote the establishment of the First Chinese Presbyterian Church. The message and the outreach of Reverend and Mrs. Condit impressed these converts to such an extent that they were not satisfied until there was an independent church for the Chinese and the Condits had returned to staff it.

In his memoirs, Condit reveals his fundamental sympathy toward the Chinese, as well as his distaste for many of their cultural practices. A man of his times and training, Condit embodied much of the nineteenth-century sense of mission of many Americans to share their "superior" culture and Protestant faith with a less-developed people. However, the clergyman also resisted anti-Asian prejudice and served as a valuable spokesman for the Chinese. He and his wife served as liaisons between white society and the Chinese community, in times when racism was violent throughout the western states. Along with the three women volunteers sent by the American Missionary Association, the Condits believed firmly in the value of education and Christianization to acculturate the Chinese as American citizens.

Los Angeles Protestants provided an unusual addition to the traditional ranks of missionaries, with the placement of volunteer female teachers in mission schools. Such work on behalf of the Chinese provided local Protestant women with the first organized opportunity to engage in service beyond immediate congregational circles. Affiliating with the American Missionary Association, the original endeavor of the Congregationalists also linked Los Angeles women, for the first time, to a national Protestant society with a heritage of female volunteer service. Work with the Chinese preceded similar catechesis of Hispanics, primarily because women perceived the Chinese to be in greater need of hearing the Christian Gospel and learning American ways.

In later years, women in the Los Angeles churches would found local chapters of the well-known denominational foreign missionary societies. Other women would devote time to assist Ida Boone in her school for Spanish-speaking children, in "Sonoratown." These and subsequent developments in the work of evangelization rested upon the significant efforts first undertaken on behalf of the Chinese, in 1871. The early outreach broadened women's sphere of activity within the church, as well as increasing mutual understanding between peoples of different races and religious traditions. Given the violence of racial prejudice among certain Angelenos, these first contacts were halting but important contributions of the women and the churches toward harmony and mutual understanding in the frontier settlement.

Missionary work among the Chinese, for example, began in the West and gradually spread out across the continent, in a reversal of the historic pattern of Christian evangelization. Los Angeles represented one of the earliest and first extensions of these ministrations outside San Francisco. Despite the frustration frequently derived from dealing with the sojourner mentality, workers made significant progress among Asian immigrants. This evangelistic outreach also provided local women with their first ties to a national voluntary Protestant society promoting female missionary benevolence.

The service-oriented approach secured for the Christian evangelizers an operational base, which gave them credibility. The Chinese were able to obtain English instruction and job references through their church connections, thus enhancing their economic mobility. These immigrants also gained valuable allies. Denominational support was no small matter in a community infamous for one of the worst outbreaks of anti-Chinese violence in the history of the country. This outreach to members of this race, however, was but one of the ministries that occupied the sects of the city.

The recourse to women in ministry came early and broadened steadily over the period under study. They provided the denominations with the flexibility to meet diverse needs and to respond to regionally specific problems. Given the presence of the Indians, Hispanics, and Chinese, the requisite breadth of ministry and array of missionaries distinguished this settlement from any frontier outside the Southwest. Amazingly pluralistic in the nineteenth century, ethnic and racial diversity has continued to challenge evangelizers in Los Angeles throughout the twentieth century as well.

7

SOLDIERS OF CHRIST, ANGELS OF MERCY

We started early on the morning of the eighteenth of October [1855]. There were five of us—three Spanish sisters and two of the three American sisters . . . for the California Mission. . . . the whole community was at Mass. The Sisters sang "Soldiers of Christ, Arise." After Mass, our lamented Father Burlando gave us his blessing and, to each sister, an umbrella.[1]

In these brief words, an aged Sister Angelita Mumbrado recalled the day, sixty years previously, on which she and her companions had set out for Los Angeles. These women were leaving from the motherhouse of their community, located in Emmitsburg, Maryland. They were destined for New York, from which they would sail on to Panama, San Francisco, and finally, southern California. All five pioneers were members of the Daughters of Charity of St. Vincent de Paul, an organization whose American roots dated from 1809.[2] Like so many other Roman Catholic women religious in the

[1] Sister Angelita Mumbrado, D.C., "Remembrance of My Youth" (typescript, [1917]), p. 6; Archives of the Central Province of the Daughters of Charity of St. Vincent De Paul, St. Louis, Missouri. Reverend Francis Burlando was the Director of the American Province of the Daughters of Charity between 1853 and 1873; see Helene Bailey de Barbery, *Elizabeth Seton* (sixth edition, New York: MacMillan Company, 1931), pp. 485, 495, 499, 541. The hymn, "Soldiers of Christ, Arise," was a composition of Charles Wesley, in 1749. It appeared most frequently in Methodist hymnals in the United States. One arrangement is found in Nathaniel J. Burton, Edwin Pond Parker, and Joseph H. Twichell, *The Christian Hymnal* (Hartford, Connecticut: Brown and Gross, 1877), #294.

[2] For the early history of this Sisterhood, see Annabelle M. Melville, *Elizabeth*

United States, their experiences on the frontier contributed to the ongoing Americanization of their denomination. The purpose of this chapter is to illustrate the challenges these women confronted and the manner in which they coped with successive difficulties in the boisterous cow town.[3]

Several recent historians have noted the neglect of so many nuns who made important contributions to the settlement of the American West. Joan M. Jensen and Darlis A. Miller called attention to the omission of these and other "gentle tamers," such as missionary teachers and wives of ministers. Polly Wells Kaufman cited the need for information regarding religious women of the antebellum era. She specifically noted that Catholic Sisters had been prominently involved in founding schools and hospitals. More recently, Margaret Susan Thompson has maintained that inattention to these women's efforts severely weakens any comprehensive understanding of the Roman Catholic experience in the United States.[4]

For Thompson, pioneering Sisters played a crucial role in the difficult adjustments that Old World Catholics faced in nineteenth-century America. Many Protestant citizens sincerely believed that Catholicism was a religion incompatible with a democratic society. For example, Reverend Lyman Beecher's 1835 tract, "A Plea for the West," expressed the fear of many evangelical Americans about Catholicism's rapid spread across the continent. Catholics in the early republic repeatedly defended themselves against Beecher's charges of being members of a foreign and despotic religion. Controversy focused on the nature of their allegiance to the pope, resident in

---

Bayley Seton, 1774–1821 (New York: Charles Scribner's Sons, 1951; reprint ed., St. Paul, Minnesota: Carillon Books, 1976).

[3] The terms "nun," "sister," and "woman religious" have technically different meanings, particularly for the years prior to the 1983 revision of canon law. I have followed common practice, however, which permits a certain interchangeable use of these terms.

[4] Joan M. Jensen and Darlis A. Miller, "The Gentle Tamers Revisited: New Approaches to the History of Women in the American West," *Pacific Historical Review*, XLIX (May 1980), p. 199; Polly Wells Kaufman, *Women Teachers on the American Frontier* (New Haven: Yale University Press, 1984), p. xix; and Margaret Susan Thompson, "To Serve the People of God: Nineteenth-Century Sisters and the Creation of an American Religious Life," Notre Dame, Indiana: University of Notre Dame, Cushwa Center for the Study of American Catholicism, Working Paper Series 18, No. 2 (Spring, 1987), pp. 4–6.

Europe, the authority of priests and bishops, and the education of Catholic children. Amidst these conflicts, the nuns confronted the stubborn dilemma that for decades bedeviled all members of their communion: how to be both Catholic and American.

Many of the clergy and bishops born and educated in Europe were thoroughly imbued with Old-World concepts of divinely ordained church-state relations. When these clerics reached American shores, they frequently could not speak English and would not accept religious pluralism as a legal principle or a legitimate practice. However, the frontier challenged not only bishops and priests, but the church's lay members as well, and it was they who, whether married or committed to religious sisterhoods, most readily adapted their religious practices to pioneer conditions. This was as true for Hispanics on the frontera of New Spain as it was for Anglo-American settlers in Kentucky, in the 1820s.

The experience of the Sisters of Charity in Los Angeles provides an excellent illustration of this process. These women repeatedly demonstrated their willingness and ability to adapt to the changing exigencies of life in this far-western community. This blue-robed band proved to be the most flexible and adaptive Roman Catholic personnel in the pueblo. Invited to found a school and orphanage, the nuns later undertook hospital nursing, disaster relief, job placement for women, parish catechism instruction, fundraising for Catholic causes, and care of smallpox victims. Because of the nuns' far greater numbers, range of ministries, and contacts with the broader community, they contended more directly than most priests with local pastoral problems.[5]

These Sisters constituted only one segment of the local female population concerned with the advance of religion in the commu-

[5] Other historians have studied the flexibility of Catholic women religious in meeting the needs of church members in the United States. See, in particular, Mary Ewens, O.P., *The Role of The Nun in Nineteenth-Century America* (New York, Arno Press, 1978), and "Leadership of Nuns in Immigrant Catholicism," in *Women and Religion in America*, ed. by Rosemary Radford Ruether and Rosemary Skinner Keller, vol. I: *The Nineteenth Century*, (San Francisco: Harper and Row, 1982), pp. 101–107; Elizabeth Kolmer, "Catholic Women Religious and Women's History: A Survey of the Literature," in *Women in American Religion*, ed. by Janet Wilson Jones (Philadelphia: University of Pennsylvania Press, 1980), pp. 127–39; and Margaret Susan Thompson, "Discovering Foremothers: Sisters, Society, and the American Catholic Church," *U.S. Catholic Historian*, V (Summer-Fall 1986), pp. 273–90.

nity. As discussed in the preceding chapter, other churchwomen in Los Angeles included parish or synagogue members, the wives of clergymen, female Chinese believers, and the teachers of the American Missionary Association and the Presbyterian Board of Home Missions. To varying degrees and in differing capacities, all these women actively spread their respective faiths. However, two circumstances set the Daughters of Charity in a category by themselves: the number of nuns who served in this settlement, and the extensive written material that survives to describe their work. Between 1856 and 1882, 126 Sisters served locally and corresponded regularly with their superiors, in Maryland and France.[6]

It is the abundance of documentation that permits this chapter's survey of the ministries of these women. Source materials on other groups of women, unfortunately, are far less complete. The minutes of the meetings of the Ladies Hebrew Benevolent Society, for example, do not exist for this early period. Only a handful of letters survive from three teachers of the American Missionary Association, between 1871 and 1875. Scattered references mention Ida Boone's labors.[7] For these reasons, a systematic comparison among the women of different denominations is not possible.

Three aspects of the Daughters of Charity's early experience warrant attention: their adaptability and willingness to respond to local needs; their creativity in funding their efforts; and their central position in pueblo society. The first evidence of the Sisters' pioneering spirit appeared shortly after their arrival in southern California, in January 1856.[8] Bishop Thaddeus Amat and a committee of prominent

[6] The register "Catalogue du Personnel–Etats Unis" listed the names of those nuns serving in Los Angeles between 1856 and 1882. Archives of the Daughters of Charity, Rue du Bac, Paris, France.

[7] None of the records of any Ladies' Aid Society or Sewing Circle remain from the early congregations known to have sponsored such organizations during this period. This includes the Northern Methodists, Episcopalians, Congregationalists, Presbyterians, Baptists, and Roman Catholics. The papers for another association, the Woman's Christian Temperance Union of Southern California, are no longer open for research. Other societies, such as the women's clubs and the Free Kindergarten Association, were not specifically religious groups, though they did attract members from the churches and synagogue. The documents of the Flower Festival Society date from 1885–88, though this too was not a specifically religious group.

[8] Their names, once again, were Sisters Scholastica Logsdon and Corsina McKay, both American-born; Ann Gillen, from Ireland; and Francesca Fernandez, Angelita Mumbrado, and Clara Cisneros, all from Spain. See "Remarks on Sister Mary Scholastica Logsdon," *Lives of Our Deceased Sisters, 1903*, (Emmitsburg, Maryland: St. Joseph's Central House, 1903), p. 109.

citizens quickly obtained a house for them and a nine-acre lot, north-east of the plaza.[9] With equal dispatch, the Sisters commenced their labors. Within five years, they had extended their property to four-teen acres, on which they located a prosperous academy, an orphan-age, a hospital, a vineyard with six thousand vines, and an orchard of three hundred fruit trees. However impressive these achievements appeared to their Angeleno neighbors, the Sisters nonetheless felt iso-lated from other houses of their sisterhood and suffered a chronic shortage of ready cash.[10]

The nearest Daughters of Charity were 350 miles to the north, in San Francisco, while an entire continent separated them from their motherhouse, in Maryland. Their Los Angeles Institución Carita-tiva remained the sisterhood's far southwestern outpost for many years. Letters in 1858 traveled at the then-remarkable rate of twenty-one days by stage from St. Louis. The hostilities of the Civil War interrupted communications, which prompted the Emmitsburg au-thorities to dispatch a priest as "Sub-Director" to assist in the man-agement of the California houses.[11] The success of the Sisters in this remote post was due in large measure to the leadership of the pioneer superior, Sister Mary Scholastica Logsdon.

Prior to her arrival in Los Angeles, Sister Scholastica had filled sev-eral different posts during her sixteen years in the sisterhood. She had worked in an orphanage in New York City, between 1842 and 1846, and then joined two Sisters in founding an asylum in Natchez, Mis-sissippi, 1846–49. Logsdon returned to her native Maryland, in 1849, and remained there until dispatched to California. Serving in the Emmitsburg motherhouse, she manifested her administrative skills in those years as the province procuratrix, or manager, of the tem-poral goods of the Sisters in the United States.[12] Logsdon's varied

[9] Letter, Bishop Thaddeus Amat to Reverend Francis Burlando, C.M., 7 May 1855, Paris, AALA; *El Clamor Público*, 12 January 1856; and Mumbrado, "Remem-brance," pp. 7–8.

[10] Illustrative of the Sisters' repeated cash-flow difficulties, the Los Angeles *Star*, of 11 May 1861, included their property on the "Delinquent Tax List," subject to auction to satisfy back taxes.

[11] In common with many Roman Catholic women's communities, the Daughters of Charity were technically subject to male superiors. The superior-general of the Congregation of the Mission in Paris appointed a priest to serve as the "director" for each province of the Sisters worldwide. In the United States, the director, Reverend Francis Burlando, C.M., was resident at the Sisters' motherhouse, in Emmitsburg, Maryland. See de Barbery, *Elizabeth Seton*, pp. 495–500.

[12] "Remarks on Sister Mary Scholastica Logsdon," p. 109.

experience and winning personality enabled her to undertake the challenging Los Angeles assignment in 1856 and to serve successfully as superior, or "Sister Servant," until 1884.

According to her journal, difficulties confronted Logsdon from the very start of the trip to California from Maryland. The six Sisters of Charity traveled in the company of Bishop Amat, eleven priests, one seminarian, and twelve Sisters of Providence. Amat booked passage for his party in New York City, on the *Empire City*. Designed to handle seven hundred passengers but carrying one thousand, the crowded vessel had a frequently stormy passage from New York City to Aspinwall. The nuns were frequently seasick, despite the administration of "old brandy" by a kindly fellow passenger. Logsdon noted, after three weeks at sea, "We are getting very tired of the ocean—we encourage ourselves that San Francisco will cure all."[13]

They entered the Golden Gate on 14 November 1855 and dispersed to their various destinations throughout the state. The nuns rested several weeks and then proceeded on to Los Angeles by steamer. Finding no one to meet them, the women arrived unannounced in the pueblo, on 6 January 1856. The committee in charge of local arrangements soon called upon the women and showed them a variety of sites for their prospective residence and orphanage. Logsdon chose a house and lot offered by Benjamin D. Wilson, much to the consternation of the gentlemen assisting her. As Wilson's agent noted,

> Some of them [the committee members] are anxious to favor some of their friends and buy some of their old adobe houses. The Sisters are equally anxious to retain the place [Wilson's] as they are much pleased with the premises.[14]

With the selection finally concluded to Logsdon's satisfaction, the Sisters commenced their school and orphanage in the unfurnished residence, in February 1856. Soon known to Spanish-speaking Angelenos as "Hermana Escolastica," Logsdon utilized the limited resources at hand to provide beds and other necessities. She instructed her companions to sew large bags, which they then stuffed with wood

---

[13] Copy of Logsdon's journal, found in ledger, "San Francisco," p. 39; AWPDC.

[14] Letter, Henry Rice Myles to Benjamin D. Wilson, 12 February 1856, Los Angeles; Wilson Papers, HL.

shavings she obtained from a carpenter's shop. These mattresses on the floor proved "awfully hard," but there was little time to complain. Soon boarding students were living with the Sisters, and the room where the girls slept served as "oratory, classroom, sewing room, and parlor." As one nun later recalled, "Only God knows what we went through . . ."[15]

A school for girls and an orphanage comprised the Institución Caritativa, an "asylum" modeled on similar worldwide institutions of the Sisters. The editor of the local Spanish newspaper monitored their progress and reported, in July 1858, an enrollment of 170 girls, of whom 45 were orphans.[16] The annual "exhibition at the Sisters' school" soon merited extensive coverage in the town's journals.[17] The success of the school prompted church authorities later to request that these women religious instruct young boys. Because of pressing local need, the Maryland superiors of the Sisters permitted an exception to the regulation that had restricted the nuns to the education of girls and boys under six years of age.[18]

Other community needs surfaced over the years and demanded initiative and imagination on the part of Logsdon and her companions. For example, the Daughters of Charity were famed for their hospital work in other portions of the United States and around the world. Citizens approached Logsdon within months of her arrival, in 1856, and requested that she open a hospital in Los Angeles. While she corresponded with Reverend Francis Burlando, the nuns' Director in Maryland, the local parish priest brought a sick man to her door for nursing.[19] The Sisters' response to this invalid encouraged several residents to renew their appeal for the establishment of a hospital.

The absence of any health care facilities in the southern portion

---

[15] Mumbrado, "Remembrance of My Youth," pp. 7–8.

[16] *El Clamor Público*, 3 July 1858.

[17] The Los Angeles *News*, of 5 July 1867, contained an account of the academy's exercises, which concluded, "Los Angeles is justly proud of her Seminary." The editor of the Los Angeles *Star* devoted virtually the entire front page of the 22 June 1872 issue to that year's exhibition. He went so far as to reprint the texts of four student speeches, as well as the name of every student awarded a prize.

[18] William E. North, *Catholic Education in Southern California* (Washington, D.C.: Catholic University of America, 1936), p. 130.

[19] Mumbrado, "Remembrance," p. 8; and Letters, Sister Scholastica Logsdon to Reverend Francis Burlando, 25 July 1856, 8 May 1857, and 9 October 1857, Institución Caritativa [Los Angeles], "Correspondence of the Director, volume II," Box III: Manuscripts, hereafter referred to as "Correspondence, II;" AWPDC.

of the state so moved Sister Scholastica, that she won permission to accept a county contract to nurse the indigent sick. The initial facilities rented by the county, in 1858, were of the most primitive sort, in a four-room adobe house, "North of the church." The only furnishings the authorities provided were cots and bedding for eight patients and two nuns. Indian women took the linens to the riverbank to be washed, and an Indian boy and girl prepared the meals, under the supervision of Sister Ann Gillen. She later recalled that providing milk for the patients was a challenge, because "the cows were not accustomed to be milked and the operation was a dangerous one."[20]

The Irish-born Gillen remained in charge of the hospital from 1858 until failing health forced her to resign, in 1881. A variety of letters and memoirs record her wit as well as her compassion. Logsdon described one religious celebration, when "dear Sister Ann threatened to dance around the wards of her Hospital . . ."[21] Gillen cared deeply for the welfare of invalids in her care, as community annals record.

It was hard for good Sister Ann to see her patients die; and when the circumstance of sickness and death were particularly touching, as in the case of two or three French boys who died regretting their mother, her tears would flow abundantly.[22]

After only four months at the initial site the county provided, Gillen and Logsdon transferred the nursing operation, in November 1858, into a residence on a lot adjoining their orphanage. Logsdon did not wait for approval from Burlando this time, but "presumed" his permission to expend $3,000 for the five-acre site.[23] The increasing numbers of patients over the years prompted the nuns to erect additional buildings on the property. After one decade of operation, the crowded conditions were no longer tolerable. As one priest wrote, in 1868, to the nuns' director in Maryland, "They [the Sisters] cannot possibly go on much longer as they are. They are obliged to put the

---

[20] Quoted in "Remarks on Sister Mary Scholastica Logsdon," p. 113.

[21] Letter, Logsdon to Burlando, 30 January 1859, Los Angeles; "Correspondence, II," AWPDC.

[22] "Remarks on Sister Mary Scholastica Logsdon," p. 114.

[23] Letter, Logsdon to Burlando, 8 October 1858, Institución Caritativa [Los Angeles], "Correspondence, II," AWPDC.

patients in the *Barn*! The *Wash-house*! and even the *Bath-house*!"[24] Late in 1869, the Sisters obtained eight acres on the northern edge of town and erected a two-story brick facility for their Los Angeles Infirmary.

This commitment to health care prompted these women to volunteer to nurse during the smallpox epidemics that repeatedly ravaged the community. As recounted in chapter 4, the nuns agreed to the requests of city and county officials to tend smallpox victims in 1861–62, 1869, and 1876–77. Logsdon and Gillen visited the initial "pest house" in 1861 and discovered a distressing situation. It was

> in a pitiable condition—the patients lying pell-mell on the floor, suffering in every way . . . Some becoming delirious from fever, would rush out over the patients thickly strewn on the floor—all was confusion and distress!"[25]

The two women decided immediately to commit the resources of their sisterhood to the care of the afflicted.

Their first act was to move the sick from the remote pest house, in the hills outside of town, to a site closer to medical facilities. The women secured a residence on the next street from their hospital and there tended between fifty and sixty victims during the three months of that first epidemic. In the removal, during the night, of the blanket-wrapped bodies of the dead, it was Gillen who held the horse and steadied the burial cart. The names of others who worked during that first siege of smallpox went unrecorded. However, Sisters Phileta McCarthy and Margaret Weber nursed in the isolated cottage in 1869, followed by Sisters Xavier Schauer and Mary Ellen Downey, in 1876–77.[26] During the course of the first epidemic, a natural disaster prompted the Sisters to undertake another mission of mercy on behalf of the suffering.

[24] Letter, Reverend James McGill to Burlando, 20 December 1868, St. Vincent's College, Los Angeles; "Correspondence," I, AWPDC.

[25] "Remarks on Sister Mary Scholastica Logsdon," p. 113. Original punctuation retained in quotation.

[26] "Remarks on Sister Mary Scholastica Logsdon," pp. 113–14. See also a Letter, Logsdon to Burlando, 21 May 1869, Los Angeles, "Correspondence, II;" Folder, "Lives of Our Deceased Sisters, 1879–1954," p. 75; and unidentified newspaper clipping, 1 December 1912, obituary for Sister Xavier Schauer, found in "Los Angeles Orphanage" box; AWPDC.

Chapter 7

The winter rains of 1862 lashed southern California with such force that rivers overflowed, fields were swept away, and streets turned into muddy bogs. Sixty miles east of Los Angeles, the raging waters of the Santa Ana River destroyed the small towns of Agua Mansa and San Salvador. Bishop Amat noted, in a letter, that Logsdon and the nuns managed the relief effort on behalf of the flood victims. ". . . the Sisters will go tomorrow throughout the town collecting something, and after tomorrow two of them will go to that place with the provisions they will be able to raise up . . ." The women gathered two wagonloads of goods, and then two of their number proceeded by stage to render what assistance they could offer.[27]

This disaster relief was not the only endeavor outside of Los Angeles that the Sisters undertook to meet pressing pastoral needs. Bishop Amat, for one, repeatedly approached these women to extend their labors throughout his vast diocese. He initially desired Sisters to teach at an Indian school one hundred miles south of Los Angeles.[28] When superiors in Maryland declined this offer, the bishop continued to appeal for the establishment of "asylums" in six other small towns across the state. Sister Scholastica weighed the merits of each case, reviewed the personnel available and the commitments already made, and eventually assigned Sisters to four locales.[29]

Church authorities in both San Diego, California, and Virginia City, Nevada, also requested that the Daughters of Charity establish schools or hospitals in their respective towns. Beginning with ninety students, the women commenced instruction in Virginia City in October 1864 and expanded to two schools and an orphanage by 1867.[30] The Sisters also opened St. Mary's hospital in that commu-

---

[27] Letter, Thaddeus Amat to Joseph S. Alemany [archbishop of San Francisco], 26 January 1862, Los Angeles, AALA; Marjorie Tisdale Wolcott, ed., *Pioneer Notes from the Diaries of Judge Benjamin Hayes, 1849–1875* (Los Angeles: Privately Printed, 1929), p. 266; and "San Francisco" ledger, p. 100, AWPDC. Concerning the destruction of the settlements of New Mexican colonists at Agua Mansa and San Salvador, see Mildred B. Hoover, et al., *Historic Spots in California*, revised by William N. Abeloe (third edition, Stanford, California: Stanford University Press, 1966), p. 325.

[28] Letter, Logsdon to Burlando, 21 November 1856, Los Angeles, "Correspondence, II," AWPDC.

[29] Letter, Thaddeus Amat to Francis Burlando, 21 December 1857, Los Angeles, "Correspondence, I,"; Letters, Logsdon to Burlando, 19 June 1859, 7 December 1861, 28 August 1862, 4 August 1863, 26 March 1867, 15 May 1867, all from Los Angeles, "Correspondence, II;" AWPDC.

[30] Letters, Reverend John Asmuth to Francis Burlando, 3 May 1864, San Fran-

nity, in 1875, the first health facility in the state of Nevada. To the south, the pastor in San Diego had written, as early as 1870, to petition for such an institution in his hamlet. The Sisters could not accept his appeal, because the extreme poverty of the place would not have permitted them to sustain themselves.[31]

From their first days in southern California, the Sisters had manifested a second distinctive trait: the ability to administer several different institutions in a community where ready cash was frequently unavailable. The Los Angeles committee of citizens, for example, had secured only half of the money needed to purchase the property for the Institución Caritativa in 1856. A drought that year had depressed the local economy, which was based on the cattle trade. Bishop Amat assisted the nuns in this instance, though it was his usual practice only to pay for the costs of the women's transportation from the motherhouse in Maryland to his diocese.[32] The only other revenue received through Amat was from an annual collection taken, after 1869, in the parishes of the poor diocese for the benefit of all its orphanages.[33]

Other than these two transfers of funds from the bishop, the Sisters were entirely responsible for the financial affairs of their institutions. They exhibited a notable creativity in responding to the ongoing demands to sustain the costs of their expanding endeavors. As recounted in chapter 4, the nuns and the "ladies of Los Angeles" commenced an annual "Orphans' Fair," in 1858. Though such a benefit was without local precedent, townspeople of all faiths generously patronized this event. Later newspaper publicity suggests the popularity which the fair came to enjoy. Numerous newspaper accounts appeared between 1856 and 1885, reporting on a host of other benefits and collections on behalf of the orphanage. These ranged from a St. Patrick's Day

---

cisco, and 5 June 1864, San Francisco, "Correspondence, I," AWPDC. See also White, *Life of Mrs. Eliza A. Seton*, p. 504.

[31] Letter, Reverend James McGill to Francis Burlando, 23 January 1870, Los Angeles, "Correspondence, I," AWPDC.

[32] Letter, Logsdon to Burlando, 23 June 1857, Los Angeles, "Correspondence, II," AWPDC.

[33] Letter, Logsdon to Burlando, 22 April 1867, Los Angeles, "Correspondence, II," AWPDC. Regarding the annual diocesan collection to benefit orphanages, see Decree 34, *Constitutiones Latae et Promulgatae ab Illmo. ac Revmo. D. Thaddaeo Amat, Congregationis Missionis, Episcopo Montereyensi et Angelorum, in Synodo Dioecesanis Prima et Segunda* (San Francisco: Mullin, Mahon and Company, 1869), p. 98.

dinner (with profits of $98.75) to a weekend performance of "Lee's National Circus."[34]

The Sisters also altered their traditional goals in education, in order to augment school revenues. Their director, Father Burlando, reminded them that their sisterhood had been founded to teach the children of the poor. Other communities of nuns existed to instruct the daughters of the wealthy. Nonetheless, the priest granted the nuns' request for permission to charge tuition and to accept boarding students. Logsdon later requested that the Sisters also might offer the "finishing school" subjects of music, drawing, and French, but only to generate additional income for the support of the orphans.[35]

The school and orphanage also benefited from other sources of income secured by these religious women. The vineyard and orchard yielded not only fruit for the table, but also cash crops, used "to buy flour and other necessary things."[36] In 1859, the state legislature also began to allocate small grants for the care of orphans. That first year, the Sisters received an appropriation of $1,000, according to an 1861 pamphlet entitled, "Report of the Trustees of the R.C. Orphan Asylum of Los Angeles." Logsdon noted in this statement that the 1861 appropriation had not yet reached her, a distressing situation, since her debts totaled $13,000.[37]

Sister Scholastica did not hesitate to press her claims on behalf of the orphans, a fact abundantly clear in her later correspondence

---

[34] *El Clamor Público*, 20 March 1858; *Southern Vineyard*, 21 December 1858; and Los Angeles *Star*, 9 January 1869. See also the programs for the Orphans' Fairs, found in the Antonio Coronel Collection of the Seaver Center for Western History Research, Natural History Museum of Los Angeles County, Los Angeles, California.

[35] Letter, Bishop Thaddeus Amat to Reverend Francis Burlando, 19 January 1857, Los Angeles, AALA; and copy of letter, Burlando to Amat, 27 February 1857, Emmitsburg, Maryland, "Correspondence, I," AWPDC. See also letters, Logsdon to Burlando, 21 November 1856 and 18 September 1861, Los Angeles, "Correspondence, II," AWPDC.

[36] Mumbrado, "Remembrance," p. 12.

[37] Sister M. Scholastica Logsdon, D.C., "Report of the Trustees of the R.C. Orphan Asylum of Los Angeles," (n.p.: Benjamin P. Avery, State Printer, 5 December 1861), pp. 1–4. For the appropriations voted by the state legislature, see *Leyes de California* (Sacramento: John O'Meara, State Printer, 1859), $1,000, pp. 239–40, (1861) $1,000, p. 49, (1862) $1,000, p. 201, (1863–64) $1,000, p. 12; and the *Appendix to the Journals of the Senate and Assembly* (Sacramento: State Printer, 1870), $1,000, p. 72.

with one prominent local citizen. Benjamin D. Wilson, though not a Roman Catholic, had generously supported the works of the nuns over the years.[38] Upon Wilson's election to the state senate, in 1869, Logsdon wrote a letter of congratulation that revealed how well she understood the processes of government.

> We expect through your influence to have this year an increased appropriation. We have written to the good Governor, who is always a kind friend to us. We are not much acquainted with the members in the Assembly, but one word from you to them will be sufficient to secure us friends."[39]

On the local level, Logsdon also understood how to manage government officials and to secure appropriations for the hospital in her care. Certain "gentlemen" she had consulted in 1857 informed her that the county supervisors budgeted $2,600 annually for the care of the impoverished sick. The Sisters would probably be able to obtain this funding, if they agreed to operate the proposed county hospital.[40] The nuns assumed operation of the new facility in 1858, receiving from the board of supervisors one dollar per day per indigent patient. Though this amount was reduced, in 1871, to seventy-five cents per day, the Sisters continued to care for those otherwise unable to afford medical treatment.[41]

[38] When the Sisters arrived in Los Angeles, in 1856, they located their Institución Caritativa in Wilson's former residence. The citizen's committee purchased the property for the asylum, and Wilson himself reduced the price by $1,000 and then contributed a further $250 to the collection. Letter, Logsdon to Burlando, 4 June 1856, Los Angeles, "Correspondence, II," AWPDC.

[39] Letter, Sister Scholastica Logsdon to Benjamin D. Wilson, 22 December 1869, Los Angeles; Wilson Collection, HL. Within four months, the Los Angeles *Republican* carried an editorial opposing a bill then pending in the state senate to appropriate $5,000 to the Los Angeles orphanage and $5,000 to the Sisters' hospital. See the issue of 5 March 1870. The *Appendix to the Journal for the Senate and Assembly* for 1872 records, on p. 67, that the legislators finally voted an appropriation for the hospital of $500.

[40] Letter, Logsdon to Burlando, 8 May 1857, Los Angeles, "Correspondence, II," AWPDC.

[41] Beginning on 9 November 1859, with the allotment of $706.00, the "Minutes" of the county board of supervisors list the dates that "Mary S. Logsdon" received payment for the services which the Sisters of Charity rendered. See vol. II, p. 299, in "Minutes," housed in the Executive Office of the Board of Supervisors, Los Angeles,

Chapter 7

The increasing demands from citizens in later years for greater economizing coincided with steps that the Daughters of Charity had taken to protect their properties and benevolent works. They formed two civil corporations, in June 1869, and became the first Los Angeles women ever to organize themselves in this manner. They constituted the orphanage and the hospital as distinct legal entities: The Los Angeles Orphan Asylum and The Los Angeles Infirmary.[42] Listing the names of the respective incorporators, the "Corporation Books" also document annual meetings, election of officers, budgets, and real-estate transactions. The nuns were following the guidelines issued from their Maryland motherhouse, which were later printed as "Remarks on Corporations."[43]

Evidence suggests that a further reason existed to compel the Sisters to seek incorporation of their institutions.[44] Disagreements apparently arose between the nuns and the local bishop, regarding who should hold title to the properties of the asylum and hospital. As head of the local diocese, the Spanish-born Thaddeus Amat evidently considered himself to be the rightful owner of this realty. Though all the documents are not available, it appears that the American-born

---

California. For the reduction in per-patient reimbursement, see Los Angeles *Star*, 7 March 1871.

[42] "Articles of Incorporation," The Los Angeles Orphan Asylum, 21 June 1869, Office of the Secretary of State, Sacramento, California; and "Corporation Book, 1869–1909," p. 1; Department of Marketing Communications, St. Vincent's Medical Center, Los Angeles, California; hereafter cited as SVMC.

[43] Letter, Reverend James McGill to Francis Burlando, 15 June 1869, Los Angeles, "Correspondence, I," AWPDC; and "Corporation Book," pp. 1–15, SVMC.

[44] All pertinent documents in this dispute are not presently available for study. The episcopal correspondence files in the Archives of the Archdiocese of Los Angeles contain materials that suggest the outline of the lengthy disagreements. See Letters, Thaddeus Amat to Francis Burlando, 30 May 1856, Santa Cruz [California]; Amat to Burlando, 18 August 1857, Santa Barbara [California]; Amat to Burlando, 21 December 1857, Los Angeles; Amat to Martin J. Spalding [Archbishop of Baltimore], 22 April 1865, Los Angeles; Alexander Cardinal Barnabo [Prefect of the Congregation of Propaganda Fide at the Holy See] to Amat, 17 December 1862, Rome; Barnabo to Amat, 25 January 1864, Rome; Amat to M. Etienne [Superior General of the Congregation of the Mission, Paris], 13 July 1864, Los Angeles; Amat to Barnabo, 13 October 1865, Los Angeles; AALA. For published summaries of additional Roman correspondence, see Finbar Kenneally, O.F.M., ed., *United States Documents in the Propaganda Fide Archives: A Calendar* (First series, Washington, D.C.: Academy of American Franciscan History, 1966–1977), vol. II, #2021; vol. III, #186, #365; vol. V, #1033, #1165.

Logsdon thwarted the bishop's designs, by recording the title to the nuns' real estate in her own name. Circumventing the bishop once more, she later transferred ownership of the hospital and orphanage land and assets to the new corporations.[45]

In the first election of officers, on 3 January 1870, Sister Scholastica and her longtime assistant, Ann Gillen, received the hospital corporation's presidency and vice-presidency, respectively. The initial financial report listed $6,000 in income, an amount comfortably exceeding the year's expenses of $5,500.[46] One of the earliest endeavors of the corporation was the construction of a new hospital. The county grand jurors, charged with reviewing expenditures of county funds, evidently did not consider the Sisters' site suitable for such a clinic. As early as May 1869, the members of this body had issued a report describing this district as unhealthful.[47]

The Sisters began the search for a better site that year and eventually decided upon property on Naud Street, in the northeastern section of town, near the river. A visiting reporter later described the completed two-story brick structure they erected as "scrupulously neat and clean" and reflecting "great credit on the management of the Sisters."[48] Such newspaper publicity became increasingly important, because French residents of Los Angeles had commenced construction of the town's second hospital, in October 1869. Though smaller and restricted to serving members of the French Benevolent Society, the Maison de Santé was located in a more desirable locale than the Sisters' older infirmary. The "French Hospital," as it came to be known, initiated the gradual proliferation of health care facilities in the settlement.[49]

The potential for competition from this Gallic operation troubled the Sisters, as did the repeated statements of the grand jurors in later years. The empaneled citizens began to complain that the wards of the facility were being filled by those who were recent, "penniless" arrivals in the county.[50] The growing populace of Los Angeles included

---

[45] "Corporation Book," p. 14; SVMC.

[46] "Corporation Book," p. 14; SVMC.

[47] Los Angeles *Republican*, 13 May 1869.

[48] Los Angeles *Star*, 20 August 1870.

[49] Los Angeles *Star*, 30 October 1869 and 30 July 1870. The French Hospital is presently known as the Pacific Alliance Medical Center.

[50] For example, see Los Angeles *Star*, 15 January 1870 and 21 February 1871.

those who were not considered true "residents," but newly settled "chronic cases." Responding to the jurors' pleas for greater economy, the board of supervisors took steps to save taxpayers' dollars. The supervisors first terminated the county contract with the Sisters, in November of 1878. Board members then opened a publicly administered county hospital, with an attached almshouse where patients would work to help support themselves.[51]

The increasing population and altered expectations regarding local health care led to important changes in the Sisters' endeavors. The nuns reevaluated their existing hospital location, because of the adverse comments on the healthfulness of the site and the proximity of the recently constructed depot and yards of the Southern Pacific Railroad.[52] The hospital's board of trustees finally decided, in March 1883, to sell the property and to purchase a six-acre site in the "Beaudry Park" development, on the north side of the city.[53] Following the real-estate practices of the times, the women subdivided the vacated site on Naud Street. The sale of lots in their "Infirmary" and "New Depot" tracts produced more than $30,000 in revenue between 1883 and 1886.[54] They also advertised for construction bids on the new infirmary, selected the contractors, and proceeded to break ground, in September 1884.

The correspondence of the corporation's president reveals the anxious moments that such financial affairs involved. Sister Emily Conway headed the hospital from 1881 to 1885, while also serving as the corporate treasurer.[55] In a letter to the director, in Emmitsburg, she explained the difficulties she faced. "There is quite a stir among the Physicians of the City to erect a Protestant Hospital . . . not far from our new place." Undaunted, she continued with the news that the

---

[51] Los Angeles *Star*, 7 March 1871; and Los Angeles *Herald*, 30 October 1878.

[52] As early as 14 December 1874, the hospital's board of trustees had voted to move the infirmary because of the new railroad depot. The president, Sister Ann Gillen, purchased property by January 1875. It is not clear from the records why the hospital was not relocated at that time. "Corporation Book," pp. 63–64, 66; SVMC.

[53] "Corporation Book," p. 152.

[54] Entries in the "Corporation Book" between March 1883, and January 1886 record a total of $30,250 in lot sales, pp. 152–88; SVMC.

[55] The presidents of the hospital corporation and their terms of office were: Sisters Scholastica Logsdon, 1870–74; Ann Gillen, 1874–81; Emily Conway, 1881–85; and Severana Brandel, 1885–86. See "Corporation Book," pp. 14, 54, 123–24, 184; SVMC.

cornerstone ceremony for the Sisters' Infirmary was slated for 8 September 1884. She also discussed the details of construction and the difficulties of finance:

> By contract the whole building will cost, I mean Mason and Carpentry work, Sixty-three thousand and some dollars, Plumbing, etc., extra or different contracts, but the whole will not cost as much as was first supposed. There is property at the rate we have been selling to cover all, and it would be a relief if we could secure the cash.[56]

Property sales evidently did not proceed as rapidly as Conway anticipated, to meet payment deadlines for construction contracts. Corporation minutes recount that the Sisters' officers over two years' time contracted a series of short-term loans totaling $35,000, to cover their obligations.[57] The range of these financial dealings demonstrates the administrative skills of these nuns. They effectively secured the necessary loans, provided the appropriate collateral, and met repayment schedules in such a way as to maintain a sound credit rating. The nuns continued to negotiate their loans with the Farmers and Merchants Bank, the oldest and most reputable firm in the community.[58]

Similar documentation exists for the other corporation the Sisters formed in 1869, the Los Angeles Orphan Asylum.[59] As noted previously, a boarding school for girls and an orphanage comprised this institution, northeast of the plaza. Enrollment by 1878 totalled 202 students and 31 orphans, with the expenses of $12,765 running within

---

[56] Sister E[mily Conway] to "Very dear Father" [Alexis Mandine, C.M.], 17 August 1884, Los Angeles Infirmary, "Early History Mss." folder, "St. Vincent's Hospital" box; AWPDC.

[57] "Corporation Book," pp. 178, 181, 184, 185; SVMC.

[58] A summary of the early history of banking in Los Angeles is found in Robert Glass Cleland and Frank B. Putnam, *Isaias W. Hellman and the Farmers and Merchants Bank* (San Marino, California: The Huntington Library, 1980), pp. 9–57.

[59] The women who founded this society, on 21 June 1869 were Sisters Scholastica Logsdon, Ann Gillen, Francis Xavier Schauer, Mary Eugenia Maginnis, Mary Corsina McKay, Theresa McDonald, Mary Ellen Downey, Mary Angela Noyland, and Rosanna Smith. "Articles of Incorporation," Office of the Secretary of State, Sacramento, California. With their facility now located in suburban Rosemead and known as Maryvale, the Sisters still continue their work in child care.

$1.25 of receipts for that year.[60] In 1884, the nuns purchased new property, in East Los Angeles, to relocate the aged facility to more spacious grounds. The women then expended so little money on the old structure that

> on one occasion as a visitor was being entertained . . . in the parlor, there was a interruption in the conversation—a foot and ankle were seen protruding through the ceiling—a Sister was coming through, but fortunately her descent was arrested.[61]

Beginning construction of the new orphanage in early 1889, the nuns transferred the 300 orphans to the completed $150,000 structure in 1890.[62] The financial dealings for this and other projects over the years brought the Sisters into contact with a broad spectrum of the local population.

The third characteristic of the nuns' pioneering spirit was their willingness to associate widely with peoples of diverse faiths and cultures. Like other members of the Catholic laity, they participated directly in joint efforts to improve and protect the community. The work of the Sisters introduced them to members of all creeds and races. Their service in the smallpox epidemics offered dramatic evidence of the commitment of these women to the neediest of the town's residents. Other activities further document the cooperation of the nuns with settlers of differing origins in the City of the Angels.

As previously noted, in chapter 5, Spaniards and Irishmen long comprised the majority of the local Roman Catholic clergy. No Spanish-speaking male from Los Angeles sought training and ordination during the period 1848–85. A different situation existed among the women. Not only did the Daughters of Charity train local females to join their sisterhood, but they also received at least four Hispanic women into their novitiate. Additional nuns from Mexico served locally, and two received election as trustees in the hospital corporation.

---

[60] White, *Life of Mrs. Eliza A. Seton*, p. 504; and "Minutes," Los Angeles Orphan Asylum Board of Trustees, vol. 1, p. 75, Maryvale, Rosemead, California.

[61] "Remarks on Sister Mary Scholastica Logsdon," p. 120.

[62] "Remarks on Sister Mary Scholastica Logsdon," pp. 121–22.

Only one document survives listing all the women who worked in the asylum and hospital between 1856 and 1882.[63] Officers at the sisterhood's Paris headquarters recorded the names of 126 nuns who served in the Institución Caritativa and the Los Angeles Infirmary in those years. The vast majority were women of Irish descent, though it is impossible to determine the exact number. Eight of the Sisters were exiles from Mexico, of whom María Chávez and Guadalupe Quirván occupied seats on the hospital board, in 1875.[64] Two more were natives of Spain.[65] The other Hispanics in the local convent were native-born Californians, trained in the seminary under the charge of Sister Scholastica.

The distance from the Maryland motherhouse had led the superiors of the religious order, in 1860, to decide upon opening a West-Coast novitiate, or training program. Reverend Francis Burlando sent orders for Logsdon to commence the new endeavor in Los Angeles, despite her protests of her inability to conduct such a project.[66] Detailed instructions guided Logsdon in opening the institute, in early 1861. Of the six young women who commenced their training as Daughters of Charity that year, four were Hispanic. Three of the four remained in the program and joined the sisterhood: Sisters Angélica Olives, Agatha Quintana, and Josephine Orduño.[67]

The completion of the transcontinental railroad led provincial superiors, in 1870, to close the Los Angeles seminary. Thereafter, all who aspired to enter the sisterhood traveled to the motherhouse, in

---

[63] Register, "Catalogue du Personnel–Etats Unis" [ca. 1873–82], pp. 143, 167–70; Archives of the Daughters of Charity, Rue du Bac, Paris, France.

[64] "Corporation Book," pp. 71, 72; SVMC; and Los Angeles *Evening Express*, 24 February 1875.

[65] The Spaniards, as noted previously, were Sisters Angelita Mumbrado and Clara Cisneros. A third, Francesca Fernández, had left the Sisters shortly after her arrival in Los Angeles, in 1856. Recruited in Spain by Bishop Amat, she was apparently mentally unstable. See Letters, Logsdon to Burlando, 7 May 1856 and 4 June 1856, Los Angeles, "Correspondence, II;" AWPDC.

[66] Copy of Letter, Burlando to Logsdon, 12 November 1860, Emmitsburg, Maryland, "Correspondence, I;" Letter, Logsdon to Burlando, 30 December 1860, Los Angeles, "Correspondence, II;" and Letter, Sister Ann Simeon to Sister [Scholastica Logsdon], n.d., n.p., found in folder, "Los Angeles Orphanage–Early History"; AWPDC.

[67] Letter, Logsdon to Burlando, 4 May 1861, Los Angeles, AWPDC; and register

Maryland, for their training. In the years of her direction, 1861–70, approximately sixty women came under Logsdon's tutelage. Incomplete records make it difficult to determine exactly how many remained with the Sisters. The Paris "Catalogue du Personnel" lists thirty-two nuns who had come into the religious community through the southern California novitiate.[68]

These women involved themselves in service to the educational and health needs of Angelenos of all ages. The breadth of the nuns' involvement with the local populace amazed their contemporaries. The Sisters dealt with people from every socioeconomic level in the pueblo. While enrolling wealthy girls alongside orphans in the asylum's classes, the religious women educated the children of the local Indians, as well. The Sisters discovered that the daughters of the Indian people were no more difficult to train than any other children. The greatest obstacle proved to be language.

The Indian girls knew no English, and their instructor was unfamiliar with Spanish. The nun in question studied, "But the mixture of the Indian and Spanish dialect[s] embarrassed her frequently."[69] A similar situation existed among the nuns themselves, because three of the first six Sisters at the Institución Caritativa were Spaniards, and spoke no English; their three American companions had no knowledge of Spanish.[70] In the process of teaching one another, the Sisters attracted the Hispanic women of the rico class to the school. Studying English in the mornings, the señoras sat down to a noontime lunch, which their servants provided at tables in the yard.[71] Class and ethnicity were irrelevant factors in this frontier academy, a policy the nuns maintained in their nursing assignments as well.

The Sisters involved in nursing tended all those in need of medical attention at the county hospital for two decades. During the recurrent

---

"Catalogue du Personnel-Etats Unis," Archives of the Daughters of Charity, Rue du Bac, Paris, France.

[68] Logsdon noted, however, that in the first four years of the Los Angeles seminary, she had already trained thirty-three Sisters, enrolled five more, dismissed three, and suffered the loss of one other from death. Letter, Logsdon to Burlando, 29 January 1865, Los Angeles, "Correspondence, II;" AWPDC; and "Remarks on Sister Mary Scholastica Logsdon," p. 120.

[69] "San Francisco" ledger, p. 97; AWPDC.

[70] "Remarks on Sister Mary Scholastica Logsdon," p. 111.

[71] Mumbrado, "Remembrance," p. 8.

smallpox epidemics, these women also tended the stricken, regardless of race. Their solicitude for the dying Indians amazed many native Californios. The Indios comprised the lowest level of Los Angeles society and worked in the homes and on the estates of the wealthy in the most menial labor. One chronicler of the religious group recalled that ministering to these afflicted people in 1861–62 brought the nuns "the respect of Jew and Gentile." [72]

The care of orphans won for the Daughters of Charity further renown, along with widespread support in the community. From the time of the nuns' arrival, in 1856, Angelenos of all classes and creeds stood ready to assist in sustaining the local shelter for children, in the custody of the Sisters. The involvement of people regardless of religious heritage long characterized these efforts. The Sisters praised local Jews, in 1869, for their "encouraging words and open purses." [73] Even the town's pioneer rabbi left a bequest for the orphanage at the time of his death, in 1907. [74]

A variety of related undertakings brought this band of women into contact with the elite and the impoverished, the Spanish-speaking and people of other languages. When an orphan came of age, for example, the Sisters arranged for some "respectable" employment, such as service as a governess or domestic. Sister Scholastica noted that she could easily find placements for these young women. [75] Logsdon was acquainted with members of the leading families in the community, and she utilized her social connections for the benefit of her wards.

---

[72] "San Francisco" ledger, pp. 97–99; AWPDC.

[73] Los Angeles *Daily Star*, 22 January 1869, as quoted in Norton B. Stern and William M. Kramer, "An 1869 Jewish Standard for Gentile Behavior," *Western States Jewish Historical Quarterly*, IX (April, 1977), p. 284.

[74] Regarding the interreligious support of the Sisters, see William H. Workman, "Sister Scholastica," Historical Society of Southern California *Annual Publication*, V (1902), p. 258. Rabbi Abraham Wolf Edelman's bequest can be found in Norton B. Stern and William M. Kramer, "Jewish Padre to the Pueblo: Pioneer Los Angeles Rabbi Abraham Wolf Edelman," *Western States Jewish Historical Quarterly*, III (July 1971), p. 221. The nuns' banker, Isaias W. Hellman, also remembered their orphanage in his will, with a bequest of $5,000, in 1921. See William M. Kramer and Reva Clar, "Emanuel Schreiber," *Western States Jewish Historical Quarterly*, IX (July 1977), p. 367.

[75] Letter, Logsdon to Burlando, 18 September 1859, Los Angeles, "Correspondence, II;" AWPDC. See also Los Angeles *Star*, 7 May 1870; and Wallace E. Smith, *This Land Was Ours: The Del Valles of Rancho Camulos* (Ventura, California: Ventura County Historical Society, 1977), p. 116.

Such contacts also proved to be valuable for the success of several projects of the local clergy, as well.

"Las Señoras del Altar," the women's society of Our Lady of the Angels Church, solicited funds, in 1869, to renovate the shrine of Saint Vibiana, the diocesan patroness. The majority of donors listed for this project were women from the wealthiest Roman Catholic families. The names of Hispanics and Irish predominate on the ledger pages. Two entries specify the gifts of the Daughters of Charity and reveal their active involvement in this society of parish women.[76] In addition to this parochial project, the Sisters were engaged in a diocesan fundraising endeavor four years later.

As recounted in chapter 8, the construction of a diocesan cathedral required five years of concentrated effort by the bishops, priests, and parishioners. All segments of the Roman Catholic population cooperated to meet the staggering challenge of raising $75,000 in building costs. The Daughters of Charity sponsored one of the major events in the early part of the campaign to raise revenues. Through their ability to bring together people of differing classes and creeds, the nuns could attract a corps of volunteers to collaborate on this highly successful project. The Sisters' Fair in 1873, on behalf of the cathedral, was one of the two most profitable benefits held during the erection of the edifice, 1871–76.[77]

This range of activities, from nursing Indians to fundraising for cathedral construction, kept the Sisters in contact with a wide array of people in the town. These involvements enabled the nuns to render what were probably their greatest services to their church and their adopted community, by bridging two major divisions within local society. The first split involved the Hispanics, who were suffering displacement within their church in the latter half of the nineteenth-century. The second chasm was found between the growing Anglo-American population and the European-born bishops and priests of the Roman Catholic communion.

Bishop Amat worked vigorously to conform local Catholicism to the norms mandated by the national hierarchy in the United States. Amat preferred rubrically precise worship, devoid of the various reli-

---

[76] "Book of Subscriptions," p. 18; AALA.

[77] The Sisters' Fair raised $1,621.70, while a Fourth of July dinner, in 1875, produced $1,622.55. "Cuentas de la Catedral de Sta. Vibiana V. y M.," p. 25; AALA.

gious customs that had evolved over two centuries on the isolated frontera. The restriction of these pious traditions alienated many local Hispanic Catholics and left them feeling like strangers in their own church. The Daughters of Charity, however, had participated in this Hispanic piety from the time of their arrival, in 1856.[78] The nuns had also served the Spanish speaking in the school and orphanage, at the hospital, and during the repeated epidemics.

In the course of educating Hispanic girls at the academy over three decades, the Sisters also welcomed several of them into the sisterhood itself. The number of Californio women to enter the religious group was small; only three are known to have joined prior to 1885. Nonetheless, there existed a mutual acceptance between the Sisters and these women that was certainly absent between the local clergy and Hispanic young men. The nuns worked to serve the various needs of this increasingly marginalized population and in the process maintained one of the few effective pastoral bridges between local Hispanics and the church of their ancestors.

The Sisters were also important intermediaries between European-born church officials and the growing local settlement. Bishop Amat showed little understanding or adaptation to the frontier community's broad-mindedness in religious matters. He recruited his clergy from his native Spain and later from Ireland. The legislation of the diocesan synods during his tenure of office mandated ever more precise and restrictive requirements for Catholic behavior. For the twenty-three years of his episcopacy (1855–78), Amat retained a thoroughly European perspective in the matters of church and society.

The nuns offered a marked contrast to their denomination's local leader and many of his clergymen. The Sisters worked beside people of all faiths, in community-service projects ranging from education to emergency health care. These women participated in the cooperative female activities in the town, as well. They were acquainted with a broader spectrum of pueblo society than most priests, because of their diverse works. While garnering the respect of fellow Angelenos

---

[78] See *El Clamor Público*, of 5 June 1858, for a typical description of the nuns' participation in the street procession on the feast day of Corpus Christi. The Sisters marshalled some one hundred orphans, dressed in white, in the march around the plaza that day.

for their care of society's unfortunates, the nuns also provided their church with a flexible corps of dedicated workers.

These women also attracted attention as the first female business executives in the community. When their property was threatened, the Sisters sought recourse, through the American legal system, to incorporate themselves and thereby insure the safe possession of their goods. Their hospital and orphanage developed into important local institutions, requiring increasingly sophisticated skills to staff, supervise, and finance. The Sisters offered local Catholic women a vocational alternative to homemaking and keeping school. As the historian Hasia R. Diner has noted, "Nuns provided role models of women engaged in a variety of educational, charitable, and social welfare activities, often doing work deemed inappropriate for women." [79]

The range of roles modeled by the Sisters for Los Angeles women exceeded those sanctioned in the Catholic church that Bishop Amat had known in Spain. Here on the frontier was an American-based group of religious women buying and selling property, in the name of legal corporations they had constituted themselves. Here, too, were nuns who negotiated with bankers, lobbied politicians, and worked alongside Protestants and Jews to benefit the health and welfare of townspeople. Such wide involvement did not take place in the Old World, where nuns led a more cloistered and restricted existence.

In offering new roles for local Catholic women, the Daughters of Charity also provided local members of their faith with an alternative model for the church itself. In their service to the civic community, they also contributed to their religious communion. The nuns struggled, as did all Catholics, to be both American and Catholic. However, the Sisters looked less frequently to Rome for their inspiration and guidance than did their clerical counterparts. This more flexible spirit, so typical of Catholic female religious in the United States, allowed these women to undertake necessary new works, to search creatively for means to fund these ventures, and to serve as unofficial bridge builders between estranged groups in both church and community.

[79] Hasia R. Diner, *Erin's Daughters in America: Irish Immigrant Women in the Nineteenth Century* (Baltimore: Johns Hopkins University Press, 1983), p. 130. Jay P. Dolan supports this idea, in his volume, *The American Catholic Experience: A History from Colonial Times to the Present* (Garden City, New York: Doubleday and Company, 1985), p. 290.

Historians have characterized this spirit of adaptation as a key trait of the truly "American" churches on the frontier in the nineteenth century. The Daughters of Charity demonstrated that members of the Roman Catholic communion could also grapple creatively with the exigencies of pioneer life in their pueblo convent. To the extent that the Sisters altered their practices, they merit recognition for their "American" accomplishments. The experiences of these women in Los Angeles offer important amplifications to historical accounts that focus so exclusively upon the accomplishments of men, particularly bishops and priests. As members of the more numerous laity, the nuns demonstrate quite clearly the willingness of this segment of their church to engage in flexible responses to frontier demands.

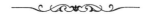
DISPLACEMENT OF ROMAN
CATHOLICS IN LOS ANGELES

Sitting down one evening with his diary, Benjamin Ignatius Hayes noted that on 1 April 1850 he had been duly sworn in as county attorney in Los Angeles. He and the other elected officials had gathered in the *sala,* the living room, of the adobe town house of Don Ygnacio del Valle, the new county recorder. Their host had prepared an altar for the occasion, a cloth-draped table surmounted with a crucifix. Señor del Valle even provided a cushion upon which to kneel. He solemnly beckoned the gentlemen forward, to sign the constitutional oath of office. The other Californios in the group hesitated, unfamiliar as they were with the customs of this new government, introduced through United States conquest.

Hayes and the Norteamericanos present indicated the new order, by declining to kneel before the cross. Hayes, a fellow Roman Catholic, noted that del Valle "was somewhat shocked at our cold, unsentimental form on such a *gran ocasión.*"[1] The pious don's sensibilities were due for many another jolt in years to come. Every aspect of pueblo life would suffer drastic change or challenge. Dispensing with customary religious trappings in government ceremonies comprised but a single instance in the unraveling of the neatly woven integration of church and state in Mexican Los Angeles. The shock that Señor del Valle suffered in his own sala symbolized the much broader clash between two cultures that emerged in the aftermath of the warfare of 1846–48.[2]

[1] Quoted in Marjorie Tisdale Wolcott, ed., *Pioneer Notes from the Diaries of Judge Benjamin Hayes, 1849–1875* (Los Angeles: Privately Printed, 1929), p. 186.
[2] Wallace E. Smith, *This Land Was Ours: The Del Valles and Camulos* (Ventura, Cali-

Chapter 8

The United States victory commenced a quarter century of tumultuous transformation in the City of the Angels. Political, social, religious, and economic practices introduced after the war eventually redefined the community's cultural orientation and self-understanding. Wholesale displacement of local Hispanics ensued, with their lands forfeited and their pastoral economy ruined. The Californios resisted the encroachments of the Yanqui, but were forced to retreat by forces they neither fully understood nor controlled. In this and the following chapter, we examine the dual dynamics operative in the religious displacement in Los Angeles between 1848 and 1880.

We consider two specific processes: in one, the ecclesial leaders of the town's oldest communion endeavored to create a distinct and separate Catholic subculture; in the second, members of arriving creeds reformed the community along American Protestant lines. Catholics followed an agenda that the assembled hierarchy of the United States dictated, in a series of nineteenth-century conclaves. Among Protestants, believers also pursued national denominational issues and dedicated themselves to bringing to Los Angeles starched-collar manners and mores, such as temperance and Sabbath observance. Members of both traditions commonly disregarded the regional heritage of the indigenous community. In this chapter, we examine the involvement of Roman Catholics in this radical redefinition of the local religious ethos. Not only were Spanish-speaking residents desperately struggling to retain their homes, property, and culture during these years, but they were clinging to traditions of faith that also were under attack during the "Americanization" of their church.

During the years 1846 to 1888, this pueblo of Hispanic and Indian Roman Catholics was the destination of Protestant home missionaries, immigrant Jews, and laboring Chinese.[3] Several scholars in re-

---

fornia: Ventura County Historical Society, 1977), pp. 166, 169, 172–73. Del Valle himself would die, debt-ridden, in 1881, having lost political prominence and most of his estate, not to mention the influence he and his family had once enjoyed. Ygnacio del Valle's eldest son, Reginaldo, first served in the California State Assembly in 1880, and the state senate in 1882. Long active in southern California political circles, he never received election to any post after his initial two victories. The most that del Valle achieved was an honorary leadership in the Hispanic community.

[3] One historian described the settlement during those years as "Californian in the center, Mexican toward the east, Yankee in the west, and cosmopolitan everywhere." Leonard Pitt, *The Decline of the Californios: A Social History of the Spanish-Speaking Californians, 1846–1890* (Berkeley: University of California Press, 1966), p. 121.

cent years have examined the intricacies of the sometimes stormy interaction among such frontier believers. If community formation often involved social conflict, as these historians have argued, pioneer church formation could be equally discordant.[4] In fact, such dissension was a constitutive dynamic in church growth. Nowhere was this more true than in the frontera wrested from Mexico. Throughout California and the Southwest, creed constituted yet another element of the new social order emerging after the war. In numerous settlements of this semiarid region, adherents of arriving creeds clashed with the pobladores, the Spanish-speaking residents, who had long cherished vastly different customs and beliefs.

The first rivulet of change began to flow in Los Angeles with the removal of Hispanics and their established faith from positions of prominence and influence in local society. This displacement coincided with those complex processes that impoverished the Spanish-speaking throughout the state after 1848. Californios first lost their lands and property and then political control and representation, which left them residing in ever more concentrated ethnic enclaves in the town. They also experienced a steady downward social mobility vis à vis employment opportunities for themselves and their children. A few of the most prominent rancheros managed to retain their patrimonies, but the vast majority of the *hijos del país,* the "sons of the land," were effectively deprived of their holdings.

Several scholars have ably documented the processes by which Hispanics lost the public and private lands underpinning the Mexican pastoral economy.[5] The Spanish-speaking were unfamiliar with the language and legal system of the United States, as well as with the procedures of a newly formed Board of Land Commissioners. Established by Congress, in 1851, this body eventually reviewed 848 private land grants in California. The commissioners sought to estab-

---

[4] See Allan G. Bogue, "Social Theory and the Pioneer," *Agricultural History,* XXXIV (January 1960), pp. 21–34; Robert R. Dystra, *The Cattle Towns* (New York: Alfred A. Knopf, Inc., 1968; reprint ed., New York: Athaneum, 1974), pp. 207–92, 371–78; Don Harrison Doyle, "Social Theory and New Communities in Nineteenth-Century America," *Western Historical Quarterly,* VIII (April 1977), pp. 151–66; and John Mack Faragher, *Sugar Creek: Life on the Illinois Prairie* (New Haven: Yale University Press, 1986), pp. 156–70.

[5] In particular, see Pitt, *The Decline of the Californios;* Robert Glass Cleland, *The Cattle on a Thousand Hills,* second edition (San Marino, California: Huntington Library, 1951); Richard Griswold del Castillo, *The Los Angeles Barrio, 1850–1890: A Social History* (Berkeley: University of California, 1979).

lish the correct ownership and boundaries of lands roughly surveyed under Spanish and Mexican regimes. The lengthy and costly judicial review of these titles compounded the host of problems the owners faced in retaining their property.[6]

Hispanic landholding was undermined by the activities of unscrupulous lawyers, usurious rates of interest on borrowed money, confiscation of land by squatters, and "confiscatory" tax rates levied by the state on unimproved land, in order to break up large landholdings. Town councils in Los Angeles and elsewhere proceeded to sell the *ejidos,* the traditional communal lands of the pueblo. Embarrassed by a lack of revenue, municipal authorities auctioned off fields that numerous residents had long utilized to graze their stock and raise small plots of produce. The booming cattle trade of the 1850s briefly masked the serious nature of these actions. The Californios enjoyed a brief period of prosperity, long remembered for its lavish fiestas, open-handed hospitality, and the extravagant betting in card games and horse races.[7]

One example will suffice to illustrate the catastrophic effects of these converging and interrelated factors. In 1851, the two leading landholders in the county both resided in Los Angeles: José Andrés Sepúlveda and Abel Stearns. Sepúlveda owned some 102,000 acres devoted to cattle grazing, assessed at $83,000. The Massachusetts-born Stearns, married to the belle of the prominent Bandini clan, had amassed 140,000 acres, valued at $90,000.[8] Over the next dozen years, the collapse of the cattle trade threw the local economy into chaos and visited ruin upon the personal fortunes of these men and their associates.

Renowned for his stable of race horses and his extravagant life

[6] The work of the Land Commission is described from differing perspectives in W. W. Robinson, *Land in California* (Berkeley: University of California Press, 1944), pp. 99–100, 105; and Paul Wallace Gates, "Adjudication of the Spanish-Mexican Land Claims in California," *Huntington Library Quarterly,* XXI (May, 1959), pp. 213–36, and *California Ranchos and Farms, 1846–1860* (Madison: State Historical Society of Wisconsin, 1967), pp. 7–16.

[7] Alberto Camarillo, *Chicanos in a Changing Society: From Mexican Pueblos to American Barrios in Santa Barbara and Southern California, 1848–1930* (Cambridge: Harvard University Press, 1979), p. 114.

[8] Los Angeles County Assessment Book for 1851, cited by Benjamin I. Hayes in *An Historical Sketch of Los Angeles County,* by J. J. Warner, Hayes, and J. P. Widney (Los Angeles: Lewis Lewin, 1876; reprint ed., Los Angeles: O. W. Smith, 1936), p. 80.

style, José Sepúlveda did not survive the disastrous drought of 1863–64. When his cattle died by the hundreds, the don turned to local moneylenders to obtain funds for the taxes due on his vast acreage. He was unable to pay off the resulting mortgages, with interest rates of seven to ten percent, compounded monthly. Moving to Sinaloa, Mexico, the former grandee died, impoverished, in 1875, after selling off the last of his estates.[9] By way of contrast, Stearns had increased his holdings to some 200,000 acres by 1860, developed his commercial properties in Los Angeles, and survived the adversities of drought and taxation, through the sale or subdivision of much of his grazing land.[10]

Similar accounts could be multiplied repeatedly, to cover the economic turmoil that American rule and natural adversity brought upon Hispanics in the southern "cow counties" of the state. The historian Richard Griswold del Castillo, in particular, has compiled convincing data for the losses suffered by all classes among the Spanish-speaking residents of Los Angeles.[11] According to his analysis of property re-

Table 2: Mexican-American Property Holders in
Los Angeles, 1850–1870[12]

Year	Number of property-holding heads of families	Number of families	% of fam. heads with prop.	Average value of property
1850	135	220	61.4%	$2,105
1860	153	530	28.8%	$1,228
1870	116	545	21.2%	$1,072

[9] Robert Glass Cleland, *The Irvine Ranch* (rev. ed., San Marino, California: Huntington Library, 1962), pp. 41–43; and *Saddleback Ancestors: Rancho Families of Orange County, California* (Orange, California: Orange County California Genealogical Society, 1969), pp. 110–11.

[10] Extensive correspondence documents the economic fortunes of Abel Stearns. See, in particular, the following: Letter, C.R. Johnson to Stearns, 7 October and 8 November 1862; Statement of Account, Juan Bandini to Abel Stearns, 28 January 1856; Letter, H.F. Teschemacher to Stearns, 13 June 1862; and Letter, Andrew Casserly to Stearns, 4 April 1863; all from the Abel Stearns Collection, HL. See also Cleland, *Cattle on the Thousand Hills*, pp. 190, 196–207; and John Quincy Adams Warren, "Letter," *American Stock Journal*, III (July 1861), reprinted in Gates, *California Ranches and Farms*, pp. 115–34.

[11] Griswold del Castillo, *Los Angeles Barrio*, pp. 46–49.

[12] Griswold del Castillo, *Los Angeles Barrio*, p. 47.

tention among Californios, town dwellers lost their properties much earlier than rural residents. This process was well underway in the 1850s. The pueblo's rapid rate of commercial activity increased the value of real estate in town and made it more difficult for Hispanic Angelenos to retain their properties, because of pressure from speculators, investors, and lawyers. The collapse of the cattle trade, expensive litigation, and the great droughts did not hit the surrounding rancheros until the early 1860s.

With the forfeiture of their lands and the means to earn a livelihood, Californios also exerted diminished political influence. As with property retention, Hispanics living in town experienced a loss of political position earlier than their compatriots in the rest of the county. Griswold del Castillo has compiled statistics that document these developments. In the period 1850–59, fifty-seven Hispanics held state, county, or town offices by election or appointment. This number fell to thirty-one in the decade 1860–69, and the total remained the same for the subsequent ten years, 1870–79.[13] In the elections after 1860, the rural Hispanic vote was necessary to carry a Spanish-speaking candidate, because of the great number of Anglo-American residents in town.

Hispanics who sought office in Los Angeles came from the ranks of the rico families that had adapted most quickly to American political life. As early as 1848, names such as Olvera, del Valle, Coronel, and Requeña appeared on the ballot, after nomination in closed *juntas,* or meetings of the elite. By 1850, two Maryland lawyers fashioned an alliance with these Hispanics, which would dominate the community for the next decade. With many of the newcomers to Los Angeles in the 1850s arriving from the South, Joseph Lancaster Brent and Benjamin Ignatius Hayes formed a coalition between these Democrats and the Californio leaders. The suave Brent and the hard-drinking Hayes learned the Spanish language, defended the land titles of the Hispanics, and moved freely in the social circles of the upper class.[14]

---

[13] Griswold del Castillo, *Los Angeles Barrio,* pp. 158–59.

[14] Hayes had the added advantage of being a Roman Catholic, in a town where the vast majority of the residents shared that faith; Pitt, *Decline of the Californios,* pp. 132–33. Brent strengthened his alliance with the prominent del Valle family by serving as *padrino,* or godfather, at the baptism of several of their children. According to the

Much of the success of Brent and Hayes in those early years arose from their understanding of voting customs among the Californios. By deciding to cast his ballot for a particular candidate, the patriarch of a Hispanic family simultaneously determined the votes of his sons, relations, and numerous retainers. Hispanic names proved to be a valuable asset to the Democratic ticket. In 1857, for example, three of the five county supervisors were native-born Angelenos, as were fifteen of the thirty-three election judges, six justices of the peace, and five constables. The advent of the Civil War fractured this coalition, but local Democrats remained a powerful force through 1864.[15]

In the late 1860s, Hispanics maintained an increasingly precarious political position, through their alliance with the Democrats. Immigration into Los Angeles resumed after the war, and new settlers strengthened the local Republican party. A high rate of residential mobility, along with the concentration of the Spanish-speaking in *barrios,* further undermined Hispanic influence in local and county politics.[16] Candidates such as Antonio Coronel and Reginaldo del Valle turned to their *compadres* in the outlying districts of the county to augment the ballots cast by their supporters in the town.[17] But this was a short-lived solution, because of the declining proportion of Hispanics in the population. The population influx of the 1880s overwhelmed Spanish-speaking voters and led to the loss of the last vestiges of Hispanic political influence.

By that time, half of the Hispanic populace was concentrated in a single area, nicknamed "Sonoratown," located east of Main Street and north of the plaza. Residentially segregated and poverty stricken, the majority of the Spanish-speaking in this and later barrios were employed in low-level occupations by 1880. The barrio, however,

---

customs of this relationship, he was further considered a *compadre,* or member of the family. See Smith, *This Land was Ours,* pp. 101, 106, 115.

[15] Pitt, *Decline of the Californios,* pp. 203–204, 241.

[16] Those Hispanics who managed to survive politically tended to come from a small group of elite families, so that year after year the same surnames appeared on the ballots. Examples of the repetition of family names among candidates can be found in the lists of county and city officials contained in J. Albert Wilson, *History of Los Angeles County, California,* (Oakland, California: Thompson and West, 1880; reprint ed., Berkeley: Howell-North, 1959), pp. 50–51, and 114–15, respectively.

[17] Camarillo, *Chicanos in a Changing Society,* p. 111; Griswold del Castillo, *Los Angeles Barrio,* p. 159; Pitt, *Decline of the Californios,* pp. 272–73.

provided a place where the traditional language and social customs might still survive. Mutual aid societies, known as *mutualistas*, and political clubs, *juntas patrióticas*, were only two of the various types of organizations by which residents rendered support to one another, deflected prejudice, and maintained their collective identity.[18] Residents here also freely practiced traditional pious customs beyond the scrutiny of the parish priest.

The "Americanization" of Los Angeles did not spare the Roman Catholic church, but introduced clerics who sought to replace the time-honored devotional customs inherited from the frontera. This spiritual displacement affected the Spanish-speaking as profoundly as their economic and political reverses. A group of new clergy set out to strengthen the institution of the formal church, often at the expense of a more spontaneous folk piety, long popular among the laity.

The faith life of the pobladores had long been a blend of church ceremony and familial piety, in which a host of religious feastdays punctuated the calendar year. Colorful processions wound their way from the church and through the dusty streets of the pueblo in honor of one or another popular saint. Religious customs marked all facets of life, from birth through death. This piety reached into every household, with a deep respect for God, the Virgin Mary, the saints, and the clergy. The community as a whole recognized the place of religion, through the allocated "sacred space," for its church on the plaza, and burial ground, or *campo santo*, on the edge of town. Families also reserved such holy space in their homes, where *altarcitos*, or shrines, were adorned with candles, flowers, and religious images.[19]

The household's day customarily began and ended with an *alabado*, or hymn of praise, while other prayers, such as the rosary or the

---

[18] The Los Angeles *Daily Star*, for 9 April 1876, described the activities of one prominent *mutualista*, the Spanish-American Mutual Benefit Society, with 128 members. The significance of such organizations in the barrio for cultural survival is discussed at length in Griswold del Castillo, *Los Angeles Barrio*, pp. 103–138; Camarillo, *Chicanos in a Changing Society*, pp. 118–20; and Antonio Ríos-Bustamente and Pedro Castillo, *An Illustrated History of Mexican Los Angeles, 1781–1985*, (Los Angeles: Chicano Studies Research Center, University of California, 1986), pp. 99–109.

[19] Antonio F. Coronel, "Cosas de California," (Dictation D-16, 1877), p. 230, BL; Arnoldo de Leon, *The Tejano Community, 1836–1900* (Albuquerque: University of New Mexico Press, 1982), pp. 139–49; and Barnabas C. Diekemper, O.F.M., "The Catholic Church in the Shadows: the Southwestern United States During the Mexican Period," *Journal of the West*, XXIV (April 1985), pp. 49–50.

Angelus, were announced by tolling church bells. Harris Newmark arrived in 1853 and later recalled, "In the first years of my residence here, the bells . . . ringing at six in the morning and at eight in the evening, served as a curfew to regulate the daily activities of the town."[20] These forms of Roman Catholicism were derived from long years on the frontera, where few priests had been present. Devotions and practices had evolved that did not require the sacramental rituals of the clergy, and which lay members could conduct. Nurtured in the family, these customs formed a communal matrix of belief that integrated the hard-won joys and the too-frequent sorrows of life on the frontier.

Foremost among these shared practices was that of *compadrazgo,* a social network binding together individuals, families, and classes under the blessing of the church. At the time of a child's baptism, the parents would ask two people well known to them to serve as godparents, to assist in the child's spiritual upbringing. In the event of the death of the parents, the *padrino* and *madrino* were expected to adopt the child. The two persons acting as godparents were related to the parents as *compadres* and were considered part of the extended family. The child grew up to treat these sponsors with the respect and honor due to parents, while the *padrinos,* in turn, remembered their ward with gifts and special affection.

Such ties, with their religious overtones, formed what one Angeleno termed *"un vínculo de afinidad,"* a tie of affinity, which bound the townspeople together. It extended from the parents and their children to the godparents, and augmented the social networks of intermarriage or blood relationship. Outsiders, such as immigrant Anglo-Americans, could easily be included within the family circle. This means of inclusion encouraged the formation of bonds by which newcomers were assimilated into the life of pueblo society. While not having the force of law, compadrazgo existed by custom throughout the Hispanic frontera and persisted well after United States conquest.[21]

---

[20] *Sixty Years in Southern California, 1853–1913,* (4th ed., revised by Maurice H. Newmark and Marco R. Newmark, Los Angeles: Zeitlin and Ver Brugge, 1970), p. 101.
[21] Coronel, "Cosas de California," p. 231, BL; Henry D. Barrows, "Captain Alexander Bell and the Bell Block," *Historical Society of Southern California Annual*

Chapter 8

The communal expression of religious beliefs occurred frequently in the life of the settlement, and pueblo residents participated according to status and station. The annual Corpus Christi procession, after Easter, for example, stopped at elaborate altars erected in front of the houses of the elite rico families. Designated leaders supervised the Christmas pastorelas, or miracle plays, performed in the church. The town's corps of soldiers conducted the mock trial of Judas Iscariot during Holy Week, followed by his execution, in effigy, in the plaza. Other customs included refraining from fiestas during the forty days of Lent, bathing in the river for good health on the feast of St. John the Baptist, and visiting the cemetery on All Souls Day, November 2, to light candles and pray for the dead.[22]

Besides these seasonal devotions, personal practices took a variety of forms, the most popular being the veneration of the saints and the Virgin Mary. People attributed special powers to their patron saints, such as restoration of health or assistance with good weather, and bound themselves by vows known as *promesas* to obtain a request. An individual might also undertake a novena, nine days of special prayers, including a visit to the church. Other forms of piety included pilgrimages to a shrine, the wearing of medals, scapulars, or crucifixes, the sprinkling of holy water on a person or place, and the burning of candles. Finally, parents, godparents, and other elders bestowed formal blessings on children and relatives before or after any absence.[23]

Publication, III, Part III (1895), p. 14; and a humorous treatment in Horace Bell, *Reminiscences of a Ranger* (Los Angeles: Yarnell, Caystile, and Mathes, 1881), pp. 179–82. For a sensitive and insightful description of persisting compadrazgo, see Bishop Henri Granjon's memoir, *A Pastoral Visit To Southwest New Mexico in 1902* (Albuquerque: University of New Mexico Press, 1986), pp. 38–39.

[22] These customs were extensively noted and reported in mid-nineteenth-century Los Angeles. For Corpus Christi, see *El Clamor Público*, 28 May 1853, 5 June 1858, and 25 June 1859; for the Christmas pastorelas, see *El Clamor Público*, 29 December 1855 and 5 January 1856; and for All Souls Day, see *El Clamor Público*, 7 November 1857 and Los Angeles *Daily Star*, 3 November 1870. The execution of Judas attracted the attention of Horace Bell, in his *Reminiscences of a Ranger*, pp. 287–88; while other practices are treated in two volumes by Ana Begue de Packman, *Early California Hospitality* (Glendale, California: Arthur H. Clark Company, 1938), pp. 157–61, and *Leather Dollar Days* (Los Angeles: Times-Mirror Press, 1932), p. 18. See also Susanna Bryant Dakin, ed., *Navidad: A Christmas Day with the Early Californians* (San Francisco: California Historical Society, 1958).

[23] Wolcott, ed., *Pioneer Notes from . . . Hayes*, p. 199.

The diversity of these personal and communal customs effectively brought religion within the daily experience of the ordinary person. As noted previously, such devotions were needed in a region where priests were few in number and frequently absent from the pueblo. Most of the practices described here required little more than an occasional visit of a clergyman. When present, the priest performed those services reserved to his ministry; only he could solemnize a marriage, celebrate the mass, or hear confessions. While an individual cleric might not inspire popularity or even respect, most Hispanics nonetheless generally revered the office he represented in local society.[24]

Under Mexican rule, Los Angeles had warranted a resident pastor, because of its size and its importance in the province. The majority of clerics tending the church on the plaza, Our Lady of the Angels, had been Frenchmen, of the Society of the Sacred Hearts. Scarcity of clergy in California had prompted church authorities to accept the services of these Gallic missionaries, in 1832. Tolerant of Hispanic religious customs, these priests withdrew for other lands in 1856, soon after Bishop Thaddeus Amat assumed leadership of the diocese. Amat named as the new pastor the Reverend Blas Raho, a Neapolitan, who had served in various posts in the southern and midwestern United States, since 1838.[25]

Bishop Amat initiated successive measures to redirect religious practices and bring them in line with those found elsewhere in the United States and in Europe. He envisioned a local Catholic communion thoroughly Roman in orientation, uniform in expression, and obedient to him in its actions.[26] His alterations were the local instances

[24] Reverend Edmond Venisse, SS.CC., recorded, in 1856, one instance in which he experienced the sincere Hispanic regard for the priesthood. Shortly after his ordination, the members of an entire congregation in Santa Barbara came forward to kneel and kiss his hands. See Venisse, "Extrait d'une lettre," *Annales* de la Propagation de la Foi (Lyon, France), XXX (1858), p. 58. For a discussion of the role of the cleric on the frontera in the Mexican era, see David J. Weber, *The Mexican Frontier, 1821–1846: The American Southwest Under Mexico* (Albuquerque: University of New Mexico Press, 1982), pp. 69–82. See also Oakah L. Jones, Jr., *Los Paisanos: Spanish Settlers on the Northern Frontiers of New Spain* (Norman: University of Oklahoma Press, 1980), pp. 149–54, 237.

[25] Harold A. Whelan, SS.CC., *The Picpus Story* (Pomona, California: Apostolate of Christian Renewal, 1980), pp. 90–93, 103–23, 175–82, 186–88.

[26] Bishop Amat reiterated his concept of episcopal authority in several letters to his flock, citing the New Testament to bolster his claims: "Obey your Prelates, and be subject to them . . . (Hebrews 13,17)," as quoted in Amat, *Pastoral Letter* (Los

of a nationwide effort the Roman Catholic hierarchy was promoting. With immigrant groups flooding the dioceses of the country, the bishops sought to meet immense pastoral needs, while at the same time countering the bitter prejudice of Know-Nothings and other nativists. They advocated the formation of a separate religious subculture within the nation. These clerics wanted to segregate Catholics culturally and socially from the mainstream of an antagonistic Protestant American society.

Distinguishing between the sacred and the secular realms, the prelates also concerned themselves with the personal morality of the laity, to the neglect of broader societal concerns. The bishops sought safety for their flock within "a uniform adherence to ritual practices, patterns of religious behavior, and forms of prayer," which bound their church together and united it more securely with the international ecclesial body.[27] Meeting in Baltimore, in 1866, the Second Plenary Council enacted particularly specific legislation regarding the devotions of the laity. These regulations covered prayer books, parish missions, devotional organizations, indulgences, and a host of other pious practices. Church authorities in Rome reviewed and amended these rules, yet never reminded the American hierarchy to attend to the social issues plaguing their flocks.

Amat, in subscribing to the new laws, pledged to make "every effort to see to it that one and the same discipline is everywhere observed."[28] Such insistence on ritual conformity insured a clerically controlled uniformity of religious expression, but it denigrated the local spiritual heritage and neglected altogether the tragic issue of Hispanic loss of economic security and political representation. Amat's policies, coinciding as they did with the dramatic decline of Hispanic fortunes, unintentionally exacerbated the woes of this increasingly marginalized portion of his flock.

Angeles: n.p., 1869), p. 10; see also his *Exhortación Pastoral* (Los Angeles: Office of the Southern Californian, 1856), p. 4; and *Pastoral Letter* (San Francisco: Smyth and Shoaff, 1872), pp. 3, 12.

[27] Joseph P. Chinnichi, O.F.M., "Organization of the Spiritual Life: American Catholic Devotional Works, 1791–1866," *Theological Studies*, XL (June 1979), p. 229.

[28] *Acta et Decreta Sacrorum Conciliorum Recentiorum Collectio Lacensis 3*, p. 502, quoted in Ann Taves, *The Household of Faith: Roman Catholic Devotions in Mid-Nineteenth-Century America* (Notre Dame, Indiana: University of Notre Dame Press, 1986), p. 118.

The historian Richard Griswold del Castillo has ventured so far as to term the results of these actions the "spiritual segregation" of the Spanish-speaking from the church of their birth.[29] Indeed, the old forms of religious expression had been integral to the cultural ethos of the community, far more so than contemporary observers recognized. These customs acquired a poignant significance with the accelerating Anglo-American transformation of the pueblo. As discussed in chapter 4, the array of clerical alterations sought to separate Catholics securely from local society.[30] Four examples illustrate how these changes Amat initiated contributed to the Hispanic sense of spiritual disorientation.

Soon after his arrival in California, the freshly consecrated bishop substituted a Roman saint in place of a Mexican madonna, as patroness of his diocese. The original had been the Virgin Mary, under the Mexican title, *Nuestra Señora del Refugio*, Our Lady of Refuge. The first bishop in California, Francisco García Diego y Moreno, had made this selection in 1841, based on the Virgin's veneration at his alma mater, the Franciscan missionary seminary of Our Lady of Guadalupe, in Zacatecas, Mexico.[31] In 1854, Pope Pius IX named Amat to the southern portion of García Diego's divided diocese. While in Rome, Amat received from the pope the recently discovered relics of a third-century martyr, Vibiana, on the condition that a cathedral be erected in her honor.[32]

Amat departed the Eternal City carrying the bones of Vibiana to California, and in 1856, he requested that she be named patroness of his diocese. Furthermore, he established a lay association known as an archconfraternity, to which the pope imparted special blessings, known as indulgences.[33] Such a subtle, though decided, alteration in

[29] *Los Angeles Barrio*, p. 161. Further comments about Amat's actions are found in Jeffrey M. Burns, "The Mexican American Catholic Community in California, 1850–1980," in *Religion and Society in the American West*, edited by Carl Guarneri and David Alvarez (Lanham, Maryland: University Press of America, 1987), pp. 258–60.

[30] See the pertinent enactments of the diocesan synods, cited in chapter 4, from the *Constitutiones Latae et Promulgatae ab Illmo. ac Revmo. D. Thaddaeo Amat, Congregationis Missionis, Episcopo Montereyensi et Angelorum in Synodo Dioecesana*, 1862, 1869, 1876.

[31] Maynard Geiger, O.F.M., "Our Lady in Franciscan California," *Franciscan Studies*, XXIII (June 1942), pp. 107–108.

[32] Santa Barbara *Gazette*, 22 May 1856.

[33] *Novena a Santa Vibiana, Virgen y Mártir, Protectora de la Diócesis de Monterey*, (San Francisco: Vicente Torras, 1856), pp. 5–6.

the heavenly protectors of the diocese underscored the determination of ecclesial leaders to foster more standardized, "Roman" forms of faith expression, at the expense of local customs on the frontier.

The second instance illustrating the changing orientation of local Roman Catholicism also derived from the relationship between the bishops in Rome and Los Angeles. To fulfill the pope's wishes, Amat undertook the construction of a suitably magnificent cathedral to enshrine the saint's relics. Such an edifice would also serve to express more concretely the importance of the office of the bishop in the local church. The design, location, and cost emphasized the enhanced status of episcopal authority. While Amat temporarily used the Hispanic church on the plaza to house the Roman relics, he judged the humble adobe building unsuitable to fulfill his pledge to the pontiff.

What the bishop had in mind was a structure of brick, capable of accommodating 3,000 worshipers, even though Los Angeles counted a total population of only 5,728, one year after the 1869 groundbreaking. The estimated cost for a church 266 feet long and 116 feet wide was $100,000,[34] although the annual income of the diocese in 1869 amounted to $20,380.78, with a surplus of a mere $1,200, after expenses.[35]

Amat selected a plan for the building that was based upon memories of the church he attended during his childhood, San Miguel del Puerto, in Barcelona, Spain. The style was classical baroque and unlike any other structure in Los Angeles in design or dimension. Amat disregarded the Hispanic colonial lines and materials of Our Lady of the Angels Church, on the plaza. Instead of adobe blocks, the new cathedral was constructed of brick, with an elaborately ornamented facade. A single mural over the door adorned the old church; the bishop's new edifice boasted a rose window of stained glass, statues of six saints, and a steeple towering 140 feet above the unpaved streets.[36]

The original site chosen, at Sixth and Main streets, had to be abandoned, in 1871, in favor of a location not so "distant" from town. The new locale, at Second and Main streets, was west of the plaza,

[34] Los Angeles *Star*, 9 October 1869.
[35] "Cash Book," vol. I, entry for 1869; AALA.
[36] Francis J. Weber, *Saint Vibiana's Cathedral: A Centennial History*, (Los Angeles: Archives of the Archdiocese of Los Angeles, 1976), pp. 16, 20–21.

in the increasingly fashionable, affluent, English-speaking residential district of the community. Hispanics, as noted in the previous chapter, were clustering east and south of Main Street, and the cathedral's dedication, in 1876, split local Catholicism along socioeconomic lines, with the Spanish-speaking remaining attached to the poorer parish of Our Lady of the Angels.[37]

The financial ledgers of the diocese faithfully record the sums slowly collected, after 1858, to finance the construction, including the thirty-eight dollars received from Angelenos in that first year.[38] By 1877, the expenses had totalled almost $75,000, and the interior furnishings were still incomplete. Fundraising for this project dwarfed all other endeavors in the diocese, as Amat, and later his assistant bishop, Francisco Mora, labored intently to complete this monument.

The efforts of Amat to build a cathedral, as a symbol of the changes in Roman Catholicism on the frontier, matched those of a contemporary Southwestern prelate, the French-born Jean Baptiste Lamy. Bishop of Santa Fe from 1850 to 1888, Lamy later inspired Willa Cather's 1927 classic, *Death Comes for the Archbishop*, which dramatized his travails in bringing French piety to Hispanic New Mexico. Lamy, like Amat, envisioned a cathedral reminiscent of his homeland. He opted for the solid Romanesque of the Midi, in France. Both Amat and Lamy broke ground for their respective structures in October 1869, immediately prior to their departures for Rome, to attend the ecumenical council, Vatican I.

Lamy superimposed his cathedral upon an adobe church, dating from 1712, while Amat chose to build an entirely new edifice. Lack of funds plagued both projects, causing periodic suspension of construction, as well as the redesign of both churches, along more modest dimensions. Both ecclesiastics solicited funds while traveling in Europe. They also received significant donations from prominent members of the local Jewish communities in their respective towns.

---

[37] Zephyrin Engelhardt, O.F.M., *San Gabriel Mission and the Beginnings of Los Angeles* (San Gabriel, California: Mission San Gabriel, 1927), p. 315; and J. Thomas Owen, "The Church on the Plaza," Historical Society of Southern California *Quarterly*, XLII (June 1960), p. 196.

[38] The total sum collected in 1858 was $1,374. See the pamphlet issued under Amat's name, "Asociación de Santa Vibiana, Virgen y Mártir, Patrona de la Diócesis de Monterey, con el objeto de erigirle una catedral," (Barcelona: Pablo Riera, 1860), p. 5. See also, "Cuentas de la Catedral de Sta. Vibiana V. y M." ("Accounts of the Cathedral of St. Vibiana, V[irgin] and M[artyr]"), p. 1, AALA.

Amat lived to see the completion of his dream, in 1876, while Lamy died in 1888, seven years prior to the consecration of the Cathedral of St. Francis, by his successor.[39]

Because a cathedral serves as the locus for the liturgical exercise of a bishop's authority, both prelates envisioned structures that would proclaim visually the importance of their office. The dimensions, materials, and rich furnishings betokened stability, strength, and superior culture. Both buildings were impressive for their age and locales. These foreign-style monuments stood in stark contrast to the wood-frame meetinghouses of other denominations, more recently arrived in the region. And the massive churches were intended to overawe worshipers accustomed to modest, whitewashed adobe chapels.

Finally, these two prelates also shared a further common challenge, in their dealings with the clergy resident in their dioceses upon their respective arrivals. Lamy assumed the see of Santa Fe in 1853, while Amat was named to Monterey in the following year. Certain prominent native-born clerics in New Mexico resented the Frenchman's appointment and quarreled bitterly with him. Padre Antonio José Martínez, pastor of Taos, figured most prominently in these disputes and eventually incurred Lamy's excommunication, in 1857.[40] In southern California, Bishop Amat also engaged in an extended altercation with the local clergy, which both parties eventually argued in the halls of Rome.

Vast differences in the approach to organized religion divided the European-born Amat from local Catholics. Members of the Order of Friars Minor, or Franciscans, had at first welcomed Amat, when he took up residence in Santa Barbara, late in 1855. The superior of the friars, Reverend José María González Rubio, O.F.M., had served in California since 1833, as missionary, secretary to the first bishop, and administrator of the diocese, from 1846 to 1850, and again in 1853, until Amat's arrival. Widely respected and admired, González Rubio

---

[39] Bruce Ellis, *Bishop Lamy's Santa Fe Cathedral* (Albuquerque: University of New Mexico Press, 1985), pp. 13–46; and Francis J. Weber, "An Historical Sketch of St. Vibiana's Cathedral, Los Angeles," *Southern California Quarterly*, XLIV (March 1962), pp. 48–52.

[40] For one version of this conflict between Lamy and Martínez, see Paul Horgan, *Lamy of Santa Fe: His Life and Times* (New York: Farrar, Straus, Giroux, 1975), pp. 129–30, 232–33, 240–45, 249–51.

shared pastoral duties in Santa Barbara with the deeply beloved Francisco Sánchez, O.F.M., later immortalized as Father Salvierderra, in the novel *Ramona*. These priests and their two confreres even surrendered their residence and church to Amat's use.[41]

Relations between the friars and Amat deteriorated rapidly, when the new bishop issued a pastoral letter, in September 1856, in which he excoriated the religious laxity of local Catholics. Having ministered to the Barbareños since the founding of the pueblo in 1782, the Franciscans were understandably shocked. Amat later widened his criticism of local piety and accused the Franciscans themselves of fostering a minimal and "superstitious" Christianity.[42] They had failed to confront the members of their flock living in an obvious state of sin, and they tolerated sexual immorality, which was reputedly widespread in the community.

The bishop sought a more precise and orderly conduct of local religion, at a time when Hispanics throughout southern California faced staggering Yanqui challenges in economics and politics. Amat did not demonstrate a pastoral concern for the vast problems crushing so many members of his flock. Instead, he turned his attention to time-honored customs of the Franciscans that distressed him far more and invited his censure. One such practice was the provision of a burial shroud for pious friends, for which a donation was expected. To the Spaniard, this suggested both simony and avarice on the part of the clergy. Amat went so far as to charge that the merit of the historic missionary work in the state was the result of the labors of Spanish Franciscans, not their Mexican brothers.[43]

The bishop found these California customs revolting, and he acted decisively to halt them. In the course of this controversy with the Franciscans, he suspended their priestly faculties, in 1858, which prevented them from administering the sacraments. González Rubio

---

[41] Maynard Geiger, O.F.M., *Franciscan Missionaries in Hispanic California, 1769–1848* (San Marino, California: Huntington Library, 1969), pp. 116–17, 215–17.

[42] An extended treatment of this clash between Amat and the Franciscans is found in Michael C. Neri, "Hispanic Catholicism in Transitional California: The Life of José González Rubio, O.F.M. (1804–1875)" (Ph.D. dissertation, Graduate Theological Union, Berkeley, 1973), pp. 138–81.

[43] Letter, Amat to the Congregation for the Propagation of the Faith, 1 February 1859, Rome, quoted in Neri, "Hispanic Catholicism in Transitional California," p. 166.

protested to Roman authorities, and local Catholics were outraged. Amat himself set sail for Rome, to argue the case, which was eventually settled by compromise, in 1861.[44] While none of this altercation directly affected Catholics in Los Angeles, the incident provides a telling insight into the mentality of Amat and his attitudes toward the clergy and laity he found in the settlements of his diocese.

Such forced alterations in the religious practice of the Spanish-speaking left them distanced from the increasingly regulated, institutional church. Clerical disregard for the once-vibrant forms of frontera piety forced Hispanics into painful choices, ranging from conformity, private continuation of old practices in their homes, or conversion to Protestantism. Year by year, personal devotion became increasingly separated from formal religion. Local Hispanics, reeling from the loss of their lands, political control, and economic influence, had seen their culture relentlessly displaced in the years after 1848. Their distress did not stop there. The clergy of their church implemented the new policies decided in far-distant Baltimore and Rome and commanded by their bishop in Los Angeles.

Immigration into southern California, steadily increasing after 1865, brought new members to Roman Catholic and other congregations, as well as introducing religious groups previously unknown in Los Angeles. The arrival of new denominations began what one historian has termed the community's "Protestantization."[45] Bishop Amat and his clergy initially extended a nervous welcome to these newcomers, but soon forbade the members of their flocks to associate with those who did not follow the Church of Rome. Diocesan regulations, enacted in the three synods that Amat convened, provide ample evidence of his increasingly skeptical attitudes toward the community's growing religious pluralism.

In May 1862, the members of the first synod met in Los Angeles and drafted 110 laws, covering fifty-three pages, when published.

---

[44] Amat was to restore the faculties of the suspended priests, but additional and more exemplary Franciscans were to be sent to Santa Barbara. These were to be friars from any country in the world; except Mexico. See Maynard Geiger, O.F.M., *Mission Santa Barbara, 1782–1965* (Santa Barbara: Franciscan Fathers of California, 1965), pp. 174–81.

[45] Gregory H. Singleton, *Religion in the City of the Angels: American Protestant Culture and Urbanization, Los Angeles, 1850–1930* (Ann Arbor, Michigan: UMI Research Press, 1979), p. 50.

Quoting the enactments of the Fourth Provincial Council of Baltimore, decrees required that pastors show particular concern for children who attended public schools. To be safe, these priests ought to found Catholic schools in their parishes and even teach the classes themselves, if necessary. Furthermore, the clergy were to be on guard against the circulation of Protestant bibles and anti-Catholic tracts, "disseminated by people of different opinions." If parishioners appeared with such volumes, the priests were to be engaged in "snatching such books from their hands . . . ," sending the books to Amat, and "meanwhile, keeping them very much closed." [46]

When the bishop again summoned his clergy into solemn conclave, in 1869, they proceeded to prohibit three areas of lay association: secret societies, mixed marriages, and social outings. Not only were groups such as the Odd Fellows and Sons of Temperance proscribed, but even "those festivities . . . which go under the name of *picnics, excursions,* or some similar name, and which very often 'offer the direct occasion of sin'. . ." Even parish fairs and dances could only be held with the approval of the bishop. Under no circumstance should the priests allow their congregants to patronize any social events if sponsored by non–Roman Catholics. [47] This legislation did not go so far as to ban "non-Catholics" from attending Roman Catholic functions, probably due to the belief in Roman Catholic religious superiority to other faiths, and to the need for revenue from the patronage of these citizens.

By the time of this 1869 meeting, Los Angeles counted five denominations in the community besides the Roman Catholic communion. All but one had appeared since the previous diocesan synod, in 1862. The increased scope and detail of the strictures suggest that the bishop and his clergy feared the increasing diversity of contacts enjoyed by members of their flock. The growth of an ever more diverse religious population within the diocese presented a situation that synod members undoubtedly interpreted as a serious threat to the fidelity of Roman Catholics to their communion.

Other restrictions issued directly from the bishop's pen several

---

[46] Decrees 22, 23, and 24 in *Constitutiones in Synodo Dioecesana Montereyensi at Angelorum Prima, Latae et Promulgatae Mense Maii, Anni 1862* (San Francisco: Vicente Torras, 1862), pp. 21–22.

[47] Decree 14, *Constitutiones . . . Synodis dioecesana Segunda*, pp. 90–91.

years later. In a pastoral letter to the diocese, in 1872, the Spanish cleric spelled out exactly which organizations the faithful might join with spiritual impunity. Amat limited these to societies with "industrial and commercial purposes." Charitable and benevolent societies must be church-blessed, with the bishop himself approving the constitutions and by-laws. Most specifically, these societies must "be composed, exclusively, of members of the Catholic Church," with priests as their official chaplains.[48] The clergy would function as arbiters of the actions of these associations regarding morals, expulsions, expenditures, and public exhibitions.

In the final years of his life, Amat continued to warn his flock of the dangers of associating with non-Catholics. The third diocesan synod, meeting in Los Angeles in 1876, reaffirmed earlier strictures on Roman Catholic membership of unapproved societies. It also expanded earlier admonitions regarding marriages between communicants of the Church of Rome and members of another faith.[49] In 1877 came the last of this ever-constricting series of prohibitions. Some measure of the mentality of the hierarchy can be deduced from the legalistic approach taken toward organizations that claimed many Roman Catholic members.

The four bishops in California had sought a clarification from Roman officials on certain organizations suspected of excessive secrecy. Like their episcopal colleagues throughout the United States, these hierarchs feared the anti-Catholicism of a variety of contemporary associations. As early as 1866, Amat had queried the archbishop of San Francisco about condemning the Fenians.[50] The "secret societies" the prelates suspected in 1877 in California included the Ancient Order of Hibernians, the French Benevolent Society, and the Saint Patrick Benevolent Society. All three groups claimed substantial Roman Catholic ethnic membership. Because of what was judged excessively restrictive membership oaths, the later two were subject to Roman censure.[51] When Roman Catholic members were instructed

[48] Thaddeus Amat, *Pastoral Letter* (San Francisco: Smyth and Shoaff, 1872), pp. 15, 17.

[49] Decree 5, *Constitutiones . . . In Sinodo Dioecesana Tertia* (San Francisco: P.J. Thomas, 1876), p. 12.

[50] Letter, Amat to Joseph S. Alemany, 13 April 1866, Los Angeles; AALA.

[51] Copy of Letter, Alexandro Cardinal Franchi to J.S. Alemany, 20 January 1877, [Rome], in Latin, AALA. The ecclesiastics requesting this clarification were Archbishop Joseph S. Alemany, of San Francisco, and Bishops Eugene O'Connell, of Grass Valley, Amat, and Francisco Mora, Amat's auxiliary.

to withdraw from these condemned organizations, the St. Patrick Benevolent Society in Los Angeles soon ceased to function.

The recourse to Roman authorities on such matters concerning local church practice exhibited the legalistic mentality of the clerics involved. Furthermore, all decrees enacted in the three diocesan synods were subject to prior review and approval by church officials in Rome. National and international mandates were now determining local affairs. Increasingly strong bonds tied the church in frontier Los Angeles to the papal curia in the Eternal City. The series of prohibitions and proscriptions issued between 1862 and 1878 highlights the skeptical attitude of Bishop Amat toward both Hispanic forms of piety and emerging religious pluralism.

The spectre of waxing Protestantism persuaded southern California's Catholic bishops and clergy that the best recourse for their flocks lay in a withdrawal from the wider society. On the one hand, these priests and bishops struggled to protect their people by following the tactics and agenda set by the national hierarchy. They subscribed to measures adopted in Baltimore and confirmed in Rome, which standardized ritual and strengthened discipline, to unify their burgeoning but badgered denomination. On the other hand, the clergy adopted procedures that alienated an already marginal segment of their congregation. A rift developed between the formal and informal religious life of Hispanic Angelenos that continues to the present.

Thaddeus Amat counted many accomplishments during his years as bishop of Monterey–Los Angeles, and it must be said that he doggedly executed the duties of his office in trying times. Together with his clergy, he steadily brought a clear order and consistent policy to the life of his denomination. However, he secured the alterations in spiritual practices at considerable price. Choosing a Roman patroness and a Spanish-style cathedral were but two of many instances by which the bishop acted to reorient local Catholicism away from its regional heritage. The extent of these changes, coupled with the immigration of Anglo-American and European Catholics, effectively displaced Hispanics from their traditional place within the local church.

The meetings of the bishops during the nineteenth century delegated the responsibility for all significant matters of congregational life to the local pastor. This clerical control deprived parishioners of a direct voice in decision-making processes. These strictures also vitiated Hispanic customs and rituals, cherished since the earliest days of the frontera. The actions of the hierarchy may have enabled the Catholic church to cope with contemporary nativist prejudice, but it came at the price of a vibrant Hispanic religious heritage. In mandating national norms, bishops and priests thwarted the local expression of initiative, energy, and interest among their parishioners. Spanish-speaking Catholics were less involved in parish life and provided fewer leaders for church positions, two circumstances that have persisted in California and the Southwest into recent times.

This portion of the city's populace increasingly experienced the immediate effects of the religious conflicts bedeviling the nation. Hispanics were the first, but not the last, Catholics to undergo a jolting socioreligious displacement in Los Angeles between 1846 and 1888. As the nineteenth century came to a close, Hispanics and later Catholics held fewer elective offices of any import. After 1900, no Roman Catholic (or Jew) would receive election as mayor of the city, nor would any person with a Spanish surname serve on the city council again, until 1949.[52] The rise of local religious pluralism actually foreshadowed the impending decline in the fortunes of the town's oldest creed. When coupled with Amat's increasingly defensive attitude, these developments hastened the "Protestantization" of Los Angeles. In the next chapter we examine how new denominations enjoyed an ever-wider public influence, at the expense of a previously prominent church.

[52] Ríos-Bustamente and Castillo, *Mexican Los Angeles*, p. 174; and Fernando J. Guerra, "Ethnic Officeholders in Los Angeles County," *Sociology and Social Research*, LXXI (January 1987), p. 93.

CREATING AN "AMERICAN" COMMUNITY OF FAITH

One sunny day in 1880, a nameless photographer lugged camera and tripod up the steeply graded hill to the corner of Fort (now Broadway) and Temple streets. Facing south, he captured a view of the burgeoning city of Los Angeles, which then boasted some twelve thousand souls. Towering church spires loomed above the skyline of business blocks, wood-frame structures, and the last of the single-story adobe residences. The clustered houses of worship announced that the godly were present and that the heyday of the pueblo's cow town morals was now past.[1]

Increasingly common in post-frontier southern California, such scenes reminded visitors of hometowns far to the east. Certainly the Presbyterian kirk would look familiar, as would the smaller Southern Methodist church, one block northeast. The presence of a Roman Catholic cathedral, however, presented a startling difference. The Spanish Baroque design contrasted sharply with the clapboard-meetinghouse architecture of its two Christian neighbors. More unique yet was the smaller and older Jewish synagogue, erected in brick in the fashionable Victorian Gothic style, surmounted with an unusual, five-pointed star. These distinct structures offered material evidence of the religious pluralism that had developed in Los Angeles and that continues to distinguish the city.

As newly settled members of denominations established their many congregations, they also started to work on reformulating the moral

---

[1] Photograph #382, "Methodist Church" file, TICOR Title Insurance (Los Angeles) Collection of Historical Photographs, the California Historical Society, at the

norms of the community. The long-desired "people of the right sort" were out to make a difference in Los Angeles. As mentioned in previous chapters, ministers had staked their hopes on the growth of Protestant churches with the immigration of settlers from other states. The decade of the 1880s witnessed an abundant answer to the preachers' prayers. New churches sprang up, and with them came demands for a new code of morality and social mores.

Change began when the Southern Pacific Railroad reached Los Angeles, in 1876, and accelerated with the arrival of the Santa Fe line, in 1885. The demographic and religious impact of these transcontinental rail connections are discernible from the data contained in the following two tables. In the first, the growth in overall population contrasts markedly with a minimal Hispanic increase. The rate of population growth in Los Angeles between 1880 and 1890 reached a dizzying 351 percent, but the proportion of the Spanish-speaking in the populace declined dramatically, decade by decade, in the face of this great immigration.[2]

Table 3: Population Growth in Los Angeles, 1850–1890.[3]

YEAR	TOTAL POPULATION	HISPANIC POPULATION	HISP. PERCENTAGE OF POPULATION
1850	1,610	1,215	75.4%
1860	4,385	2,069	47.1%
1870	5,728	2,160	37.7%
1880	11,183	2,166	19.3%
1890	50,393	unavailable	unavailable

Regional History Center, University of Southern California, Los Angeles, California.

[2] Robert M. Fogelson, *Fragmented Metropolis: Los Angeles, 1850–1930* (Cambridge: Harvard University Press, 1967), p. 79, Table 5: "Rates of Population Growth in Selected Cities, 1890–1930."

[3] U.S. Census Office, *Social Statistics of Cities*, Part II: *The Southern and Western Cities*, (Washington, D.C.: Government Printing Office, 1887), p. 779; Fogelson, *Fragmented Metropolis*, p. 67. Griswold del Castillo provides the data concerning Hispanics, in *Los Angeles Barrio*, p. 35. In an appendix explaining his methodology in computer tabulations, Griswold del Castillo listed his criteria for identifying an individual as "Hispanic." Such a person had to possess a Spanish surname, or have been born in Mexico or California, prior to 1848; see pp. 180–82.

Complementing these figures are the religious statistics, compiled by federal enumerators for the first time in 1890. The eleventh census reported data for denominational affiliation in a volume later published as the *Report on Statistics of Churches in the United States*.[4] When earlier church membership rosters are consulted, the increase by 1890 stands out more clearly.

Unfortunately, more complete figures are unavailable, though charter memberships show the initial size of pioneer congregations. Thirty-two Jews formed Congregation B'nai B'rith, in 1862, while ten communicants constituted St. Athanasius Episcopal Church, three years later. In 1867, six Congregationalists organized their First Church. Approximately fifteen Northern Methodists gathered

Table 4: Figures for Communicants, Los Angeles, 1870–1890.[5]
(With Year of Congregational Founding)

YEAR	RC 1822	JW 1862	EP 1865	CG 1867	ME,N 1867	AME 1869	ME,S 1870	BP 1874	PB 1874	UN 1885
1870			40	37	60	12	11			
1875			112	62				13	51	
1880			81	303	[25]			65	216	
1885	[5,000]	[50]	200	301	999		160	233	[300]	40
1890	6,154	460	979	1,082	3,002	121	885	1,282	1,873	750

[4] U.S. Census Office, Washington, D.C.: Government Printing Office, 1894.

[5] *Report on Statistics of Churches in the United States*, pp. 112–13; *Minutes*, Southern California Methodist Episcopal Church, North, Annual Conference, 1875, 1880, 1885; "Register A," St. Athanasius–St. Paul Episcopal Church, Los Angeles, California; *Journal*, Annual Convention of the Protestant Episcopal Church of the Diocese of California, (1875), p. 55, and (1886), p. 77; Los Angeles *Star* 25 September 1869; J.C. Simmons, *Southern Methodism on the Pacific Coast* (Nashville: Southern Methodist Publishing House, 1886), p. 378; J. Albert Wilson, *History of Los Angeles County, California* (Oakland, California: Thompson and West, 1880; reprint ed., Berkeley: Howell-North, 1959), p. 120; *Minutes* of the Annual Meeting of the General Session of California [Congregationalists], 1875, 1880, 1885; Pat Hoffman, *History of the First Presbyterian Church, Los Angeles* (Los Angeles: United University Church, 1977), p. 5; "Official Records," vol. I, pp. 124–26, First Baptist Church, Los Angeles, California; and "History, Preamble and Constitution of the Church of Unity, Los Angeles, Cal.," p. 2, First Unitarian Church, Los Angeles. The Los Angeles *Times* of 7 March 1886 supplied the statistics for Roman Catholics, Jews, Southern Methodists, and Presbyterians for the 1885 entries; these cannot be considered official reports from those congregations.

that same year, followed by eleven of their Southern brethren, who founded Trinity Church, in 1869. Twelve blacks also gathered in 1869, to form the local African Methodist Episcopal Church. Two other Protestant congregations formed in 1874, the first being the eight Presbyterians who organized themselves in February, followed in September by eleven Baptists.[6]

The prosperity of the 1880s eclipsed these humble beginnings, when pioneer folk first met in front parlors of homes or in rented halls. Counting some 18,229 members by 1890, the seventy-eight religious organizations in Los Angeles ranged from the Pilgrim faith of the Congregationalists to Japanese Buddhism. Most Western cities were less religious than their counterparts in other regions of the country, but not the City of the Angels. Churchgoers in 1890 constituted 36 percent of the local populace of 50,395, and outranked comparably sized Omaha, where the godly mustered only 32 percent of the cityfolk.[7] Religious affiliation had attained an importance to Angelenos that would characterize the community into the twentieth century.

The history of one of these denominations illustrates well the growth in numbers, resources, and influence that Protestant congregations enjoyed. The Northern Methodists had supplied Angelenos with ministers on an irregular basis since 1853, but not until 1867 did a permanent congregation survive. When the Reverend A.M. Hough arrived, in 1868, he found about 15 regular worshipers at the Fort Street church. Within two years, he had boosted those weekly numbers to between 50 and 70, with 108 children in the Sunday school.[8]

---

[6] Los Angeles *Star*, 19 August 1872, cited in Thomas Owen, "The First Synagogue in Los Angeles," *Western States Jewish Historical Quarterly*, I (October, 1968), p. 9; *Journal*, Annual Convention, Protestant Episcopal Church, Diocese of California (1865), quoted in Stephen C. Clark, *The Diocese of Los Angeles: A Brief History* (Los Angeles: Committee on Diocesan Anniversaries, 1945), p. 16; *Minutes* of the Annual Meeting of the General Session of California [Congregationalist], 1867; Reverend A.M. Hough, "Dictation of A Life's Story," (typescript, n.d.), p. 2, BL; Edward Drewry Jervey, *The History of Methodism in Southern California and Arizona* (Nashville, Tennessee: Historical Society of the Southern California–Arizona Conference, 1960), p. 36; Delilah L. Beasely, *The Negro Trail Blazers of California* (Los Angeles: Privately Printed, 1909), pp. 109–10; Los Angeles *Star*, 25 September 1869; "Official Records," vol. I, p. 124, First Baptist Church, Los Angeles; and Hoffman, *History of the First Presbyterian Church*, p. 5.

[7] *Report on the Statistics of Churches*, pp. 91, 112; Lawrence H. Larsen, *The Urban West at the End of the Frontier* (Lawrence, Kansas: Regents Press of Kansas, 1978), p. 29.

[8] Hough Dictation, p. 2, BL; and Los Angeles *Star*, 26 March 1870.

Table 5: Annual Membership, Fort Street
Methodist Episcopal Church, with Sunday
School Attendance Figures.[9]

YEAR	MEMBERSHIP	SUNDAY SCHOOL
1876	247	220
1877	253	250
1878	255	unavailable
1879	267	205
1880	303	225
1881	362	370
1882	437	620
1883	385	360
1884	483	450
1885	550	425

Membership gradually increased annually, until 1879, and then experienced the sharp and continuing rise shown in the following table.

Not only did the Fort Street congregation grow and thrive, but additional Northern Methodist churches became necessary. The dip in the number of communicants in the above table undoubtedly reflects the subdivision of a parish from the parent church. Two formed in 1881, two more in 1882, one in 1883, and yet another in 1885.[10] In addition to these houses of worship, local blacks separated into the First African Methodist Church, while the Northern Methodists also initiated a mission to the German-speaking in the community. This outreach became a formal station in 1876, and three years later counted a pastor, 38 communicants, 65 children in the Sunday school, and a chapel worth $750.[11]

With membership increasing, facilities under construction, and societies organizing, the Northern Methodists took a hard look at the shortcomings of Los Angeles. The journals of their Southern California Annual Conference record the formation and reports of committees charged with monitoring the town's manners and mores.

[9] *Minutes*, Southern California Annual Conference, 1876–1885.

[10] 1881: University Church and the Rose Street Chapel; 1882: Asbury and Boyle Heights churches; 1883: Grace Church; and 1885: Main Street Chapel. See *Minutes*, Southern California Annual Conference, (1881–1885), passim.

[11] Beasley, *Negro Trail Blazers*, p. 110; *Minutes*, Southern California Annual Conference, 1876–1885, passim; and *Minutes* of the California Annual Conference (1879), pp. 42–43.

In their opinion, education was woefully inadequate in the mid-1870s. The conference initially sponsored the Los Angeles Academy, in 1876, and this school's enrollment soon eclipsed that of the older St. Vincent's College. In 1880, the academy trustees voted to merge with the grandly named University of Southern California. Laity and clergy closed ranks behind this new institution and launched it on the wave of the greatest real-estate speculation that the town had yet known.

The prospects of developing their surrounding lands led three local entrepreneurs to disregard sectarian differences and bestow 308 lots on the nascent school. Ozro W. Childs, John Gately Downey, and Isaias W. Hellman were the generous benefactors: a Yankee Episcopalian, an Irish Catholic, and a German Jew. In ceremonies in a dusty field, five miles southwest of town, two Methodist bishops laid the cornerstone for the first building, on 4 September 1880. The Northern Methodists sponsored the institution, but advertisements nonetheless heralded the school as "in no sense sectarian," and a true "community project." In 1883, the president chose to stress the curriculum's contributions to a general set of "Christian morals and ethics . . . as the basis of every successful life." [12]

This emphasis on the school's broad Christian character appears to have been a deliberate attempt to emphasize (and retain) wide Protestant support. To consider such a university as a specifically communal project also underlies a shift in the city's religious sensibilities. Similar nondenominational assertions had once described Bishop Amat's 1865 undertaking, St. Vincent's College. Even earlier, the Sisters of Charity had initiated their school and orphanage, with widespread endorsement, as a community project, in 1856. [13]

The emphasis on education as a road to reform accelerated in later years and expanded to surrounding communities. In 1884, the Presbyterians began Sierra Madre College, in South Pasadena. While that failed, Occidental College, where instruction would be "evangelical

---

[12] Leslie F. Gay, Jr., "The Founding of the University of Southern California," *Historical Society of Southern California Annual Publication*, VIII, Part I (1909–1911), pp. 42, 45; and Reverend Marion M. Bovard, "University of Southern California," in the special edition of the Los Angeles *Illustrated Herald*, September 1883, p. 12.

[13] Regarding St. Vincent's College, see Los Angeles *News*, 16 May 1865 and 2 July 1867; regarding the Sisters of Charity and their works, see: *El Clamor Público*, 12 January 1856 and 18 July 1857; Los Angeles *News*, 5 July 1867.

rather than sectarian," followed, three years later. That same year, the Congregationalists opened Pomona College, east of Los Angeles. German Dunkards followed, in 1891, with Lordsburg College (now known as the University of La Verne), while Quaker and Baptists efforts, respectively, culminated in the foundation of Whittier College and the University of Redlands, after a variety of initial setbacks. Aside from the Catholic college and a branch of the state normal school, local higher education was a Protestant-sponsored undertaking.[14]

The Northern Methodists in Los Angeles took an early lead in another movement then attracting considerable attention across the nation. The annual conference, in 1877, recommended that temperance be taught in the public schools and a temperance society be formed in every Methodist congregation. In 1883, a delegate of the Woman's Christian Temperance Union addressed the yearly gathering. The following year, the Temperance Committee endorsed a proposed amendment to the state constitution, permitting local legislative control of alcoholic consumption. For good measure, the committee also included a condemnation of the use of tobacco.[15]

Urging total abstinence from alcoholic spirits, southern California Baptists had sounded the tocsin in the battle against liquor as early as 1872. In 1880 and 1882, the Los Angeles Baptist Association endorsed state laws to ban liquor in California, and in 1884 they went a step further. Assembled saints declared that it was "unbecoming to the Christian position" to raise and sell grapes intended for wine. Like their Methodist colleagues, local Baptists also considered the use of tobacco "contrary to the spirit and teaching of God's word." An attempt to repeat this resolution in 1883 proved unsuccessful, due to divergent opinions among the animated discussants.[16]

---

[14] Robert Glass Cleland, *The History of Occidental College, 1887–1937* (Los Angeles: Ward Ritchie Press, 1937), p. 5; Glenn S. Dumke, *The Boom of the Eighties in Southern California* (San Marino, California: Huntington Library, 1944), pp. 249–56; E. Wilson Lyon, *The History of Pomona College, 1887–1969* (Claremont, California: Pomona College, 1977), pp. 4–6. It should also be noted that F.C. Woodbury opened his Woodbury Business College in 1884, with a curriculum consisting of bookkeeping, English, penmanship, and spelling. See *Woodbury University: 100th Anniversary Year* (Los Angeles: Woodbury University, 1984), [p. 3].

[15] *Minutes*, Southern California Annual Conference (1877), pp. 12–13; (1883), p. 18; and (1884), pp. 35–38.

[16] *Minutes* of the Los Angeles Baptist Association, (1872), pp. 56–57; (1880), p. 198;

One final topic, that of Sabbath observance, merited interdenominational endorsement at annual gatherings of the various faiths. Leading Protestants were concerned about the lack of enforcement of state laws passed in 1855 and 1861. The Northern Methodists heard repeatedly from their conference committee on the subject, and the 1876 report provided a clear idea of what was then considered improper behavior. The Lord's Day was not the time for picnics, excursions, social visits, or any public sports.[17] Once again, Baptists expressed similar concern about the subject from time to time, by considering resolutions in favor of dutiful recognition of a day of rest.[18] Presbyterians and Congregationalists also condemned desecration of the Lord's Day.[19]

Throughout the state, the issue of Sabbath observance became more heated in the early 1880s, when Seventh-Day Adventists challenged the laws.[20] Angelenos entered the fray in December 1881, when mass meetings heard the pastors and leaders of the Presbyterian, Baptist, and Northern Methodist congregations demand local enforcement of existing laws. Opposing residents gathered at the Germans' Turnvereien Hall to organize themselves as the "League of Freedom." In the course of electing officers and signing petitions, one speaker proclaimed: "We are mostly foreigners in this hall. . . . You know the movers in this thing [Sunday law enforcement] come from the rank and file of the Puritan churches."[21] The voters of the state decided the matter in 1882, by electing Democrats to the legislature who were committed to repealing the blue laws. The governor's signature on the repeal legislation, in 1883, was a setback for evangelical Christianity at the state level, which spurred local Protestants to greater

---

(1882), pp. 254, 255; (1884), p. 4; all cited in Leland D. Hine, *Baptists in Southern California* (Valley Forge, Pennsylvania: Judson Press, 1966), pp. 42–43.

[17] *Minutes*, Southern California Annual Conference, (1876), p. 24.

[18] Hine, *Baptists in Southern California*, p. 43.

[19] For example, see the resolutions adopted by assembled Presbyterians, as reported in the *Minutes* of the Synod of the Pacific (1873), pp. 25–26, and (1884), pp. 24–25; and a report of a sermon preached at the Annual Meeting of the Congregationalists' General Association, as noted in the *Pacific*, 4 November 1875.

[20] For a clear and insightful analysis of this confrontation, see Sandra Sizer Frankiel, *California's Spiritual Frontiers: Religious Alternatives in Anglo-Protestantism, 1850–1910* (Berkeley: University of California Press, 1988), chapter 4: "Sacred Time and Holy Community," pp. 47–58.

[21] Los Angeles *Times*, 6, 11, 12, 13, 14 December 1881.

vigilance over local morals. There were collaborative efforts on several fronts.

The Northern Methodists, for example, increasingly interacted directly with the leaders of other churches, at the annual conference gatherings. The *Minutes* faithfully acknowledge the presence of invited ministers from other denominations at the sessions.[22] Such invitations were more than an exchange of courtesies; they were a continuation of a decade of collaboration among the town's Protestant bodies. The manifestations of this mutual assistance included joint prayer meetings, temperance lectures, Thanksgiving services, "union street preaching," and clergy meetings.[23] Chinese evangelization, later in the decade, had strong cooperative overtones as well, particularly between Congregationalists and Presbyterians. By 1881, there existed a ministerial association, where "most" of the Protestant pastors selected a common topic upon which all would preach on a given Sunday.[24]

Local newspapers were quick to notice the growth of the different Protestant sects, with their array of Sunday schools, youth groups, ladies' aid societies, and construction projects. The Los Angeles *Times* titled the community a "City of Churches," in its first edition, in 1881. Moreover, the editors took heart that new schools and congregations, "the pulse and heart . . . of every community," were appearing "with such rapidity in this city."[25] Church building was only one means by which these growing numbers of newcomers struggled to replicate a Christian way of life resembling hometowns beyond the Sierra Nevadas. Several important organizations also made their appearance in Los Angeles in the 1880s. Drawing their membership from the ranks of the believers, the leaders of these societies spearheaded a variety of additional projects to further improve the manners and mores of Angelenos.

[22] For example, see *Minutes*, Southern California Annual Conference, (1880), p. 7.
[23] Los Angeles *Republican*, 25 November 1869; Los Angeles *Star*, 17 April 1869, 8 and 22 January 1870, and 20 November 1870; unidentified newspaper clipping, 23 October 1869, Benjamin Hayes Scrapbooks, vol. 54.2, #22, BL; Los Angeles *Express*, 7 December 1878. Baptist participation in these activities included "union prayer meetings" with the Northern Methodists, as in January of 1879. See "Official Records," vol. I, p. 83, First Baptist Church, Los Angeles.
[24] Los Angeles *Times*, 4 December 1881.
[25] Los Angeles *Times*, 4 December 1881.

Chapter 9

Anglo-American Protestants had long exhibited an abiding interest in the direction of public elementary and secondary education, particularly in the training of teachers. The first Teachers' Institute had met in 1870, under the direction of State Superintendent of Public Instruction, the Reverend O.P. Fitzgerald, later a bishop in the Methodist Episcopal Church, South. Hoping to influence the assembled teachers, local ministers actively participated in this and subsequent meetings.[26] In the following year, the Episcopalian pastor and the Southern Methodist minister engaged in a debate with one of the teachers regarding the advisability of Bible reading in the public school. One instructor noted that Jews would find the New Testament offensive, and Bible reading would also disturb the "conscience of the [Latter-Day] Saint."[27]

A later development revealed another aspect of the involvement of Reformed Christians in local public education. In 1881, the state legislature authorized the construction of a branch of the state normal school in Los Angeles. Located on what was known as "Pound Cake Hill," at Fifth and Grand streets, the school opened, in 1882, with an enrollment of eighty-five students. The three-story brick structure included a chapel, in which all students gathered daily for a morning prayer service.[28] Faculty members, such as Melville Dozier, were prominent members of local congregations, while the wife of the second principal actively participated in temperance activities.[29]

Churchgoers took an active interest in an additional project, commenced in the same year that the normal school opened its doors. In January of 1882, a group of men gathered at Trinity Southern Methodist Church to found a branch of the Young Men's Christian

[26] Los Angeles *Star*, 25 and 27 October 1870.

[27] It is not clear whether teachers read the Bible in the classrooms of Los Angeles. Los Angeles *Star*, 16, 17, 18 November 1871. See also Los Angeles *Times*, 11 April 1883.

[28] Emma H. Adams, *To and Fro in Southern California* (Cincinnati: W.M.B.C. Press, 1887; reprint ed., New York: Arno Press, 1976), p. 140; and James R. Martin, *The University of California (in Los Angeles)* (Los Angeles: Privately Printed, 1925), pp. 35–36.

[29] Herbert L. Sutton, *Our Heritage and Our Hope* (Los Angeles: First Baptist Church of Los Angeles, 1974), p. 20; Melville Dozier, "Reminiscences," Historical Society of Southern California *Annual Publication*, XV (1933), pp. 105–106; and Mary Alderman Garbutt, *Victories of Four Decades, 1883–1924* (Los Angeles: Woman's Christian Temperance Union of Southern California, 1924), p. 21.

Association.[30] The organizer and first president was Samuel Ingham Merrill, a Baptist hardware-store proprietor. Like other concerned Protestants, Merrill hoped that the Y.M.C.A. would help young Christian males to retain their faith, amidst the temptations of urban living. The twenty-one signers of the constitution created eight committees to meet men's needs, through services such as devotions, visiting and relief work, lectures and entertainment, publications, and employment. Membership was open to parishioners of any "evangelical" denomination, though "associate" affiliation was permitted those who did not frequent any church but were of good moral character.[31]

By the time of the first anniversary celebration, in 1883, membership had risen to nearly 150 men. President Merrill welcomed the general secretary of the San Francisco Y.M.C.A., Henry McCoy, to the program at Trinity Southern Methodist Church. Hymns were interspersed with the speeches of Merrill, McCoy, and the two ministers listed on the program.[32] The speakers recounted the accomplishments of the first year, outlined the dreams for the future, and took up a collection to fund these projects. With donations that evening totaling only $500, McCoy proceeded to meet with "the ladies," to form a women's auxiliary for the support of the Y.M.C.A.[33]

Reports delivered in October 1883 outlined the activities in which members of the "Y" had been engaged over the preceding five months. The devotional committee had been responsible for 44 prayer meetings, at which a total of 4,000 people had attended. The head of the room committee asked for more books and papers, in order to meet the growing demands of readers. Other chairmen listed visits on 159 occasions to the sick or handicapped; employment

---

[30] Theodore Grivas, "The History of the Los Angeles Young Men's Christian Association" (typescript, 1957), pp. 4–6; Box, "Historical Data Compiled in Research, 1957," Office of the President, Metropolitan Los Angeles YMCA, Los Angeles, California; hereafter cited as LA-YMCA.

[31] Los Angeles *Times*, 4 April 1882.

[32] Merrill and a later Y.M.C.A. president, Lyman Stewart, collaborated on another project of Christian outreach to urban residents. In 1891, they founded the Pacific Gospel Mission, now known as the Union Rescue Mission. See notes on Samuel I. Merrill, found in Box, "Historical Data Compiled in Research, 1957," LA-YMCA.

[33] The ministers were Reverend Thomas R. Curtis, of Trinity Church, and P.W. Dorsey, of First Baptist Church of Los Angeles. See Los Angeles *Times*, 30 January 1883.

located for 78 men, and financial assistance rendered to 10 others; and numerous meetings held in the city jails, where volunteers distributed tracts, flowers, and fruit to inmates.[34] In these and other ways, the men of the "Y" sought "to develop the spiritual, mental, moral and physical condition of its members, and by them to impart comfort and assistance to strangers and others requiring it."[35]

In the first ten years of its existence, officers of the Y.M.C.A. legally incorporated their organization, greatly expanded their membership, and initiated an ambitious campaign to erect their own headquarters. In 1887, they had commenced a $50,000 fundraising drive, to complete their structure on Fort Street.[36] This building included a gymnasium, reading room, and offices, as well as meeting space for other evangelical Christians. Association members had previously opened their rented hall, in 1885, to the gatherings of a society that was rapidly becoming one of the great Protestant organizations of Los Angeles.[37] Sharing similar sentiments regarding their community's need for moral improvement, the men of the Y.M.C.A. welcomed the formation of a local branch of the Woman's Christian Temperance Union.

In April 1883, Frances E. Willard, national president of the W.C.T.U., had addressed the women of Los Angeles, exhorting them to form the first female temperance group, or "union," in their community. After speaking in the Fort Street church of the Northern Methodists, Willard participated in a series of meetings, over three days, which achieved the results she desired, before continuing her cross-country organizing tour to other cities in southern California. By the time of Willard's departure, the Los Angeles branch of the association counted one hundred, members under the presidency of Mrs. Will D. Gould. The interest among women was so high that an additional meeting was necessary, by September of that year, to form a state organization.[38]

---

[34] Unidentified newspaper clipping, October, 1883; Box, "Historical Data Compiled in Research, 1957," LA-YMCA.

[35] Los Angeles *Times*, 4 April 1882.

[36] "Articles of Incorporation," 6 January 1889, in Box, "Historical Data, 1882–1909;" LA-YMCA. See also Los Angeles *Times*, 24 February 1886 and 7 December 1887.

[37] Los Angeles *Times*, 6 January 1885.

[38] Los Angeles *Times*, 1, 3, 4 April 1883.

One of the first officers later wrote that the size of the state and the expense of travel necessitated the formation of the Woman's Christian Temperance Union of Southern California. Though affiliated with their sisters headquartered in San Francisco, the members in the southernmost five counties of the state desired easier access to their officers.[39] Delegates from thirteen unions, representing 427 local members, met at First Presbyterian Church, Los Angeles, to organize their society on 20 and 21 September 1883. The 38 women drafted a constitution, in which they declared, "We, the Christian women of Southern California, covenant together in a sacred and enduring compact against the liquor traffic, and pledge ourselves to work till our purpose is accomplished."[40]

Having stated their organization's purpose, the delegates proceeded with the election of officers and the creation of the first two committees. Miss Martha Hathaway, a relation of the prominent Bixby family, assumed the presidency, while Miss Alice Miller and Mrs. Susan B. Dorsey filled the positions of recording secretary and treasurer, respectively. Dorsey, wife of the pastor of First Baptist Church, would later play an increasingly prominent role in the city's public school system.[41] Hathaway, a native of Maine and member of an ardent temperance family, was an articulate speaker, whom one pioneer recalled as possessing "rare executive ability." In her two terms as state president, Hathaway selected the leaders of the "departments," or committees, brought lecturers and organizers to the Pacific coast, and planned the organization's work on a broad scale.[42]

Los Angeles women were prominent leaders in the state orga-

---

[39] *Annual Report*, Woman's Christian Temperance Union of Southern California (1885), p. 24, cited in Betty Jane Woods, "An Historical Survey of the Woman's Christian Temperance Union of Southern California as It Reflects the Significance of the National W.C.T.U. in the Woman's Movement of the Nineteenth Century" (unpublished M.A. thesis, Occidental College, Los Angeles, 1950), pp. 105–106. Because the records of the W.C.T.U. of Southern California are no longer open for research, my treatment of this organization relies upon the Woods thesis and the Garbutt history of the association, *Victories of Four Decades*. Both authors made extensive use of the primary documents previously available. Garbutt was also a leader in the state organization, from the time of its founding.

[40] Garbutt, *Victories of Four Decades*, p. 17.

[41] A biographical sketch of Dorsey can be found in Margaret Romer, "Pioneer Builders of Los Angeles," Historical Society of Southern California *Quarterly*, XLIII (March 1961), p. 343.

[42] Garbutt, *Victories of Four Decades*, p. 18.

nization and furnished nine of the fourteen presidents who served between 1883 and 1924. Sharing in the "Do Everything" spirit of national leader Frances Willard, these women adopted the motto, "The battle is not yours but God's."[43] Not only did they zealously take up the challenge of temperance work, but they also served as fervent guardians of the community's virtue. The exact number of members is not known, because statistics are not available for Los Angeles. However, the state organization for southern California did not count more than 2,000 members until 1900. In 1884, 22 local unions, with 632 members, existed in 6 counties. Ten years later, the 84 branches in the same territory counted 1,737 women who wore the White Ribbon of the W.C.T.U.[44]

While never successful in securing the locally legislated prohibition of the liquor trade, the Los Angeles Central Union was nonetheless an active group. The Los Angeles *Times* highlighted their various campaigns and printed numerous stories on the consequences of drinking alcoholic beverages. In May of 1884, W.C.T.U. members sought city abatement of "the demoralizing features" of a local theatre, along with enforcement of the city's ordinance regulating saloon hours of operation. In the following month, the women petitioned the city council again, this time to protest a proposed licensing of "bawdy houses."[45]

The city fathers of Los Angeles proceeded with a noticeable lack of enthusiasm when it come to regulating prostitution. The women of the W.C.T.U. badgered these worthies over a period of thirty years, until passage of the "Red Light Injunction and Abatement Law," in 1913.[46] One member's irritation with such slow progress led her to muster forces, in 1889, to rescue "fallen" women. The "cribs" of prostitutes on Alameda Street so outraged a Mrs. Spencer, that she spearheaded the formation of the Social Purity League, which established a "rescue home" for women, early in 1889. Named for an early

[43] *Annual Report*, W.C.T.U. of Southern California (1885), p. 19, as cited in Woods, "Historical Survey of the W.C.T.U.," p. 119.

[44] *Annual Report*, W.C.T.U. of Southern California (1885, 1895, 1900), passim, as cited in Woods, "Historical Survey of the W.C.T.U." p. 125.

[45] City Council "Minutes," vol. 17, pp. 776, 799; vol. 18, pp. 85–86; vol. 19, p. 525; Archives of the City of Los Angeles, Piper Technical Center, Los Angeles, California.

[46] Garbutt, *Victories of Four Decades*, p. 104.

benefactor, the Los Angeles Central Union assumed sponsorship of the Eleanor Ransom Home, in December of that year, and operated the facility for the next three decades.[47]

Later campaigns of the members of the Los Angeles branch of the W.C.T.U. brought two important victories, in 1890. In July of that year, it became illegal to sell cigars, cigarettes, and tobacco to minors under the age of sixteen; this became state law in the following year. In December 1890, the women secured passage of a city ordinance requiring the closure of saloons on Sundays.[48] In addition to these local activities, many Los Angeles women actively participated in projects for which the state organization requested their aid. The most important of these crusades was the drive to secure temperance instruction in all of California's public schools.

The first attempt to gain such legislation occurred in 1884, but the letters and petitions sent to Sacramento did not achieve the desired objective. When Lucy Drew More, of Los Angeles, assumed the presidency of the state society, in 1886, she renewed efforts on behalf of this educational proposal. As the wife of the state normal school principal in Los Angeles, she was well acquainted with the men responsible for guiding the state's academic institutions. More first secured the active cooperation of the W.C.T.U. based in San Francisco. Together, the two organizations sent delegations of women to lobby every member of both houses of the legislature. The women arrived in the capital carrying hundreds of petitions and the endorsements of numerous church groups. When the lawmakers convened in 1887, they enacted the Scientific Temperance Instruction Bill, which mandated compulsory temperance education in public schools throughout the state.[49]

The Los Angeles members also participated in several other projects ardently championed by the officers of the state W.C.T.U. In 1886, the women began a seven-year drive to raise the $46,000 needed

---

[47] *White Ribbon*, (October, 1893), p. 1, (May, 1894), p. 3, (July, 1895), p. 2, as cited in Woods, "Historical Survey of the W.C.T.U.," pp. 145–47.

[48] *White Ribbon*, (January, 1890), p. 4, and (December, 1890), p. 1, as cited in Woods, "Historical Survey of the W.C.T.U.," pp. 128, 141.

[49] *Annual Report*, W.C.T.U. of Southern California (1884), p. 37, cited in Woods, "Historical Survey of the W.C.T.U.," p. 37; and Garbutt, *Victories of Four Decades*, pp. 118–20.

to pay the mortgage on their six-story headquarters building.[50] From their Temperance Temple, as the structure in Los Angeles was known, the members issued their first ringing call for women's suffrage, in 1887. Their ongoing commitment to this cause later prompted national leader Susan B. Anthony to write that the woman's movement of southern California was a W.C.T.U. movement.[51] Reports of the members' many activities appeared on the pages of the *Southern California White Ribbon*, a monthly newspaper that the state society began publishing in 1889.

The W.C.T.U. remained a politically important organization in the southern end of the state throughout the first three decades of its existence. Despite repeated attempts, the women of the Central Union were never successful in securing prohibition of the liquor trade by means of a "local option" ordinance in Los Angeles. Their sisters in surrounding communities, such as Pasadena, enjoyed greater success. The City of the Angels would not "go dry" until 1920, when the Volstead Act became the law of the land. In the years prior to the attainment of this goal, the state and local W.C.T.U. members pursued a wide variety of other legislative reforms, such as women's suffrage, the minimum wage, the regulation of child labor, and the eight-hour working day for women.[52]

The crusaders of the temperance unions were not the only women working locally for improvements in social morality and civic virtue. While less directly religious in their societies' stated goals, the members of the first women's clubs were equally committed to many of the same causes as the crusaders of the W.C.T.U. In fact, of the same names appear on the rosters of both sets of organizations. While occupied in establishing the town's first Unitarian church, Caroline Seymour Severance also organized the Woman's Club of Los Angeles, in May 1878.[53] A handful of followers met in this pioneer club for

[50] *White Ribbon*, (April, 1893), p. 1, as cited in Woods, "Historical Survey of the W.C.T.U.," pp. 132–33.

[51] Susan B. Anthony, *Scrapbook*, XXII (1896), p. 126, as cited in Woods, "Historical Survey of the W.C.T.U.," p. 167.

[52] Other matters of concern to the W.C.T.U. were smoking in street cars, dancing in public schools, drinking at the State University, "impure post cards," saloon licensing, regulation of hours for pool-hall operation, and curfew laws; see Garbutt, *Victories of Four Decades*, pp. 125–29.

[53] "Constitution & By-laws and Secretary's Minutes of the Woman's Club of Los

slightly more than one year and engaged in one of the first attempts by Los Angeles women to gain political office.

According to the recollections of one participant, the club women petitioned the city council, in 1879, to appoint a woman as city librarian. That year's revised city charter designated the council members and mayor as the ex officio trustees of the new municipal public library. The women decided upon one of their number as the best person for the post. As the witness recalled,

> We went in full force, twenty in all, before the honorable body
> . . . with our petition. They listened to us in respectful silence and
> then requested us to retire, which we did, gracefully, of course.
> They then promptly elected Pat Connolly librarian, as previously "fixed." [54]

Connolly, a housepainter, remained in the job for only one year. By then the club had disbanded, but the council members appointed a recent female graduate of the high school as the next librarian.

When Mrs. Caroline Severance moved from Los Angeles with her husband, in 1880, both the Unitarian Church and the woman's club lost momentum and disbanded. Soon after her return, in 1884, Mrs. Severance was again calling on her friends from a wide spectrum of faiths, to undertake two new projects. The first was the Public Kindergarten Society, under the auspices of the First Congregational Church. The members of this organization dedicated themselves to providing the benefits of kindergarten schooling to lower-class children, primarily Hispanics. [55] From this project arose the movement

---

Angeles," pp. 1, 2–4, 14, 34; Box 27, Caroline Severance Papers, HL. Having helped found one of the nation's first woman's clubs, in 1868, Severance had a long association with club work. Her associates in the New England Woman's Club were Lucy Stone and Julia Ward Howe, reformers who shared her concern for the needs of American women. See Jane Jensen's entry on Severance, in *Notable American Women*, ed. by Edward T. James et al. (Cambridge: Belknap Press, 1971), vol. III, pp. 265–68.

[54] Jane E. Collier, "Early Club Life in Los Angeles," Historical Society of Southern California *Annual Publication*, IV, Part III (1899), p. 218.

[55] The officers of the Public Kindergarten Association for 1886 included the president, Mrs. Severance (Unitarian); vice-presidents, Mrs. I.W. Hellman (Jewish), Mrs. E. Miller (Presbyterian), Mrs. A.J. Hudson, Mrs. H.G. Otis (Presbyterian), Mrs. J. Bixby (Congregationalist); secretary, Mrs. L.V. Newton (Congregationalist); and the treasurer, Mrs. Alice Seamans. The Board of Managers included Mrs. R.M.

that incorporated the kindergarten into the public school system of Los Angeles, in 1890.[56]

Caroline Severance once again sought out friends from the churches, when she attempted to revive the Los Angeles Woman's Club, in 1885. Her pastor, Reverend Eli Fay, and a "Reverend Mr. Cronin," both spoke at the group's organizational meeting.[57] Serving again as a founding president, Severance also became engaged in another attempt to involve women in political office. The members sought the election of one of their own to the city's board of education. A committee of three women called upon the town's political leaders and persuaded each of them to place Mrs. Anna Averill's name on the respective party's ticket. A former member of the faculty of the University of Southern California, Averill possessed impressive credentials for the post she sought. The politicians concurred, listed her name on the ballot, and Averill was elected to the school board, in November 1886.[58]

The club also launched another highly successful project to improve the condition of women. In March of 1885, the three members of the Work Committee delivered a report, entitled "Conditions and Wages of Working Women in Los Angeles." The audience heard that local working women suffered from many problems, including salaries as low as seven dollars per week. Extensive and serious discussion ensued for several months. The club women decided that an inexpensive boarding house was needed to assist newly arrived young women seeking employment in Los Angeles. From this grew the plan of the "Woman's Union," to raise funds by holding a flower festival, under the leadership of Severance's friend, Mary Barnes Widney. So successful was this event, in the spring of 1886, that it became an annual affair. Legally incorporating as the Flower Festival Home

Widney (Northern Methodist), Mrs. E.F. Spence (Northern Methodist), and Reverend A.J. Wells (Congregationalist). Los Angeles *Daily Herald*, 8 October 1886.

[56] Edward W. Splitter, "Education in Los Angeles, 1850–1900," part II, Historical Society of Southern California *Quarterly*, XXXIII (June 1951), p. 234.

[57] "Minute Book of the Los Angeles Woman's Club," vol. I, p. 1, 4; Box 27, Caroline Severance Papers, HL; Los Angeles *Times*, 11 February 1885.

[58] Collier, "Early Club Life," p. 221; and Los Angeles, City Auditor's Office, *Annual Report of the City of Los Angeles* (Los Angeles: City Printing Office, 1905), p. 90.

Society, the women purchased a lot at Fourth and Main streets and erected a three-story house, as a residence for female laborers.[59]

The involvement of its members in this new society so sapped the energies of the Woman's Club that it ceased to exist, in 1888. Not until 1891 would a more lasting woman's club arise, and once again Severance would serve as organizer and first president. Like its two predecessors, this Friday Morning Club was not an overtly religious organization. However, it too owed its establishment and much of its membership to the involvement of prominent churchwomen. Dedicated to social and intellectual pursuits, each of these three organizations also exhibited a strong humanitarian concern deeply rooted in the prevailing Protestant ethos of the nation. These clubs were important social institutions, which introduced Angelenos to the nationally prominent movements of the age.

Two other institutions owed their foundation to the efforts of local women dedicated to community improvement. Interestingly, both supplemented the pioneer orphanage and hospital of the Sisters of Charity in Los Angeles. In 1880, the Los Angeles Orphans' Home Society appeared and was caring for thirty-one children within one year.[60] In 1884, Episcopal Bishop William Ingraham Kip dispatched Sister Mary Wood, of the Order of the Good Shepherd, from San Francisco to Los Angeles. Within the year, the Canadian-born nun had established a nine-bed facility she titled the Los Angeles Hospital and Home for Invalids. The local Episcopal parish, and later the Diocese of Los Angeles, assumed sponsorship of what soon became known as the Hospital of the Good Shepherd.[61]

Taken together, the Y.M.C.A., the W.C.T.U., the first two woman's clubs, the Flower Festival Home Society, the Public Kindergarten Society, the Orphan's Home Society, and the Los Angeles Hospital were organizational manifestations of a changing commu-

[59] Los Angeles *Times*, 1 March 1887; Jane Apostol, "They Said It With Flowers: The Los Angeles Flower Festival Society," *Southern California Quarterly*, LXII (Spring 1980), p. 70; Collier, "Early Clubs," pp. 220–21; Adams, *To and Fro in Southern California*, pp. 267–75; Workman, *The City That Grew*, pp. 188–89.

[60] Los Angeles *Times*, 3 January 1882; and *Fifth Annual Report of the Los Angeles Orphans' Home Society* (Los Angeles: Daily Herald Printing Office, 1885), p. 5.

[61] Stephen C. Clark, *The Diocese of Los Angeles: A Brief History* (Los Angeles: Diocese of Los Angeles, 1945), p. 47. See also the centennial publication, *A Heritage of Caring* (Los Angeles: Hospital of the Good Samaritan, 1985).

nity consciousness. The activities of these associations reveal the areas of civic life that aroused deep concern among new residents in Los Angeles. Beginning in the 1880s, these newcomers championed causes of a decidedly Protestant Christian origin. In the course of that decade, growing numbers of citizens sought public recognition of virtues and values that differed greatly from those of the pueblo past. Crusades on behalf of temperance and female suffrage introduced issues that affected both religious sensibilities and challenged the established political alliances in the community.[62]

Los Angeles in the 1880s was firmly in the grip of a powerful "machine," which certain business and government leaders had formed over the years since 1865. The Southern Pacific Railroad offered leadership in the person of Walter Parker, while corporate utilities officers, public works contractors, and liquor dealers supplied necessary funds to elect city officials friendly to their own interests. Municipal employees were expected to contribute labor in electoral campaigns. Political power in this era rested in the local wards, where the machine's neighborhood leaders and "captains" assured the choice and election of candidates from either the Democratic or Republican parties. By loaning funds and providing campaign assistance, these hand-picked officials were indebted to the machine and attentive to requests from its "bosses."[63]

Machine leaders successfully controlled the current majority party, dominated the city council, and ruled the city of Los Angeles virtually unchallenged. Among the citizens immigrating to the community in the 1880s were increasing numbers who took offense at the open prostitution, gambling, and municipal graft that enriched the bosses. These irate residents involved themselves in efforts to destroy the influence of the deeply entrenched members of this "political ring." Led by dissident Republicans, the first reform effort failed at the ballot box, in 1887. In the following decade, these disgruntled Angelenos organized themselves into the Municipal Reform Association, the Direct Legislation League, and the League for Better City Government. City charter reform failed again in 1896, but succeeded

---

[62] Further discussion of these altered social relationships can be found in Fogelson, *Fragmented Metropolis*, pp. 185–92.

[63] Robert M. Fogelson, *Fragmented Metropolis*, pp. 206–209.

in 1903 and spurred the crusaders on to capture the majority of seats on the city council, in 1906.[64]

This dedication to the reformation of Los Angeles society was the special contribution of recently arrived members of the more "evangelical" Christian denominations.[65] These believers worked to change the city's moral climate, as well as to supplant the attitudes and practices of a waning Hispanic and Roman Catholic ethos. Their view of the role of government differed markedly from the concept of earlier residents. These Protestants, many of whom were Republicans, believed it right and proper for citizens to establish and maintain specific standards of conduct by means of government action. The attitude toward government among members of an "ecclesiastical" church, such as Catholicism, prompted some Angelenos to conclude that communicants of the "Roman" faith were unfriendly toward municipal reform.

Many of these new residents brought with them a strongly held bias against, for example, Roman Catholicism, Judaism, and Unitarianism. Aversion to the social and political practices in Los Angeles and the struggle to replace the indigenous political machine with its links to Catholicism reinforced prejudice. The result was increasingly common and open expression of religious intolerance. Some new citizens joined the American Protective Association, in the 1890s

[64] Fogelson, *Fragmented Metropolis*, p. 210; George E. Mowry, *The California Progressives* (Berkeley: University of California Press, 1951; reprint ed., Chicago: Quadrangle Books, 1963), pp. 39–44; W.W. Robinson, *Lawyers of Los Angeles* (Los Angeles: Los Angeles Bar Association, 1959), pp. 110–13; and Tom Sitton, "California's Practical Idealist: John Randolph Haynes," *California History*, LXVII (March 1988), pp. 3–17, 67–69.

[65] Philip R. Van der Meer discusses the different social and political perspectives of churches, denominations, and sects vis à vis the theology and polity of these religious groups. According to his thesis, "ecclesiastical" denominations, such as Roman Catholic, Episcopalian, and some Lutheran bodies, advocated the right of a church to determine moral values and to regulate the behavior of its members. Methodists, Christians, Quakers, Congregationalists, most Presbyterians, and some Baptists and Lutherans constituted the "evangelical" denominations. These groups believed that communicants must aid in redeeming the world and use the state to promote moral living. They supported the Republican and Prohibitionist parties, which prompted ecclesiasticals to sympathize with the Democrats. See "Religion, Society, and Politics: A Classification of American Religious Groups," *Social Science History*, V (February 1981), pp. 3–24.

and supported that organization's boycott of Catholic-owned businesses in Los Angeles.[66] One A.P.A. member went so far as to charge, in 1894, that Catholics were storing arms in the basement of St. Vibiana's Cathedral, on Main Street.[67] As early as 1886, it was no longer uncommon for the local press to carry articles with condescending or negative references to religious societies outside of mainstream American Protestantism.[68]

Members of the local Jewish community found that they were less welcome than previously, in social settings. Pioneer merchant Harris Newmark noted that religious tolerance waned when the city population rapidly increased. Leaders of various new community organizations placed religious and ethnic restrictions in the membership requirements of these societies. Newmark contrasted this behavior with the customs of the frontier era:

> Speaking of social organizations, I may say that several Los Angeles clubs were organized in the early era of sympathy, tolerance, and good feeling, when the individual was appreciated at his true worth and before the advent of men whose bigotry has sown intolerance and discord, and has made a mockery of both religion and professed ideals.[69]

Whether religious or racial in nature, prejudice was not a new phenomenon in the community. What was startlingly novel and troublesome to people like Newmark, was the growing social acceptance of such discrimination at the turn of the century.

Among contemporary Protestant Angelenos, attention was shifting to ministries on behalf of their newly arrived coreligionists. Many of these transplanted residents not only moved from the Midwest to southern California, but from rural to urban settings. Founders of the Y.M.C.A., the Flower Festival Home Society, and the Orphans' Home Society displayed particular concern for young Christians. Members of other societies turned their attention to the abatement

[66] Patrick W. Croake, "The Tidings," in *The Centennial, 1840–1940,* ed. by Charles C. Conroy (Los Angeles: Archdiocese of Los Angeles, 1940), p. 174.

[67] Donald L. Kinzer, *An Episode in Anti-Catholicism: The American Protective Association* (Seattle: University of Washington Press, 1964), p. 108.

[68] Los Angeles *Times,* 7 March 1886, and Los Angeles *Express,* 7 October 1886.

[69] Newmark, *Sixty Years in Southern California,* p. 383.

of social evils that contributed to the corruption of adolescents and youthful adults. The Social Purity League and the W.C.T.U. were particularly noteworthy for the projects they launched for the sake of society's junior members. Seeking further vehicles of community change, evangelical Christians also attempted to influence the teacher formation and curriculum of the public schools, locally and throughout the state.

It is important to note that the limited successes of the W.C.T.U. in Los Angeles contrasted with the victories achieved by White Ribbon members elsewhere. Surrounding towns, such as Pasadena, Compton, and Hollywood, "went dry" as a result of the active efforts of vociferous Protestant prohibitionists. Los Angeles, however, was a far more complex political community, in which "machine" leaders had entrenched themselves since 1865. Christian reformers would have to battle earnestly and repeatedly to achieve the kind of municipal reform they desired. More socially and religiously homogeneous, inhabitants of nearby towns were able to achieve objectives such as church foundation and prohibition well in advance of their Angeleno sisters and brothers.

Protestants in Los Angeles responded to other needs when they founded the Y.M.C.A., the Ransom Home, the Flower Festival Home, and the new orphanage and hospital. Like their fellow believers across the nation, local Christians were increasingly concerned with the survival of faith among new residents flocking to urban centers. Saloons, pool halls, and the "cribs" of prostitutes were evidence of the iniquities of city life. The growth of the city's population prompted movements of both reform and outreach. Settlement houses in Los Angeles would grow out of this tradition, after 1890, as well as the Pacific Gospel Mission, founded by leaders of the Y.M.C.A. Taken together with the ethnic missions discussed in chapter 5, these projects involved the energies of dedicated workers concerned about the role of Christianity in an expanding urban center.

In a wide variety of ways, Angelenos played out on the hometown stage the drama engaging their fellow Christians nationwide. Both personal morality and public decorum involved evangelical Christians in numerous campaigns in late-nineteenth-century America. Growing numbers of such believers in Los Angeles initiated a far-reaching "Protestantization" of city life. The hard-won local traditions of religious tolerance and mutual assistance gave way to interdenominational cooperation of a more exclusively Protestant nature. Diverse national movements, Protestant and Catholic, collided in Los Angeles in the later decades of the nineteenth century.

The religious order between 1850 and 1880, which congregational members fashioned amidst considerable conflict, distinguished this city as a community of southern California. Regionally distinctive factors that influenced this process included the settlement's Catholic origins, the arrival of subsequent denominations, the races and ethnicity of participants, and the divergent views of private morality and public virtue. By 1890, the changing socioreligious character of Los Angeles had reached a new stage of its evolution. During this phase, evangelical Christians achieved a prominence that would persist well into the twentieth century. One casualty of this development was the spirit of tolerance and cooperation that pioneers had laboriously learned and struggled to preserve.

CONCLUSION

Whether they term it "the city of the future" or "Lost Angeles," numerous books and articles continue to appear that describe the phenomenal growth of Los Angeles in recent years. There is both fascination and fear in the presence of a city growing and changing as rapidly as this sprawling urban center. Economic and technological changes tell part of the story; demographic shifts and political realignments furnish further dynamism in the story of this "new Ellis Island." As the daily newspaper reveals, the multicultural populations face serious tensions and conflict in adjusting to one another. It is all the more striking to discover that in nineteenth-century Los Angeles, the struggles with racial and ethnic diversity were equally difficult and daunting. The startling turns by which religious pluralism appeared prompted citizens then to make repeated efforts to broaden the extent of the tolerance they practiced in their settlement.

The evidence presented in this volume reveals that the greater the threat to the community, the higher was the level of cooperation in that frontier era. Combined efforts, such as those during smallpox epidemics, provided the first precedents for early interdenominational cooperation. The legacy of working in concert produced an abiding good will toward those involved in such service: for example, the nursing Daughters of Charity and the Jewish chairman of smallpox relief efforts. This is not to imply, however, that a vibrant ecumenism flourished in this corner of frontier America, far in advance of twentieth-century accomplishments. Yet, for certain periods and under certain conditions, cooperation and mutual forbearance existed to a greater degree than has been previously acknowledged in Los

Angeles. The tolerance involved was a fragile commodity, growing out of the interaction of people relying upon one another for survival, support, and safety.

Despite its later demise, the tradition of religious cooperation derived a large measure of its vigor from struggles to improve the community. Religious leaders shared in the "booster" mentality of many of their congregants, particularly when it came to founding schools and colleges. One earnest pastor, using the jargon of a real-estate "boomer," even urged his parishioners to invest in "choice lots" in the "new Jerusalem."[1] Church structures and hospitals were "ornaments" of the community, tangible signs of progress and sophistication. Again and again, the members of the town's common council would emphasize the importance of such construction, by attending en masse the groundbreaking or dedication of new houses of worship.[2]

The promotional attitudes among clerics, however, possessed a darker side, as well. Those who wished to attract new settlers frequently scorned the Indian populace and glossed over elements of anti-Hispanic prejudice inherent in the drive to "civilize" and "Americanize" the former pueblo. One also looks in vain for strong and clear church protests against the conditions under which the Chinese suffered in the community, or against the prejudice that African Americans endured. Certain pastors seemingly muted their concern for the urban poor and dispossessed. The desire for civic growth coincided with contemporary cultural biases against people differing in language, color of skin, economic status, or cultural heritage. Even those ministering to the Chinese and the Spanish-speaking often exhibited the condescending attitudes of racial and religious superiority that were so widespread throughout American society in that century.[3]

Other instances of the subtle forms of bias emerged in the reactions

---

[1] Cited in Henry D. Barrows, "Early Clericals in Los Angeles," Historical Society of Southern California *Annual Publication*, V, Part II (1900–1902), p. 133.

[2] Two examples illustrate this practice. When Reverend William Boardman's congregation laid the cornerstone for their church, the common council members marched in the procession to the site; see Los Angeles *Star*, 4 May 1861. A dozen years later, members of the same body attended the dedication of Congregation B'nai B'rith's synagogue; see Los Angeles *Star*, 9 August 1873.

[3] Reverend Ira M. Condit, who dedicated his life to evangelization of the Chinese,

of newer settlers to the Hispanic forms of Christianity. The spiritual heritage of the Californios confronted all church groups and forced church leaders to decide how to evangelize in such a religiously distinct region. This was as true for Roman Catholic priests as it was for Protestant parsons. Few clerics showed much respect for either the language or the customs of the former Mexican *frontera*. Pastoral work with the Spanish-speaking demonstrated the severe cultural limitations and inflexibility of most ministers, when it came to preaching their Gospel message. Even dedicated evangelizers, such as William Mosher, Carlos Bransby, and Ida Boone, displayed the tendency among the majority of the clergy to conform Hispanics to other practices, another language, or different beliefs.

Early Hispanic padres and parishioners in the Southwest and in California, however, had long molded their religion to life on the *frontera*. In Los Angeles, they later struggled to retain those faith expressions, so well suited to their culture and locale through decades of life on the rim of Christendom. The Daughters of Charity are notable for their sensitive regard for these religious traditions, while Bishop Thaddeus Amat took a much sterner approach toward the rites of Spanish-speaking Catholics.[4] Following the prescripts of the national hierarchy, Amat and his Spanish and Irish priests were the architects of the altered Roman Catholic customs and discipline. Matters of ritual and devotion were increasingly standardized and inflexible. The resultant displacement of Hispanics within their traditional communion coincided with their political and economic

---

nonetheless exhibited a deep ethnocentrism. See his *The Chinaman as We See Him* (Chicago: Fleming H. Revell Company, 1900), pp. 49–54. Agnes McCormick, who also worked with the Chinese in Los Angeles, indicated her ambivalent reactions in a published letter: "They [the Chinese] are *very* industrious, and their ruling motive is love of money." Printed in the American Missionary Society *Annual Report*, XXVI (1872), p. 74. The Sisters of Charity sought to move their orphanage from their Alameda Street location, not only because of the increasing commercialization of the neighborhood, but also because the presence of growing numbers of Chinese was a "more objectionable feature." See "Remarks on Sister Mary Scholastica Logsdon," *Lives of Our Deceased Sisters, 1903* (Emmitsburg, Maryland: St. Joseph's Central House, 1903), p. 120.

[4] For another instance of Amat's strict approach to church discipline, see Francis J. Weber, *Century of Fulfillment: The Roman Catholic Church in Southern California, 1840–1947* (Mission Hills, California: The Archival Center, Archdiocese of Los Angeles, 1990), p. 136.

dislocations, suffered after 1848. Hispanics who found their traditional piety disparaged or disregarded grew increasingly distant from
these institutional forms of religion and took refuge in their family-
centered piety. These domestic customs, however, brought them less
frequently into formal contact with their church and allowed Hispanics to form a subgroup within local Roman Catholicism that en-
dures in the twentieth century.

Another aspect of the shortcomings of the denominations in meeting local needs appears in another area of church life. The early
geographic and cultural isolation rendered religious groups amenable
to assisting one another in fundraising to meet construction costs
of churches and schools. The breadth of cooperation exceeded that
found on other frontiers and extended even to Roman Catholics and
Jews, for approximately three decades of the mid-nineteenth century. The bounds of liberality, however, excluded certain peoples,
in particular the so-called "heathen" Chinese.[5] In anti-Asian feeling,
Los Angeles equalled other Western settlements in the violence of its
antipathy, as demonstrated in the riot of October 1871.[6] On the spectrum of religious coexistence, Angelenos ranged widely, from toleration to murderous discrimination, reflecting an ongoing struggle
to define the cultural identity of a settlement passing from Hispanic
pueblo to American town.

This changing milieu of the City of the Angels between 1848 and
1880 originated in the shifting composition of the local population.
Thus, when Rabbi Abraham Edelman altered synagogue ritual with
services partially in English, mixed seating of worshipers, and the
addition of women to the choir, he did so in response to his rapidly

---

[5] Angelenos had initially tolerated and even respected their Latter-Day Saint
neighbors, to the east in San Bernardino, between 1851 and 1857. News of the Mountain Meadows Massacre, however, terrified residents of Los Angeles and planted
seeds of lasting suspicion about this religious group. For instances of changing Angeleno attitudes toward the followers of Joseph Smith, see Los Angeles *Estrella*, 17 July
and 14 August 1852; Los Angeles *Star*, 22 October 1853; and *El Clamor Público*, 5 September, 17 October, 28 November, and 19 December 1857.

[6] To place the anti-Chinese violence of the nineteenth century in context, see
Shih-Shan Henry Tsai, *The Chinese Experience in America* (Bloomington: Indiana Uni-
versity Press, 1986), pp. 67–72. Besides the Los Angeles massacre, Shih-Shan notes
that other serious incidents occurred in Denver (1880); Rock Springs, Wyoming
Territory (1885); Seattle and Tacoma, Washington (1885); and on the Snake River,
Oregon (1887).

Americanizing congregation. More than any other single cleric, Edelman initiated the greatest religious change in response to local conditions. This is all the more remarkable because he represented the oldest and most traditional of the Occidental creeds. This also stands in stark contrast to the Roman Catholic experience, in which Bishop Amat promoted close adherence to nationally standardized norms of discipline and discouraged the members of his flock from interacting with peoples of other faiths.

The Daughters of Charity, however, quietly went about their works of mercy and adapted themselves to meet the needs of local society's unfortunate members. These women exhibited the greater readiness of the lay members of their church to confront creatively the conditions they faced in this remote cow town. Enough of the nuns mastered the Spanish language to serve as effective emissaries of their faith to Hispanic Angelenos. They legally incorporated their institutes, in order to insure the survival of their ministries. Willing to assist those in greatest need, the nuns provided Roman Catholicism with a flexible corps of personnel, capable of responding to crises or rendering a variety of vital social services.

The role of these and other women in frontier evangelization was far more extensive in Los Angeles than has been previously understood or acknowledged. Like their sisters across the nation, female members formed the largest segment of any local congregation and worked consistently in fundraising, Sabbath schools, social events, mission societies, and benevolence endeavors.[7] The exception was among the Chinese, where cultural restrictions precluded a wider public role for the few resident Asian women. Among the Jews and Christians, however, women utilized the congregations as means to extend their influence and involvement beyond the circle of home

---

[7] Two examples demonstrate women's widespread involvement. The vestry minutes of St. Athanasius Episcopal Church record that in times of financial distress, the trustees turned to the Ladies' Aid Society for relief. This was particularly the case in July 1875, September 1876, and again in February 1877. Perhaps tiring of this practice, the women loaned the vestry the needed funds in the last instance cited, but at one percent interest, compounded monthly. See "Minutes of the Vestry," volume I, pp. 63, 79, 88, 89; St. Athanasius–St. Paul Episcopal Church, Los Angeles, California. A similar society of women at the First Presbyterian Church purchased more than one valuable lot for church structures, first in 1876 and again several years later. See the *Manual of the First Presbyterian Church* (Los Angeles: First Presbyterian Church, 1884), pp. 4–5.

and family. The range of their achievements was as impressive in its diversity as was its impact upon the community.

Such godly progress greatly cheered Reverend James Woods, the pioneer Presbyterian divine who was so dismayed in the 1850s at the spectacle of bull fights on the Sabbath. Returning to the community in 1880, Woods marveled at all he saw.[8] Los Angeles had ceased to be the "city of Demons" he had noted and the "moral desert" that Congregationalist Alexander Parker discovered in 1866.[9] The newspaper editors no longer lamented that ministers preached to empty benches. Articles had stopped appearing that described the settlement as one "where society is disorganized, religion scoffed at, where violence runs riot, and even life itself is unsafe . . ."[10] By the mid-1880s, "the "Queen of the Cow Counties" had become "a city of churches." The process accelerated at a dizzying rate in the last years of the 1880s.

In his landmark study of the real-estate boom of 1886–87, the late Glenn S. Dumke examined the far-reaching changes that overtook Los Angeles in a flurry of land subdivisions and the founding of new towns. Noting the advances in agriculture, education, population, transportation, and other fields, Dumke concluded that the events of those years finally Americanized the community: "The gold rush made northern California a real part of the United States; the boom of the eighties did precisely that for the south."[11] Another source documents the dramatic shift in demography that further confirms Dumke's assessment. The federal census of 1900 revealed that in only five large cities in the United States did American-born whites born of American-born parents constitute an absolute majority of the population. Three of those five cities were located west of the Missis-

[8] James L. Woods, *California Pioneer Decade of 1849* (San Francisco, 1922), pp. 124–25, cited in Lindley Bynum, ed., "Los Angeles in 1854–5: The Diary of Rev. James Woods," Historical Society of Southern California *Quarterly*, XXIII (June 1941), p. 68; see also James Woods, *California Recollections* (San Francisco: J. Winterburn and Company, 1878), p. 200.

[9] Woods diary entry for 12 November 1854, found in Lindley Bynum, ed., "Los Angeles in 1854–5: The Diary of Rev. James Woods," p. 70; and Letter, Alexander Parker to M[ilton] Badger, 27 August 1866, Los Angeles, Microfilm C-B 393, reel 3, American Home Missionary Society file, "California: 1866, A-P, section 1," BL.

[10] This quotation appeared in an article entitled "Our Moral Destitution," on the occasion of the resignation of Reverend Thomas K. Davis as Presbyterian pastor. See the Los Angeles *Star*, 16 August 1856.

[11] Dumke, *The Boom of the Eighties in Southern California* (San Marino, California: Huntington Library, 1944), p. 276.

sippi River; Los Angeles was one of those urban centers, along with Kansas City and St. Joseph, Missouri.[12]

While the city rapidly assumed a midwestern, Anglo-American civic culture after 1885, Hispanics, Chinese, and African Americans survived in some of the oldest barrios and poorest neighborhoods of Los Angeles. Religion continued to play an important role in the lives of these residents, while a vibrant Protestant Christianity assumed a position of prominence. The historian Gregory H. Singleton notes that members of these new growing congregations sought to build a Protestant community free from the corrupting influences that industrialization and immigration inflicted upon the eastern cities of the United States.[13] According to Robert M. Fogelson, newly arrived Angelenos wanted a community that avoided "the blight of 'demoralizing metropolitanism.'"[14] Instead, they heralded an earthly paradise with a small-town atmosphere, which was spared labor strife, crime-ridden tenements, and hordes of immigrants speaking a babel of languages.

With their widespread advertising, city boosters succeeded in capturing the imagination of people throughout the Midwest—and across the globe. The continued phenomenal growth of Los Angeles boosted it to the rank of the largest city in California by 1920.[15] The city expanded in all directions, in a decentralized sprawl of newly mapped suburbs alongside suburban small towns. Those who chose to make their homes in the City of the Angels also included peoples of a widening range of ethnic and racial backgrounds. The drive to increase the population of the city also had the unintended result of stimulating a renewal of the community's demographic and religious diversity.

Hispanics were the first to grow in numbers, when railroad and agricultural interests began importing workers after 1900. The Mexican revolution sparked additional emigration, as did later *bracero,* or

---

[12] U.S. Bureau of the Census, *Twelfth Census of the United States: 1900,* vol. I: *Population,* Part I, p. cxxii, quoted in John J. Harrigan, *Political Change in the Metropolis* (third ed., Boston: Little, Brown and Company, 1985), p. 49.

[13] Singleton, *Religion in the City of the Angels: American Protestant Culture and Urbanization, Los Angeles, 1850–1930* (Ann Arbor, Michigan: UMI Research Press, 1979), pp. 54–57.

[14] Robert M. Fogelson, *The Fragmented Metropolis: Los Angeles, 1850–1930* (Cambridge: Harvard University Press, 1967), p. 192.

[15] Fogelson, *Fragmented Metropolis,* p. 78.

Conclusion

farm labor, programs, beginning in World War II. Roman Catholicism in Los Angeles became again a church composed of significant numbers of the Spanish-speaking.[16] African Americans began migrating from southern states to Los Angeles after 1900, in a process similar to the "Great Migration" to northern cities after 1915. By 1920, most blacks were living along approximately thirty blocks of Central Avenue, where they built most of their churches and businesses.[17] Concentrated in their historic district until 1938, the Chinese increased slowly, until Congress revised the racist immigration laws of the nineteenth century.[18] Beginning with the 1943 repeal of the Chinese Exclusion Acts, new legislation permitted Chinese and other Asians to emigrate to the United States. Thousands moved to Los Angeles and brought with them religious customs and beliefs long observed in the local community.

Members of other religious groups had also read the literature of the chamber of commerce and moved to Los Angeles by the thousands. Russian Jews and Molokans, Italian and Slavic Catholics, Swedish Baptists, and Japanese Buddhists were only some of the newcomers heading toward the City of the Angels after 1900. Fogelson notes that the mainline churches attracted few new members from the new migration in the years after the first World War. New denominations appeared, either as transplants from other cities or local creations, and included Christian Science, Theosophy, New Thought, and the Church of the Nazarene. Given the mobility of southern California's population, these newer religious groups attracted people in search of meaning in their lives, which they could not discover in older Christian churches. Sandra Sizer Frankiel notes that the appearance of these later churches fractured the hegemony of Protestant power in Los Angeles after 1900, because of the religious alternatives they offered to the restless.[19]

[16] Antonio Ríos-Bustamente and Pedro Castillo, *An Illustrated History of Mexican Los Angeles, 1781–1985* (Los Angeles: Chicano Studies Research Center, University of California, 1986), pp. 127–34.

[17] Lawrence B. De Graaf, "The City of Black Angels: Emergence of the Los Angeles Ghetto, 1890–1930," *Pacific Historical Review*, XXXIX (August 1970), p. 335.

[18] Suellen Cheng and Munson Kwok, "The Golden Years of Los Angeles Chinatown: The Beginning," in *The Golden Years, 1938–1988* (Los Angeles: Los Angeles Chinatown Corporation, 1988), pp. 39–41.

[19] Frankiel, *California's Spiritual Frontiers: Religious Alternatives in Anglo-Protestantism, 1850–1900* (Berkeley: University of California Press, 1988), p. 62.

Both the "metaphysical" and conservative churches posed challenges to the prevalent American Christian ethos in local denominational life. Without threatening the existence of mainline congregations, the newer religious associations offered other forms of faith than the traditional Protestantism found in Los Angeles. Revivalists Aimee Semple McPherson and Robert Schuler developed followings, which further diminished the influence of the older congregations in the 1920s. These trends continued to the close of the 1930s, and World War II ended the phase of the community's religious history dating back to 1885. The post-war population boom transformed the metropolis as drastically as the boom of 1886–87, and international developments in ecumenism inspired local leaders to broaden religious harmony.

Given our contemporary consciousness of the demands of social justice, civil and human rights, and ecumenical relations, the religious community in Los Angeles of the last century at first glance appears backward. However, when assessed in the context of their frontier conditions, the courage and accomplishments of these residents emerge more clearly. They faced geographic isolation, inadequate funding, and ill-prepared ministers on this religious frontier. Amidst the struggles with religious prejudice and racial violence, there is also a record of accomplishments that would reflect well upon any American settlement in the nineteenth century. Churches and synagogues were built with the aid of people of all religions; Sabbath schools were integrated; English-language classes were offered to Asian immigrants; and women were enlisted in the efforts to expand religious influence.

These examples of accomplishments, as well as the contrasting failures in toleration, are important episodes in the broader saga of the American West. In her provocative and insightful scholarship, the historian Patricia Nelson Limerick has noted that the history of such frontier settlements continually involved struggles over issues of religion, language, and culture.[20] This grappling for "cultural dominance" enveloped the residents of Los Angeles between 1846 and 1888. It is apparent that further study of the religious life of Angelenos is needed to carry the story of conflict and cooperation

---

[20] Limerick, *The Legacy of Conquest: The Unbroken Past of the American West* (New York: W. W. Norton and Company, 1988), pp. 27–29.

Conclusion

into the twentieth century. Then it would be possible to understand these nineteenth-century experiences as part of a broader pattern of struggle among residents to cope with the consequences of conquest, diversity, and growth.

There remains a second need for additional study to compare the religious experience of this community with parallel developments in other settlements in southern California and the Southwest. A growing body of community, Chicano, and Asian-American historical literature suggests the profitability of such work. A number of scholars, for example, have documented the role that religion played in sustaining cultural cohesion among Spanish-speaking populations from Santa Barbara to San Diego, and from Tucson to Laredo and El Paso.[21] Hispanics coped with the consequences of conquest in a variety of means, and their religious customs and beliefs offered solace and strength during times of assault and misunderstanding.

In these and other ways studied in this volume, Los Angeles offers a microcosm of one of the many frontiers that made up American society in the West. The history of the one-time pueblo offers the reminder that pioneers created complex social arrangements, spoke a variety of languages, and worshipped more than one god. Here it was that those who cherished a constitutional theory of religious freedom began to advance, slowly and painfully, toward living out that legal ideal, with all its unexpected demands. Here it was that local events tested and tried those Angelenos whose spiritual convictions included respect for the beliefs of their fellow human beings. A hard-won mutual tolerance among members of diverse creeds developed over several decades in cow town Los Angeles, only to disappear in later years under shifting demographic tides.

When Bishop Francisco Mora retired, in 1896, he recalled the fading spirit of the "sympathy, tolerance, and good feeling" that he and

[21.] Albert Camarillo, *Chicanos in a Changing Society: From Mexican Pueblos to American Barrios in Santa Barbara and Southern California, 1848–1930* (Cambridge: Harvard University Press, 1979); Richard Griswold del Castillo, *The Los Angeles Barrio, 1850–1890: A Social History* (Berkeley: University of California Press, 1979); Ricardo Romo, *East Los Angeles: History of a Barrio* (Austin: University of Texas Press, 1983); Thomas E. Sheridan, *Los Tucsonenses: The Mexican Community in Tucson, 1854–1941* (Tucson: University of Arizona Press, 1986); Gilberto Miguel Hinojosa, *A Borderlands Town in Transition: Laredo, 1755–1870* (College Station: Texas A & M University Press, 1983); and Mario T. Garcia, *Desert Immigrants: The Mexican Immigrants of El Paso, 1880–1920* (New Haven: Yale University Press, 1981).

other pioneers had once known. Mora reminded the members of his flock, in his farewell address, that people of all faiths share a common creator and "are your brethren. . . . let no animosity ever exist between you; have confidence in them. Such has been my endeavor always . . ."[22] Here is the spirit that Angelenos from Harris Newmark to Biddy Mason had followed in their struggles to transcend differences among creeds and races. They could nod their heads in knowing recognition of Mora's sentiments and recall their own battles with prejudice and narrow-mindedness. These residents forged new patterns of mutual respect and in the process accomplished far more for local society than has been previously acknowledged. Though changing times erased much of the progress they made, Los Angeles in the mid-nineteenth century witnessed achievements that can be considered notable for any frontier community, of any age.

---

[22] [Los Angeles], *The Tidings*, 24 October 1896.

APPENDIX

Clergy Assigned to Service in Los Angeles, 1846–1888.
(Denominations Listed in Order of Founding)

Denom.	Station Clergyman	Dates of Service
Roman	Our Lady of Angels ("Plaza Church")	
Catholic	Blaz Ordaz, OFM	1845–48
	Sebastian Bongiami	1849–50
	P.J. Doubet	1850–51
	Francisco Sanchez, OFM	1851
	Jose J. Jimeno, OFM	1851
	Anacletus Lestrade, SS.CC.	1851–56
	Edmund Venisse, SS.CC.	1854–55
	Blas Raho, C.M. (rector)	1856–62
	Thaddeus Amat, C.M.	1859–76
	Francisco Mora (rector)	1862–73
	Peter Sastre (rector)	1873
	Pedro Verdaguer (rector)	1874–89
	St. Vibiana's Cathedral	
	Thaddeus Amat	1876–78
	Francisco Mora	1876–96
	Hugh McNamee (rector)	1882–3
	Joaquin Adam (rector)	1884–99
Jewish	Congregation B'nai B'rith: Rabbis	
	Abraham Wolf Edelman	1862–85
	Emanuel Schreiber	1885–89
Episcopal	St. Athanasius/St. Paul's: Pastors	
	Elias Birdsall	Dec. 1864–66
	H.H. Messenger	1866–67
	J.J. Talbot	1868
	C.F. Loop	1869

Appendix

	George Burton	June 1869–70
	J.B. Gray	Nov. 1870–Feb. 1874
	W.H. Hill	1874–79
	Elias Birdsall	1880–89

Congreg.	First Congregational Church: Pastors	
	Alexander Parker	July 1866–July 1868
	Isaac W. Atherton	Oct. 1868–Nov. 1871
	J.T. Wills	Nov. 1871–Aug. 1873
	D.T. Packard	Jan. 1874–1878
	C.J. Hutchins	Mar. 1879–Oct. 1882
	Andrew J. Wells	Oct. 1882–Apr. 1887

Methodist (Northern)	Los Angeles Circuit/District	
	Adam Bland	1854
	J.M. McCaldwell	1855
	N.P. Peck	1856
	Elijah Merchant	1857
	David Tuthill	1858

	Fort Street Methodist Episcopal Church: Pastors	
	Columbus Gillett	1868
	A.P. Henden	1868
	A. Coplin	1869
	A.M. Hough	1870
	P.Y. Cool	1871
	S.G. Stump	1871–73
	J.M. Campbell	1873–76
	Geo. S. Hickey	1876–78
	M.M. Bovard	1878–80
	E.S. Chase	1880–83
	P.F. Bresee	1883–86

Methodist (Southern)	Los Angeles Circuit/District	
	E.B. Lockley	1855
	J.F. Blythe	1856
	J.W. Ellis	1856
	T.O. Ellis	1857–58
	C.H.E. Newton	1859
	Wm. A. Spurlock	1860
	J.S. Stewart	1861–63
	S.W. Davies	1864
	C.M. Hogue	1865–66
	J.C. Miller	1867

Trinity Methodist Church, South: Pastors
  Abram Adams   1869
  A.M. Campbell   1873
  Richard Pratt   1873
  A.M. Campbell   1875–?
  Th. R. Curtis   1881–?

African Methodist Episcopal

First African Methodist Episc. Church: Pastors
  Jesse Hamilton   ca. 1870
  —Morton   ?
  S. Brown   ?
  Stephen Savins   Sept. 1885–?

Baptist

First Baptist Church: Pastors
  Wm. Hobbs   Sept. 1874–June 1875
  Winfield Scott   Sept. 1876–Jan. 1878
  H.J. Parker   Feb. 1878–April 1878
  Henry Angell (stated supply) 1879
  P.W. Dorsey   Aug. 1881–Sept. 1887

Second Baptist Church: Pastors
  S.C. Pierce   1885–87

Presbyterian Missionaries
  John W. Douglas   Nov. 1850–Aug. 1851
  Samuel H. Willey   Jan.–Aug. 1851
  James Woods   Nov. 1854–Sept. 1855
  Th. K. Davis   Sept. 1855–Aug. 1856
  Wm. E. Boardman   May 1859–Mar. 1862
  Wm. C. Harding   1870
  Wm. C. Mosher   1871
  Th. Fraser (Synodal Missionary)

First Presbyterian Church: Pastors
  A.F. White   Aug. 1875–Jul. 1877
  W.F.P. White (stated supply) 1877
  F.M. Cunningham (stated supply) 1878
  W.J. McKnight (stated supply) 1878
  J.W. Ellis   Nov. 1879–Sept. 1885
  W.J. Chichester   1885–88

Disciples of Christ

First Christian Church: Pastors, Presiding Elders
  W.J.A. Smith   Aug. 1875–Dec. 1876
  John C. Hay   ?
  B.F. Coulter   ?

Appendix

Lutheran (Missouri Synod)	Trinity Evangelical Luthern Church: Pastor George Runkel	March 1883–1905

LIST OF ABBREVIATIONS

AALA	Archives of the Archdiocese of Los Angeles, Mission Hills, California
ACLA	Archives of the City of Los Angeles, Piper Technical Center, Los Angeles, California
AHMS	American Home Mission Society microfilm
APSAC	Archives of the Pacific and Southwest Annual Conference of the United Methodist Church, Claremont, California
APWCM	Archives of the Province of the West of the Congregation of the Mission, Montebello, California
ASFTS	Archives of the San Francisco Theological Seminary, San Anselmo, California
AWPDC	Archives of the Western Province of the Daughters of Charity of St. Vincent de Paul, Seton Provincialate, Los Altos Hills, California
BL	Bancroft Library, Berkeley, California
CA-CO, AMA	California-Colorado Correspondence files, American Missionary Association Manuscripts, Amistad Research Center, Tulane University, New Orleans, Louisiana
Constitutions	"Constitution and By-Laws of the First Protestant Society of Los Angeles," Huntington Library, San Marino, California
FAME	First African Methodist Episcopal Church, Los Angeles, California
FBC	First Baptist Church, Los Angeles, California
Hayes	Judge Benjamin Hayes Scrapbooks, Bancroft Library
HL	Huntington Library, San Marino, California
LA-YMCA	Office of the President, Metropolitan Los Angeles Young Men's Christian Association, Los Angeles, California

Abbreviations

PBFM	Presbyterian Board of Foreign Missions files, Presbyterian Office of History.
POHP	Presbyterian Office of History, Philadelphia, Pennsylvania
Records	Records of Lodge 42, Free and Accepted Masons, Los Angeles, California
SVMC	Saint Vincent's Medical Center, Los Angeles, California

SELECTED BIBLIOGRAPHY

I. Manuscript Collections.

Berkeley, California. Bancroft Library.
Baptist Home Missionary Society. Correspondence. Typescript, n.d. #C-C
   215.
American Home Missionary Society. California Correspondence. Micro-
   film #C-B 393, rolls 1–6.
Coronel, Antonio F. "Cosas de California." 1877. Document CB-75.
Hayes, Benjamin I. Scrapbooks. 138 volumes.
Hough, Reverend A.M. "Dictation of a Life's Story." Typescript, n.d.
   #C-D 810.
Knighten, Reverend Willian Ammon. "Dictation Concerning His Life."
   Typescript, 1887. #C-D 810.
Maclay, Charles. "Dictation." Typescript, n.d. #C-D 817.
Owen, Reverend Isaac. "Correspondence." Transcript, Part I, n.d. #C-B
   337.
Verdaguer, Reverend Peter. "Dictation." Transcript, n.d. #C-D 810.

Berkeley, California, Graduate Theological Union Library.
"American Home Missionary Society Papers, 1816–1894." Microfilm #24,
   6 reels.
Fleming, Sanford. "Baptist History in Southern California: Source Material
   Listed." Typescript, 1941.
Warren, Reverend James Henry. "Album of all Congregational Ministers
   who labored as pastors, acting pastors, stated supplies, educators, edi-
   tors, etc., in California during the first 25 years, 1849–1874."

*Claremont, California. Archives of the Pacific and Southwestern Annual Conference
   of the United Methodist Church. Claremont School of Religion.*

Bibliography

"Anniversary Celebration and History." Los Angeles: First United Methodist Church, 1973.
"Centennial Anniversary." Los Angeles: Trinity United Methodist Church,
1969.
"Minutes." Pacific Annual Conference. Methodist Episcopal Church, South.
2 vols.
"Trinity Methodist Church Yearbook, 1928." Los Angeles: Trinity Methodist Church, South, 1928.

*Los Altos Hills, California. Archives of the Western Province of the Daughters of
Charity of St. Vincent de Paul. Seton Provincialate.*
Manuscripts, Box 3: "Correspondence of the Director." Vols. I–II.
"San Francisco" ledger.
"Los Angeles Orphanage" Collection.
"Los Angeles Infirmary" Collection.

*Los Angeles, California. Regional History Center. Department of Special Collections.
University of Southern California.*
California Historical Society. TICOR Title Insurance (Los Angeles) Collec-
tion of Historical Photographs.

Los Angeles, California. City of Los Angeles. City Archives. Piper Technical Center.
"Minutes" of the Common [later City] Council, Vols. VII, XII, XV–XX.
City Treasurer Collection. Bills Paid Files: "Pest House Warrants, 1877."

*Los Angeles, California. City of Los Angeles. Department of Public Works. Public
Reference Office. City Hall.*
Historical Map Collection.

Los Angeles, California. County Board of Supervisors. Executive Office.
"Minutes." Vols. I–VII.

Los Angeles, California. First African Methodist Episcopal Church.
Baker, Fred M., and Sterling, Jesse H. "History." Typescript, n.d.
"History of the First African Methodist Episcopal Church of Los Angeles."
Typescript, n.d.

Los Angeles, California. First Baptist Church.
"Official Records," Vols. I and II.
"Minutes of the Board of Trustees."
"Constitution and By-Laws, Articles of Faith, Church Covenant and Roll
of Members."

Bibliography

Los Angeles, California. First Congregational Church.
"Clerk's Records," Vols. I, III.

Los Angeles, California. First Unitarian Church.
"History, Preamble and Constitution of the Church of the Unity, Los Angeles, Cal." [Minutes of the Trustees, 1886–92].

Los Angeles, California. First United Presbyterian Church.
"Minutes." Vol. I.
"100th Anniversary, First United Presbyterian Church, 1883–1983."
"75th Anniversary, First United Presbyterian Church, 1883–1958."

Los Angeles, California. Free and Accepted Masons. Lodge #42.
"Records," Vols. I–VI.
"Rollbook."

Los Angeles, California. French Benevolent Society. Pacific Alliance Medical Center.
"Minutes," Vols. II–IV.
"Registre des décès et lieux d'inhumations des Societaires."
"Registre des Membres."

Los Angeles, California. Los Angeles County Medical Association. Library.
"Minutes." Los Angeles County Medical Association. Microfilm 4-A L89, reel 2.

Los Angeles, California. Natural History Museum of Los Angeles County. Seaver Center for Western Historical Research.
Antonio Coronel Collection.

Los Angeles, California. St. Athanasius–St. Paul Parish.
"Minute Book of St. Athanasius Protestant Episcopal Church, Los Angeles, California, from Easter Monday, April 1st, 1872."
"Minutes of the Vestry," Vols. I–II.

Los Angeles, California. St. Vincent's Medical Center. Department of Marketing Communications.
"Corporation Book."

Los Angeles, California. Wilshire Boulevard Temple. Office of the Executive Director. Historic Documents file.
Breuer, Stephen E. "Cowtown Congregation: The Early Jewish Settlement of Los Angeles, From 1850 Through 1885." Typescript, 1958.

Bibliography

Los Angeles, California. Young Men's Christian Association of Metropolitan Los Angeles. Office of the President.
"Historical Data" boxes.

Mission Hills, California. Archives of the Archdiocese of Los Angeles.
"Book of Buildings."
"Cash Book of Income and Expenses," Vol. I.
"Cuentas de la catedral de Santa Vibiana, V. y M."
Episcopal correspondence files, 1855–1890.
"Libro Primero de Gobierno."

Montebello, California. Archives of the Province of the West for the Congregation of the Mission. St. Vincent de Paul Center.
"Annals of St. Vincent's College," Vol. I.
"Records," Vol. I. [Minutes of the Board of Trustees, St. Vincent's College].

New Orleans, Louisiana. Tulane University. Amistad Research Center. American Missionary Association Manuscripts.
California-Colorado file. Microfilm #1060. Reel 1.

Paris, France. Archives of the Daughters of Charity of St. Vincent de Paul. Rue du Bac.
"Catalogue du Personnel—Etats Unis."

Philadelphia, Pennsylvania. Office of History. Presbyterian Church, U.S.A.
Board of Foreign Missions. Records, 1829–1895. Record Group 31, Box 45.
Davis, Thomas K. "Autobiographical Sketch." January, 1867. Manuscript D2971.
Los Angeles, California. First Presbyterian Church. Session. Minutes and Records, vol. 1, 1874–1879; and vol. 2, 1874–1892; and Trustees. Minutes, 1879–1894.
Los Angeles Presbytery (Presbyterian Church in the United States of America). Presbyterial Register, 1876–1958; Records, 1873–87; and Trustees. Minutes, 1883–1916.
"Who's Who in Presbyterian Missions" File.

Rosemead, California. Maryvale, Los Angeles Orphan Asylum.
Minutes of the Board of Trustees.

Sacramento, California. Office of the Secretary of State.
Articles of Incorporation. The Los Angeles Orphan Asylum.

Bibliography

St. Louis, Missouri. Archives of the Central Province of the Daughters of Charity of St. Vincent de Paul. Marillac Provincialate.
Mumbrado, Sister Angelita, D.C. "Remembrance of My Youth." Typescript [1917].

San Anselmo, California. San Francisco Theological Seminary. Archives.
Thomas Fraser Papers.
Los Angeles Presbytery Papers.
"Minutes of the Synod of Alta California." Typescript, 1939.
"Minutes of the Synod of the Pacific." Typescript, 1939.
James Woods Papers.

San Marino, California. Henry E. Huntington Library.
Sarah (Johnson) Barnes. Diary.
E.S. Field. "Historical Address." Typescript, 1894.
"Constitution and By-Laws of the First Protestant Society of Los Angeles."
Reverend William C. Mosher. Journal and Scrapbook.
"Program 75-järhrige Jubiläums-Feir der Ersten Deutsche Methodisten-Kirke." Los Angeles: [German Methodist Church], 1951.
Caroline M. Severance Papers.
Abel Stearns Papers.
Joseph Pomeroy Widney. "History of the Early Methodist Church in Los Angeles." Typescript, 1938.
Benjamin D. Wilson Papers.
Reverend James Woods. Diary.
Frances Widney Workman. "The Life of Mary Barnes Widney." Typescript, 1956.

Santa Barbara, California. Mission Santa Barbara. Archives-Library.
College of Our Lady of Sorrows Collection.
De la Guerra Collection.

II. Church Publications.

American Home Missionary Society. Report. New York: Executive Committee of the American Home Missionary Society, 1871–76.
American Missionary Association. Annual Report. New York: American Missionary Association, 1870–77.
California Annual Conference. Methodist Episcopal Church, North. Minutes. San Francisco: Methodist Book Depository, 1879, 1881.
California Baptist State Convention. Minutes of the Fourth Anniversary of the

Bibliography

California Baptist State Convention Co-operating with the American Baptist Home Mission Society. San Francisco: n.p., 1870.

General Association of California. [Congregationalist] *Minutes of the Annual Meeting.* San Francisco: by the General Association, 1857–76, 1877–88.

Pacific Annual Conference. Methodist Episcopal Church, South. *Minutes of the Sixth Session.* San Francisco: n.p., 1856.

Presbyterian Board of Home Missions. *Annual Reports.* New York: Presbyterian Board of Home Missions, 1875–77.

Protestant Episcopal Church in California. *Journal of the Proceedings of the Annual Meeting.* San Francisco: n.p., 1853–56, 1858–59, 1861–64, 1866–84, 1886.

St. Vincent's College. *Catalogues.* Los Angeles: St. Vincent's College, 1877, 1880–86.

Southern California Annual Conference. Methodist Episcopal Church, North. *Minutes.* Los Angeles: Southern California Annual Conference, 1876–85.

Synod of the Pacific [Presbyterians]. *Minutes.* San Francisco: Synod of the Pacific, 1870–83.

III. Newspapers and Periodicals

American Missionary. 1870–77.
Gum Saan Journal. 1978–87.
Home Mission Monthly. 1887.
Los Angeles Daily News. 1880.
Los Angeles. El Clamor Público. 1855–59.
Los Angeles Evening Express. 1874–78.
Los Angeles Herald. 1878–86.
Los Angeles News. 1864–65.
Los Angeles Republican. 1867–70.
Los Angeles Star. 1851–64, 1868–79.
Los Angeles Tri-Weekly News. 1862–69.
Los Angeles. Southern Vineyard. 1858–59.
Los Angeles. The Tidings. 1896, 1931.
Los Angeles Times. 1881–87.
San Francisco. The Pacific. 1851–85.
San Francisco. The Occident. 1868–85.

IV. Government Documents.

California. State Legislature. *Appendix to the Journals of the Senate and Assem-*

bly . . . of the Legislature of the State of California. Sacramento: State Printer, 1868, 3 vols.; 1870, 2 vols.; 1872, 4 vols.

————. *Leyes de California.* Thomas R. Eldredge, trans. Sacramento: State Printer, 1859, 1861–64.

Los Angeles. City Auditor's Office. *Annual Report for the City of Los Angeles.* Los Angeles: City Printing Office, 1905.

U.S. Census Office. 7th Census, 1850. *The Seventh Census of the United States, Embracing a Statistical View of Each of the States and Territories.* Washington, D.C.: Robert Armstrong, Public Printer, 1853.

————. *Statistical View of the United States.* Washington, D.C.: Government Printing Office, 1854; reprint ed., New York: Gordon and Breach Science Publishers, 1970.

U.S. Census Office. 8th Census, 1860. *Agriculture of the United States.* Washington, D.C.: Government Printing Office, 1866.

————. *Population of the United States.* Washington, D.C.: Government Printing Office, 1864.

————. *Statistics of the United States (Including Mortality, Property, etc.) in 1860.* Washington, D.C.: Government Printing Office, 1866.

U.S. Census Office. 9th Census, 1870. *A Compendium of the Ninth Census.* Washington, D.C.: Government Printing Office, 1872.

————. *Statistics of the United States.* Washington, D.C.: Government Printing Office, 1872.

U.S. Census Office. 10th Census, 1880. *Report on the Productions of Agriculture.* Washington, D.C.: Government Printing Office, 1883.

————. *Social Statistics of Cities.* Part II: *Southern and Western States.* Washington, D.C.: Government Printing Office, 1887.

————. *Statistics of Population of the United States.* Washington, D.C.: Government Printing Office, 1883.

U.S. Census Office. 11th Census, 1890. *Report of the Statistics of Churches in the United States.* Washington, D.C.: Government Printing Office, 1894.

V. Books.

Acuña, Rudolfo. *Occupied America: A History of Chicanos.* 2nd ed. New York: Harper and Row, 1981.

Adams, Emma H. *To and Fro in Southern California.* Cincinnati: W.M.B.C. Press, 1887; reprint ed., New York: Arno Press, 1976.

Ahlstrom, Sidney E. *A Religious History of the American People.* New Haven: Yale University Press, 1972.

Amat, Thaddeus. *Asociación de Santa Vibiana, Virgen y Mártir, Patrona de la Diócesis de Monterey, con el objecto de erigirle una catedral.* Barcelona: Pablo Riera, 1860.

Bibliography

————. *Exhortación Pastoral*. Los Angeles: Office of the Southern Californian, 1856.

————. *Pastoral Letter*. Los Angeles: n.p., 1869.

————. *Pastoral Letter*. San Francisco: Mahon, Rapp, Thomas, and Company, 1870.

————. *Pastoral Letter*. San Francisco: Smyth and Shoaff, 1872.

————. *Treatise on Matrimony According to the Doctrine and Discipline of the Catholic Church*. San Francisco: Michael Flood, 1864.

Annual Register. Los Angeles: Fort Street Methodist Episcopal Church, 1889.

Anthony, Charles V. *Fifty Years of Methodism: A History of the Methodist Episcopal Church, within the Bounds of the California Annual Conference, from 1847 to 1897*. San Francisco: Methodist Book Concern, 1901.

Archdeacon, Thomas J. *Becoming American: An Ethnic History*. New York: The Free Press, 1983.

Ash, James L. *Protestantism and the American University: An Intellectual Biography of William Warren Sweet*. Dallas: Southern Methodist University Press, 1982.

Bakker, Elna. *An Island Called California: An Ecological Introduction to Its Natural Communities*. 2nd ed. Berkeley: University Of California Press, 1984.

Bancroft, Hubert Howe. *The Works of Hubert Howe Bancroft*. Vols. 18–24: *History of California*. San Francisco: The History Company, 1886–90; reprint ed., Santa Barbara, California: Wallace Hebberd, 1970.

————. *Chronicles of the Builders of the Commonwealth*. 7 vols. San Francisco: The History Company, 1892.

Barber, Ruth, and Agnew, Edith. *The Sowers Went Forth: The Story of Presbyterian Missions in New Mexico and Southern Colorado*. Albuquerque, New Mexico: Menaul History Library of the Southwest, 1981.

Barth, Gunther. *Bitter Strength: A History of the Chinese in the United States, 1850–1870*. Cambridge: Harvard University Press, 1964.

Beasley, Delilah L. *The Negro Trail Blazers of California*. Los Angeles: Privately Printed, 1909.

Bell, Horace. *On the Old West Coast, Being Further Reminiscences of a Ranger*. Edited by Lanie Bartlett. New York: William Morrow and Company, 1930.

————. *Reminiscences of a Ranger*. Los Angeles: Yarnell, Caystile, and Mathes, 1881.

Bender, Thomas. *Community and Social Change in America*. New Brunswick, New Jersey: Rutgers University Press, 1978.

Benton, Joseph A., ed. *Religious Progress on the Pacific Slope*. Boston: Pilgrim Press, 1917.

Bicentennial Digest: A Perspective of Pioneer Los Angeles Jewry. Los Angeles: Jewish Federation–Council of Greater Los Angeles, 1976.

Bibliography

Billington, Ray Allen. *The Protestant Crusade, 1800–1860*. New York: Mac-Millan Company, 1938; reprint ed., Chicago: Quadrangle Books, 1964.

Bland, Sister Joan. *Hibernian Crusade: The Story of the Catholic Total Abstinence Union of America*. Washington, D.C.: Catholic University of America Press, 1951.

Boardman, William E. *The Higher Christian Life*. Boston: Hoyt, 1858.

Boardman, Mrs. [William E.] *Life and Labours of the Rev. W. E. Boardman*. New York: D. Appleton and Company, 1887.

Boles, John B. *The Great Revival, 1787–1805: The Origins of the Southern Evangelical Mind*. Lexington: University Press of Kentucky, 1972.

Bond, J. Max. *The Negro in Los Angeles*. San Francisco: S & E Research Associates, 1972.

Brackenridge, R. Douglas, and García-Treto, Francisco. *Iglesia Presbiteriana: A History of Presbyterians and Mexican Americans in the Southwest*. San Antonio: Trinity University Press, 1974.

Bucke, Emory Stevens, ed. *The History of American Methodism*. 3 vols. New York: Abingdon Press, 1964.

Burton, Nathaniel J., Parker, Edwin Pond, and Twichell, Joseph H. *The Christian Hymnal*. Hartford, Connecticut: Brown and Gross, 1877.

Camarillo, Alberto. *Chicanos in a Changing Society: From Mexican Pueblos to American Barrios in Santa Barbara and Southern California, 1848–1930*. Cambridge: Harvard University Press, 1979.

Carpenter, Edwin H. *Early Cemeteries of the City of Los Angeles*. Los Angeles: Dawson's Book Shop, 1973.

Caughey, John, and Caughey, LaRee, eds. *Los Angeles: Biography of a City*. Berkeley: University of California Press, 1977.

Chan, Sucheng. *The Bitter-Sweet Soil: The Chinese in California Agriculture, 1860–1910*. Berkeley: University of California Press, 1986.

Chinn, Thomas W., Lai, H. Mark, and Choy, Philip P. *A History of the Chinese in California: A Syllabus*. San Francisco: Chinese Historical Society of America, 1969.

Christ in the Army: A Selection of Sketches of the Work of the U. S. Christian Commission. Philadelphia: Ladies Christian Commission, 1865.

Church, Robert L. *Education in the United States: An Interpretive History*. New York: Free Press, 1976.

Clark, Francis D. *The First Regiment of New York Volunteers, Commanded by Colonel Jonathon D. Stevenson in the Mexican War*. New York: George S. Evans and Company, 1882.

Clark, Stephen C. *The Diocese of Los Angeles: A Brief History*. Los Angeles: Committee on Diocesan Anniversaries, 1945.

Cleland, Robert Glass. *The Cattle on a Thousand Hills*. 2nd ed. San Marino, California: Huntington Library, 1951.

Bibliography

————. *The History of Occidental College, 1887–1937*. Los Angeles: Ward Ritchie Press, 1937.

————. *The Irvine Ranch*. Revised ed. San Marino, California: Huntington Library, 1962.

Cleland, Robert Glass, and Putnam, Frank B. *Isaias W. Hellman and the Farmers and Merchants Bank*. San Marino, California: Huntington Library, 1980.

Cole, Clifford A. *The Christian Churches of Southern California*. St. Louis: Christian Board of Publication, 1959.

Condit, Ira M. *The Chinaman as We See Him and Fifty Years of Work for Him*. Chicago: Fleming H. Revell Company, 1900.

Conroy, Charles C. *The Centennial, 1840–1940*. Los Angeles: Archdiocese of Los Angeles, 1940.

Constitution and By-Laws of the Hebrew Benevolent Society of Los Angeles, California. Los Angeles: Office of the Southern Californian, 1855.

Constitutiones Latae et Promulgatae ab Illmo. ac Revmo. Thaddaeo Amat, Congregationis Missionis, Episcopo Montereyensis et Angelorum, in Synodo Dioecesana Prima. San Francisco: Vicente Torras, 1862.

Constitutiones Latae et Promulgatae ab Illmo ac Revmo. Thaddaeo Amat, Congregationis Missionis, Episcopo Montereyensis et Angelorum, in Synodo Dioecesana Segunda. San Francisco: Mullin, Mahon, and Company, 1869.

Constitutiones Latae et Promulgatae ab Illmo. ac Revmo. Thaddaeo Amat, Congregationis Missionis, Episcopo Montereyensis et Angelorum, in Synodo Dioecesana Tertia. San Francisco: P.J. Thomas, 1876.

Cook, Sherburn F. *The Population of the California Indians*. Berkeley: University of California Press, 1976.

Crompton, Arnold. *Unitarianism on the Pacific Coast: The First Sixty Years*. Boston: Beacon Press, 1957.

Cross, Whitney B. *The Burned-Over District: The Social and Intellectual History of Enthusiastic Religion in Western New York*. New York: Harper and Row, 1950.

Crumlish, Sister John Mary. *1809–1959*. Emmitsburg, Maryland: St. Joseph's Central House, 1959.

Dakin, Susanna Bryant, ed. *Navidad: A Christmas Day with the Early Californians*. San Francisco: California Historical Society, 1958.

Davis, Royal G. *Light on a Gothic Tower*. Los Angeles: First Congregational Church, 1967.

Davis, Thomas Kirby. *The Davis Family*. Norwood, Massachusetts: The Plimpton Press, 1912.

de Barbery, Helene Bailly. *Elizabeth Seton*. 6th ed. New York: MacMillan Company, 1931.

Del Castillo, Richard Griswold. *The Los Angeles Barrio, 1850–1890: A Social History*. Berkeley: University of California Press, 1979.

De Leon, Arnoldo. *The Tejano Community, 1836–1900.* Albuquerque: University of New Mexico Press, 1982.

Diner, Hasia R. *Erin's Daughters in America: Irish Immigrant Women in the Nineteenth Century.* Baltimore: Johns Hopkins University Press, 1983.

Directory of Los Angeles for 1875. Los Angeles: Mirror Book and Job Printing, 1875.

Dolan, Jay P. *The American Catholic Experience: A History from Colonial Times to the Present.* Garden City, New York: Doubleday and Company, 1985.

———. *Catholic Revivalism; The American Experience, 1830–1900.* Notre Dame, Indiana: University of Notre Dame Press, 1978.

Doyle, Don Harrison. *The Social Order of a Frontier Community: Jacksonville, Illinois, 1825–1870.* Urbana, Illinois: University of Illinois Press, 1978.

Drury, Clifford M. *The Centennial of the Synod of California.* San Francisco: Office of the Stated Clerk, 1952.

———. *Presbyterian Panorama: One Hundred and Fifty Years of National Missions History.* Philadelphia: Board of Christian Education, Presbyterian Church of the U.S.A., 1952.

Du Brau, Richard T. *The Romance of Lutheranism.* St. Louis: Concordia Publishing House, 1959.

Dumenil, Lynn. *Freemasonry and American Culture, 1880–1930.* Princeton: Princeton University Press, 1984.

Dumke, Glenn S. *The Boom of the Eighties in Southern California.* San Marino, California: Huntington Library, 1944.

Dykstra, Robert R. *The Cattle Towns.* New York: Alfred A. Knopf, Inc., 1968; reprint ed., New York: Athaneum, 1974.

Elliott, C. E. *A History of the Methodist Episcopal Church in the Southwest.* Cincinnati: Poe and Hitchcock, 1868.

Ellis, Bruce. *Bishop Lamy's Santa Fe Cathedral.* Albuquerque: University of New Mexico Press, 1985.

Engelhardt, Zephyrin, O.F.M. *Missions and Missionaries in California.* 4 vols. San Francisco: James H. Barry Company, 1915.

———. *San Gabriel Mission and the Beginnings of Los Angeles.* San Gabriel, California: Mission San Gabriel, 1927.

Ewens, Sister Mary. *The Role of the Nun in Nineteenth-Century America.* New York: Arno Press, 1978.

Faragher, John Mack. *Sugar Creek: Life on the Illinois Prairie.* New Haven: Yale University Press, 1986.

Ferrier, William W. *Congregationalism's Place in California History.* Berkeley: n.p., 1943.

———. *Pioneering Church Beginnings and Educational Movements in California.* Berkeley: Privately Printed, 1927.

Fields, Richard. *How the Swans Came to the Lake: A Narrative History of Bud-*

dhism in America. Revised ed. Boston: Shambhala Publications, Incorporated, 1986.

The First Los Angeles City and County Directory, 1872. Los Angeles: n.p., 1872; reprint ed., Los Angeles: Ward Ritchie Press, 1963.

The First Unitarian Church of Los Angeles Centennial Celebration, 1877–1977. [Los Angeles: First Unitarian Church, 1977].

Fitzgerald, O.P. *California Sketches*. 4th ed. Nashville: Southern Methodist Publishing House, 1880.

———. *California Sketches*. 2nd Series. 2 vols. Nashville: Southern Methodist Publishing House, 1889.

Fleming, Sanford. *God's Gold: The Story of Baptist Beginnings in California, 1849–1860*. Philadelphia: Judson Press, 1949.

Fogelson, Robert M. *The Fragmented Metropolis: Los Angeles, 1850–1930*. Cambridge: Harvard University Press, 1967.

Foster, Charles I. *An Errand of Mercy: The Evangelical United Front, 1790–1837*. Chapel Hill: University of North Carolina Press, 1960.

Frankiel, Sandra Sizer. *California's Spiritual Frontiers: Religious Alternatives in Anglo-Protestantism, 1850–1910*. Berkeley: University of California Press, 1988.

Gandolfo, A.H. *Notes on Our Venerated and Beloved Father, Very Rev. James Francis Burlando, C.M., Director of the Province of the United States*. Emmitsburg, Maryland: St. Joseph's Central House, 1873.

Garbutt, Mary Alderman. *Victories of Four Decades, 1883–1924*. Los Angeles: Woman's Christian Temperance Union of Southern California, 1924.

Garcia, Mario T. *Desert Immigrants: The Mexicans of El Paso, 1880–1920*. New Haven: Yale University Press, 1981.

Garrison, Winfred Ernst. *Religion Follows the Frontier: A History of the Disciples of Christ*. New York: Harper and Row, 1931.

Gates, Paul Wallace, ed. *California Ranchos and Farms, 1846–1862*. Madison: State Historical Society of Wisconsin, 1967.

Gaustad, Edwin S. *Religion in America: History and Historiography*. Washington, D.C.: American Historical Association, 1973.

———. *A Religious History of America*. 2nd ed. New York: Harper and Row, 1974.

Geiger, Maynard, O.F.M. *Franciscan Missionaries in Hispanic California, 1769–1848*. San Marino, California: Huntington Library, 1969.

———. *Mission Santa Barbara, 1782–1965*. Santa Barbara, California: Franciscan Fathers of California, 1965.

Glazier, Nathan. *American Judaism*. 2nd ed., revised. Chicago: University Of Chicago Press, 1972.

The Golden Years, 1938–1988. Los Angeles: Los Angeles Chinatown Corporation, 1988.

Bibliography

Golder, Frank A., Bailey, Thomas A., and Smith, J. Lyman, eds. *The March of the Mormon Battalion from Council Bluffs to California: Taken from the Journal of Henry Standage*. New York: The Century Company, 1928.

Goodykuntz, Colin B. *Home Missions on the American Frontier, with Particular Reference to the American Home Missionary Society*. Caldwell, Idaho: Caxton Printers, 1939.

Gonzalez, Roberto O., O.F.M., and La Velle, Michael. *The Hispanic Catholic in the United States: A Socio-Cultural and Religious Profile*. New York: Northeast Catholic Pastoral Center for Hispanics, 1985.

Granjon, Henry. *Along the Rio Grande: A Pastoral Visit to Southwest New Mexico in 1902*. Ed. by Michael Romero Taylor. Trans. by Mary W. de Lopez. Albuquerque: University of New Mexico Press, 1986.

Graves, Jackson A. *Seventy Years in California, 1857–1927*. Los Angeles: Times-Mirror Press, 1927.

Grenier, Judson A., with Gillingham, Robert. *California Legacy*. Los Angeles: Watson Land Company, 1987.

Guarneri, Carl, and David Alvarez, eds. *Religion and Society in the American West: Historical Essays*. Lanham, Maryland: University Press of America, 1987.

Guilday, Peter. *A History of the Councils of Baltimore, 1791–1884*. New York: MacMillan Company, 1932.

Handy, Robert T. *A History of the Churches in the United States and Canada*. New York: Oxford University Press, 1976.

Hayes, Florence. *Daughters of Dorcas: The Story of the Work of Women for Home Missions Since 1802*. New York: Board of National Missions, Presbyterian Church of the U.S.A., 1952.

Heizer, Robert F., ed. *The Indians of Los Angeles County: Hugo Reid's Letters of 1852*. Los Angeles: Southwest Museum, 1968.

Hennesey, James, S.J. *American Catholics: A History of the Roman Catholic Community in the United States*. New York: Oxford University Press, 1981.

Heritage of Caring. Los Angeles: Hospital of the Good Samaritan, 1985.

Hickey, Edward J. *The Society for the Propagation of the Faith: Its Foundation, Organization and Success*. Washington, D.C.: Catholic University of America Press, 1922.

Hill, Laurence L., ed. *Six Decades: The Growth of Higher Education in Southern California*. Los Angeles: Security First National Bank, 1929.

Hine, Leland D. *Baptists in Southern California*. Valley Forge, Pennsylvania: Judson Press, 1966.

Hine, Robert V. *Community on the American Frontier*. Norman, Oklahoma: University of Oklahoma Press, 1980.

Hinojosa, Gilberto M. *A Borderlands Town in Transition: Laredo, 1755–1870*. College Station, Texas: Texas A & M University Press, 1983.

Bibliography

History of the American Missionary Association, with Facts and Anecdotes Illustrating Its Work in the South. Rev. ed. New York: American Missionary Association, 1874.

History of the First Baptist Church of Los Angeles. [Los Angeles: First Baptist Church], 1949.

Hoffman, Pat. *History of the First Presbyterian Church of Los Angeles.* Los Angeles: United University Church, 1977.

Holland, Clifford L. *The Religious Dimension in Hispanic Los Angeles: A Protestant Case Study.* South Pasadena, California: William Carey Library, 1974.

Hoover, Mildred B., Rensch, Hero E., and Rensch, Ethel G. *Historic Spots in California.* 3rd ed., revised by William N. Abeloe. Stanford: Stanford University Press, 1966.

Horgan, Paul. *Lamy of Santa Fe.* New York: Farrar, Straus, and Giroux, 1975.

The Horizon. Los Angeles: First Methodist Church, 1938.

Instrucción y Breve Compendio de Oraciones para Uso de los Miembros de la Obra de la Propagación de la Fé; de la Archicofradia del Santisimo e Inmaculado Corazón de María, y de la Asociación para la Conversión de los Hereges. San Francisco: Vicente Torras, 1856.

James, Edward T., James, Janet Wilson, and Boyer, Paul S., eds. *Notable American Women.* 3 vols. Cambridge: Harvard University, Belknap Press, 1971.

Jervey, Edward D. *The History of Methodism in Southern California and Arizona.* Nashville: Parthenon Press, 1960.

Johnson, Bernice Eastman. *California's Gabrielino Indians.* Los Angeles: Southwest Museum, 1964.

Johnson, Charles A. *The Frontier Camp Meeting: Religion's Harvest Time.* Dallas: Southern Methodist University Press, 1955.

Johnson, Paul E. *A Shopkeeper's Millennium: Society and Revivals in Rochester, New York, 1815–1837.* New York: Hill and Wang, 1978.

Jones, Helen L., and Wilcox, Robert F. *Metropolitan Los Angeles: Its Governments.* Los Angeles: The Haynes Foundation, 1949.

Jones, Janet Wilson, ed. *Women in American Religion.* Philadelphia: University of Pennsylvania Press, 1980.

Jones, Oakah L., Jr. *Los Paisanos: Spanish Settlers on the Northern Frontier of New Spain.* Norman, Oklahoma: University of Oklahoma Press, 1979.

Jordan, Winthrop S. *Religion in America.* 2nd ed. New York: Charles Scribner's Sons, 1973.

The Journal of Lt. John McHenry Hollingsworth of the New York Volunteers. San Francisco: California Historical Society, 1923.

Kaufman, Polly Wells. *Women Teachers on the American Frontier.* New Haven: Yale University Press, 1984.

Kelley, Douglas O. *History of the Diocese of California, from 1849 to 1914*. San Francisco: Bureau of Information and Supply, Diocese of California, 1915.

Kenneally, Finbar, O.F.M., ed. *United States Documents in the Propaganda Fide Archives: A Calendar*. 7 vols. Washington, D.C.: Academy of American Franciscan History, 1966–77.

King, Ethel Thompson. *St. Athanasius Episcopal Church, Los Angeles, California, 1864–1969*. [Los Angeles: St. Athanasius Church, 1969].

Kip, William Ingraham. *The Early Days of My Episcopate*. New York: T. Whittacker, 1892.

Kramer, William M., ed. *The American West and the Religious Experience*. Los Angeles: Privately Printed, 1975.

Lapp, Rudolph M. *Blacks in Gold Rush California*. New Haven: Yale University Press, 1977.

Larsen, Lawrence H. *The Urban West at the End of the Frontier*. Lawrence, Kansas: Regents Press of Kansas, 1978.

Limerick, Patricia Nelson. *The Legacy of Conquest: The Unbroken Past of the American West*. New York: W.W. Norton and Company, 1988.

Linking Our Lives: Chinese American Women in Los Angeles. Los Angeles: Chinese Historical Society of Southern California, 1984.

Lives of Our Deceased Sisters, 1903. Emmitsburg, Maryland: St. Joseph's Central House, 1903.

Loofburrow, Leon L. *In Search of God's Gold*. San Francisco: Historical Society of the Northern California–Nevada Conference, Methodist Church, 1950.

Los Angeles City and County Directory for 1881–2. San Francisco: Southern California Directory Company. 1881.

Los Angeles City and County Directory for 1883–84. San Francisco: A.J. Leary, 1883.

Los Angeles City and County Directory, 1884–5. Los Angeles: Atwood and Ernst, 1885.

Los Angeles City Directory, 1878. Los Angeles: Mirror Printing, Ruling, and Binding House, 1878.

Los Angeles Orphan's Home Society. *Annual Report*. Los Angeles: Los Angeles Orphans' Home Society, 1883, 1885, 1889.

Loveland, Anne C. *Southern Evangelicals and the Social Order, 1800–1860*. Baton Rouge: Louisiana State University Press, 1980.

Loyer, Fernand, and Beaudreau, M.C. *Le Guide Français de Los Angeles et du Sud de la Californie*. English Edition. Los Angeles: Franco-American Publishing Company, 1932.

Ludwig, Salvator, Archduke of Austria. *Los Angeles in the Sunny Seventies: A Flower from the Golden Land*. Trans. by Marguerite Eyer Wilbur. Los

Bibliography

Angeles: Bruce McAllister and Jake Zeitlin, 1929.

Lyon, E. Wilson. *The History of Pomona College, 1887–1969*. Claremont, California: Pomona College, 1977.

Manual of the First Congregational Church of Los Angeles, Cal. Los Angeles: First Congregational Church, 1886.

Manual of the First Presbyterian Church of Los Angeles. Los Angeles: First Presbyterian Church, 1884.

Martin, Helen Eastman. *The History of the Los Angeles County Hospital (1878–1968) and the Los Angeles County-University of Southern California Medical Center (1968–1978)*. Los Angeles: University of Southern California Press, 1979.

Martin, James R. *The University of California (in Los Angeles)*. Los Angeles: Privately Printed, 1925.

Marty, Martin E. *Pilgrims in Their Native Land: 500 Years of Religion in America*. Boston: Little, Brown, and Company, 1984.

———. *Righteous Empire: The Protestant Experience in America*. New York: Dial Press, 1970.

Mathews, Donald G. *Religion in the Old South*. Chicago: University of Chicago Press, 1977.

McGloin, John B., S.J. *California's First Archbishop: The Life of Joseph Sadoc Alemany, O.P., 1814–1888*. New York: Herder and Herder, 1966.

———. *Eloquent Indian: The Life of James Bouchard, California Jesuit*. Stanford: Stanford University Press, 1949.

McLoughlin, William G. *Revivals, Awakenings, and Reforms: An Essay on Religion and Social Change in America, 1607–1977*. Chicago: University of Chicago Press, 1978.

McNeill, J.T., Spinka, Matthew, and Willoghby, Harold R., eds. *Environmental Factors in Christian History*. Chicago: University of Chicago Press, 1939.

Melville, Annabelle M. *Elizabeth Bayley Seton*. New York: Charles Scribner's Sons, 1951; reprint ed., St. Paul, Minnesota: Carillon Books, 1976.

Miyakawa, T. Scott. *Protestants and Pioneers: Individuality and Conformity on the American Frontier*. Chicago: University of Chicago Press, 1964.

Mowry, George F. *The California Progressives*. Berkeley: University of California Press, 1951; reprint ed., Chicago: Quadrangle Books, 1963.

Muir, Gladys E. *Settlement of the Brethren on the Pacific Slope*. Elgin, Illinois: Brethren Publishing House, 1939.

Muir, Leo J. *A Century of Mormon Activities in California*. 2 vols. Salt Lake City: Deseret News Press, [1952].

Nadeau, Remi. *City-Makers: The Story of Southern California's First Boom, 1868–1876*. Los Angeles: Trans-Anglo Books, 1965.

Neal, Thomas A. *St. Vibiana's: Los Angeles Cathedral, 1876–1950*. Los Angeles: Dawson's Book Shop, 1950.

Nelson, Howard J., and Clark, William A.V. *Los Angeles: The Metropolitan Experience*. Cambridge: Ballinger Publishing Company, 1976.

Newmark, Harris. *Sixty Years in Southern California, 1853–1913*. 4th ed., revised by Maurice H. Newmark and Marco R. Newmark. Los Angeles: Zeitlin and Ver Brugge, 1970.

Newmark, Maurice H., and Newmark, Marco R., eds. *Census of the City and County of Los Angeles, California, for the Year 1850*. Los Angeles: Times-Mirror Press, 1929.

1981 Historical Journal: Pacific and Southwest Annual Conference. Pasadena, California: United Methodist Center, 1981.

North, William E. *Catholic Education in Southern California*. Washington, D.C.: Catholic University of America Press, 1936.

Northrop, Marie E. *Spanish-Mexican Families of Early California, 1769–1850*. 2 vols. Burbank, California: Southern California Genealogical Society, 1976, 1984.

Novena a Santa Vibiana, Virgen y Mártir, Protectora de la Diócesis de Monterey. San Francisco: Vicente Torras, 1856.

Nunis, Doyce B., Jr., ed. *Los Angeles and Its Environs in the Twentieth Century: A Bibliography of a Metropolis*. Los Angeles: Ward Ritchie Press, 1973.

Nye, Russell B. *Society and Culture in America, 1830–1860*. New York: Harper and Row, 1974.

Packman, Ana Beguede. *Early California Hospitality*. Glendale, California: Arthur H. Clark Company, 1938.

———. *Leather Dollars: Short Stories of Pueblo Los Angeles*. Los Angeles: Times-Mirror Press, 1932.

Perry, John D. K. *A History of the First Unitarian Church of Los Angeles, California, 1877–1937*. Los Angeles: First Unitarian Church, 1937.

Pitt, Leonard. *The Decline of the Californios: A Social History of the Spanish-Speaking Californians, 1846–1890*. Berkeley: University of California Press, 1966.

Pond, William C. *Gospel Pioneering: Reminiscences of Early Congregationalism in California, 1853–1920*. Oberlin, Ohio: Privately Printed, 1921.

Posey, Walter B. *Frontier Mission: Religion West of the Southern Appalachians to 1861*. Lexington: University Press of Kentucky, 1966.

Ruether, Rosemary Radford, and Keller, Rosemary Skinner, eds. *Women and Religion in America*. 3 Vols. San Francisco: Harper and Row, 1982. Vol. I: *The Nineteenth Century*.

Rice, William B. *The Los Angeles Star, 1851–1864*. Berkeley: University of California Press, 1947.

Bibliography

————. *William Money: A Southern California Savant*. Los Angeles: Privately Printed, 1943.

Ríos-Bustamente, Antonio, and Castillo, Pedro. *An Illustrated History of Mexican Los Angeles, 1781–1985*. Los Angeles: Chicano Studies Research Center, University of California, 1986.

Rischin, Moses, ed. *Jews of the West: The Metropolitan Years*. Waltham, Massachusetts: American Jewish Historical Society, 1979.

Robinson, Alfred. *Life in California During a Residence of Several Years in That Territory*. New York: Wiley and Putnam, 1846; reprint ed., Salt Lake City: Peregrine Publishers, 1970.

Robinson, John W. *Los Angeles in the Civil War Days, 1860–1865*. Los Angeles: Dawson's Book Shop, 1977.

Robinson, W. W. *Land in California*. Berkeley: University of California Press, 1944.

————. *Lawyers of Los Angeles*. Los Angeles: Los Angeles Bar Association, 1959.

————. *Maps of Los Angeles: From Ord's Survey in 1849 to the End of the Boom of the Eighties*. Los Angeles: Dawson's Book Shop, 1966.

Roemer, Theodore, O.F.M. Cap. *Ten Decades of Alms*. St. Louis: B. Herder Book Company, 1942.

Rolle, Andrew. *California: A History*. 2nd ed. New York: Thomas Y. Crowell Company, 1969.

————. *Los Angeles: From Pueblo to Modern City*. San Francisco: Boyd and Fraser Publishing Company, 1981.

Romo, Ricardo. *East Los Angeles: History of a Barrio, 1900–1930*. Austin: University of Texas Press, 1983.

Ruddy, Ella G., ed. *Mother of Clubs: Caroline M. Seymour Severance*. Los Angeles: Baumgardt Publishing Company, 1906.

Ryan, Mary P. *Cradle of the Middle Class: The Family in Oneida County, New York, 1790–1865*. Cambridge: Cambridge University Press, 1981.

Saddleback Ancestors: Rancho Families of Orange County, California. Santa Ana, California: Orange County Genealogical Society, 1969.

Sandberg, Neil C. *Jewish Life in Los Angeles: A Window to Tomorrow*. Lanham, Maryland: University Press of America, 1986.

Sandoval, Moises, ed. *Fronteras: A History of the Latin American Church in the U.S.A. Since 1513*. San Antonio, Texas: Mexican American Cultural Center, 1983.

Senkewicz, Robert M., S.J. *Vigilantes in Gold Rush San Francisco*. Stanford: Stanford University Press, 1985.

Servin, Manuel P., and Wilson, Iris Higbie. *Southern California and Its University: A History of the University of Southern California, 1880–1964*. Los Angeles: Ward Ritchie Press, 1969.

Bibliography

Sheridan, Thomas E. *Los Tucsonenses: The Mexican Community in Tucson, 1854–1941*. Tucson, Arizona: University of Arizona Press, 1986.

Sherwood, Midge. *Days of Vision, Years of Vintage*. 2 vols. San Marino, California: Orizaba Press, 1982, 1987.

Simmons, J.C. *The History of Southern Methodism on the Pacific Coast*. Nashville: Southern Methodist Publishing House, 1886.

Singleton, Gregory H. *Religion in the City of the Angels: American Public Culture and Urbanization, Los Angeles, 1850–1930*. Ann Arbor, Michigan: UMI Research Press, 1979.

Smith, George G. *The Life and Times of George F. Pierce, D.D., L.L.D.* Sparta, Georgia: Hancock Publishing Company, 1888.

Smith, Sarah Bixby. *Adobe Days*. 4th ed., revised. Fresno, California: Valley Publishers, 1974.

Smith, Timothy L. *Revivalism and Social Reform: American Protestantism on the Eve of the Civil War*. 2nd ed. Baltimore: Johns Hopkins University Press, 1980.

Smith, Wallace E. *This Land Was Ours: the Del Valles and Rancho Camulos*. Ventura, California: Ventura County Historical Society, 1977.

Sorrentini, Cayetano. *Panegírico en honor de Santa Vibiana*. Paris: Adriano LeClere, 1857.

Spalding, William A. *History and Reminiscences of Los Angeles City and County, California*. 3 vols. Los Angeles: J.R. Finnell and Sons, 1931.

Sturtevant, William C., gen. ed. *Handbook of North American Indians*. 20 vols. Washington, D.C.: Smithsonian Institution, 1978. Vol. 8: *California*, ed. by Robert F. Heizer.

Sutton, Herbert L. *Our Heritage and Our Hope: The History of the First Baptist Church of Los Angeles, California, 1874–1974*. Los Angeles: First Baptist Church, 1974.

Sweet, William Warren. *The American Churches: An Interpretation*. New York: Abingdon-Cokesbury Press, 1948.

———. *Religion in the Development of American Culture, 1765–1840*. New York: Charles Scribner's Sons, 1952.

———. *Religion on the American Frontier*. Vol. 1: *The Baptists, 1783–1830*. New York: Henry Holt, 1931. Vol. 2: *The Presbyterians, 1783–1840*. New York: Harper and Brothers, 1936. Vol. 3: *The Congregationalists, 1783–1850*. Chicago: University of Chicago Press, 1939. Vol. 4: *The Methodists, 1783–1840*. Chicago: University of Chicago Press, 1946.

———. *Revivalism in America: Its Origin, Growth, and Decline*. New York: Charles Scribner's Sons, 1944; reprint ed., Gloucester, Massachusetts: Peter Smith, 1965.

———. *The Story of Religions in America*. New York: Harper and Row, 1930.

Swett, John. *History of the Public Schools in California*. San Francisco: A. L.

Bibliography

Bancroft Company, 1876.

Szasz, Ferenc Morton. *The Protestant Clergy in the Great Plains and the Mountain West, 1865–1915*. Albuquerque: University of New Mexico Press, 1988.

Taves, Ann. *The Household of Faith: Roman Catholic Devotions in Mid-Nineteenth-Century America*. Notre Dame, Indiana: University of Notre Dame Press, 1986.

Taylor, George Rogers, ed. *The Turner Thesis*. Boston: D. C. Heath and Company, 1956.

Toll, William. *The Making of an Ethnic Middle Class: Portland Jewry over Four Generations*. Albany, New York: State University of New York Press, 1982.

A Treasury of Tradition, Innovation and Hope: History of Second Baptist Church, Los Angeles. Los Angeles: Second Baptist Church, 1975.

Tsai, Shih-Shan Henry. *The Chinese Experience in America*. Bloomington: Indiana University Press, 1986.

Tyler, David. *A Concise History of the Mormon Battalion in the Mexican War*. Salt Lake City: n.p., 1881; reprint ed., Chicago: Rio Grande Press, 1964.

Vallier, Ivan. *Catholicism, Social Control, and Modernization in Latin America*. Englewood Cliffs, New Jersey: Prentice-Hall, Inc., 1970.

Vorspan, Max, and Gartner, Lloyd P. *History of the Jews of Los Angeles*. San Marino, California: Huntington Library, 1970.

Ward, David. *Cities and Immigrants: A Geography of Change in Nineteenth-Century America*. New York: Oxford University Press, 1971.

Ware, E.B. *History of the Disciples of Christ in California*. Healdsburg, California: [F.W. Cooke], 1916.

Warner, J.J., Hayes, Benjamin I., and Widney, J.P. *An Historical Sketch of Los Angeles County, California*. Los Angeles: Louis Lewen, 1876; reprint ed., Los Angeles: O.W. Smith, 1936.

Weber, David J. *The Mexican Frontier, 1821–1846: The American Southwest Under Mexico*. Albuquerque: University of New Mexico Press, 1982.

Weber, David J., ed. *New Spain's Far Northern Frontier: Essays on Spain in the American West, 1540–1821*. Albuquerque: University of New Mexico Press, 1979.

Weber, Francis J. *A Biographical Sketch of Right Reverend Francisco García Diego y Moreno, O.F.M.* Los Angeles: Borromeo Guild, 1961.

———. *California's Reluctant Prelate*. Los Angeles: Dawson's Book Shop, 1964.

———. *Century of Fulfillment: The Roman Catholic Church in Southern California, 1840–1947*. Mission Hills, California: Archival Center, Archdiocese of Los Angeles, 1990.

———. *Francisco Mora, Last of the Catalans*. Los Angeles: Westernlore Press, 1967.

————. *St. Vibiana's Cathedral: A Centennial History*. Los Angeles: Archives of the Archdiocese of Los Angeles, 1976.

Weber, Francis J., comp. *Necrologium, Sacerdotum Saecularium, qui et in territorio Archdioecesis Angelorum et in finibus eidum juristictioni jure antea adnexis, laboraverunt vel obierunt*. Los Angeles: Chancery Archives, 1966.

Weber, Francis J., ed. *The Old Plaza Church: A Documentary History*. Los Angeles: Privately Printed, 1979.

————, ed. *The Religious History of Southern California*. Los Angeles: Inter-religious Council of Southern California, 1976.

Whalen, William J. *Christianity and American Freemasonry*. Milwaukee: Bruce Publishing Company, 1958.

Whelan, Harold A., SS.CC. *The Picpus Story*. Pomona, California: Apostolate of Christian Renewal, 1980.

White, Charles J. *Life of Mrs. Eliza. A. Seton*. 10th ed. New York: P.J. Kenedy and Sons, [1879].

Wicher, Edward A. *The Presbyterian Church in California, 1849–1927*. New York: Frederick H. Hitchcock, 1927.

Wiggin, Kate Douglas. *My Garden of Memory: An Autobiography*. Boston: Houghton Mifflin Company, 1923.

Willey, Samuel H. *Thirty Years in California*. San Francisco: A.L. Bancroft and Company, 1879.

Wilson, J. Albert. *History of Los Angeles County, California*. Oakland, California: Thompson and West, 1880; reprint ed., Berkeley: Howell-North, 1959.

Wilson, Iris Higbie. *William Wolfskill, 1798–1866: Frontier Trapper to California Ranchero*. Glendale, California: Arthur B. Clark Company, 1965.

Wolcott, Marjorie Tisdale, ed. *Pioneer Notes from the Diaries of Judge Benjamin Hayes, 1849–1875*. Los Angeles: Privately Printed, 1929.

Woodbury University: 100th Year Anniversary. Los Angeles: Woodbury University, [1984].

Woods, James. *Recollections of Pioneer Work in California*. San Francisco: Winterburn and Company, 1878.

Woods, James L. *California Pioneer Decade of 1849*. San Francisco: Privately Printed, 1922.

Woods, Samuel D. *Light and Shadows of Life on the Pacific Coast*. New York: Funk and Wagnalls Company, 1910.

Workman, Boyle. *The City That Grew*. Los Angeles: Southland Publishing Company, 1935.

Young, Nellie Mae. *William Stewart Young*. Glendale, California: Arthur H. Clark Company, 1967.

Bibliography

VI. Articles.

Apostol, Jane. "They Said It With Flowers: The Los Angeles Flower Festival Society." *Southern California Quarterly* LXII (Spring 1980), pp. 67–78.

Ash, James L. "American Religion and the Academy in the Early Twentieth Century: The Chicago Years of William Warren Sweet." *Church History* L (December 1981), pp. 450–64.

Barrows, Henry D. "Captain Alexander Bell and the Bell Block." Historical Society of Southern California *Annual Publications* III, Part III (1895), pp. 11–18.

———. "Early Clericals of Los Angeles." Historical Society of Southern California *Annual Publications* V, Part II (1900–1902), pp. 127–33.

Barrows, June, ed. "A Vermonter's Description of a Sunday in Los Angeles in 1852." *Vermont History* XXXVIII (Summer 1970), pp. 192–94.

Bogue, Allan G. "Social Theory and the Pioneer." *Agricultural History* XXXIV (January 1960), pp. 21–34.

Bohme, Frederick G. "Episcopal Beginnings in Southern California." *Southern California Quarterly* XLVII (June 1965), pp. 171–90.

Bynum, Lindley, ed. "Los Angeles in 1854–5: The Diary of Reverend James Woods." Historical Society of Southern California *Quarterly* XXIII (June 1941), pp. 65–86.

Chace, Paul G. "The Turtledove Messenger, A Trait of the Early Los Angeles Chiao Ceremony," *Gum Saan Journal* of the Chinese Historical Society of Southern California, XII (December 1989), pp. 1–9.

Chan, David R. "The Chinese Experience in Los Angeles." Chinese Historical Society of America *Bulletin* XV (March 1980), pp. 3–16.

Chinnici, Joseph P., O.F.M. "Organization of the Spiritual Life: American Catholic Devotional Works, 1791–1866." *Theological Studies* XL (June 1979), pp. 229–55.

Cohen, Thomas. "First Jewish Community Site: Los Angeles." *Western State Jewish Historical Quarterly* I (April 1969), pp. 89–101.

Collier, Jane E. "Early Club Life in Los Angeles." Historical Society of Southern California *Annual Publications* IV, Part III (1899), pp. 216–22.

Cook, Louis. "Parish Missions in 1885." *Academy Scrapbook* I (July 1950), pp. 19–26.

Cooley, Laura C. "The Los Angeles Public Library." Historical Society of Southern California *Quarterly* XXIII (March 1941), pp. 5–23.

Cott, Nancy F. "Young Women in the Second Great Awakening." *Feminist Studies* III (February 1977), pp. 15–29.

De Falla, Paul M. "Lantern in the Western Sky." Historical Society of Southern California *Quarterly* XLII (March 1960), pp. 57–88; and (June 1960), pp. 161–85.

Bibliography

de Graaf, Lawrence B. "Race, Sex, and Region: Black Women and the American West, 1850–1920." *Pacific Historical Review* XLIX (May 1980), pp. 285–313.

del Castillo, Richard Griswold. "Myth and Reality: Chicano Economic Mobility in Los Angeles, 1850–1880." *Aztlán* VI (April 1975), pp. 151–71.

Diekemper, Barnabas C., O.F.M. "The Catholic Church in the Shadows: the Southwestern United States During the Mexican Period," *Journal of the West*, XXIV (April 1985), pp. 46–53.

Dorland, C.P. "The Chinese Massacre in Los Angeles in 1871." Historical Society of Southern California *Annual Publications* III, Part II (1894), pp. 22–26.

Doyle, Don Harrison. "The Social Functions of Voluntary Associations in a Nineteenth-Century Town." *Social Science History* I (Spring 1977), pp. 333–55.

———. "Social Theory and New Communities in Nineteenth-Century America." *Western Historical Quarterly* VIII (April 1977), pp. 151–66.

Dozier, Melville. "The Reminiscences of Melville Dozier." Historical Society of Southern California *Annual Publications* XV (1933), pp. 65–111.

Drury, Clifford M. "A Chronology of Protestant Beginnings in California." California Historical Society *Quarterly* XXVI (June 1947), pp. 163–74.

Engelhardt, Zephyrin, O.F.M. "The First Ecclesiastical Synod in California, March 19–23, 1852." *Catholic Historical Review* I (April 1915), pp. 30–37.

Gates, Paul Wallace. "Adjudication of the Spanish-Mexican Land Claims in California." Huntington Library *Quarterly* XXI (May 1958), pp. 213–56.

Gay, Leslie F., Jr. "The Founding of the University of Southern California." Historical Society of Southern California *Annual Publications* VIII, Part I (1909–11), pp. 37–50.

Geiger, Maynard, O.F.M. "Our Lady in Franciscan California." *Franciscan Studies* XXIII (June 1942), pp. 99–112.

Guerra, Fernando J. "Ethnic Officeholders in Los Angeles County." *Sociology and Social Research* LXXI (January 1987), pp. 89–94.

Guinn, James M. "Los Angeles in the Later Sixties and Early Seventies." Historical Society of Southern California *Annual Publications* III, Part I (1893), pp. 63–68.

———. "Los Angeles in the Adobe Age." Historical Society of Southern California *Annual Publications* IV, Part I (1897), pp. 49–55.

———. "Pioneer School Superintendents of Los Angeles." Historical Society of Southern California *Annual Publications* IV, Part I (1897), pp. 76–81.

———. "Schools and Schoolmasters of Los Angeles." Historical Society of Southern California *Annual Publications* III, Part IV (1896), pp. 7–14.

Bibliography

Harrington, Marie. "A Rancho Celebrates La Fiesta de la Santa Cruz." *Masterkey* XLII (April-June 1968), pp. 75–78.

Hayden, Dolores. "Biddy Mason's Los Angeles, 1856–1891," *California History*, LXVIII (Fall 1988), pp. 86–99, 147–49.

Jensen, Joan M., and Miller, Darlis A. "The Gentle Tamers Revisited: New Approaches to the History of Women in the American West." *Pacific Historical Review* XLIX (May 1980), pp. 173–213.

"Journal of John McHenry Hollingsworth, A Lieutenant in Stevenson's Regiment in California." California Historical Society *Quarterly* I (January 1923), pp. 207–70.

Kelsey, Harry. "A New Look at the Founding of Los Angeles." *California Historical Quarterly* LV (Winter 1976), pp. 326–39.

Kramer, William M., and Clar, Reva. "Emanuel Schreiber." *Western States Jewish Historical Quarterly* IX (July 1977), pp. 354–68; and X (October 1977), pp. 48–55.

Kramer, William M., and Stern, Norton B. "Isaac Lankershim and the San Fernando Valley." *Southern California Quarterly* LXVII (Spring 1985), pp. 25–34.

Kramer, William M., and Stern, Norton B. "The Layman as Rabbinic Officiant in the Nineteenth Century." *Western States Jewish History* XVI (October 1983), pp. 49–53.

Kramer, William M., and Stern, Norton B. "The Major Role of Polish Jews in the Pioneer West." *Western States Jewish Historical Quarterly* VIII (July 1976), pp. 326–44.

Laslett, Barbara. "The Household Structure of an American Frontier: Los Angeles, California, in 1850." *American Journal of Sociology* LXXXI (July 1975), pp. 109–28.

———. "Social Change and the Family: Los Angeles, California, 1850–1870." *American Sociological Review* XLII (April 1977), pp. 268–90.

Layne, J. Gregg, ed. "The First Census of the Los Angeles District." *Historical Society of Southern California Quarterly* XVIII (September-December 1936), pp. 81–99.

Locklear, William R. "The Celestials and the Angels: A Study of the Anti-Chinese Movement in Los Angeles to 1882." *Historical Society of Southern California Quarterly* XLII (September 1960), pp. 239–56.

Lyman, Edward L. "The Demise of the San Bernardino Mormon Community, 1851–1857." *Southern California Quarterly* LXV (Winter 1982), pp. 321–40.

Mason, William. "Indian-Mexican Cultural Exchange in the Los Angeles Area, 1781–1834." *Aztlán* XV (Spring 1984), pp. 123–44.

———. "The Chinese in Los Angeles." *Museum Alliance Quarterly* V (Fall 1967), pp. 15–20.

Bibliography

Mason, William, and Duque, Jeanne. "Los Angeles Plaza: Living Symbol of Our Past." *Terra* XIX (January-February 1981), pp. 14–22.

Mathews, Donald G. "The Second Great Awakening as an Organizing Process, 1780–1830: An Hypothesis." *American Quarterly* XXI (Spring 1969), pp. 23–43.

McGloin, John C., S.J. "The California Catholic Church in Transition, 1846–1850." California Historical Society *Quarterly* XLII (March 1963), pp. 39–48.

Mead, Sydney E. "Professor Sweet's *Religion and Culture in America*: A Review Essay." *Church History* XXII (March 1953), pp. 33–49.

"Mrs. Cordelia Mallard." Historical Society of Southern California *Annual Publications* IV, Part III (1899), pp. 280–82.

Muller, Dorothea R. "Church Building and Community Making on the Frontier, A Case Study: Josiah Strong, Home Missionary in Cheyenne, 1871–1873." *Western Historical Quarterly* X (April 1979), pp. 191–216.

Newmark, Marco R. "The Story of Religion in Los Angeles, 1781–1900." Historical Society of Southern California *Quarterly*, XXVIII (March 1946), pp. 35–50.

Northrop, Marie E., ed. "The Los Angeles *Padron* of 1844." Historical Society of Southern California *Quarterly* XLII (December 1960), pp. 360–417.

Ostergren, Robert C. "A Community Transplanted: The Formative Experience of a Swedish Immigrant Community in the Upper Midwest." *Journal of Historical Geography* V (April 1979), pp. 189–212.

———. "Geographic Perspectives on the History of Settlement in the Upper Middle West." *Upper Midwest History* I (1981), pp. 27–39.

Owen, J. Thomas. "The Church on the Plaza: A History of The Pueblo Church of Los Angeles." Historical Society of Southern California *Quarterly*, XLII (March 1960), pp. 5–28; and (June 1960), pp. 186–204.

———. "The First Synagogue in Los Angeles." *Western States Jewish Historical Quarterly* I (October, 1968), p. 9–13.

Packman, Ana Begue. "Landmarks and Pioneers of Los Angeles in 1853." Historical Society of Southern California *Quarterly* XXVI (June-September 1944), pp. 57–95.

"Parson's Progress to California." Historical Society of Southern California *Quarterly* XXI (June-September 1939), pp. 45–78.

Phillips, George Harwood. "Indians in Los Angeles, 1781–1875: Economic Integration, Social Disintegration." *Pacific Historical Review* XLIX (August 1980), pp. 427–51.

Pritchard, Linda K. "A Comparative Approach to Western Religious History: Texas as a Case Study, 1845–1890." *Western Historical Quarterly* XIX (November 1988), pp. 413–30.

Bibliography

Romer, Margaret. "Pioneer Builders of Los Angeles." Historical Society of Southern California *Quarterly*, XLIII (March 1961), pp. 342–49.

Seager, Robert, II. "Some Denominational Reactions to Chinese Immigration to California, 1856–1892." *Pacific Historical Review* XXVIII (February 1959), pp. 49–66.

Sheridan, Thomas E. "Peacocks in the Parlor: Frontier Tucson's Mexican Elite." *Journal of Arizona History* XXV (Autumn 1984), pp. 245–64.

Sitton, Tom. "California's Practical Idealist: John Randolph Haynes," *California Historian*, LXVII (March 1988), pp. 3–17, 67–69.

Splitter, Henry H. "Education in Los Angeles, 1850–1900." Historical Society of Southern California *Quarterly* XXXIII (June 1951), pp. 101–18; (September 1951), pp. 226–44; and (December 1951), pp. 313–30.

Stern, Norton B. "The First Jew to Run for Mayor of Los Angeles." *Western States Jewish Historical Quarterly* XII (April 1980), pp. 246–58.

———. "Jews in the 1870 Census of Los Angeles." *Western States Jewish Historical Quarterly* IX (October 1976), pp. 71–87.

———. "Location of Los Angeles Jewry at the Beginning of 1851." *Western States Jewish Historical Quarterly* V (October 1972), pp. 25–31.

———. "Myer J. Newmark." *Western States Jewish Historical Quarterly* II (April 1970), pp. 136–71.

Stern, Norton B., and Kramer, William M. "An 1869 Jewish Standard for Gentile Behavior." *Western States Jewish Historical Quarterly* IX (April 1977), pp. 282–85.

Stern, Norton B., and Kramer, William M. "Jewish Padre to the Pueblo: Pioneer Los Angeles Rabbi Abraham Wolf Edelmen." *Western States Jewish Historical Quarterly* III (July 1971), pp. 192–226.

Stimson, Marshall. "History of Los Angeles High School." Historical Society of Southern California *Quarterly* XXIV (September 1942), pp. 98–109.

Sweet, William Warren. "The Churches as Moral Courts of the Frontier." *Church History* II (June 1933), pp. 3–21.

———. "Some Significant Factors in American Church History." *Journal of Religion* VIII (January 1927), pp. 1–15.

Temple, Thomas Workman. "Se Fundaron Un Pueblo de Españoles." Historical Society of Southern California *Annual Publications* XV (1931), pp. 69–98.

Thompson, Margaret Susan. "Discovering Foremothers: Sisters, Society, and the American Catholic Church." *U.S. Catholic Historian* V (Summer-Fall 1986), pp. 273–90.

Van der Meer, Philip R. "Religion, Society, and Politics: A Classification of American Religious Groups." *Social Science History* V (February 1981), pp. 3–24.

Bibliography

Venisse, Edmond, SS.CC. "Extrait d'une lettre de M. Venisse." *Annales de la Propagation de la Foi* (Lyon, France) XXX (1858), pp. 57–68.

Weber, David J. "Failure of a Frontier Institution: The Secular Church in the Borderlands Under Independent Mexico, 1821–1846." *Western Historical Quarterly* XII (April 1981), pp. 125–43.

Weber, Francis J. "An Historical Sketch of St. Vibiana's Cathedral, Los Angeles." *Southern California Quarterly* XLIV (March 1962), pp. 43–56.

————. "Joaquin Adam y Tous." *Southern California Quarterly* LXVII (Summer 1985), pp. 135–152.

————. "Precedent for Ecumenism." *Western States Jewish History*, XIX (January 1987), pp. 158–60.

Wittenburg, Sister Mary Ste. Therese. "A California Girlhood: Reminiscences of Ascencion Sepulveda y Avila." *Southern California Quarterly* LXIV (Summer 1982), pp. 133–39.

Workman, William H. "Sister Scholastica." Historical Society of Southern California *Annual Publications* V (1902), pp. 256–58.

75-Jährige Jubliäums-Feier der Ersten Deutschen Methodisten-Kirche Los Angeles: First German Methodist Church, 1951.

VII. Theses and Papers.

Campbell, Frances M. "American Regional Catholicism: Dichotomous Developments in Anglo and Hispano Traditions, 1776–1885." Paper delivered at the 64th Annual Meeting of the American Catholic Historical Association, San Francisco, California, 28 December 1983.

Ellis, Ivan C. "Baptist Churches in Southern California." Ph.D. dissertation, Northern Baptist Theological Seminary, Chicago, 1948.

Gjerde, Jon. "The Seacoast of Iowa: Chain Migration from the Middle West to California, 1880–1930." Paper delivered at the 78th Annual Meeting of the Organization of American Historians, Minneapolis, Minnesota, 20 April 1985.

Harkness, E.J. "History of the Presbytery of Los Angeles, 1850–1928." Ph.D. dissertation, University of Southern California, 1929.

Hogue, Harlan E. "A History of Religion in Southern California, 1846–1880." Ph.D. dissertation, Columbia University, 1958.

Lewis, Albert L. "Los Angeles in the Civil War Decades, 1850–1868." Ph.D. dissertation, University of Southern California, 1970.

Liu, Felix. "A Comparative Study of Selected Chinese Churches in Los Angeles County." Ph.D. dissertation, Fuller Theological Seminary, Pasadena, 1981.

Lou, Raymond. "The Chinese-American Community of Los Angeles, 1870–1900: A Case of Resistance, Organization, and Participation." Ph.D.

dissertation, University of California, Irvine, 1982.

Neri, Michael C. "Hispanic Catholicism in Transitional California: The Life of José González Rubio, O.F.M. (1804–1875)," Ph.D. dissertation, Graduate Theological Union, Berkeley, 1973.

Schippling, Roy F. "A History of the Diocese of Los Angeles." S.T.M. thesis, Nashotah House, 1972.

Thompson, Margaret Susan. "To Serve the People of God: Nineteenth-Century Sisters and the Creation of an American Religious Life." Notre Dame, Indiana: University of Notre Dame, Working Paper Series of the Cushwa Center for the Study of American Catholicism, Spring, 1987.

Walker, Randi Jones. "Protestantism in the Sangre de Cristos: Factors in the Growth and Decline of the Hispanic Protestant Churches in New Mexico and Southern Colorado." Ph.D. dissertation, Claremont School of Religion, 1983.

Woo, Wesley S. "Protestant Work Among the Chinese in the San Francisco Bay Area, 1850–1920." Ph.D. dissertation, Graduate Theological Union, Berkeley, 1983.

Woods, Betty Jean. "An Historical Survey of the Woman's Christian Temperance Union of Southern California As It Reflects the Significance of the National W.C.T.U. in the Woman's Movement of the Nineteenth Century." M.A. thesis, Occidental College, Los Angeles, 1950.

Workshops on Hispanic Liturgy and Popular Piety. "Faith Expressions of Hispanics in the Southwest." San Antonio, Texas: Mexican American Cultural Center, 1977.

INDEX

Index